BACK TO DARWIN

*The Scientific Case for
Deistic Evolution*

M.A. Corey

UNIVERSITY
PRESS OF
AMERICA

Lanham • New York • London

Copyright © 1994 by
University Press of America®, Inc.
4720 Boston Way
Lanham, Maryland 20706

3 Henrietta Street
London WC2E 8LU England

Library of Congress Cataloging-in-Publication Data
Corey, Michael Anthony.
Back to Darwin : the scientific case for Deistic evolution /
M.A. Corey.
p.   cm.
Includes bibliographical references and index.
1. Evolution—Religious aspects.   2. Evolution (Biology)
3. Deism.   I. Title.   II. Title: Deistic evolution.
BL263.C774   1993   213—dc20   93–34539 CIP

ISBN 0–8191–9306–2 (cloth : alk. paper)
ISBN 0–8191–9307–0 (pbk. : alk. paper)

The paper used in this publication meets the minimum requirements of
American National Standard for Information Sciences—Permanence
of Paper for Printed Library Materials, ANSI Z39.48–1984.

For my parents, Mike Sr. and Jeanette, and my two brothers, Johnny and Danny

Acknowledgments

I would like to thank the following individuals for their help in making this book possible: David Ray Griffin, Robert Newman, Barbara Oden, James Brimhall, Julie Kirsch, Helen Hudson, John Sisk, Lynn Gemmell, Steve Davis, John Hick, John B. Cobb, Jr., Mike and Jeanette Corey, Father Olof Scott, Jeannie Poulsen, Lucretia Lyons, Linda Hill, Nahia Khoury, Johnny and Danny Corey, Beth Najjar, Elliot and Gina Namay, Steve and Susan Levine, Talal, the Maloneys, Sammy Ghareeb, Zegeer Hardware, Ellen and Henry Sun, Steve Lewis, Elizabeth and Janice Nassany, John Karl and Adele Adams, Paula and Marvin, Dr. Steve Zekan and staff, Bonnie Maddox, Charlotte Pritt, Louise Lewis and the entire Lewis family, Billie McNabb, Julie Hughes, Tina and Tamara Namay, Mary and John Townshend, Mr. and Mrs. Parker and family, Stewart and Susan May, Therese Cox, Bill Watkins, Denis and Jane Clarke, Samuel Jordan, Dr. Alan Scott Levin, Kevin Abdalla, Greg Ammar, Ernestine Bsharah, John Hyde, Greg Summers, Eli and Brandon Namay, and the entire staff of The Claremont Graduate School.

Contents

Contents

PART II
DIRECTED EVOLUTION

Contents

It has been said that the highest praise of God consists in the denial of Him by the atheist, who finds creation so perfect that he can dispense with a creator.

Marcel Proust

Preface

Copernicus' discovery that the earth revolves around the sun undoubtedly ranks as one of the most significant discoveries in the entire history of science. It removed humanity from the geographical center of the universe and forced scientists and philosophers to take a sobering new look at our position in the cosmos. Indeed, some have gone so far as to use the Copernican principle to argue that there is nothing special about our place in the heavens at all.

However, it doesn't necessarily follow that, just because our position in the universe isn't privileged in *every* way, it isn't privileged in *any* way. It was this realization that led Brandon Carter in 1974 to limit the Copernican dogma through his radical assertion that "our location in the universe is necessarily privileged to the extent of being compatible with our existence as observers."[1]

This assertion came to be known as the Anthropic Principle, and in the years following Carter's initial paper a great deal of scientific evidence has been marshalled in support of it. The essence of the Anthropic Principle can be found in the mystifying relationship between our own self-awareness and the existence of a physical universe that was somehow capable of producing beings like ourselves.[2] As we now know, a vast array of very precise physical parameters must simultaneously have been fulfilled if any sort of biological life was to ever have been capable of evolving on this planet (or on any other planet for that matter). Fortunately for us, each and every one of these necessary parameters have in fact obtained, in spite of the fact that most of them have been judged to be profoundly improbable on *a priori* grounds.

Many authors have examined these "cosmic coincidences" and have concluded that the most likely explanation is theistic in nature.[3] As many physicists have come to realize, the evidence strongly suggests that the universe has been deliberately designed by a Higher Power for the expressed purpose of sustaining life on earth. For instance, the fundamental constants of nature occupy precisely those values that make life possible, while the expansion dynamics surrounding the Big Bang are now understood to have been exquisitely "fine-tuned" in such a manner as to produce the only type of universe that is capable of generating intelligent observers. Indeed, had any of these fundamental physical parameters occupied even slightly different values, we would not be here to discuss the fact.[4]

Remarkably, the current values of these physical parameters seem to have been "chosen" out of an infinite range of possible values. More remarkable still is the fact that each of these fundamental parameters is now known to play a crucial cooperative role in the facilitation of life. As a consequence, it appears as though the stipulation that life should be able to exist may have been the cosmic criterion that was operative in the selection of the present values out of the infinite range of possible choices.

However, it is the uncanny relationship between our own existence and entire constellations of these fundamental parameters that is the most astonishing feature of modern science. For it is now known that life was only able to evolve because of the cooperative interaction of a large number of cosmic "coincidences" between distant branches of physics, each of which was wildly improbable in its own right. Indeed, had even a single one of these "coincidences" not occurred, life could never have evolved on this planet. Taken together, these life-facilitating "coincidences" have an almost unmistakable air of deliberateness about them. It was this realization that led physicist Freeman Dyson to remark the following:

> As we look out into the Universe and identify the many accidents of physics and astronomy that have worked together to our benefit, it almost seems as if the Universe must in some sense have known that we were coming.[5]

Indeed, the evidence for Deliberate Design from these cosmic "coincidences" is so compelling that they amount to a strong probabilistic "proof" of a Grand Designer.[6] It is my intention in this book to add to this probabilistic proof by showing that the process of biological evolution is not only fully consistent with the existence of a Grand Designer, it is also positively unintelligible in the absence of one. While other hypotheses regarding the cause and meaning of evolution may be possible, it is my contention that they are not nearly as persuasive as the theistic hypothesis, especially given the biocentric nature of the universe as a whole.

Creation vs. Evolution: The Modern Debate

It is commonly believed that there are only two possible ways for life to have arisen on earth: through a random and mindless process of gradual evolution, or through an instantaneous creation by an all-powerful Creator. Indeed, it is this dichotomy that appears to be the chief reason why many scientists and other intellectuals have chosen to reject the idea of a Divine Creator altogether God in favor of an autonomous realm of natural cause-and-effect processes: because through innumerable scientific observations it has become apparent that both the world and the larger universe have slowly arisen over billions of years through the various natural processes that are inherent in matter. This fact is taken to be *prima facie* evidence against the possibility of a deliberate creation by a Supreme Being, as the following quote makes clear:

> That organisms have evolved rather than having been created is the single most important and unifying principle of modern biology.[7]

However, the above-stated dichotomy between gradual evolution and Divine Creation is grossly in error. Like many provocative issues that are divided into two opposing camps, the truth concerning the origin of life lies in the *middle* of the ideological battleground. From this intermediate perspective, it is possible to state that the universe may indeed have arisen gradually through natural evolutionary processes, but not blindly or randomly. Rather, the Supreme Being Himself could have found it necessary to utilize these natural evolutionary processes as His Divine Creative Tools. Stated another way, it is possible that God may have created the universe all right, but not instantaneously through Divine Fiat. Instead, He could have created it in a gradual, stepwise fashion, by utilizing the natural evolutionary processes that are inherent in matter.

In this way of thinking, creation and evolution aren't mutually exclusive alternatives at all. They simply refer to different issues in the overall question of the origin of life. Howard J. Van Till beautifully summarizes this point in his book *The Fourth Day*:

> "Creation" and "evolution" are not contradictory answers to the same question; each speaks to distinctly different issues. "Creation" is the answer to the question of what status the material world has. "Evolution" is an answer to the question of what material process characterizes the temporal development of the universe. "Evolution" provides answers to a set of questions that belong in the category of "internal affairs," while "creation" provides answers to the basic questions in the category of "external relationships." The concepts of creation and evolution are not contradictory. Nor do they provide supplemental answers to a common set of questions. Rather, they provide appropriately different answers to categorically complementary questions.[8]

For some reason, both scientists and laymen alike find it difficult to conceive of a God who acts largely through natural processes; even Christians find such a "naturalistic" God difficult to fathom. Such individuals prefer to imagine a God who is similar to the magical Barbara Eden of "I Dream of Jeannie" fame, who does everything by miraculous, instantaneous Fiat, instead of through gradual physical processes. I would like to propose that, on the basis of the available evidence at hand, this conception of the Deity is patently false, and is thus based more on wishful thinking than cosmic reality. Rather, God seems to act almost exclusively through the use of natural cause-and-effect processes—which He Himself designed into matter—for two reasons: 1) because it is a more appropriate form of creativity, given the intrinsic character of the end product (humanity) that He has chosen to create, and 2) because it is more consistent with His own internal nature. This book is based on an ideological synthesis that posits the existence of just such a naturalistic Creator—who consistently uses the natural "evolutionary" processes that are inherent in matter to do His creating.

This synthesis between evolution and creation is known in philosophical circles as Theistic Evolution. (Deistic Evolution is actually a subset of Theistic Evolution, insofar as the latter designation refers to the general position that God is ultimately behind the evolutionary process in one way or another.) Like many syntheses, it purports to heal the split between two radically opposing points of view, which in this case is non-theistic evolutionism and non-evolutionary creationism. Moreover—and this is the surprising thing—this scientifically-based synthesis also has the advantage of being totally compatible with most forms of traditional theology. Consequently, the doctrine of Theistic (or Deistic) Evolutionism can be used by both physical scientists and theistic believers alike without any compromise in the integrity or fundamental convictions of either group. It can therefore be used to heal the ever-widening schism between scientific evolutionism and special creationism.

In this book we will be fleshing out this theistically-based position with the most recent discoveries in evolutionary biology and molecular genetics. Our goal will be to address the major points of disagreement between science and religion, so as to be able to obtain a unified view of the rise of life.

Notes

1. Brandon Carter, "Large Number Coincidences and the Anthropic Principle in Cosmology," *Confrontation of Cosmological Theories With Observation*, ed. M.S. Longair (Dordrecht: Reidel, 1974), p. 291.
2. There are actually two different arguments imbedded in the Anthropic Principle, which are discussed at length in my previous book *God and the New Cosmology* (Lanham, MD.: Rowman and Littlefield, 1993). They are: 1) a general argument for contrivance in the universe, which I termed the Biocentric Principle, and which only requires the existence of some sort of generic life to be valid, and 2) the anthropocentric argument that humans were intended all along, which I termed the Anthropic Principle, and which requires the existence of uniquely human life in order to be valid. For my purposes in this book, however, this distinction is not particularly important, so I will be grouping both the Biocentric Principle and the Anthropic Principle together into one general argument for Intelligent Contrivance in the universe, which for the sake of convenience I shall term the "Anthropic Principle."
3. See John Leslie's "Anthropic Principle, World Ensemble, Design," in *American*

Philosophical Quarterly 19 (1982): 141–151, and my own *God and the New Cosmology* (Lanham, MD: Rowman and Littlefield, 1993).

4. See John D. Barrow and Frank J. Tipler's *The Anthropic Cosmological Principle* (New York: Oxford University Press, 1986).

5. Taken from John L. Casti's *Paradigms Lost* (New York: William Morrow and Company, 1989), p. 484.

6. Probabilistic proofs for the existence of God are to be distinguished from formal proofs in that they don't argue that God's existence inevitably follows from a certain set of fundamental premises. They simply argue that, given the present nature of the universe, it is more likely that God exists than that He does not.

7. Daniel R. Brooks and E.O. Wiley, *Evolution as Entropy* (Chicago: University of Chicago Press, 1986), p. xi.

8. Howard J. Van Till, *The Fourth Day* (Grand Rapids: Eerdmans Press, 1986), pp. 246–247.

CHAPTER 1
The Deistic Roots of Modern Darwinism

> What a magnificent idea of the infinite power to cause the causes of effects,
> rather than to cause the effects themselves.
>
> ERASMUS DARWIN

Popular opinion has it that Charles Darwin was a radical atheist who
devised his famous theory of evolution by natural selection to show how life
could have evolved in the absence of an Intelligent Designer. This belief is
so widespread that almost everyone, from the average person in the street
to the evolutionary theorist, believes it to some extent.

The fact is, however, that Darwin wasn't an atheist at all. He was a radical
deist, which is to say that he believed in the existence of a distant primordial
Creator, who would have originally created self-organizing atoms and molecules, and who would have then allowed them to evolve on their own according to natural law. This radical deism is to be distinguished from classic
eighteenth-century deism, which asserted that all the major kinds of creatures were miraculously created fully formed, and were then allowed to
evolve from there. This is why Darwin didn't attempt to explain the origin
of life or the ultimate source of variations in *The Origin of Species*: because
he attributed these phenomena to the activities of a Grand Designer. The
following quote makes Darwin's position with regard to God absolutely unmistakable:

> If we admit, *as we must admit*, that some few organic beings were *origi-
> nally created*, which were endowed with a high power of generation &
> with the capacity for some slight inheritable variability, then I can see no
> limit to the wondrous & harmonious results which in the course of time
> can be perfected through natural selection (italics mine).[1]

The French mathematician and philosopher René Descartes initiated the
deistic movement with his idea that God could have brought about the existence of our present world through the use of natural mechanistic processes:

> In Descartes's interpretation of the "mechanical philosophy," the earth
> was formed by natural means from matter distributed in space—but be-
> cause God created both the original distribution and the laws that govern
> the behavior of matter, He had clearly foreseen the end product and could

thus be said to have designed the evolutionary process itself. Even Darwin accepted the concept that God had established the general laws by which life evolves, although he was forced to concede that the details of what happened were not the result of divine forethought.[2]

Darwin expressed this deistic tone of the *Origin* from the very outset, quoting from William Whewell's Bridgewater Treatise "On Astronomy and General Physics" opposite his title page:

> But with regard to the material world, we can at least go so far as this;— we can perceive that events are brought about, not by insulated interpositions of Divine power exerted in each particular case, but by the establishment of general laws.[3]

Darwin's central purpose in the *Origin* was thus to show how the various species in existence could have evolved entirely on their own according to natural law, after having been initially given the impetus to evolve at the beginning of time by the Creator. He openly expressed this belief in the last paragraph of the *Origin* with the following oft-quoted words:

> There is grandeur in this view of life, with its several powers, *having been originally breathed by the Creator into a few forms or into one*; and that, whilst this planet has gone cycling on according to the fixed law of gravity, from so simple a beginning endless forms most beautiful and most wonderful have been, and are being evolved (emphasis mine).[4]

In this one paragraph Darwin shows himself to be in full agreement with the central tenet of Deistic Evolutionism, insofar as he admits that the ultimate power behind the evolutionary process was "originally breathed by the Creator into a few forms or into one." Although Darwin is said to have added this deistic proviso in the second edition of his book in order to quell religious opposition to his theory, he nevertheless believed in its validity to an important extent, as we can clearly see by examining other passages in the *Origin*. Consider, for instance, the following quote:

> Authors of the highest eminence seem to be fully satisfied with the view that each species has been independently created. To my mind it accords better with what we know of the laws impressed on matter by the Creator, that the production and extinction of the past and present inhabitants of the world should have been due to secondary causes, like those determining the birth and death of the individual. When I view all beings not as special creations, but as the lineal descendants of some few beings which lived long before the first bed of the Silurian system was deposited, they seem to me to become ennobled.[5]

In the above passage, Darwin explicitly *assumes* the existence of a deistic Creator, insofar as he assumes that a certain set of laws were impressed on matter "by the Creator." *This is certainly not a statement that would be made by an atheist or even an agnostic.*

Darwin further assumed that this sort of deistic Creator was no less worthy of our deepest worship and admiration, just because He tended to create indirectly through secondary causes:

> It is just as noble a conception of the Deity to believe that he created a few original forms capable of self-development into other and needful forms.[6]

Darwin also assumed the existence of a Creator when he considered the evolution of the eye, and questioned whether we can properly draw an analogy between the creative mechanisms employed by God and those employed by man:

> Have we any right to assume that the Creator works by intellectual powers like those of man?[7]

Indeed, Darwin believed certain aspects of the traditional Design Argument to be so convincing that he sometimes felt compelled to openly confess its overall validity, as the following quote well illustrates:

> One cannot look at this Universe with all living productions and man without believing that all has been intelligently designed. . . . [8]

Darwin thus appears to have been fully convinced of the existence of a deistic Creator. For Darwin, then, the primary issue wasn't God's existence or non-existence *per se*, but rather the specific *mechanism* the Creator would have used to impart His creative will to the earth. Two different options immediately presented themselves to Darwin. Either: 1) God directly caused each specific change in the biological realm through a miraculous intervention in worldly affairs, or 2) He indirectly caused the causes of events in the biological realm, as Darwin's grandfather Erasmus believed.

Put another way, the central issue of relevance to Darwin was whether God created the species all at once in their final form, or whether He simply allowed them to gradually evolve to their present state of complexity from humble beginnings. Either way, the existence of an Intelligent Creator was not in dispute; rather, it was the Creator's chosen method of generating species on earth that was the central point of contention for Darwin.

On this one point Darwin can hardly be gainsaid, because God is clearly *not* directly acting as an efficient cause for each and every event in the natural realm. Rather, He has given nature a certain amount of behavioral freedom, through which it can act in accordance with the laws that God Himself set up when He originally created the world. As Darwin rightfully declares, there truly *is* grandeur in this view of life, since a self-organizing natural realm is clearly more impressive than a lame one that has to be tinkered with each step of the way by an inefficient Designer. Other authors, such as Neal Gillespie[9] and John Greene[10] have acknowledged Darwin's belief in a deistic Creator:

According to this reading, Darwin did not abandon design but realized that the Creator had decided to work in a less directly obvious way. His references to the laws of nature achieving a higher purpose through evolution are genuine expressions of his faith that, despite its superficial air of harshness, natural selection does work for the good of all living things. Adapatations, even progress, *are* brought about in the long run, and the Creator's intentions fulfilled. Ospovat . . . even has suggested that in Darwin's early formulations, the selection mechanism was intended explicitly to bring about a state of "perfect" adaptation, in which there was no need for further struggle until the next change in the environment occurred. Several writers have drawn attention to Darwin's use of the analogy of a "Being" who superintends the operations of natural selection . . . This Being takes the place of the human breeder in artificial selection, and by using such language Darwin invites us to imagine that the Creator is really in charge of natural evolution. It was all too easy to think of nature as a conscious selecting agent and thus as an arm of divine providence. In his more hard-headed moments, Darwin certainly appreciated that this was only an anthropomorphic way of describing the effects of struggle, yet his decision to use this analogy may reflect an inability to throw off the influence of the design argument.[11]

Another member of the Darwin family who was also a deist was Charles' grandfather Erasmus. A physician by trade, Erasmus Darwin believed that God had designed living organisms to be self-improving through time. This belief led to the first[12] evolutionary theory of the transmutation of species, which was set forth in Dr. Darwin's famous work *Zoonomia*. Indeed, many have argued that Charles Darwin's theories were only an elaboration of his grandfather's original beliefs. This is significant for our purposes in this book because Erasmus Darwin was a confirmed deist, and not an atheist or agnostic.

Charles Darwin's theological beliefs are thus not at all surprising when we consider his family's long history of theological belief, the predominance of deism in England during the nineteenth century, and the nature of Darwin's chief training at Cambridge, which was in *theology*, not science. Indeed, Darwin's goal at one time was to become an actual clergyman, and he even admitted to being a Bible-quoting fundamentalist while on the H.M.S. Beagle:

Whilst on board the Beagle I was quite orthodox, and I remember being heartily laughed at by several of the officers (though themselves orthodox) for quoting the Bible as a unanswerable authority on some point of morality.[13]

However, despite his clear theological underpinnings, Darwin was haunted throughout the remainder of his life by the question of *why* an all-powerful Deity would have utilized such a painful and wasteful evolutionary process to do His creating, when presumably a much easier and more straightforward process was available to Him.

A being so powerful and so full of knowledge as a God who could create the universe, is to our finite minds omnipotent and omniscient, and it revolts our understanding to suppose that his benevolence is not unbounded, for what advantage can there be in the sufferings of millions of the lower animals throughout almost endless time?[14]

Darwin also found the existence of a benevolent Deity difficult to reconcile with the existence of cold-hearted violence in the animal world:

Did He [God] cause the frame and mental qualities of the dog to vary in order that a breed might be formed of indomitable ferocity, with jaws fitted to pin down the bull for man's brutal sport?[15]

Darwin's inability to reconcile theism with the apparent "immorality" exhibited throughout the animal world caused him to grow increasingly distant from his underlying deistic beliefs in the latter part of his life, so that eventually, he came close to abandoning them altogether. This "flight from theism" was exacerbated by the obvious opportunism that is displayed throughout the living world, which seemed to Darwin to indicate that amoral physical processes alone were responsible for creating the entire natural order.[16]

Darwin's alienation from God was further compounded by the fact that his deistic beliefs encouraged him to relegate God to the very periphery of the created universe. This meant that every component of the evolutionary process was understood to be entirely naturalistic in origin and function, apart from the self-organizing atoms and molecules that Darwin believed God Himself had made. For Darwin, then, the role of the Creator in evolution could more or less be ignored once the initial creation of the atoms and molecules in the universe had taken place. It is this "sideline status" of the deistic Creator during the actual evolutionary process itself, along with Darwin's absolute emphasis on natural cause and effect processes during the history of life, that Darwin's followers have confused for frank atheism or agnosticism. And admittedly, it is quite difficult to maintain an active belief in a Supreme Being when: 1) He has been pushed back into the cosmological distance as much as possible, 2) He cannot be directly observed in action, and 3) when He fails to directly intervene to halt worldly evil. When all of these considerations are factored in together, it isn't surprising that Darwin almost lost sight of his deistic Creator altogether.

In other words, Darwin seems to have been so confused by the extraordinary tenets of radical deism that he was often unable to determine God's precise role during the evolution of life. Indeed, there is no question that the very concept of deism is fraught with many philosophical, theological, and emotional difficulties, as Bowler has aptly pointed out:

> As long as one believed that the original form of the universe was created by God, the idea could be accepted that any later developments occurred in accordance with his wishes. Many of Descartes's followers, nevertheless, began to lose sight of this point as they concentrated more on the mechanical processes themselves. It was difficult to imagine that God really superintended or even cared about the actual details of what happened in the world, because He had delegated all responsibility to the laws of nature. At best, one might suppose that He had planned the general outline of what happened, but to believe that every minute detail of nature's activity was intended by divine forethought seemed unreasonable. Thus emerged the clock-maker God of the deists and an increasing suspicion that such a God had no relevance for human affairs.[17]

Few people want to believe in a Deity who can never be counted on to become directly involved in their lives, even if He has very good reasons for not doing so. Indeed, the popular image of God has become so dependent on His presumed Coercive Power over everything in existence that the very notion of deism—that is to say, of a remote and indirect Universal Power—is for many tantamount to no Creator at all. No wonder most readers of the *Origin* have made Darwin's deistic views virtually synonymous with outright atheism, as Darwin himself at times seems to have done.

It is important to keep in mind, however, that Darwin's chief complaint against the notion of Intelligent Design wasn't scientific in nature; it was moral and theological.[18] Darwin simply found it difficult to believe that an omnipotent and omniscient Deity would have used such a "higgledy-piggledy" way of creating the world, when presumably a much easier and less painful means was available to Him. In his more skeptical moments, this sort of reasoning led Darwin to seriously question his underlying deistic beliefs. Nevertheless, the obvious element of Design that was apparent throughout the natural world kept bringing Darwin back to his deistic roots time and time again, as the following quote from Darwin's *Autobiography* well illustrates:

> Another source of conviction in the existence of God, connected with the reason and not with the feelings, impresses me as having much more weight. This follows from the extreme difficulty or rather impossibility of conceiving this immense and wonderful universe, including man with his capacity of looking far backwards and far into futurity, as the result of blind chance or necessity. When thus reflecting I feel compelled to look to a First Cause having an intelligent mind in some degree analogous to that of man; *and I deserve to be called a theist* (italics mine).[19]

This passage leaves little doubt as to Darwin's underlying theological beliefs. And even though Darwin found it difficult to imagine why an omnipotent God would allow so much pain and suffering in the world (as many of us do today), this difficulty itself does not necessarily preclude belief in God, since there is always the chance that there could be a higher, and therefore justifiable, reason why God would have created the world through such a pain-filled process of evolution and decay. In his more lucid moments, Darwin seemed to have been aware of this possibility, since, as we have seen, he often confessed outright belief in the notion of Intelligent Design.

One of the central tenets of Darwin's radical deism is that God works primarily (some would say exclusively) through secondary causes in nature. This is an idea that has confused a great many people through the years, as it is tempting to lose sight of God altogether when secondary causes seem to be doing all the work in the universe. Such a conclusion, however, clearly doesn't follow from the implied premises, and our own experience with creativity confirms this. We routinely utilize secondary causes like mechanical and electrical tools in our creative efforts, but this fact doesn't render us any less responsible for the creative acts themselves. Similarly, God's apparent use of secondary causes in nature doesn't necessarily make Him any less responsible for bringing the entire universe about, and Darwin seems to have been aware of this important distinction.

In short, although Darwin clearly had reservations about the role God may have played in the evolutionary process, he almost certainly believed in *some* sort of Creator, since he had no other explanation for the obvious self-organizing power of nature's most fundamental constituents. Darwin simply had a hard time understanding, as we all do, why God would have created the world the way He did.

We thus should be careful not to allow Darwin's theological doubt to deter us from concluding that he was ultimately a theist (or more accurately, a deist). It is the rare person indeed who has absolutely no doubt at all as far as the existence of God is concerned; most believers are stricken with doubt from time to time, and scientists seem to experience this problem more than most people, due to their inherently questioning nature. Indeed, the very word "belief" implies a distinct element of doubt, for if there were no doubt at all in one's belief structure, one would not longer believe but *know.* With this in mind, it would be a mistake to confuse Darwin's frequent doubting concerning the nature of God with frank atheism. There seems little question that if Darwin were forced to choose between either the existence or non-existence of some type of Creator, he almost certainly would have gone the theistic route.

He did, however, eventually come to reject both orthodox biblicism and traditional Christianity out of hand, and this has only served to compound the historical confusion regarding Darwin's theological beliefs. It would be a mistake, though, to confuse his rejection of the standing orthodoxy of his day with outright atheism or even agnosticism, as Gillespie has clearly pointed out.[20] One does not have to accept the tenets of traditional Christianity in order to be religious, as there are any number of theological conceptualizations that are incompatible with religious orthodoxy. Indeed, Darwin's own "hopelessly muddled theology" was anything but orthodox, but it was nevertheless a theology centered around some type of Creator.

It is thus safe to say that Darwin remained a deist to the very end of his life (though again not without reservation). Curiously, however, this is not the picture of Darwin that is presented in most evolutionary texts. To the contrary, Darwin is repeatedly described as being the most hardened of theological cynics, who allegedly was so opposed to the idea of Intelligent Design that he came up with the theory of evolution by natural selection in order to do away with the idea of a Creator altogether. In reality, though, Darwin was merely opposed to the twin ideas that: 1) God had created an immutable series of creatures in their final form during the initial creation of the world, and 2) that God had personally directed the evolutionary process during each major historical transformation. Rather, Darwin believed, along with many of the fellow deists of his day, that God was only responsible for creating the original atoms and molecules themselves, and that they were subsequently allowed to evolve into complex life forms "on their own" in response to the miraculous self-organizing ability that God had originally designed into them.

Darwin had thus immersed himself:

> . . . in the orthodox Newtonian view that the system of natural laws, in biology no less than in physics, formed a set of secondary causes to carry out the Divine Will, without being guided by that will in matters of detail. The principle of natural selection could thus execute God's aim to produce, by operation of natural law itself, an evolutionary creature who could discern these very processes with his very well-adapted but fully natural mind, and so engage in a free man's worship (Ospovat, 1981).[21]

Darwin's central revelation, then, was not that life had evolved by blind, undirected chance, or that *no* form of Intelligent Design could be deduced by the evidence of descent with modification in nature. It was simply that life had evolved into its myriad of present-day forms by natural processes alone, and not through any direct sort of Divine Intervention *per se*. In short, Darwin merely rediscovered that which his grandfather Erasmus had pointed out long before him: that God acts in the world chiefly through secondary (i.e., indirect) causes, and not primary (i.e., direct) ones. But as we have seen, even Erasmus Darwin assumed the ultimate existence of a Divine Creator behind the evolutionary process, as the following quote from the elder Darwin's *Zoonomia* well illustrates:

> What a magnificent idea of the infinite power to cause the causes of effects, rather than to cause the effects themselves.[22]

Unfortunately, many people have a hard time imagining how a God who creates exclusively through indirect, secondary causes is as good or better than one who creates through direct, primary ones. Some even find such a "hopelessly distant" Creator to be tantamount to no Creator at all, despite the profound illogic of such reasoning. Indeed, this is precisely what many scientific historians have concluded with their inaccurate rendition of Darwin as a materialistic atheist. These individuals have taken unfair advantage of: 1) the distant nature of Darwin's deistic Creator, 2) Darwin's many theological doubts and questions (which we all have), and 3) his absolute rejection of orthodox biblicism, and have concluded that Darwin must have been a thoroughgoing atheist. We have seen, however, that this is far from an accurate rendition of the truth.

The reality of the situation is that these agenda-bearing authors have whiggishly imposed their own anti-theistic bias on Darwin's world-shaking ideas, as they have done with most of the other founding fathers of the modern scientific movement. Copernicus, for instance, is routinely credited in the scientific literature for the downfall of the anthropocentric world view because of his bold discovery that the earth revolves around the sun, but the historical record indicates that Copernicus was nevertheless a committed anthropocentrist who was absolutely convinced of the existence of God. Similarly, Newton is routinely credited with the creation of an entirely mechanistic world view, with no place in it for a larger Creator, but history again indicates that Newton was one of the greatest scientific supernaturalists of all time. In the same way, Galileo is typically referred to as the very symbol of science's antagonism with religion, but in actuality Galileo was also a supremely devoted theist as well.

The picture we see emerging is one of a deliberate alteration of the basic historical facts in science, whose purpose has been to help further the cause of scientific atheism, which has almost universally taken hold since the turn of the century. Nowhere is this historical perversion more evident than in the case of Charles Darwin, who is routinely said to have driven the final nail into the coffin of "theological superstitionism."

My purpose in this book is to set the record straight by arguing for Darwin's original position with regard to the origin of species. I will do this by presenting the case for *Deistic Evolutionism*, which refers to the idea that God has indirectly guided the evolutionary process along by designing the miraculous property of self-organization into the first atoms and molecules. In the process, I will be distinguishing between four different views of the origin of species: 1) the non-theistic evolutionary view, which is the one that is propounded by most neo-Darwinian evolutionists today, 2) the anti-evolutionary "creation-science" view, which asserts that no natural form of macroevolution has occurred, 3) the theistic evolutionary view, which holds that God has directly guided the evolutionary process along by intervening in worldly affairs at various points in the history of life, and 4) the deistic evolutionary view, which holds that God originally created the propensity to evolve into the first atoms and molecules, and then allowed them to develop on their own entirely according to natural cause-and-effect processes.

Although I will ultimately be arguing in behalf of Darwin's deistic Creator, most of the argumentation will be directed *against* the modern interpretation of Darwin's ideas, for two reasons: 1) because most of Darwin's ideas have been incorporated into an undirected, non-theistic evolutionary stance by modern evolutionists, and 2) because in his desire to remain true to his positivist underpinnings (which he saw as being essential to the practice of science itself), Darwin tended to present his own ideas in a non-theistic, "objective" manner, even though deep down he was a committed deist.[23]

In other words, my attack of orthodox neo-Darwinian theory isn't directed against the fact of evolution *per se;* it is directed against the non-theistic *version* of the theory that has become orthodox dogma in modern evolutionary circles. My basic argument will be that the reality of evolution is unintelligible in the absence of an Intelligent Designer, even if His Creative Activity is to be confined to the initial moments of creation. I will thus ultimately be arguing for Darwin's original idea of Deistic Evolution, since I am convinced, as he himself seemed to be, that God *indirectly* controls the evolutionary process through the self-organizing power that He originally built into atoms and molecules. This view of the Creator is to be distinguished from one in which He *directly* controls worldly events through the first-hand manipulation of primary terrestrial causes.[24]

However, before continuing on, I should hasten to point out that my position in this book is by no means identical with Darwin's own version of deism. There is, in point of fact, a significant difference between our two views having to do with the important issue of God's foreknowledge and control over the evolutionary process. Darwin believed that God had instituted the evolutionary system of natural law without directly knowing how it would all turn out in the end. He therefore believed that God did not directly intend the specific results of evolution in matters of detail. This is how Darwin chose to distance God from all the pain and suffering that have ostensibly been produced by the evolutionary process throughout the millennia.

In contradistinction to Darwin's brand of deism was the providential evolutionism of such influential nineteenth-century thinkers as Robert Chambers, Richard Owen, and St. George Jackson Mivart. Although these indivduals were also deists in the classic sense, they sought to retain God's ultimate control over the evolutionary process by arguing that God was indeed capable of foreseeing the eventual results of His creative actions.

While the theoretical differences between these two forms of deism are significant, they are trivial when compared to their enormous similarities. Both views, for instance, posit the existence of a deistic Creator who creates almost exclusively through an elaborate system of natural law and secondary causes. Both views also assert that, for the most part, God's initial creation of these secondary causes was so thorough and complete that there was little or no subsequent need for miraculous intervention following the first act of creation.

Nevertheless, despite these similarities, it is important to note that the Deistic Evolutionism I will be advocating in this book is more in line with the providential evolutionism of Chambers and Mivart than it is with the views of Darwin himself. I too believe that God had complete control over the evolutionary process of secondary causes, not in the sense of directly causing each specific event in the world, but rather in the sense of being able to completely foresee the eventual results of His actions, and being able to adjust His initial creation of the universe accordingly.

However, because providential evolutionism is actually a subset of Deistic Evolutionism, I will be retaining the latter designation throughout the remainder of this book, not because my views are identical with Darwin's, but because the similarities between our two views vastly outweigh their differences. Indeed, I will be issuing a vigorous argument for the truth of Deistic Evolutionism in the upcoming pages, because I am convinced that this general position is firmly supported by the existing scientific evidence.

The first step, however, in any full-scale defense of Deistic Evolutionism is to show how the notion of deism itself is not necessarily opposed to the tenets of traditional theology. We will concern ourselves with this issue in the upcoming section. Once this task is completed, we will then begin our full-scale assault on non-theistic evolutionism, with the intention of simply showing how the process of evolution fails to make any real sense apart from the creative activity of an Intelligent Designer. This being accomplished, we will then turn our attention to the intriguing concept of designed or providential evolution. In this section we will offer an alternative deistic interpretation of the evolutionary process, and from there we will move on to consider a possible rationale for why God would have used the process of biological evolution to do His creating, when presumably a much less painful and time-consuming process was available to Him. In order to find a plausible answer to this question, though, we must endeavor to look beyond the confines of the empirical sciences only, since the primary issue at stake here is a *theological* one. (Darwin's chief mistake is that he sought to answer this theological problem from within the ranks of the empirical sciences *only.*) Finally, we will explore the many ramifications that are entailed in any religious view of biogenesis.

1.1 A Theological Defense of Deism

Webster's New World Dictionary defines deism as "belief in the existence of a God on purely rational grounds without reliance on revelation or authority, especially the 17th- and 18th-century doctrine that God created the world and its natural laws, but takes no further part in its functioning."

The first part of this definition isn't so objectionable; it is the latter part about God's relative lack of involvement with the world following His initial creative activity that causes the most problems with theologians and philosophers, because it seems to imply a lack of Divine caring towards the world. If such a Creator never intervenes in worldly affairs, it is tempting to conclude that He mustn't care at all about mankind, because there is so much apparent need for Divine Intervention throughout the world.

However, the very idea of an uncaring God is a contradiction in terms, for a God who is uncaring cannot really be God at all. This is why most orthodox theologians have opted to reject deism altogether.

Nevertheless, there are two possible ways to reconcile a limited form of deism with a traditional view of God's relationship to the world: 1) we can posit that God has voluntarily chosen not to intervene in worldly affairs for a higher (and therefore justifiable) reason, or 2) we can posit that God's lack of intervention during the evolutionary process doesn't necessarily carry over into His present dealings with mankind.

As far as choice (1) is concerned, it is important to understand that as long as we can come up with a justifiable reason for God's non-intervention in worldly affairs, then it no longer follows that a non-intervening God is uncaring towards mankind. This position has been vigorously defended by John Hick, who believes that our behavioral freedom is contingent upon the existence of a certain amount of "epistemic distance" between humankind and God.[25] The basic idea here is that if we were able to directly perceive the existence of the Creator, our freedom to act would be totally overwhelmed by God's utter Magnificence and Infinitude. For Hick, then, God's policy of non-intervention towards mankind is evidence *for*, rather than against, His love of the world, since it is a necessary precondition for the existence of human freedom (which Hick takes to be more or less synonymous with our humanity).

From this point of view, a deistic Creator is actually *more* caring towards the world than one who frequently intervenes in it, because this non-interventionist policy is itself a foundational prerequisite for genuine human freedom. On this highly compelling view, a God who frequently intervenes in worldly affairs would end up doing far more harm than good, because such actions would minimize the epistemic distance between humanity and God, and this in turn would presumably destroy the chance for genuine human freedom in the world.

Of course, one could validly counterargue that these Divine Interventions wouldn't necessarily minimize the epistemic distance between humanity and God, because it is always possible that God's Interventions could be discrete enough to avoid outright human detection. While this may be the case, it nevertheless remains true that explicit Divine Intervention as a general rule cannot be maintained along with the possibility of genuine human freedom. The direct, unmistakable evidence of God's Creative Hand that would result from such explicit Interventions would itself shrink the epistemic distance between humanity and God to the point that human freedom would be an almost certain casuality. So we see that deism in some respects isn't necessarily incompatible with the existence of a personal, loving Creator who truly cares about humanity.

As far as the nature of a deistic Creator is concerned, common sense tells us that such a deistic Being is inherently more impressive from a creative standpoint than a merely theistic one, since He is clever enough to create a self-organizing universe once its fundamental laws have been laid down. A God who continually has to intervene to accomplish His creative purposes is clearly inferior to such a deistic Being, in the same way that a car-maker who is clever enough to design self-building cars is far more impressive than one who has to be directly involved during each step of the creative process. From this point of view, a deistic Creator is more worthy of our worship and admiration than a merely theistic one, since He is so inherently powerful and clever.

Nevertheless, this notion of a deistic Creator has traditionally been frowned upon in orthodox circles, because it seems to render God impotent as far as the day-to-day events of human history are concerned. But even though this concept of a non-intervening Creator seems to be entirely consistent with the details of our past history, it doesn't necessarily follow that such a Being has played no direct role in the evolution of the universe or in human affairs. To the contrary, it is possible to imagine such a Creator continually "intervening" in the affairs of the physical universe through the upholding of its very existence and coherence as a functional system. On this view, God would indeed have created a self-organizing universe, but His Divine Power would still be needed at all times to supply the metaphysical foundation for the universe's continued existence from moment to moment. The data from modern particle physics supports this contention, as it recognizes the need for a deeper metaphysical principle to bring concrete existence to the shadowy quantum world of subatomic particles. Because these particles are said to only possess the "tendency" to exist, some deeper principle must constantly be at work to bring definite reality and internal fidelity to these slippery quantum images. Either the deistic or the theistic type of Creator is fully capable of performing this all-important function.

The distinction we are drawing here is thus between: 1) God acting as an efficient cause within the present universal system and, 2) His acting as a sustaining cause for the universe as a whole. It is one of the chief tenets of radical deism that God doesn't interject efficient causes into the world as a general rule (though He probably could from time to time to effect strategic outcomes). Nevertheless, such a deistic Being can still act as a direct sustaining cause for the entire universe, as we have seen. Thus, it isn't technically accurate to say that a deistic Creator takes *no* further part in the workings of the world once He has created it.

With this in mind, we are now in a position to at least partially reconcile the existence of a deistic Creator with the Sovereign God of traditional theism. On the one hand, we have a deistic God, who could have created a self-organizing universe that in turn could have brought about life entirely through natural means once the universe was set up in a certain way. On the other hand, this self-organizing universe nevertheless would have required a metaphysical foundation for its very existence and capacity to function as a coherent system, which of course would have been provided by this same deistic Being. It is thus only at the level of efficient causation within the physical universe that the notion of deism has any relevant meaning. Once we get beyond this to the metaphysical ground of all being itself, we find that the traditional notion of God as the Sovereign Sustainer of all existence still holds, whether that Being is theistic or deistic in nature.

Moreover, once the world has been created through natural, secondary causes, it doesn't necessarily follow that a deistic Creator will follow such a non-interventionist policy throughout human history. To the contrary, a tremendous distinction exists between the evolution of the physical universe, on the one hand, and the development of human affairs, on the other. With this distinction in mind, it is possible that the same deistic God who would have created a self-organizing universe could have also reserved the right to intervene in worldly affairs whenever the need presented itself.

Indeed, given God's supreme power to create the world in any coherent way He sees fit, it is possible to hold, as Thomas Burnet[26] did in the seventeenth century, that God could have slanted the initial creation of matter in such a way that He could have predetermined all subsequent physical events from the very beginning of time, even to the point of "causing" specific events in the distant future, like the great Lisbon earthquake or hurricane Hugo. This immense power to act at the very beginning of time, which is entirely plausible given the existence of a Supremely Powerful Deity, blurs the distinction between deism and traditional theism, since a deistic God could conceivably accomplish just about any desired "intervention" in worldly affairs without having to directly intervene in them. This adds more credibility to the deistic hypothesis, since it doesn't seem to require us to give up the important theological idea of God's Sovereignty over the entire universe.

It is even possible to maintain an active belief in traditional Christianity within a general deistic framework. While there is a definite sense in which the Incarnation was miraculous, it didn't directly appear to be that way to most people, since Jesus was born in the same way that all humans are born. Hence, Jesus' arrival on earth was accomplished in so discrete a manner that the epistemic distance between humanity and God was hardly disturbed. This would have preserved human freedom in spite of the tremendous Intervention that had actually occurred. While the adult Jesus did allegedly perform a large number of miracles, no one's freedom was directly opposed by them (Jesus even required people to have faith in their own healing before He would agree to cure them). Moreover, it is distinctly possible that Jesus used higher levels of natural causation to effect His miracles, instead of sheer supernatural power *per se*. This contention is supported by Jesus' own admission that we too will eventually be able to perform even greater miracles than He did (John 14:12). Indeed, to the extent that Jesus was a literal human being, nothing He did in the world could be considered to be a genuine Divine Intervention, because humans are inherently unable to accomplish such ends.

The overall picture we see emerging here is that of a deistic Creator who creates a self-organizing universe in the beginning and then leaves it alone to evolve intelligent life in the fulness of time. Once humans arrive on the scene, He continues this non-interventionist policy whenver it is deemed appropriate, which is to say that He also intervenes to some limited extent in worldly affairs whenever appropriate as well. The chief criterion we can use here to ascertain whether or not such a deistic Being would choose to intervene in the world is the overall good of humanity as far as human growth towards the kingdom of God (i.e., self-actualization) is concerned. If a given Intervention (such as the Incarnation) is deemed to be the best alternative for the greatest number of people, we can coherently expect our deistic Creator to have gone ahead with it, despite His overall policy of non-intervention. It is in this manner that the radical deism of Darwin can be reconciled with the basic tenets of historical Christianity.

It simply isn't true, then, that deistic ideas are inherently opposed to the tenets of traditional theism. If anything, they are a positive adjunct to them, since 1) a deistic Creator is more impressive overall than one who must create piecemeal, 2) a general policy of non-intervention is evidence for, rather than against, God's caring for mankind, and 3) it doesn't necessarily follow that a deistic Creator will not intervene from time to time in worldly affairs once the general world order has been established. This being the case, we see that it is quite possible to hold deistic beliefs without having to give up one's belief in a traditional Creator or in the physical independence of the universe from external "intervention."

Indeed, once the idea of an all-knowing and all-powerful God is affirmed, the chief deistic tenet, which states that God was clever enough to have created a totally self-organizing universe from the very beginning, seems to follow naturally, since we would expect any creator to avail himself of the most advanced possible techniques in his creation (when appropriate, of course). This being so, we would expect a supremely competent Creator to have used the most advanced possible creative techniques whenever He would set about creating something, and this would seem to necessarily entail some form of self-organization (since a self-organizing universe is inherently more advanced than one that has to gradually be assembled piecemeal).

If anything, it is the standard theistic assumption—namely that God is intimately involved in all aspects of the present world order—that seems to infringe upon God's supreme competency as Creator, since it implies that He was unable to get all His creating done at the beginning of time. Even the Bible implies that God created the universe in a deistic manner, insofar as it delegates several creative mechanisms to the earth (i.e., "and the earth brought forth living creatures" Gen. 1:11–12) and states that God rested after the first six "days" of the creation. Both of these points imply that God created a natural realm that was largely capable of creating itself once a sufficient metaphysical foundation had been laid.

Once some form of deism is affirmed, we find that a universal process of evolution is also simultaneously affirmed, since the very concept of self-organization *implies* an evolutionary ascent from relatively simple beginnings. The etymology of the word "evolution" supports us in this contention, since it comes from the Latin *evolutio*, meaning "to unroll." Darwin's deistic universe, therefore, was one in which increasing forms of complexity steadily unraveled themselves in response to self-organizing cause-and-effect processes.

1.2 Deism and Natural Theology

In this book we will be making a bold return to an area of intellectual inquiry that enjoyed tremendous influence and popularity in the past. Known simply as "natural theology," this mode of rational thought attempts to deduce the existence of a Supreme Being from the power of logical reasoning, coupled with the observable (scientific) facts of the natural world.

Deism was centered around the pursuit of natural theology, insofar as its founders believed that the traditional design argument could provide one with important information about the Creator. This deistic emphasis on natural theology, as opposed to pure revelation, is theologically defensible when we consider the fact that millions of people throughout history have not had access to any sort of Divine Revelation. Hence, if God is ultimately to be fair with His creatures and if all people are to have a more or less equal chance of entering the kingdom of heaven, there must be *another* way to become aware of God's Presence in the universe besides pure revelation. This is the role that has traditionally been ascribed to natural theology.

Such an assertion turns out to be in full agreement with the Bible, where we are told in the book of Romans that "since the creation of the world His [God's] invisible attributes . . . [have been] clearly seen, being understood by the things that are made, even His eternal power and Godhead, so that they [those who haven't been directly exposed to the revelation of God] are without excuse" (Rom. 1:20).

At the same time, though, the possible existence of Divine Revelation in the world doesn't contradict the basic tenets of deism, since revelation can always be used as a helpful adjunct to the deistically inspired design argument. The central problem with this approach, however, is that one cannot ultimately tell which purported piece of revelation is genuine and which is not. This problem doesn't exist in the natural realm, however, since the reality we perceive is always genuine (though it can often be misunderstood). Since reality can always be counted on to be genuine, we can count upon the deistic use of the design argument to tell us important things about the Creator, when different forms of purported revelation may or may not be helpful in this capacity.

1.3 Natural Theology and the Validity of Objective Reasoning

At one time natural theology was the dominant mode of reasoning employed by the majority of scientists and theologians, especially in England. Indeed, it is a little-known fact that the foundations of our modern scientific understanding of the world were laid by scientists and philosophers who were strongly committed to the precepts of natural theology. Newton, Boyle, Leibniz, along with a whole host of other scientific pioneers, were convinced that the many physical details of the natural world contained incontrovertible evidence of Intelligent Design. This is why they made such a serious attempt to deduce the order of the natural realm in the first place: because they were convinced that a universe created by a Supernatural Being would display a comprehensible degree of order and design. It was in this fashion that the discipline of natural theology set the stage for the bold scientific discoveries of the Enlightenment and post-Enlightenment periods.

However, the gradual rise of the modern world view—which posits a non-animistic, deterministic, reductionistic type of non-theistic materialism—also saw the concommitant decline of natural theology in both scientific and philosophical circles. As David Ray Griffin explains in *God and Religion in the Postmodern World*,[27] the very assumptions of the modern world view precipitated the collapse of theistic naturalism into a purely non-theistic materialism. The very definition of the scientific method—which dictated that only those objects and processes that were amenable to objective study could fall under the proper domain of science—added to the decline of natural theology. Since the claims of the natural theologian could not be verified (or falsified) by any conceivable type of experimental protocol, they came to be dismissed by the majority of scientists as "unscientific."

However, as I will seek to show throughout the remainder of this book, the details of the natural world *do* in fact have something important to say about the possible existence of a Supreme Being, but only if we allow ourselves to duly consider them with with an open mind and an inquiring heart.

Such an assertion, of course, brings with it the question of whether such an endeavor is worth pursuing in the first place. Answering this question in the negative is the philosophical position known as *fideism*, which claims that objective reasoning is entirely inappropriate for religious belief. The Danish philosopher Soren Kierkegaard (1813–1855), for instance, believed that faith, and not reason, was the primary essence of the religious life. Other fideists have adopted a similar position, agreeing with the third-century theologian Tertullian that religious faith is both against and beyond mere human reason.

There is, to be sure, a certain sense of the religious life in which this emphasis on inner subjectivity and faith, as opposed to reason, is entirely appropriate and to be desired. As Kiekegaard has correctly pointed out, the only way in which one can exercise true religious passion is in a cognitive environment in which one is *not* absolutely convinced of the validity of the various theistic truth-claims.

On the other hand, one needs to have *some* justifiable reason for ascribing to this sort of subjective religious faith in the first place. In times past, this justifiable reason often amounted to nothing more than the simple assent to a long-standing cultural tradition. Kierkegaard's own justifiable reason was more subjectively based, as it had to do with the utter meaninglessness of life in the absence of faith in God. For many people today, however, this sort of negative reasoning is inappropriate, since a more concrete, rationally-based justification for being "religious" seems to be required. In the pre-scientific era this sort of "doubting Thomas" attitude was probably less widespread than it is today, because there are now millions of people around the world who have been weaned on the gospel of scientific revelation, and who as a consequence require belief in God to be rational before they will allow themselves to subscribe to it.[28]

Michael Scriven, a philosopher at the University of California at Berkeley, argues that this mode of reasoning is eminently justifiable, insofar as "faith" should mean faithfulness to a reasonable commitment, not to an unreasonable one.[29] On this view, if theists cannot put forth a sufficiently persuasive body of evidence supporting the assertion that God exists, then atheism, or at most agnosticism, can be the only rational response.

For Scriven, the choice of atheism or agnosticism depends on the intrinsic persuasiveness of the theist's evidence for the existence of God. If this evidence amounts to a 50 percent probability that God exists, then agnosticism is judged to be the most rational response. If, however, the evidence reveals a significantly less probability for the existence of God, then atheism is judged to be the most rational choice.

Although Scriven's point is clearly debatable, there are nevertheless a large number of individuals who subscribe to this sort of rationale. It is partly for the benefit of these evidence-seeking people that the natural theologian seeks to delineate a body of rational evidence that supports the existence of a Divine Being. For while the natural theologian freely admits that absolute proof of God's existence is intrinsically impossible, he also points out that absolute proof is *not* what is required in this instance. As Scriven has shown, it is the overall *probability* of theism that renders it either acceptable or unacceptable to the rational individual, not its absolute proof or disproof *per se*. Thus, if the natural theologian can provide evidence that is sufficiently persuasive to render theism more probable overall than atheism, then belief in a Creator will (on Scriven's terms) be justified.

The creation versus evolution controversy, of course, has given a large number of people sufficient reason for rejecting the "theistic hypothesis." As we will be seeing throughout the remainder of this book, however, the theoretical foundation for this controversy is entirely inappropriate, as it is based on a fallacious interpretation of the presenting problem, as well as a faulty interpretation of both the scientific and theological evidence at hand. As a consequence, an adequate resolution of this problem can only serve to advance the cause of the natural theologian in making a rational case for theism.

It is perhaps an unfortunate sign of our times that many people no longer have a sufficient inner reason to subscribe to a theistic point of view.[30] Rather than attempt to show how religious belief can be rational in the absence of convincing evidence (this point has already been well demonstrated by Hick[31] and Plantinga, among others), I will simply concentrate in the remainder of this book on showing that there is in fact *plenty* of evidence for the existence of God, if evidence is what one truly desires. My overall point will be that when all the possibilities are duly considered, the best explanation for the existing scientific evidence is indeed theistic in nature.

1.4 A New Level of Debate

The central argument in this book differs significantly from most other theistically-oriented books on evolution. Instead of trying to argue that no form of evolution could have ever occurred, as fundamentalist creationists have been trying to do, the Deistic Evolutionist fully affirms the reality of the evolutionary process at all levels of cosmic reality. It is only the non-theistic *version* of evolutionary theory which the Deistic Evolutionist finds to be inconsistent with the known facts.

Hence, the primary question that will be debated in the ensuing pages isn't whether evolution has actually occurred or not, but whether it is coherent to believe that it could have happened in the absence of an Intelligent Designer. This radical question raises the traditional creation-evolution debate to a significantly higher level of argument, because the Deistic Evolutionist is fully prepared to accept the reality of *all* legitimate forms of evolution in nature. He can do this because he is convinced that the only way *any* kind of evolution can make sense is if it is being directed by some form of larger Intelligence.

Such an up-front affirmation of the reality of evolution makes the doctrine of Deistic Evolutionism especially hard to refute by the orthodox neo-Darwinist, because he is no longer being expected to prove that *some* form of evolution has actually occurred. Rather, he is now expected to show that the non-theistic theory of evolution is the best type of evolutionary theory to account for the existing evidence, and this is a *far* more difficult thing to do by its very nature, because almost all of the known facts point in the *opposite* direction, namely to the existence of an Intelligent Designer behind the evolutionary process. We will now turn out attention to an in-depth consideration of these basic evolutionary facts.

Notes

1. Taken from Neil C. Gillespie's *Charles Darwin and the Problem of Creation* (Chicago: The University of Chicago Press, 1979), pp. 130–131.
2. Peter J. Bowler, *Evolution: The History of an Idea* (Berkeley: University of California Press, 1983), p. 6.
3. Quoted in Ronald W. Clark's *The Survival of Charles Darwin* (New York: Random House, 1984), p. 121.
4. Taken from Michael Denton's *Evolution: A Theory in Crisis*, p. 37.
5. Charles Darwin, *The Origin of Species* (London: Penguin Books, 1968), p. 458.
6. Quoted in Barrow and Tipler, p. 85.

7. Darwin, *The Origin of Species*, p. 219.
8. Quoted in Ronald W. Clark's *The Survival of Charles Darwin*, p. 454.
9. Neal C. Gillespie, *Charles Darwin and the Problem of Creation* (Chicago: University of Chicago Press, 1979).
10. John C. Greene, *Science, Ideology, and World View: Essays in the History of Evolutionary Ideas* (Berkeley: University of California Press, 1981).
11. Peter J. Bowler, *Evolution: The History of an Idea*, p. 169.
12. Ibid., p. 82.
13. F. Darwin, ed., *The Life and Letters of Charles Darwin*, (London: John Murray, 1888), Vol. 1, p. 307.
14. Quoted in Ronald W. Clark's *The Survival of Charles Darwin*, p. 77.
15. Ibid., p. 53.
16. Darwin's chief problem with theism was thus more philosophical than scientific. Indeed, it was the overwhelming evidence of design throughout the natural world that kept Darwin coming back to some form of religion, in spite of the moral repugnance he felt at the very thought of a Divinely directed evolutionary process.
17. Peter J. Bowler, *Evolution: The History of an Idea*, p. 28.
18. D.R. Oldroyd, *Darwinian Impacts* (Atlantic Highlands, NJ: Humanities Press, 1980), p. 248.
19. Taken from Neil Gillespie's *Charles Darwin and the Problem of Creation*, p. 141.
20. Neal Gillespie, *Charles Darwin and the Problem of Creation*, pp. 134–145.
21. David J. Depew and Bruce H. Weber, *Evolution at a Crossroads* (Cambridge: The MIT Press, 1985), p. 252.
22. Erasmus Darwin, *Zoonomia* (London, 1974).
23. I will also be rejecting the non-evolutionary creation-science position out of hand, because of the overwhelming amount of scientific evidence indicating that *some* form of evolution has undoubtedly occurred.
24. Interestingly enough, the Deistic Evolutionist's tremendous emphasis on natural cause and effect processes during evolution opens this position up to some degree of scientific analysis and potential verification, since the chief domain of science is in the realm of natural processes. Fundamentalist creationism, on the other hand, must be placed outside the realm of true scientific investigation, since it relies on repeated miraculous interventions of the Creator to explain the existence of life on this planet.
25. John Hick, *Evil and the God of Love* (New York: Harper & Row, 1977), pp. 280–291.
26. See Thomas Burnet's *Sacred Theory of the Earth* (1691), London: reprinted by Centaur Press, 1965.
27. David Ray Griffin, *God and Religion in the Postmodern World* (Albany: SUNY Press, 1989).
28. Indeed, as Ayer has pointed out, the rise of science has indirectly contributed to the decline of religious feeling in modern people, insofar as the intelligibility of the world that has been made possible by the modern scientific movement "tends to destroy the feeling of awe with which men regard an alien world." (Alfred Jules Ayer, *Language Truth and Logic* (1936), p. 117.)
29. See Michael Scriven's "The Presumption of Atheism," in Louis P. Pojman's *Philosophy of Religion* (Belmont, CA: Wadsworth Publishing Co., 1987), pp. 364–372.
30. Throughout the remainder of this book I will be respecting existing convention by using the term "theism" to refer to the general view that God exists and is

responsible for creating the world in one way or another. Although I believe that a limited form of Darwin's radical deism does actually apply to the Godhead, this distinction between theism and deism is largely irrelevant to the basic case being argued in the rest of this book, which is whether or not some type of Creator has superintended the evolutionary process on this planet. From here on out, then, I will be using the terms "deism" and "theism" interchangably.

31. See John Hick's "Rational Theistic Belief Without Proof," in *Arguments for the Existence of God* (London: Macmillan, 1971), and Alvin Plantinga's "Religious Belief Without Evidence," in *Rationality and Religious Belief*, C.F. Delaney, ed., (University of Notre Dame Press, 1979).

PART I

The Implausibility
of Non-Theistic Evolution

CHAPTER 2
Spontaneous Generation

A fool sees not the same tree that a wise man sees.

WILLIAM BLAKE

Approximately four billion years ago the earth was still in the process of cooling down from its fiery beginnings as the third planet in our solar system. At that point there were as yet no life forms in existence on this planet. As time progressed, however, something miraculous happened—inanimate matter somehow became transformed into "living" tissue, and earthly life was born. The big question in evolutionary biology concerns exactly *how* this process took place.

Both the non-theistic evolutionist and the Deistic Evolutionist agree that this "spontaneous generation" of living tissue did in fact occur (it *had* to have occurred or else we would not be here); they only differ on *how* this critical event took place. The non-theistic evolutionist believes that when the conditions on the early earth were sufficiently favorable, complex macromolecules, which were themselves the result of undesigned physical processes, began forming all by themselves in a random fashion, until one day a simple living organism was produced. He believes that this was a totally haphazard occurrence, and so was not directed by any type of external Intelligence whatsoever. The Deistic Evolutionist, on the other hand, believes either of two distinct possibilities: 1) that God Himself directly acted upon non-living matter so as to bring about life when the time was right, or 2) that God constructed matter in such a way that when the conditions were right, matter was able to utilize its God-given ability for spontaneous order by coming together "on its own" to form the first living cell.

Thus, the bottomline issue here isn't whether spontaneous generation actually took place or not; it is whether spontaneous generation occurred *with or without* God's Intelligence and Divine Superintendence. Interestingly enough, we can find part of the answer to this problem right within the known rules of biology itself.

2.1 The Implausibility of Non-Theistic Biogenesis

Before they knew better, people used to think that life could spontaneously arise from non-living matter. Flies and maggots, for instance, were thought to form spontaneously from putrid organic matter. However, the experiments of Redi (c. 1688), Spallanzani (c. 1780), and Pasteur (c. 1860), proved this notion worthless once and for all.[1]

Today, the impossibility of spontaneous generation has risen to the level of a biological axiom, for everyone knows that life cannot spontaneously arise from dead matter. In fact, it has been said that "to today's biologist, with his extended knowledge of the intricate physiochemical complexity of the living cell, the sudden, spontaneous appearance of even a simple living organism is inconceivable."[2]

Australian physician and molecular biologist Michael Denton agrees:

> The complexity of the simplest known type of cell is so great that it is impossible to accept that such an object could have been thrown together by some kind of freakish, vastly improbable, event. Such an occurrence would be indistinguishable from a miracle.[3]

Given Denton's unequivocal rejection of gradualism throughout his book *Evolution: A Theory in Crisis*, the above statement can only be taken to represent an indirect admission on Denton's part that the spontaneous appearance of life on Earth was indeed miraculous after all.

Even devout evolutionist George Gaylord Simpson agrees that the appearance of the first living cell was at least as impressive as the entire remainder of evolutionary history *put together*:

> Above the level of the virus, the simplest fully living unit is almost incredibly complex. It has become commonplace to speak of evolution from amoeba to man, as if the amoeba were the simple beginning of the process. On the contrary, if, as must almost necessarily be true, life arose as a simple molecular system, the progression from this state to that of the amoeba is at least as great as from amoeba to man.[4]

More specifically, the odds for the spontaneous appearance of the first living cell have been conservatively calculated[5] to be approximately 1 in $10^{78,436}$, a number so vast that it is trillions of times greater than the total number of vibrations experienced by *all* the subatomic particles in the universe from the beginning of time until the present!

Astronomer Hugh Ross comes up with a much more outlandish figure for the probability that life could have evolved by pure chance.[6] Reasoning that the simplest possible form of life is a virus, Ross proceeds to calculate the odds for the spontaneous evolution of the simplest conceivable type of virus. He assumes that such a creature would have to possess a bare minimum of 239 protein molecules in order to reproduce itself, each possessing an average of 445 amino acids, and all precisely positioned with regard to all the others. He further assumes that each amino acid must first be activated by the appropriate set of enzymes, and that the only amino acids that can be used are of the left-handed variety (all of which are very reasonable biochemical assumptions). When all of these factors are taken into consideration, Ross comes up with the spectacular figure of 1 in $10^{15,000,000,000}$ for the spontaneous evolution of the first living creature! And this is assuming the prior existence of all the right conditions for the evolution of life, which by no means can be taken as a given.[7]

The emergence of the first living cell, then, was undoutedly the single most miraculous phenomenon in all of evolutionary history, yet non-theistic evolutionists refuse to accept the obvious religious implications surrounding this event. Instead, they work around this great pitfall by arguing that the conditions on the early earth were so different from the way they are now that spontaneous generation was entirely possible then, even though it clearly *isn't* possible now.

Unless we first postulate the prior existence of self-organizing atoms and molecules that have deliberately been given the power to gradually develop into living cells by the Creator, it is difficult to see how *any* set of environmental conditions *alone* could have possibly been so different as to enable the miracle of life to form spontaneously, even over vast eons of time. Indeed, it is difficult to see how any coherent set of environmental conditions *at all* could have existed apart from the activity of an Intelligent Designer. We mustn't make the mistake of assuming the prior existence of a material realm that is independently capable of self-organization, because as we will be seeing throughout the remainder of this book, it is this very capacity for self-organization that is the ultimate question in any study of life's origins.

In other words, just because we know that our universe possesses the complex capacity for self-organization doesn't explain the need for God away, because we still have to find some way to account for the origin of this self-organizing power, and there doesn't seem to be any reasonable way of doing this apart from the prior existence of an Intelligent Designer. As many scientists and philosophers are increasingly coming to realize, it is quite possible that God could have infused this capacity for self-organization (and hence for the natural evolution of life itself) into the Big Bang at the beginning of time. To the extent that this possibility turns out to be true, natural processes "alone" would have been responsible for evolving the first life form, *but only because God had previously designed this capacity into matter from the very beginning*, not because natural processes alone are capable of evolving life in the eternal absence of God. As far as the Deistic Evolutionist is concerned, then, there would be no natural processes *at all* in the absence of Divine Input.

On this view, the question of *how* God would have given the universe the capacity to evolve life is almost beside the point. What is important is simply *that* He has somehow given the universe this power. Thus, He might have externally imposed life-giving levels of order onto inanimate matter in the primordial seas, as many creationists believe. Or, He might simply have infused ordinary matter with the intrinsic capacity to evolve life "on its own" whenever the time was right.

It seems reasonable to suppose that if different environmental conditions *alone* were the sole prerequisite for the spontaneous origin of life, scientists would have almost surely been able to create life in the laboratory by now. Needless to say, they haven't been able to come *close* to doing so, despite countless attempts and the frequent utilization of extremely clever methodologies. But if man in all his cleverness has been unable to create life in the lab, then perhaps the missing element isn't a particular type of physical condition *per se*, but rather a particular type of supernatural Ingenuity.

It seems clear that the capacity to create life out of non-living matter requires far more intelligent "know how" than man has yet been able to provide. To the extent that this is true, it follows that the initial origin of life on this planet must have required *far more* intelligence than humans are currently able to muster. It is hard to see how random natural processes alone could have ever provided this intelligence, unless of course it was built into matter from the very beginning by the Creator.

It was this realization of the utter impossibility of spontaneous generation that led Nobel laureate Sir Francis Crick, one of the co-discoverers of the DNA double helix, to postulate the idea of *Directed Panspermia*, which is simply the proposal that the seeds for life may have been deliberately sent here by a higher intelligence from another world. Such a proposal is disingenuous, however, for two convincing reasons: 1) it doesn't truly solve the problem of the origin of life; it only removes it from the earth and places it somewhere else, and 2) it recognizes the need for an "otherworldly intelligence" to explain the miraculousness of spontaneous generation, but cleverly sidesteps the attribution of this intelligence to God by attributing it to other "hypothetical beings." But then the existence of these other beings would have to be explained, and so on, *ad infinitum*. Clearly God is the only extraterrestrial intelligence who is capable of solving the problem of spontaneous generation, since any other "explanation" only passes the ultimate creative "buck" somewhere else. God is the only being who is self-caused by definition.[8]

The notion of Directed Panspermia is the closest scientists have yet been able to come to a theistic description of the origin of life, as it explicitly acknowledges the need for a creative extraterrestrial intelligence. It falls short, however, insofar as it fails to attribute this extraterrestrial intelligence to God. Indeed, as Michael Denton has pointed out:

Nothing illustrates more clearly just how intractable a problem the origin of life has become than the fact that world authorities can seriously toy with the idea of [non-theistic] panspermia.[9]

Interestingly enough, the Bible seems to indicate that God Himself may have used the natural conditions on the early earth to help Him bring about the first life forms. The book of Genesis repeatedly tells us that it was the earth itself that "brought forth" living creatures.[10] Considering God's apparent propensity to delegate creative responsibility to His creation whenever possible, it seems likely that God would have in fact utilized the vastly different conditions on the early earth in some capacity during the initial creative process. This, of course, would have the effect of partly substantiating the non-theistic evolutionist's claims regarding the initial origin of life. On this view, life would have arisen on the early earth in response to natural processes, but *only* because of God's prior manipulation of the natural processes themselves, most probably in the form of His creation of the material property of self-organization. The non-theistic evolutionist, then, would only be accurate insofar as he would be describing the physical processes that God used to bring about life. He would *not* be accurate, though, in describing a process that could have occurred in God's absence.

The work of Stanley Miller and Harold Urey is often cited as convincing evidence that conditions on the early earth were such that life could indeed have spontaneously generated in the absence of God. In an experiment designed to mimic the supposed conditions of the early earth, Miller and Urey were able to produce a racemic mixture[11] of several different amino acids, which are the building blocks of proteins, simply by sending electrical discharges (to simulate lightning) through a flask containing what were thought to have been the most abundant gases in the primordial atmosphere: hydrogen, hydrogen sulfide, water, ammonia, and methane.

At first, Miller and Urey's results were taken to be convincing evidence that life did in fact evolve all by itself billions of years ago, in direct response to the drastically altered conditions of the early earth. Gradually, however, a number of severe criticisms have effectively disposed of this conclusion.

To begin with, as Jeremy Rifkin argues in his book *Algeny*, there is absolutely no proof whatsoever that the chemicals Miller and Urey used in their experiment were actually indicative of the conditions seen on the early earth. In fact, there is currently a great deal of debate in the scientific community over just what the conditions on the early earth actually were.

Initially it was believed that the earth's primordial atmosphere was reducing in nature, meaning that it contained little or no oxygen. The reason for this scientific dogma had very little to do with any actual evidence for a reducing atmosphere *per se*.[12] Rather, the dogma was primarily conceived in order to facilitate *our own* conception of how life must have originated. Since *we* couldn't see how life could have ever evolved in an oxidizing atmosphere, it was simply assumed that life must have *therefore* evolved in a reducing atmosphere.

The underlying reason for this assumption has to do with the belief that an oxidizing atmosphere would have broken down the incipient macromolecules that were destined to evolve into life long before they would have ever become alive. Therefore, since life clearly did evolve long ago, it was assumed that the earth's primordial atmosphere couldn't have been oxidizing in nature. But if this were indeed the case, even deeper problems would have resulted. For if there were no oxygen in the primeval atmosphere, there couldn't have been an ozone shield to protect fledgling organisms from the sun's extremely damaging ultraviolet rays, since ozone is a molecule that is comprised of three oxygen atoms. Scientists have attempted to get around this nagging problem by saying that life first evolved under water, where it would have been shielded from the sun's ultraviolet rays. But if this is true, then it would never have had access to the lightning that is supposed to have been the energy catalyst for life's humble origins.[13]

Even worse, the presence of excess water would have broken down any complex macromolecules into their constituent parts long before they would have ever had the chance to evolve into life.[14] This is due to the fact that the proteins that are necessary for the formation of life are themselves comprised of long chains of amino acids called polypeptides. However, polypeptide chains cannot form in the presence of excess water, since water chemically reacts with polypeptides to break them down into their constituent parts.[15] This simple biochemical fact is utterly devastating to the nontheistic theory of biogenesis, because it is universally agreed that life *had* to have initially evolved in the "hot organic soup" that allegedly formed in the primordial sea!

Scientists attempt to get around this problem by saying that perhaps the organic soup existed in a warm pond that slowly evaporated, thus preventing water from interfering with the process of polypeptide synthesis. The trouble with this *ad hoc* sort of reasoning is threefold: 1) Other unwanted substances would also tend to get concentrated by the evaporation, such as salt and various other minerals, and this would have vastly lowered the chances of the "correct" molecules coming together in any meaningful pattern. 2) Without water to protect them, fledgling life forms would undoubtedly have gotten cooked into an early death by both the heat and ultraviolet radiation from the sun, since the earth presumably had not yet developed a protective ozone layer. 3) There is absolutely no geological evidence[16] that any sort of "prebiotic soup" ever existed on the earth, even though geological evidence for such a rich mixture would probably have been preserved had one ever really existed.

Recent evidence, however, indicates that the primeval atmosphere may not have been reducing after all.[17] Rocks over 3.5 billion years old, for example, show evidence of oxidized mineral deposits and oxygen-producing life forms.[18] Furthermore, calculations have shown that a significant amount of oxygen could have been produced by the photodissociation of water, which results when light energy acts to break water down into its constituent hydrogen and oxygen atoms.[19] If this is true, then such an oxidizing primeval atmosphere would have allowed for the existence of a protective ozone layer around the earth. However, it would also have made it extremely difficult for simple organic molecules to link together (polymerize) to form incipient life forms, since the atmospheric oxygen would have had the effect of breaking down any organic polymers into their constituent monomers long before anything even remotely resembling life could have been formed. Thus, the existence of an early oxidizing atmosphere seems to necessitate the External Contrivance of either a pre-assembled life form, or the spontaneous assembly of organic molecules through an as yet unknown mechanism.

Still more evidence against the scientific notion of unassisted spontaneous generation comes from the realm of "stereochemistry," which concerns itself with the three-dimensional configurations of atoms and molecules. In the same way that there are both right-handed and left-handed gloves that are not superimposable on one another, there are also distinct right-handed and left-handed forms of amino acids that cannot be superimposed on one another. Significantly, living organisms only utilize the *left-handed* forms of amino acids. Their right-handed counterparts are *never* utilized, and may even be harmful. Notably, however, Miller and Urey's experiment only produced equal quantities of both right-handed *and* left-handed amino acids (called racemates), not the excess of left-handed forms that would seem to be essential for the evolution of even the most elementary forms of life. While it is possible to imagine a principle that would exclusively bring left-handed molecules together into meaningful patterns, out of a larger solution containing equal quantities of both right-handed and left-handed molecules, such a principle cannot be demonstrated to exist today. And given the validity of the Principle of Universality—which assumes that physical and chemical laws have not changed significantly over time—it is unlikely that such a principle existed solely in the distant past.[20]

Harold Urey was once asked about this very problem concerning racemates, and his answer was enlightening:

Well, I have worried about that a great deal and it is a very important question . . . and I don't know the answer to it.[21]

But it isn't as if amino acids provide the only example of an absolute cellular preference for one "stereoisomer" (molecular mirror-image) over another. Nucleic acids (which comprise the informational "rungs" of the DNA double helix) are also absolutely "stereospecific" in this regard, only in this case it is the *right-handed* versions of the molecules that are exclusively utilized by the cell! But why should it be the case that different stereoisomers are used for amino acids and nucleic acids? If a non-intelligent principle were responsible for the origin of life, one would assume *a priori* that the *same* type of stereoisomer would be used in both cases. While it is possible that some factor intrinsic to the structure or function of nucleic acids requires the exclusive use of right-handed stereoisomers, and that some naturalistic principle not demonstrable today was able to physically extricate them from a racemic mixture (in defiance of the Principle of Universality), the fact that: 1) only right-handed nucleic acids are used by the cell, and 2) different stereoisomers are used for both nucleic acids and amino acids, seems to indicate some sort of Intelligent Contrivance in their origin. After a detailed examination of this information, Rifkin concludes that:

> Miller and Urey's much-fussed-over experiments turn out to be of absolutely no redeeming scientific value when it comes to addressing the question of the origin of life. Like so many other speculations that have characterized the evolutionary literature, their work, if it proves anything, proves how difficult it is to sustain a theory that is confounded at each step of the way by a reality that steadfastly refuses to be accommodated to its governing assumptions.[22]

Biochemist Peter Mora of the National Cancer Institute agrees, insofar as he believes that any experiments that attempt to duplicate the ancient conditions of the primeval world are "no more than exercises in organic chemistry."[23]

Before we move on, it should be pointed out that other scientists have also synthesized certain organic compounds in the laboratory that seem to have been important for the evolution of life, using only the basic materials that were thought to have been present on the early earth. Sidney Fox of the University of Miami, for instance, has allegedly heated dry mixtures of amino acids and obtained conglomerations called *protenoids*, which upon exposure to water become concentrated still further into *microspheres*.[24] Some believe that these microspheres may have been one of the biochemical precursors of the first cellular membrane.

In a similar vein, the Russian biochemist Alexander Oparin—who first proposed that life may have originated in a type of "primordial soup"—has allegedly produced polymer-rich colloidal droplets that concentrate further in water into what are known as *coacervates*, which are also thought to have been a possible biochemical precursor of the first lipid membrane.[25]

It is important to note that the intrinsic validity of these experiments is totally unrelated to the question of whether or not God was involved in the spontaneous generation of the first living cell. For one thing, there is a huge chasm separating the spontaneous origin of amino acids, lipids, and nucleic acids from the spontaneous origin of the first living cell. Therefore, merely showing that certain biochemical constituents of the living cell can evolve spontaneously is a long way from showing that *life itself* can spontaneously evolve in a similar fashion.

Furthermore, by using pre-existing substances that they didn't create, and then subjecting them to the artificial conditions of the laboratory, scientists are hardly duplicating the supposedly random processes of the distant past. They are rather utilizing their considerable intelligence to set up a contrived situation that is anything *but* random. To the extent, then, that they may have been successful in duplicating some of the naturalistic steps that led to life, their elaborate experimental contrivances only illustrate the much larger Contrivance that probably existed on the early earth.[26] Indeed, the simple fact that so much intelligent contrivance is required to produce simple organic molecules in the laboratory would *itself* appear to be powerful evidence that a good deal *more* Intelligence was probably involved in the spontaneous appearance of the first living cell.

2.2 Discussion

During any study of prebiotic evolution we must strongly avoid the tendency to believe that the existence of a Creator would somehow be disproven by the discovery of a series of natural evolutionary steps that would have led to the rise of the first living cell. For even if we were able one day to elucidate all of the natural steps that led to the first life form, it *still* would not constitute persuasive evidence against Intelligent Design, because the tantalizing possibility would always remain that this was the mechanism the Creator would have deliberately chosen to create life. We mustn't forget that God seems to cause only the *causes* of events, and not the events themselves. To the extent that this may be true, it does not seem unreasonable to suppose that we might one day be able to duplicate all of the natural processes God would have employed to create the first living cell.

Surely it is a false inference that a supernatural Creator would have for some reason been compelled to create supernaturally (that is, apart from natural cause-and-effect processes). But if this is true, then it is also true that science will never be able to disprove the possibility of Intelligent Design on the basis of any set of discoveries regarding the naturalistic origin of life.

In other words, even if scientists are able one day to duplicate all the natural steps that led to the evolution of the first living cell, this would at best only show the physical mechanisms that God would have used to build the basic biochemical structures of life. It would by no means show that this spontaneous appearance could have happened in the absence of an Intelligent Designer. Indeed, the simple fact that molecules can spontaneously organize themselves into increasingly complex forms "on their own" indicates a profound degree of intelligent contrivance in and of itself, because an extreme amount of subatomic sophistication is required to produce this capacity. Thus, the reality of our self-organizing universe cannot be used to count against the Creatorship of God, because the Deity could have easily designed the building blocks of life in such a way that they would *automatically* organize themselves into more complex forms whenever the right conditions would present themselves.

If we were to put the various pieces of a puzzle into a box and then shake them up incessantly for several days, we would expect that a few of the pieces might eventually hook up together "on their own," purely by virtue of their interlocking shapes. However, if this did actually happen, it would never prove that fully-assembled puzzles could ever spontaneously form in nature with no outside help. It would only prove that the manufacturer had designed enough order into the original pieces to enable a few of them to spontaneously hook up together when the external conditions were right.

Thus, even if we concede for the sake of argument that the experiments of Fox, Oparin, Miller and Urey all duplicated the actual conditions of the early earth, and that all were successful in creating the most rudimentary building blocks of life, this ends up proving *absolutely nothing* in relation to God. They didn't create life or anything that closely resembles life. They simply caused a mixture of chemicals to react in such a way as to initiate the formation of several different (but still dead) organic molecules, which are themselves the constituent parts of proteins and other biochemical substances essential to life. Thus, instead of showing how life could have originated in a totally non-theistic environment, these scientists have at best only demonstrated some of the natural processes that God may have used to create amino acids and other biochemical building blocks.

2.3   The "Chicken and Egg" Paradox

The reason life can only develop from pre-existing life is that each of the essential biochemical components of the cell requires the prior existence of all the other components before they can be formed. These essential components are comprised of the following: 1) proteins, which function as the structural building blocks of cells, 2) enzymes, which are the molecular catalysts that help to assemble proteins (and which are proteins themselves), 3) nucleic acids, which make up the genetic material of the cell, and 4) lipids, which help to form the critical cell wall or membrane that separates the cell from its environment.

Proteins themselves are comprised of long chains of amino acids, which must be assembled one step at a time. This gradual process of assembly is necessary because the amount of energy that is needed to synthesize proteins is so great that if it were to be supplied all at once, it would destroy the entire process altogether.[27] In order for proteins to properly be assembled in this step-wise fashion, though, other proteins called enzymes are first needed to carry out the various structural routines. Since enzymes are themselves manufactured by this very same step-wise process, they couldn't have originally been created in this manner.

Moreover, the genetic information contained in the DNA must also be called upon to provide the proper structural format for the various chains of amino acids in protein molecules. DNA, on the other hand, requires the prior existence of enzymatic proteins before *it* can be properly assembled! And to top things off, both nucleic acids and proteins require a functional lipid membrane to protect them from the larger environment and to provide a coherent structural format for the cell's many activities.

In other words, all of the cell's fundamental building blocks must first exist before a living cell can come into being. Proteins must exist in order to provide the necessary enzymes for the assembly of both DNA and structural proteins, while DNA must also exist in order to provide the structural information for the assembly of *all* proteins. The precursors of the first cell, however, had *neither* the DNA *nor* the necessary enzymes to enable it to actually construct the first protein molecules. Similarly, the first DNA molecule could not have been assembled through traditional means, as there were as yet no enzymatic proteins available to do the job. As John Wiester has pointed out, you can't make steel (the structural material) without tools that are also made out of steel; similarly, you can't have the genetic blueprint of DNA without the right enzymes as tools, but you can't make the right tools without first utilizing the proper genetic blueprint![28] It's the classic paradox of the chicken and the egg. Without an external Creator to break the deadlock, the problem of life's origin appears to be utterly insoluble.

The difficulties don't stop here, though. A viable cell also needs a protective lipid membrane comprised of fatty acids to surround it, but lipids have never been synthesized even under the most "favorable" laboratory conditions.[29] How they originally formed is still a complete mystery to chemical evolutionists.

In short, the synthesis of each of the components of the first living cell "presupposes the already existing system of the living organism." It seems, therefore, that the "synthesis of the requisite organic compounds cannot be presumed prior to the emergence of the first living system itself."[30] This in turn seems to make the creation of the first living cell dependent on some sort of outside creative power.

However, it is always possible that a simpler type of self-replicating organic molecule could have evolved on the primordial earth in response to Divinely-designed natural processes alone. In this case, the very simplicity of this organic precursor to life would have presumably been responsible for its spontaneous origin, and its capacity for self-replication would have propelled it in the eventual direction of living matter (through the action of natural selection).

Indeed, scientists may have already discovered the identity of this primordial replicator. In 1981 Thomas Cech, of the University of Colorado at Boulder, and Sidney Altman of Yale, discovered a type of bacterial RNA that can partially function as its own enzyme, thereby enabling it to catalyze its own self-replication.[31] Building on this important discovery, Harry Noller, a biochemist at the University of California at Santa Cruz, discovered a type of RNA that can splice together amino acids, the building blocks of proteins, all by itself.[32]

While these discoveries are impressive, they still aren't enough to explain the evolution of life. For that we need to find a type of RNA that can string together proteins, which can then turn around and make more RNA.[33] Even so, Cech, Altman, and Noller's highly touted discoveries provide tantalizing evidence that some form of RNA might have catalyzed the origin of the first living cell, and this, in turn, would seem to bypass the need for DNA and enzymatic proteins in the origin of self-replicating molecules.

On the other hand, there is a very large chasm between the existence of self-replicating molecules and the simplest conceivable form of life. Hence, the mere fact that self-replicating RNA molecules may have evolved "by themselves" on the early earth doesn't at all mean that life itself could have evolved through similar means. Moreover, even this "simple" form of self-catalyzing RNA is nevertheless profoundly complex, comprised as it is of 30 atoms that are interconnected in a very precise and intricate network. Therefore, it isn't at all clear that such a complex organic molecule could have evolved by chance processes alone. Indeed, at a 1986 meeting of the International Society for the Study of the Origin of Life, Robert Shapiro demonstrated conclusively that it is essentially impossible for RNA to be synthesized under prebiotic conditions.[34]

But even if, for the sake of argument, some form of self-catalyzing RNA molecule did arise naturalistically and did lead to the evolution of the first living cell, this could still never be construed as being convincing evidence against a Divine Creator, because the possibility would always remain that this would have been the physical mechanism God would have ordained to create the first life form. Again we find that no degree of self-organization on the way to life is capable of obviating the need for a larger Creator, because we will always have to explain the origin of this exceedingly clever self-organizing capacity.

It is the phenomenal degree of complexity displayed by even the "simplest" living organism that makes this notion of unfacilitated spontaneous generation untenable. As physicist Paul Davies has pointed out, it seems almost impossible for the huge threshold separating life from non-life to be passed without some form of Outside Help:

> Only when organic molecules achieve a certain very high level of complexity can they be considered as 'living,' in the sense that they encode a huge

amount of information in a stable form and not only display the capability of storing the blueprint for replication but also the means to implement that replication. The problem is to understand how this threshold could have been crossed by ordinary physical and chemical processes without the help of some supernatural agency.[35]

However, let us assume, again for the sake of argument, that lipids, proteins, nucleic acids, and the proper enzymes all just happened to form on the early earth by the most improbable of accidents and then found themselves lying fortuitously next to one another. Would it then be credible to suppose that they could somehow have organized themselves into a living cell with no Outside Help?[36]

As we will see a bit later, in order for the thousands of components that comprise even the simplest living cell to work properly, they have to all fit together in an absolutely precise fashion, in the same way that a key fits in its own corresponding lock, and no other. It is ludicrous to assume that all of these constituent structures could have just happened to evolve the right functional shape to subsequently enable them to spontaneously cooperate with the multitude of other structures in their immediate vicinity, so as to eventually enable them to form the first living cell.

It is precisely this coordinated interaction between thousands of different biochemical structures that is utterly fatal to non-theistic evolutionary theory. Given the proper circumstances (which are themselves extremely improbable), one might expect an isolated protein or nucleic acid to form spontaneously over millions of years, but one would never expect *many* proteins, nucleic acids, enzymes, and lipids to *all* spontaneously evolve in such a way that they would *all* happen to fit perfectly together to form a stupendously complicated living cell. It would be like expecting each member of a 1000-piece orchestra to start randomly playing a tune, and then expecting all 1000 members to eventually start playing the *same* sonata, in perfect tune and with the proper tempo, harmonies, melodies, and so on. It is obvious that in even an *infinite* amount of time this could never happen. In the same way, it seems apparent that even the most rudimentary living cell could never have spontaneously formed with no Outside Help, not even given an infinite amount of time. As Davies explains:

There is no reason to suppose that, left to itself, [a primordial organic soup] . . . would spontaneously generate life, even after millions of years, merely by exploring every combination of chemical arrangements. Simple statistics soon reveal that the probability of the spontaneous assembly of DNA—the complex molecule that carries the genetic code—as a result of random concatenations of the soup molecules is ludicrously—almost unthinkably—small. There are so many combinations of molecules possible that the chance of the right one cropping up by blind chance is virtually zero.[37]

According to Denton, the problem of the origin of life is not unusual, insofar as it represents the general universal principle that "complex systems cannot be approached gradually through functional intermediates because of the necessity of perfect coadaptation of their components as a pre-condition of function. Transitions to function are of necessity abrupt. The origin of life problem lends further support to the notion that the divisions of nature arise out of the necessities rooted in the logic of the design of complex systems."[38]

But if life could only have evolved abruptly out of non-living precursors, this can only mean that some type of Divine Intervention had to have occurred, either directly on the earth when the time was right, or at the very beginning of time, when God could have designed atoms and molecules in such an ingenious fashion that they would have been capable of organizing themselves into living cells when the circumstances on the earth became sufficiently favorable.

2.4   Why Natural Selection Cannot Account for the Origin of Life

It is commonly believed in non-theistic evolutionary circles that non-living compounds were able to spontaneously organize themselves to the point that they were capable of a rudimentary form of replication. Natural selection is then thought to have acted upon these self-replicating molecules through millions of generations until eventually, a living cell was finally produced.

A serious problem, however, lies at the center of this assumption. Since natural selection only eliminates the unfit members of any self-replicating species, it cannot in itself have generated any new variations in the chain of self-replicating molecules that led to life; the molecules themselves had to have done this. But there is no evidence whatsoever that primitive self-replicating molecules could have ever spontaneously developed the means for producing the beneficial molecular variations that would have led to the origin of the first living cell. Lacking any significant capacity for self-adaptation, these self-replicating molecules would have simply disintegrated whenever they would have confronted hostile environmental conditions. Philosopher of science Errol Harris agrees:

> Natural selection can operate only upon an already reproducing creature, whose progeny differ from their progenitor by slight variations sufficient to give them an advantage over other competing phenotypes for survival and further reproduction. These prerequisites are not present in a non-

auturgic (i.e., non-self-maintaining) coacervate that does not adapt spontaneously to potentially hostile conditions, and would simply be extinguished if such conditions occurred. Once a self-reproducing auturgic (self-maintaining) system has come into existence, life is already present, so it cannot be the product of natural selection, to which it is necessarily prior . . . Adaptation is inherent in the very nature of life and cannot originally have depended on natural selection, because, without it, natural selection could have never begun to operate. This point has to be made before any sensible discussion of evolution can begin, for if it is overlooked, serious misconceptions are liable to arise.[39]

Once the first proto-cell had come into being, evolutionary theorists believe that it somehow developed the crude ability to further replicate itself, such that successive beneficial changes were selectively preserved until a viable living cell eventually resulted. In order for this to have occurred, though, this proto-cell had to have synthesized a certain minimum number of enzymatic proteins, but as we have seen, this would have required a pre-existing set of functional proteins. In other words, this original proto-cell was faced with the following impossible dilemma: in order to develop a more accurate protein-synthesizing capacity, it had to synthesize proteins more accurately!

Even worse, an imperfect protein-synthesizing apparatus would have tended to become magnified in successive generations, and not minimized, as has been traditionally believed. In Denton's words:

If translation is inaccurate, this leads in turn to a more inaccurate translational apparatus which leads inevitably to further inaccuracies, and so forth. Each imperfect cycle introduces further errors. To improve itself, such a system would have to overcome its fundamental tendency to accumulate errors in exponential fashion. The very cyclical nature of cellular replication guarantees that imperfections inexorably lead to autodestruction. It is difficult enough to see how an imperfect translational system could ever have existed and achieved the synthesis of one single protein let alone the many necessary for the life of the cell. That such a cell might undergo further evolution, improving itself by "selecting" advantageous changes which would be inevitably lost in the next cycle of replication, seems contradictory in the extreme . . . That an error-prone translational system would lead inevitably to self-destruction is not only a theoretical prediction but also a well-established empirical observation.[40]

In view of these facts, we are compelled to postulate that some Larger Force, wholly adequate to the task, probably enabled the first living cell to spontaneously come into existence in a fully-functional format. However, this isn't necessarily to say that God *directly* intervened in our fledgling world to bring this initial life form into being. As we have seen time and time again, it is also possible that He could have designed the miraculous property of biotic self-assembly into the first subatomic particles when He originally created the universe during the primordial Big Bang explosion. Either way, a Transcendent Creator would have been responsible for creating the miracle of life.

2.5   The Inherent Limitations of Trial and Error Problem-Solving

At its most fundamental level, the spontaneous origin of life by random molecular shuffling represents a biological method of trial and error problem-solving. Different molecular combinations are explored at random, and those that happen to produce a functional unit are allowed the luxury of continued existence.

The trouble with this traditional neo-Darwinian scenario is that it is a well-known fact that nothing of significance can be produced by a random trial and error search through a large number of different possibilities.[41] It doesn't matter whether the possibilities to be explored are found in chess, checkers, or in the evolution of life. When the number of possible combinations becomes sufficiently great, the number of meaningless combinations so outweigh the meaningful ones that virtually nothing of value can be obtained in this manner. In order for such a random search to even be minimally successful, it needs to be directed by some sort of intelligent algorithm.[42]

This realization has important implications as far as the random evolution of life is concerned. For if an unguided process of trial and error problem-solving is intrinsically unable to produce anything but the most trivial of ends, then in all likelihood it probably had little or nothing to do with the origin of life.[43] This criticism becomes all the more valid when we realize that neither the available time span, nor the number of potential candidates for this kind of random evolution, was large enough to compensate for the immense improbability of life's evolving by pure chance, which has been estimated to be anywhere between[44] 1 in $10^{78,436}$ and[45] 1 in $10^{15,000,000,000}$. Either one of these probabilities is so inconceivably remote that they in all likelihood could not have been reached in a finite amount of time, even if the entire universe were made out of organic soup.[46] (Remember, there are only 10^{70} atoms in the entire universe.)

Denton is so convinced by these figures and by the utter lameness of the trial and error method of problem-solving that he actually believes that they come close to constituting a formal disproof of the neo-Darwinian paradigm:

> The only warrant for believing that functional living systems are probable, capable of undergoing functional transformation by random mechanisms,

is belief in evolution by the natural selection of purely random changes in the structure of living things. But this is precisely the question at issue.

If complex computer programs cannot be changed by random mechanisms, then surely the same must apply to the genetic programmes of living organisms. The fact that systems in every way analogous to living organisms cannot undergo evolution by pure trial and error and that their functional distribution invariably conforms to an improbable discontinuum comes, in my opinion, very close to a formal disproof of the whole Darwinian paradigm of nature. By what strange capacity do living organisms defy the laws of chance which are apparently obeyed by all analogous complex systems?[47]

2.6 Was There Enough Time for Life to Form?

Time is the savior of the non-theistic evolutionist, as he routinely hides behind huge stretches of time in order to defend the cogency of his theory. In his way of thinking, it doesn't matter that the odds are overwhelmingly against the accidental formation of life, because the amount of time that was supposedly available in the distant past was so huge that it is thought to have been entirely capable of compensating for these miniscule odds. As far as the devout evolutionist is concerned, *anything* can, and probably will, happen if enough time goes by, even something so utterly improbable as the spontaneous development of life. As George Wald wrote in 1954:

Time is in fact the hero of the plot. The time with which we have to deal is the order of two billion years . . . Given so much time, the 'impossible' becomes possible, the possible probable, and the probable virtually certain. One has only to wait: time itself performs the miracles.[48]

Recent scientific discoveries, however, have pretty much destroyed the miracle-producing power of time in the evolutionary scheme. The earliest fossil remains of life are now estimated to be nearly 4 billion years old,[49] yet the age of the earth itself is only around 4.5 billion years. Thus, at the most only a few hundred million years were available for life to spontaneously originate on this planet, and during most of this time the earth was simply too hot to support any type of life at all, since it was still cooling down from the enormous heat of its initial formation.

It follows, then, that life "probably arose as soon as the earth became cool enough to support it."[50] Davies agrees:

In geological terms, life was quick to establish itself on our newly-cooled planet once the birth trauma of the solar system had subsided. This suggests that whatever mechanisms were responsible for the generation of life, they were quite efficient, an observation that has prompted some scientists to conclude that life is an almost inevitable result given the right physical and chemical conditions.[51]

Applied physicist and theologian Gerald L. Schroeder concurs on this point as well. Schroeder notes that the transition from single-celled life to multicellular life took approximately 2.5 billion years.[52] However, the fossil record shows that the transition from the non-living to the living occurred in only one-tenth that amount of time.[53] If the evolution of life were dependent only upon the random forces of nature, one would naturally expect the transition from non-life to life to have taken by far the most time of all, since the ontological distance that had to have been traversed in this process is incalcuably great. However, once life had already formed, one would naturally expect the subsequent transition from single-celled life to multicellular life to have taken far less time, since the ontological distance between single-celled and multi-celled organisms is vastly less than the ontological distance between the non-living and the living. Yet, precisely the opposite is what actually happened. This would seem to indicate beyond reasonable doubt that the spontaneous generation of life was *not* a truly random occurrence.

This observation in and of itself is absolutely devastating for the non-theistic evolutionist, because in his way of thinking, life only formed after eons and eons of trial and error aggregations of simpler molecules. And, at least in terms of his underlying assumptions, he is absolutely correct: wildly improbable accidents don't immediately happen; they take time, huge stretches of time, if indeed they can happen at all.

For instance, if our goal was to consecutively flip a trillion quarters until they all turned up heads, we would undoubtedly be waiting a long time for our goal to finally occur. In fact, such an occurrence could very well be a real-world impossibility.[54] Yet, the spontaneous appearance of even the "simplest" life form is a vastly more unlikely occurrence. This is why the evolutionist is forced into relying on vast stretches of time for his non-theistic theory of biogenesis to be even remotely tenable.

As we have seen, the odds for the spontaneous appearance of the simplest living cell[55] have been calculated to be at least $10^{-78,436}$, which is a number so large that it cannot even be conceived, being hundreds of orders of magnitude larger than the total number of vibrations of all the atomic particles in the entire universe! However, since the statistical range that specifies nonpossibility[56] is between 10^{-30} and 10^{-50}, it follows that the odds for the random origin of life are so vanishingly small as to be far beyond any rational consideration. And this is only for a "simple" one-celled organism. According to Huxley, the probability for the emergence of the horse is $10^{-3,000,000}$. Now we can understand how Fred Hoyle can compare the odds for the spontaneous organization of even a simple living cell to the chance of a tornado sweeping through a junkyard accidentally assembling a Boeing 747![57] In reality, though, the odds for the spontaneous organization of a "simple" living cell *vastly exceed* those of a 747, because the complexity of even the "simplest" living thing far exceeds that of anything which man has made.[58]

When these outrageously small probabilities are coupled with the surprisingly small amount of time life had to evolve in, it becomes apparent that life could *never* have spontaneously appeared without some form of Outside Help. There is simply no other way to reconcile the inconceivably low probability of life's spontaneous formation with the small amount of time life *actually took* to develop.

In response to these considerations, the more reasonable members of the scientific community are finally beginning to come to their senses. For instance, Nobel laureate Albert Szent-Gyorgyi, the scientist who first crystalized Vitamin C, admits that he could never accept the fact that there was enough time for life in all its complexity to form by random movements alone:

> I could never accept this answer. Random shuffling of bricks will never build a castle or Greek temple, however long the available time.[59]

Szent-Gyorgyi's point seems like such a simple notion to grasp, and it is. Even a child of five can understand it. Incredibly, though, most scientists continue to believe in the "creative ability" of pure chance, at least as far as the origin and proliferation of life is concerned. It isn't enough to argue that "God is not a scientific explanation," because the Principle of Objectivity (upon which the whole scientific enterprise is supposed to be based) obliges us to explain the origin of life *in whatever way we can*, as Monod has pointed out.[60]

Indeed, the appeal to a Divine Creator to explain life's origins is actually *less* at odds with the Principle of Objectivity than the appeal to blind chance, for while we know for a fact that an intelligent designer can produce prodigious amounts of order, we have no evidence whatsoever that true randomness can do the same.[61] While it may be impossible to scientifically measure the creative power of either God or chance in the laboratory, it *is* possible to see which alternative is more consistent with the known facts. One simply cannot deny that the existence of any given functional design is, on the whole, more consistent with the prior existence of an intelligent designer than it is with mindless chance.

The evidence against the random origin of life on earth is so overwhelming that even champion anti-creationist Stephen Jay Gould has wondered "why the old, discredited orthodoxy of gradual origin ever gained such strong and general assent. Why did it seem so reasonable? Certainly not because any direct evidence supported it. . . . Gradualism, the idea that all change must be smooth, slow, and steady, was never read from the rocks. It represented a common cultural bias, in part a response of nineteenth-century liberalism to a world in revolution. But it continues to color our supposedly objective reading of life's history.[62]

Of course, the reason why gradualism has been such an important part of orthodox neo-Darwinism is because it follows necessarily from its fundamental premise that life evolved accidentally. Although it is possible to argue, through verbal sleight of hand, that saltationism[63] is still compatible with traditional evolutionary dogma (as Gould and Eldredge try to do with their theory of punctuated equilibria), the fact remains that *any* type of saltational theory is very much at odds with the neo-Darwinian paradigm. No one was more aware of this than Darwin himself, who openly admitted that:

> I do believe that natural selection will generally act very slowly, only at long intervals of time. As natural selection acts solely by accumulating slight, successive, favourable variations, it can produce no great or sudden modifications; it can act only by short and slow steps. . . .
>
> He who believes that some ancient form was transformed suddenly through an internal force or tendency . . . will further be compelled to believe that many structures beautifully adapted to all the other parts of the same creature and to the surrounding conditions, have been suddenly produced; and of such complex and wonderful co-adaptations, he will not be able to assign a shadow of an explanation. . . . To admit all of this is, as it seems to me, to enter into the realms of miracle, and leave those of Science.[64]

This is undoubtedly why Gould doesn't even attempt to explain how life could have sprung into existence abruptly from non-living precursors as soon as it possibly could: because such an event is tantamount to a miracle. This makes it all the more difficult to see how Gould can possibly maintain his commitment to the traditional neo-Darwinian paradigm while simultaneously rejecting gradualism, one of its most fundamental tenets.

While it is possible to imagine that relatively rapid speciation could have taken place within small populations in peripherally isolated regions and without any significant fossil evidence getting left behind (Gould's theory of punctuated equilibria in a nutshell), this extremely hypothetical scenario *cannot* be applied to the origin of life itself, because there were no living populations in existence at that point in time. This leaves only one other possible alternative (apart from the nonsense of directed panspermia) to account for the origin of life on this planet: that life suddenly evolved here in response to some form of Intelligent Contrivance.

2.7   Life from Life

In his textbook *Philosophy: An Introduction to the Art of Wondering*, James L. Christian answers his own question regarding spontaneous generation and the origin of life. While comparing the different theories of biogenesis, he says that:

> Creationism is the belief that life can originate only by a touch of the supernatural, and vitalism is the hypothesis that a special "life force" must infuse non-living matter before it can come alive. Both theories are widely held, but their viability depends partly upon whether it can be shown that living organisms can develop from inorganic matter. If this can be demonstrated, then hypotheses involving creationism will be unnecessary.[65]

Conversely, Christian is saying that if it can be shown that living organisms *cannot* originate all by themselves from inorganic matter, then hypotheses involving non-theistic evolution will be unnecessary. He actually chooses between these extremes two paragraphs earlier when he says:

> The theory of spontaneous generation was believed for thousands of years until the experiments of Louis Pasteur *proved* it false . . . our knowledge of microscopic life forms renders this notion *worthless* (emphasis mine).[66]

If spontaneous generation is such a worthless notion, then the theory of non-theistic evolution, which presupposes the spontaneous generation of life apart from God, is equally worthless. If living matter cannot spontaneously generate out of non-living matter, regardless of the surrounding conditions, then non-theistic evolutionists have nothing more to argue about.

Of course, non-theistic evolutionists get around this severe blow to their theory by saying that things were significantly different billions of years ago than they are today.[67] This assertion doesn't amount to much of anything, though, because things *obviously* had to have been different back then, or else we wouldn't be here *today*. Thus, the primary issue at hand here isn't *whether* things were different in the distant past, but precisely *what* those differences actually were comprised of. Even more telling is the question of why those differences were sufficient to bring life into being in the first place.

Non-theistic evolutionists believe that conditions on the early earth were so different from the way they are now that they were able to work together with random molecular rearrangements to accidentally bring about life. The Deistic Evolutionist, on the other hand, believes that it was some form of Divine Activity that was able to bring about the first life form. This Divine Activity is postulated to have either occurred: 1) at the specific moment when life itself evolved, or 2) at the very beginning of the creation, when the entire universe may have been programmed to bring forth life at some point in the future.

It is significant to note that the Deistic Evolutionist's position on this issue is not at odds with the standing scientific view, since *both* acknowledge that conditions on the early earth were different enough to allow life to spontaneously come into being. The Deistic Evolutionist simply postulates a sufficient and reasonable explanation for this difference, while the non-theistic evolutionist offers no larger explanation at all (apart from the non-explanation of chance).

All in all, the scientific texts assure us that life can only come from pre-existing life. This is a law we can sink our teeth into, so to speak, not only because it seems to be intuitively correct, but also because it has never been found to be in error. However, if we take this law back to the time of life's beginning, we find that it requires us to find a pre-existing Life Form to bequeath the miracle of life to the very first primordial cell. The Deistic Evolutionist, of course, believes that this pre-existing Life Form was none other than God Himself. The non-theistic evolutionist, on the other hand, believes that *no* such pre-existing Life Form was really necessary, since he assumes that the conditions on the early earth were sufficiently different at that time to preclude the validity of this biological law.

It should be pointed out, however, that virtually all of our known physical and biological laws have, to the best of our knowledge, retained their essential character at all times, and in all places (otherwise they would never be called laws). Given this prime scientific postulate, is it reasonable to assume that the law banning spontaneous generation from non-living matter was itself originally non-existent on the primordial earth, just because its alternative, a Divine Creator, is ideologically unacceptable to modern evolutionists?

In the final analysis, non-theistic evolutionary theory is obviously correct in its assumption that life spontaneously generated from non-living matter a long time ago. It is also obviously correct in its assumption that the natural conditions on the early earth had to have been instrumental in the initial formation of life. It is only the metaphysical postulate that no larger Creative Force was needed to enable these things to come about that seems to be mistaken, because there seems to be no other way to generate life from non-life than through the direct or indirect activity of a Supreme Being.

However, to invoke an Intelligent Designer here to explain the rise of life isn't a weak-hearted retreat to a "God-of-the-gaps" explanation, because the Deistic Evolutionist isn't necessarily arguing that God acted as an efficient cause within the world system when life first originated.[68] It could just as well be the case that self-organizing natural processes alone were able to bring life into being. But since God would have ultimately been responsible for creating this material capacity for self-organization, He would remain the ultimate cause for the existence of life.

Thus, to the extent that life did actually arise in response to the naturalistic forces that are inherent in matter, the non-theistic evolutionist would appear to be correct in saying that natural processes were directly responsible for the formation of life, but only in the same way that the natural processes of Leonardo de Vinci's paintbrush were directly responsible for the Mona Lisa. In the same way that it would be absurd to say that de Vinci's paintbrush alone was responsible for the Mona Lisa, it appears to be equally absurd to think that any set of natural processes alone would be capable of generating the first living cell with no Outside Help. To produce a painting, a paintbrush needs to be used by an artist, and to produce life through natural evolutionary pathways, the physical processes inherent in the earth need to be "used" by the Great Creator Himself.

In his popular book *Cosmos*, Carl Sagan has written that:

> Using only the most abundant gases that were present on the early earth and almost any energy source that breaks chemical bonds, we can produce the essential building blocks of life [As we have just seen, this isn't wholly true]. But in our vessel are only the notes of the music of life, *not the music itself.*[69]

At this point it doesn't appear as though man will ever be able to create the music of life, because all indications are that only God Himself can be the "Conductor." The best that man can apparently do is to duplicate some of the conditions on the early earth that God initially used to create life.

2.8 Self-Organization and Biogenesis

As we have seen, non-theistic evolutionists appear to be correct in their assertion that life probably arose just as soon as it possibly could on the newly-formed earth. This in turn implies that the molecular substrates of life were somehow able to associate themselves into a life-giving pattern just as soon as environmental conditions on the earth would allow it. Once again, as far as the Deistic Evolutionist is concerned, it doesn't really matter whether God directly intervened to create this initial life form, or whether this self-organizing capacity was built into matter from the very beginning. The evidence itself seems to suggest that matter has had this self-organizing capacity all along.

It is this self-organizing ability of material systems that has led non-theistic scientists to conclude that life must have evolved without the help of an Intelligent Designer. The basic idea here is that if natural processes "alone" are capable of producing everything we see in the physical universe, why should the unproven and unconfirmable existence of an Intelligent Designer be invoked at all? The Principle of Theoretical Parsimony would seem to legislate against such an idea.

The problem with this sort of reasoning is that the stated conclusion does not follow from the assumed premise. For while it may be the case that physical processes "alone" are capable bringing the entire universe into being, we still have to explain the miraculous self-organizing nature of matter itself, and modern science has virtually nothing at all to say about this vexing issue. This question becomes all the more perplexing when we attempt to take account of the various physical principles acting at the subatomic level that make self-organization possible, such as the Pauli Exclusion Principle and the quantum nature of the atom. Physicists have absolutely no idea where these subatomic principles originally came from or why they behave as they do, but they *do* know that without them, the property of self-organization could not possibly exist. Accordingly, it does not appear to be very sensible to attribute the appearance of this self-organizing ability to chance alone.

Put another way, the mere existence of a self-organizing system is clearly much more consistent with the activity of an Intelligent Designer than it is with blind chance. We can better illustrate this point by means of an analogy with self-assembling automobiles. It is plainly evident that the hypothetical existence of such self-assembling machines would be far more indicative of intelligent design than it would be of blind chance. Indeed, we can go so far as to say that it would be utterly ridiculous to argue otherwise, because the alternative explanation is clearly incoherent.

This being the case, the burden of proof concerning the origin of self-organization must therefore lie with the non-theistic evolutionist, for the following reason: since the property of self-organization is itself much more consistent with Intelligent Design than blind chance, this must stand as the default assumption until the non-theistic evolutionary community can prove otherwise by showing how this self-organizing capability could have come into being by chance alone.

2.9 Positivistic Science and the God of Deism

As we have seen, the Deistic Evolutionist doesn't require direct creative input from God along each step of the way in the rise of life. Indeed, if God originally elected to delegate *all* direct creative activity to the atoms and molecules themselves at the Big Bang, He would not have been directly involved at all in the subsequent evolution of the universe (in the sense of interjecting a series of efficient causes within the system of the universe itself).

This deistic possibility leads to an interesting dilemma. If all of the efficient causes in the evolution of the universe have been naturalistic (in the sense of being internal to the evolutionary process itself), *no* amount of literal scientific analysis will ever yield direct evidence of God. But since scientists have only been commissioned to study that which is physically measurable in the universe, this sort of deistic Creator seems to be forever beyond the reach of modern positivistic science.

It is only when one leaves the direct realm of positivistic analysis and begins to consider the intrinsic qualities of the natural processes themselves, that the Activity of an Intelligent Designer becomes apparent. What is called for here isn't a physical act of measurement *per se*, but the subtler act of *noticing*—noticing the larger metaphysical character of the physical processes themselves. Once this act of noticing begins to take root in one's mind, the discovery of God as Creator won't be far behind.

2.10 Antichaos and the Origin of Species

The pioneering work of biophysicist Stuart A. Kauffman in the area of biological self-organization has helped to shed new light on the process of evolution. Kaufman has discovered a miraculous property of matter called "antichaos," which enables highly disordered systems to spontaneously crystallize into much more ordered states. This amazing property of self-organization, which appears to be intrinsic to atoms and molecules themselves, is believed by Kauffman to have been an instrumental force in the origin of species.[70]

One of the most tantalizing implications of Kauffman's theory of antichaos is that it seems to render life a latent property of inanimate atoms and molecules. For if highly disordered systems can spontaneously crystallize into highly ordered states all by themselves, then several continuous cycles of this antichaotic phenomenon could very well end up producing life out of inanimate matter. If this is in fact the case, then once again we are compelled to credit the amazing self-organizing power of atoms and molecules with generating the miracle of biological life. Such a realization, of course, begs the deeper question of where atoms and molecules *themselves* originally got this miraculous power of self-organization to begin with. Since blind chance doesn't seem to be capable of infusing matter with this miraculous capability, we are again left with the enterprising work of an Intelligent Designer as the most sensible explanation for this property.

Kauffman's notion of antichaos fits in well with the Deistic Evolutionist's idea of a "distant" Creator, who delegates as much creative responsibility onto the creation as possible, so that it in turn can dignify itself to the greatest possible extent through its own process of self-development. Indeed, the very ingeniousness of this antichaotic principle would seem to bear direct witness to God's Creative Hand.

2.11 The Second Law of Thermodynamics

The Second Law of Thermodynamics further supports the idea that the spontaneous generation of living matter could never have occurred without the cooperation of some form of Higher Intelligence. Briefly, the Second Law says that time causes disorganization and decay. We know this to be true from our own everyday experience in the real world. Buildings decay, people decay, and, as the Second Law assures us, the universe itself also decays with the passage of time. Indeed, decay over time is so much in the natural order of things that scientists are able to envision a day when our sun will run out of fuel, and when all life on earth will be extinguished. But if all are agreed that time causes decay, then how on earth (or anywhere else) could life—which is the most complex thing we know of—have spontaneously originated here?

V.F. Weisskoff, one-time President of the American Academy of Arts and Sciences, has described the problem posed by the Second Law of Thermodynamics in the following way:

> The evolutionary history of the world from the "big bang" to the present universe is a series of gradual steps from the simple to the complicated, from the unordered to the organized, from the formless gas of elementary particles to the morphic atoms and molecules and further to the still more structured liquids and solids, and finally to the sophisticated living organisms. There is an obvious tendency of nature from disorder to order and organization. Is this tendency in contradiction to the famous second law of thermodynamics, which says that disorder must increase in nature? The law says that entropy, the measure of disorder, must grow in any natural system.[71]

Scientists get around this problem by pointing out that the Second Law only requires entropy (i.e. disorder) to go up in a completely self-contained system. Within such a closed system, however, a small isolated region can conceivably experience a spontaneous *rise* in order without contradicting the Second Law, but only at the thermodynamic "cost" of more disorder in the overall system.

Austrian physicist Ludwig Boltzmann relied on this apparent "loophole" in the Second Law to explain the current existence of order in the universe. Boltzmann reasoned that our present universe might only be an incredibly rare and isolated statistical fluctuation from the much more normal cosmic condition of complete featureless disorder. On this view, the only reason why we are aware of this phenomenon at all is because we happen to exist in that part of the universe where this fluctuation occurred.

At first glance, it might seem as though Boltzmann has a point. It is possible to imagine untold eons of time going by in a completely chaotic universe,[72] only to have an unbelievably rare statistical fluctuation acciden-tally produce a world containing human beings. To these humans, their spontaneous appearance would seem miraculous, but in reality it would simply be the result of the universe having an infinite amount of time to work out all possible combinations of molecular order. Eventually, an accidental combination would supposedly be produced that by chance would allow for the existence of human beings.[73]

The logical basis for this type of thinking has to do with the hypothesis that given an infinite amount of time, all the particles in the universe will spontaneously go through all possible combinations, not just once, but an infinite number of times. According to this rationale, the reason why there is a universal tendency towards disorder is simply because at any one time, there are many more disordered states possible than ordered ones.

There is, however, no good reason for supposing that, given an infinite amount of time, all the particles in the universe will ever go through all possible combinations *even a single time*. For while certain relatively unso-phisticated patterns of order can conceivably result from time to time during an infinite succession of events, it does not necessarily follow that the ex-tremely-contrived objects of human or supernatural design could ever result *even a single time*. It is doubtful to the highest degree, for example, that all of the literary works that have ever been created by the human race could ever be duplicated by an infinitely long dance of cosmic particles. Even if these particles were somehow given the shapes of letters and the capacity to stick together (two huge concessions, to be sure), it still seems almost infinitely unlikely to suppose that even a single volume of the Encyclopedia Britannica would ever get randomly formed verbatim, not even over an infinite duration of time.

It is difficult to see how one can use an infinite number of particles and an infinite amount of time to make up for a task which, by all reasonable accounts, seems to be explicitly impossible. For instance, the odds for a single line of text to be correctly formed at random have been shown to be 1 in 10^{110}, which is more than the total number of vibrations made by all the atoms in existence since the beginning of time.[74] Thus, the odds for an entire book being accidentally constituted in this manner are so far beyond the realm of statistical nonpossibility as to be virtually incalcuable. With this in mind, what good reason do we have to suppose that an infinite duration of time would somehow render such a statistically nonpossible event, possible? The extra time, in and of itself, would seem to have little or no effect at all on whether such an event could ever occur. For while it could conceivably magnify the probability that a certain unlikely event might occur, it would also seem to magnify its *unlikelihood* as well, especially in a task which is, in and of itself, sufficiently unlikely.

Indeed, to suppose that an infinite number of particles, as well as an infinite duration of time, could somehow render that which is statistically impossible, possible, is to commit an egregious category mistake between two unrelated factors. The intrinsic probability that a given event will occur constitutes one category of explanation, which, depending on the unlikelihood of the proposed task, may or may not be time independent. The amount of time and/or number of particles that are entailed, constitute a second category of explanation. Now, in a task that is sufficiently likely, it may be possible for these two categories to collapse into one another, such that the number of particles, as well as the amount of time available, could possibly make up for the inherent improbability of the proposed task. For instance, given enough time and enough coins, it is possible that a trillion consecutive "heads" could be flipped. In this case, what is possible on the small scale (say with 20 coins), may become possible on the large scale (with a trillion coins), but only if enough time and coins are allowed.

On the other hand, if the proposed task, such as the haphazard assembly of an entire book from scratch, is sufficiently unlikely on the small scale (the spontaneous assembly of a single sentence), it does *not* appear likely that even an infinite amount of time or particles could ever make up for a task that is far more prodigious on the large scale (the haphazard assembly of all the books ever written). If this conclusion does not immediately appear to be apparent, one can simply magnify the task until it *does* become apparent: Instead of having all the books ever written haphazardly put together by chance, one could further require that, after the first book has been assembled, all the remaining books be haphazardly assembled in direct succession *without a single mistake*. Since each step of this proposed task is not logically impossible, it is not logically impossible that such a prodigious task be accomplished without a single mistake. Yet, no one in their right mind would ever concede that such a ludicrous "possibility" could ever occur, not even given an infinite amount of time.

The natural theologian, of course, asserts that the chance conglomeration of particles into our present biocentric universe is a far more unlikely event than the literary task proposed above. As a consequence, his position is not threatened by the positing of an *infinite* amount of time and particles, since he is convinced that even the simplest constituents of our universe, the atoms and molecules themselves, could *never* have attained their present degree of order in the absence of an Intelligent Designer. Though such a supposition cannot be scientifically proved, it nevertheless strikes the individual who has sufficiently contemplated it "with irresistible force" (to quote the skeptic David Hume's own admission).

It must continually be borne in mind that there is no empirical reason whatsoever for supposing that our own "oasis of order" on this planet is anything other than the *status quo* for the whole universe. There is not a shred of evidence indicating that true disorder exists anywhere at all in the entire realm of physical reality.

While it is possible that the entire visible universe is *itself* a random fluctuation from disorder, contained within a much larger realm of disorder, such an idea is impossible to verify by definition. It is also very hard to believe, in view of the fact that *all* the scientific evidence amassed thus far reveals the existence of order in the farthest reaches of the heavens, as well as in the tiniest areas of the subatomic realm. If order is known to exist across such a huge range of sizes (from 10^{-13} to 10^{25} cm), doesn't it make more sense to conclude that order is an intrinsic feature of the *whole* of reality, and not just of the region that we can see or measure?

The intrinsic quality of order in the universe also provides a strong intuitive reason for supposing order to be the status quo of all of reality, and not just of our relatively small, isolated region. That is to say, all of the specific examples of order that scientists have been able to document thus far are so compelling that it seems possible to extrapolate them out to the nature of the entire universe itself. The rationale here is that if the specific examples of order in our world are *so* transcendently impressive, and if similar examples of order have been discovered in the farthest reaches of the heavens, then we are probably justified in extrapolating this relation out to the whole of physical reality.

It is interesting to note that some of the most highly-ordered structures and processes in existence can be found at the largest cosmological levels of reality. Indeed, if it weren't for the intimate cooperation of these highly-ordered cosmic forces, beginning with the Big Bang and carrying through to the present day, our biocentric universe could never have come into being. Similarly, human life is dependent on a wide variety of highly-ordered forces[75] in our own solar system, many of which cooperate with one another to precisely determine the luminosity of our sun, for instance, and the earth's orbital distance from it. Going down to the level of the biosphere, there are literally thousands of distinct structures and forces on the earth which, by virtue of their highly-ordered nature, enable our world to support biological life. In addition, there are countless numbers of highly-ordered structures in our own bodies that enable us to remain alive. Most impressive of all, however, is the fact that *all* of these forces somehow conspire *together* to make the miracle of life possible.

This same argument applies to the phenomenon of single-step selection, upon which the phenomenon of life is presumably based: it just doesn't seem possible that so many statistical fluctuations could have happened in such a coordinated fashion as to accidentally produce the highly complicated process of single-step selection. Being both mindless and aimless, these fluctuations *might* have been able to produce a few isolated instances of order, but not the marvelous edifice of complexity that makes single-step selection possible.

It is clear that the many structures and forces of nature that have conspired together to make life possible are somehow coordinated with one another, as it is only because of this larger coordination that biological life is possible in the first place. But is it possible that some type of random universal fluctuation could have accidentally produced so many separate structures that are nevertheless coordinated with one another to such an incredibly precise degree? *Coordination between distinct structures implies communication, and communication is the very antithesis of genuine randomness.*

Being mindless, it doesn't seem possible that a random universal fluctuation from disorder could have ever endowed two distinct objects with a mutually complementary structure, not even through the gradual process of cumulative selection, because the process of cumulative selection *itself* requires *its own* level of cooperation between distinct parts in order to be fully operational. So, while cumulative selection can produce impressive levels of order "on its own," all we have to do to indicate the presence of Intelligent Design is to push the argument back one step, to the origin of those metaphysical constituents that make single-step and cumulative selection possible in the first place. We mustn't forget that the process of selection is *itself* a highly refined capacity that depends on a multitude of different factors to be operational, yet there seems to be no way to explain how these constituent factors could have come together in so elaborate a form in the absence of an Intelligent Designer.

If we were to come upon a group of functional, yet ontologically distinct, objects that possessed a mutually complementary structure, would we not automatically regard this as *prima facie* evidence for some sort of intelligent design? Would it even be *coherent* to insist otherwise? The odds for the random assembly of just two functionally complementary objects are outrageous enough, but the addition of *further* functionally complementary objects has the effect of multiplying these odds astronomically. When one performs the mathematics associated with this probability, it quickly becomes apparent that no ontologically distinct, yet mutually complementary, objects could have ever formed by chance alone, even given an infinite amount of time. When this type of probabilistic thinking is extended to the trillions of distinct complementary objects in the universe, it immediately becomes apparent that chance alone could never have been responsible for creating them, especially given the relatively small amount of time since the beginning of the Big Bang.[76]

It's as if we were to find a separate musical score for each of the many instruments in an orchestra. If they all turned out to be separate pieces to the same song, no one in their right mind would ever assume that they had achieved their coordinated nature by chance alone. The very fact that each of the musical scores fits in perfectly with all the others *proves* a common intelligent origin for the music. Similarly, the very fact that the many instances of order in our universe all work together to support the phenomenon of life proves a common Intelligent Origin for these items.[77] This is an item that has not received enough attention in the anti-evolution literature: while a design may demand a designer, a complex coordination between two or more objects demands a common coordinator. Random fluctuations may be able to produce a few isolated instances of order, but not trillions and trillions of them, *all* obviously coordinated together in the support of life.

In short, even if we grant that the universe has the ability to randomly achieve instances of order on its own, three aspects of the present universal character prevent us from concluding that the universe itself was the result of pure chance: 1) the existence of atoms and molecules, which, by virtue of their own internal design, are capable of interacting with one another to produce order out of apparent chaos, 2) the separate existence of so many distinct life-supporting objects and processes, and 3) the tremendous amount of coordination that is regularly exhibited between all of these items, which in turn makes life possible.

Regarding point #1 above, it doesn't appear that true randomness could *ever* be said to exist in a universe that is populated with self-organizing atoms and molecules. These cleverly designed atomic and subatomic particles "load the cosmic dice," as it were, by making it a virtual certainty that instances of order will be able to spontaneously arise out of apparent chaos. Hence, the only time when one could truly be justified in referring to a genuinely random process is *before* self-organizing atoms and molecules ever existed in the first place.

That is to say, the only way randomness can be said to be the ultimate creator of a current ordered design is if the atoms and molecules *themselves* were *also* created by an entirely random process long ago. If they were, then it seems as though the tremendous variety of ordered objects which we presently observe in the universe could legitimately be said to be the result of genuine random processes. Yet, as Barrow and Tipler have pointed out, the degree of subatomic order found in the atom is exceedingly profound.[78] Not only must the various fundamental constants of nature all work together in an extremely precise fashion if atoms and molecules are to be capable of existing at all, other, equally mysterious phenomena, such as the Pauli Exclusion Principle and the existence of discrete quantum states, must also be operative if the atom is to be stable enough to allow for the evolution of life.[79] It would seem that such a prodigious level of coordination between so many distinct branches of physics would be unlikely to the highest degree in the absence of a Larger Designer.

Once we assume the prior existence of atoms and molecules, it almost becomes self-defeating to attribute the origin of a self-ordered design to a genuinely random process, *because we can never be sure whether the atoms and molecules themselves were originally the product of Intelligent Design or not.* To be sure, within the already highly-ordered arena of pre-designed atomic particles, it is possible for non-randomly produced atoms and molecules to behave in a "random" fashion, and even to produce impressive levels of order as a direct result of this type of "random" interaction. Yet, we cannot attribute the origin of this ordered design to random processes alone, since it was the non-randomly designed atoms and molecules *themselves* that made this self-ordered design possible in the first place.

In short, there are two types of randomness being referred to here: first-order randomness, which applies to the random origin of all things, including atoms and molecules, and second-order randomness, which applies to those processes that take place *after* highly-ordered atoms and molecules have already come into existence. Scientists regularly confuse second-order randomness for first-order randomness, and this is why they are so apt to attribute the origin of a self-ordered design to random processes alone instead of to God. They regularly observe the "creation" of highly-ordered designs out of the "random" interactions of atoms and molecules, and then conclude that the ultimate creator of this design had to have been randomness as well. It is important to understand, though, that the only way this conclusion could possibly be correct is if the notion of first-order randomness *itself* is correct. If it isn't, then the observation that second-order randomness can produce prodigious amounts of order *cannot* be used to count against Divine Creatorship, because second-degree randomness is entirely compatible with the activity of an Intelligent Designer, i.e., God could very well have utilized "random" processes with His non-randomly produced atoms and molecules to produce the entire physical universe. It is thus only first-degree randomness that is incompatible with Divine Creatorship, yet it is impossible to prove with even a marginal degree of certainty whether true first-order randomness ever existed in the first place. The most recent evidence in the field of particle physics indicates that first-order randomness probably never existed to begin with, since subatomic processes are now known to be incomparably complex and well-ordered phenomena that vastly exceed our current ability to fully understand them.

Thus, it all comes down to whether or not one believes that the atom in all its magnificent complexity could have evolved by chance alone. I, for one, find the atom's internal structure to be far too complex to be able to attribute its origin to mere chance.

2.12 Discussion

As we have seen, if our biocentric world really were the result of an exceedingly rare statistical fluctuation, one would naturally expect to find at least as many examples of cosmic disorder in the universe as one finds order. While it is possible that the entire visible universe is an "oasis of order" in a vastly larger "desert of disorder," there isn't a shred of evidence indicating that this may in fact be the case. Even the so-called "chaos" that scientists have been studying recently acts as a powerful stimulus for the development of still higher degrees of order. This cosmic "monopoly on order" is powerful evidence that our universe is not merely the result of a blind quantum fluctuation, even though order *can* spontaneously form in an open system without contradicting the Second Law.

Indeed, while it may be true that an open system allows for the development of order without any contradiction of the Second Law, it is important to understand that this is only a *necessary* condition for the development of order; it isn't a *sufficient* condition. That is to say, while an open system may be required to allow for the generation of order in the universe, it isn't *all* that is required. Many additional factors are required before this can take place. In the case of living tissue, a truly *phenomenal* number of additional factors are required. The most important of these factors is *information*.

Life, the temporary reversal of a universal trend towards maximum disorder, was brought about by the production of information mechanisms. In order for such mechanisms to first arise it was necessary to have matter capable of forming itself into a self-reproducing structure that could extract energy from the environment for its first self-assembly. Directions for the reproduction of plans, for the extraction of energy and chemicals from the environment, for the growth of sequence and the mechanism for translating instructions into growth all had to be simultaneously present at that moment. This combination of events has seemed an incredibly unlikely happenstance and often divine intervention is prescribed as the only way it could have come about.[80]

This is an excellent summarization of the Deistic Evolutionist's position with regard to the origin of life. The spontaneous appearance of such an enormously complicated system as a living cell appears to be strictly unintelligible in the absence of a larger Creator.

The fact is, scientists are still almost completely in the dark as to how and why life first arose. In the words of Freeman Dyson:

We are still at the very beginning of the quest for understanding of the origin of life. We do not yet have even a rough picture of the nature of the obstacles that prebiotic evolution has had to overcome. We do not have a well-defined set of criteria by which to judge whether any given theory of the origin of life is adequate.[81]

Given this almost complete lack of knowledge about how life first arose on this planet, along with the many complex obstacles that we know had to have been overcome en route, it would seem that the theistic hypothesis is by far the most likely explanation at the present time.

Notes

1. James L. Christian, *Philosophy: An Introduction to the Art of Wondering* (New York: Holt, Rineheart, and Winston, 1977), p. 353.
2. Quoted in Marshall and Sandra Hall's *The Truth: God or Evolution?* (Grand Rapids: Baker Book House, 1973), p. 24.
3. Michael Denton, *Evolution: A Theory in Crisis* (Bethesda, MD: Adler & Adler, 1986), p. 264.
4. George Gaylord Simpson, *The Meaning of Evolution* (New Haven: Yale University Press, 1967), pp. 15–16.
5. John R. Hadd, *Evolution: Reconciling the Controversy* (New Jersey: Kronos Press, 1979), p. 31.
6. Hugh Ross, *Genesis One: A Scientific Perspective* (Sierra Madre, CA: Wisemen Productions, 1983), pp. 9–10.
7. See my book *God and the New Cosmology* (Lanham, MD: Rowman and Littlefield, 1993) for more on the immense unlikelihood of our life-supporting universe coming into being by chance alone.
8. This is a version of the famous Cosmological Argument for the existence of God, applied to the problem of the origin of life. It claims that God is by definition the only type of being who could have started off the chain of events leading to life.
9. Michael Denton, *Evolution: A Theory in Crisis*, p. 271.
10. Gen. 1:11–12, 20, 24.
11. A racemic mixture consists of equal quantities of right-handed and left-handed molecules.
12. Rifkin, *Algeny* (New York: The Viking Press, 1983), p. 149.
13. Ibid.
14. Ibid., p. 150.
15. Ibid.
16. Michael Denton, *Evolution: A Theory in Crisis*, p. 263.
17. Ibid.
18. John Wiester, *The Genesis Connection* (Nashville: Thomas Nelson Publishers, 1983), pp. 103–105.
19. Ibid., pp. 98–99.
20. For more on the Principle of Universality, see James Trefil's *Reading the Mind of God: In Search of the Principle of Universality* (New York: Charles Scribner's Sons, 1989).
21. Quoted in Rifkin's *Algeny*, p. 151.
22. Ibid.
23. Quoted in Rifkin's *Algeny*, p. 148.
24. Gordon Rattray Taylor, *The Great Evolution Mystery* (New York: Harper & Row, Publishers, 1983), p. 201.
25. Ibid.
26. This of course is just another way of saying that Fox and Oparin may have merely discovered the natural processes that God may have indirectly used to create the first life form.

27. Errol E. Harris, *Cosmos and Anthropos* (Atlantic Highlands, New Jersey: Humanities Press International, Inc., 1991), p. 67.
28. John Wiester, *The Genesis Connection*, p. 91.
29. Ibid., p. 92.
30. Harris, *Cosmos and Anthropos*, p. 67.
31. Peter Radetsky, "How Did Life Start?" in *Discover*, Vol. 13, No. 11, Nov., 1992, p. 76.
32. Lori Oliwenstein, "All the Way With RNA," *Discover*, Vol. 14, No. 1, Jan., 1993, p. 69.
33. Ibid.
34. Robert Shapiro, "Prebiotic Ribose Synthesis: A Critical Analysis," *Origin of Life and Evolution of the Biosphere*, 18, (1988), pp. 71–85.
35. Paul Davies, *God and the New Physics* (New York: Simon & Schuster, 1983), p. 68.
36. Once again, it doesn't matter whether this "Outside Help" is in the form of a direct intervention during the actual biogenetic process itself, or in the form of cleverly designed natural processes that are able to spontaneously generate life "on their own." In either case, some form of Outside Help would be required to get life "off the ground."
37. Ibid., p. 69.
38. Michael Denton, *Evolution: A Theory in Crisis*, p, 270.
39. Errol E. Harris, *Cosmos and Anthropos*, pp. 68, 78.
40. Michael Denton, *Evolution: A Theory in Crisis*, pp. 266–267.
41. Ibid., pp. 309–316.
42. Ibid., p. 313.
43. Ibid., p. 314.
44. John R. Hadd, *Evolution: Reconciling the Controversy*, p. 31.
45. Hugh Ross, *Genesis One: A Scientific Perspective*, pp. 9–10.
46. Fred Hoyle and Chandra Wickramasinghe, *Evolution from Space* (London: J.M. Dent and Sons, 1981), p. 24.
47. Michael Denton, *Evolution: A Theory in Crisis*, pp. 315–316.
48. Quoted in Stephen Jay Gould's *The Panda's Thumb* (W.W. Norton & Company, 1980) pp. 218–219.
49. Ibid., p. 220.
50. Ibid., p. 225.
51. Davies, *God and the New Cosmology*, p. 68.
52. Gerald L. Schroeder, *Genesis and the Big Bang* (New York: Bantam Books, 1990), p. 144.
53. Ibid.
54. Statistically, there is a finite probability that a trillion quarters flipped simultaneously will eventually turn up all heads. Realistically, though, it doesn't seem likely that such a thing could ever actually happen, no matter how much time is available. It's easy to say that such a thing could eventually happen if one had trillions of years to work with, but no one has ever had this much time to empirically confirm such a prediction.
55. John R. Hadd, *Evolution: Reconciling the Controversy*, p. 31.
56. Rifkin, *Algeny*, p. 153.
57. Ibid., p. 152.
58. As we will see in more detail a bit later, the notion of cumulative selection, in which each selective step builds upon previous successes, cannot rescue the non-theistic evolutionist from the need for Intelligent Design in our world, be-

cause he still needs to provide a plausible explanation for how matter achieved the capacity for cumulative selection to begin with. Indeed, it is difficult to see how matter could have even been capable of single-step selection in the absence of an External Divine Contrivance. Biologists such as Richard Dawkins (author of *The Blind Watchmaker*), who think that the process of cumulative selection itself is capable of producing elaborate designs in the absence of a larger Designer, commit the fallacy of positing their conclusion—which they are trying to prove—in their basic premise. In this case, matter is assumed to have the prior capacity to evolve by way of both single-step and cumulative selection, yet it is by no means clear that these miraculous capacities can be taken as mere "givens." Indeed, considering the unfathomable complexity of the subatomic realm (which enables macroscopic order to exist in the first place), we cannot take *any* material process for granted, especially one that is so complicated that it can enable single-step and cumulative selection to occur. This proviso becomes doubly important when we consider the fact that non-theistic evolutionists are trying to explain *everything* in terms of material and accidental processes alone, and this would include the process of selection itself. Yet, it is hard to see how matter could have ever acquired the miraculous capacities for replication and subsequent selection by chance alone.

59. Rifkin, p. 200.
60. Jacques Monod, *Chance and Necessity* (New York: Alfred A. Knopf, 1971), pp. 21–22.
61. Although order has been shown to be capable of arising spontaneously from "chaos," this chaos is only apparent. Behind it is the stupendous order of coherent atoms and molecules that are capable of all sorts of complex physical and chemical interactions.
62. Stephen Jay Gould, *The Panda's Thumb*, pp. 225–226.
63. Saltationism refers to the doctrine that life evolved abruptly through major leaps across "bridgeless gaps." It is the direct opposite of gradualism, which states that life evolved gradually through a great many intervening steps.
64. Charles Darwin, *The Origin of Species* (New York: P.F. Collier & Son, 1909), pp. 114, 242, 468.
65. James L. Christian, *Philosophy: An Introduction to the Art of Wondering*, p. 353.
66. Ibid.
67. Things couldn't have been *too* different back then or else we would be totally unable to speculate about life's origins.
68. A "God-of-the-gaps" explanation, of course, is simply one that credits a Creator for producing any given effect in the physical universe. The weakness of this type of explanation is that it instantly fails as soon as a naturalistic cause for the effect is discovered. But the Deistic Evolutionist isn't trying to use God as a direct explanation for any given cause or effect in the universe; he is using Him as an explanation for the entire natural order itself. It is for this reason that the Deistic Evolutionist cannot fall victim to a God-of-the-gaps explanation: because the nature of his Deistic Creator places Him entirely outside the realm of efficient causation in the universe.
69. Carl Sagan, *Cosmos* (New York: Random House, 1980), p. 39.
70. Stuart A. Kauffman, "Antichaos and Adaptation," *Scientific American*, Vol. 265, No. 2, Aug. 1991, pp. 78–84.
71. Victor F. Weisskopf, "The Frontiers and Limits of Science," *American Scientist*, Vol. 65, July-August, 1977, p. 409.
72. A completely chaotic universe is actually a contradiction in terms, since the

very word "universe" entails a unified cosmic whole comprised of fully integrated parts.

73. This "random fluctuation" hypothesis is at best incomplete, as it neither accounts for the initial existence of matter, nor for the particular structural characteristics of atoms and molecules which enable them to spontaneously order themselves with no Outside Help.

74. See Guy Murchie's, *The Seven Mysteries of Life* (Boston: The Houghton Mifflin Company, 1978).

75. The word "force" in this context does not refer directly to any of the four fundamental forces of physics. It merely refers to any type of composite force that is capable of acting on matter in an influential way.

76. Compared with eternity, 15 billion years is a very short period of time. In fact, it is *infinitely* shorter.

77. For more on the biocentric nature of our entire universe, please refer to my book *God and the New Cosmology*.

78. Barrow and Tipler, *The Anthropic Cosmological Principle*, pp. 302–305.

79. Ibid.

80. Stanley W. Angrist and Loren G. Hepler, *Order and Chaos* (New York: Basic Books, Inc., 1967), pp. 203–204.

81. Freeman Dyson, "Honoring Dirac," *Science*, Vol. 185, September 27, 1974, p. 1161.

CHAPTER 3
Mutations

We know virtually nothing about the genetic changes that occur in species formation.

RICHARD LEWONTIN

The probability of dust carried by the wind reproducing Durer's *Melancholia* is less infinitesimal than the probability of copy errors in the DNA molecule leading to the formation of the eye.

PIERRE GRASSÉ

Non-theistic evolutionary theory holds that a new species is formed when the genetic material of the old species is changed to the point that interbreeding with the parent species no longer occurs. A variety of mechanisms are said to mediate this genetic change, chief among them being random mutation, gradual adaptation to a changing environment, and geographically-induced reproductive isolation.

As an example of the speciation process, let us consider a local population of finches. Although all are members of a single species, minor variations in the population render some individuals slightly better adapted to a given portion of the local environment. Being better adapted, these individuals are favored by the process of natural selection, so they survive long enough to pass their genes on to the next generation. Unless it is genetically masked, this new generation will also possess the advantageous variation, which in turn will lead it to further reproductive success, and so on. Eventually, this type of selection-based radiation into different niches is thought to produce a new species.

In order for this to be an effective mechanism for speciation, there must be a vehicle for introducing genetic variation into a given population. Although there is a certain amount of variation that is inherent in any species by virtue of genetic recombination, an additional source of *new* genetic material must also be made available to an evolving species, in order to provide new variations for natural selection to act on. Random mutation—which is the spontaneous and directionless appearance of new genetic material, in response to genetic copying errors—is thought to be the primary mechanism through which new variations are able to enter an evolving population.

Mutations

Once again both the non-theistic evolutionist and the Deistic Evolutionis. are agreed that the genetic material of the original life forms on this planet had to have been changed over and over again in order for there to have been as many different species of plants and animals as have existed throughout history. The two positions only differ on *how* these changes allegedly took place. The non-theistic evolutionist believes that random genetic mutation is the chief mechanism by which the genetic material becomes transformed, whereas the Deistic Evolutionist believes that through one naturalistic mechanism or another, God Himself programmed these genetic changes in such a way that the variations which actually appeared were already more or less coherent and fully formed.

Once these new species were formed, though, the Deistic Evolutionist believes that they became subject to the full selective pressure of the environment. On this view, when the environment began to change, species were forced to either adapt or die. By virtue of the various adaptations that they were somehow able to acquire, many creatures were lucky enough to adapt and survive. Others weren't so fortunate, so extinction followed.

With this in mind, is it any wonder that the vast majority of animals that have ever existed on this planet are now extinct? Because of their rigid genetic makeup, animals are able to adapt only so much to a changing environment. Consequently, when environmental change proceeds faster than organismic adaptation, extinction, not evolution, is the usual result.

Extinction occurs when a given species fails to experience enough internal variation to allow it to develop an adaptive response to its changing environment. While random mutations do occur, they rarely add to an organism's ability to escape death, since in the vast majority of cases[1] they are deleterious. If anything, they facilitate the process of extinction by rendering the organism less adaptable to its particular niche. Thus, random mutations appear to be one of the primary reasons why evolutionary history has been more fraught with extinction than with proliferation over the years.

It is sometimes claimed that a mutation that is deleterious in one niche can be beneficial in another niche. This seems to be an exceedingly unlikely prospect indeed, since each organism is exquisitely adapted to its own niche through the information contained in its genes; therefore, we would expect that almost any change in this genetic information would cause the organism to become less adapted to its own niche, all things considered, and that this in turn would cause it to be in immediate danger of being selected *against*. While it is conceivable that a deleterious mutation in one niche could end up being beneficial in another niche, this seems unlikely to the highest degree in the absence of any useful communication between the status of the new niche, on the one hand, and the form taken by the mutation itself, on the other. This unlikelihood is compounded by the fact that it almost always takes several genetic mutations to actually code for a single phenotypic (i.e.

69 ↲. And since the odds for a single beneficial mutation are so
ıds for several related mutations to happen *together* in a posi-
re downright astronomical. Thus, it seems as though random
ɔne cannot be the physical vehicle though which new genetic
materɪaɪ ⌐ ɛrs a species. Darwin would have agreed, for he "did not consider them [mutations] important because they nearly always represented
obviously disadvantageous modifications from the point of view of the struggle for existence; consequently they would most likely be rapidly eliminated
in the wild state by the operation of natural selection."[2]

With these things in mind, it would appear as though non-theistic evolutionists are only deceiving themselves with their emphasis on random mutations as the ultimate creative force of evolution. On the one hand, they say
that mutations are the ultimate source of genetic variation, while on the
other hand, they argue that mutant genes are "actually harmful because
they replace adaptive genes that have evolved and served the organism well
through its long evolution."[3]

Hence, even though mutation is "the ultimate source of all genetic variation,"[4] the vast majority of mutations are deleterious to the organism, so
that "it does not seem . . . that the central problem of evolution can be
solved by mutations."[5] It is this realization that has led more than one
evolutionary scientist to conclude once and for all that "mutations do not
guide evolution."[6]

But if random mutations do not guide evolution, what does? In order to
find an adequate answer to this question, we must endeavor to go beyond
the traditional boundaries of evolutionary biology.

3.1 Three Types of "Mutations"

In traditional neo-Darwinian theory there is only one type of mutation
for evolution to work on: the random variety. In this case, the word "random" isn't taken to mean *truly* random in a genuine mathematical sense; it
is taken to mean directionless genetic change with no foresight or previously-
intended adaptive significance. In this way of thinking, it is natural selection
that has the marvelous capacity for sifting through these randomly-occurring
genetic changes and choosing the most adaptively significant ones for continued survival.

One piece of evidence that superficially seems to favor the traditional
neo-Darwinian scenario is that random mutations in the above-stated sense
comprise the vast majority of those genetic changes that scientists can document in the laboratory. It is apparent, however, that this type of genetic
change alone could not have been responsible for producing the immense
amount of diversity and complexity that we currently observe in the biosphere, simply because random mutations are almost always deleterious,

and for good reason: whenever a randomly-occurring genetic change happens within a genome that is already well-adapted to its environment, destructive consequences are bound to result.

The hope of the neo-Darwinian evolutionist, of course, is that when these random mutations are multiplied over millions of organisms and billions of years, natural selection alone will be able to marshall out those rare mutations that are able to foster survival in local environments, with the result that a large variety of new species will eventually be formed. However, given the reality of relatively rapid speciation in the fossil record, along with the fact that any given phenotypic trait is generally comprised of a number of separately-occurring genetic changes that are both simultaneous and fully coordinated with one another, the odds that any coherent morphogenetic changes will appear purely by chance would seem to be vanishingly slim.

Hugh Montefiore agrees that there must be some type of order-promoting internal bias in living matter:

Although there is no external force imposed on species, and in particular on their genetic systems, mutations occur which would not be expected by random mutation. This is not because of external pressures but because of the bias implanted in matter. Such a bias is not, of course, to be detected by scientific measurement (and so the hypothesis is not testable) since there is no possibility of setting it alongside matter which is not implanted with this bias towards complexity and organization. Another way of describing this bias would be to call it the Holy Spirit working within the matter of the universe, unfolding the purpose of the Creator by immanent operation.[7]

There is, however, a way to test for the existence of this sort of internal bias in matter, as John Polkinghorne has suggested.[8] It is simply to compare the relative probabilities of those mutations that possess this internal bias to those that do not. When we do this and look at the actual odds for truly random mutations, we find that the odds are much too slim to ever represent an actual description of why mutations in the living world have actually occurred the way they did.

It is for this reason that we can postulate the existence of three different types of genetic changes (e.g. mutations) that have occurred throughout evolutionary history: 1) genuinely random (first-order) mutations, which are "unintended" and are almost always deleterious, 2) weak (second-order) orthogenetic "mutations,"[9] which are more "directed" than random mutations, but which only vaguely point in a certain adaptive direction (being diffuse rather than specific), and 3) "strong" (third-order) orthogenetic "mutations," which are strongly oriented in a certain adaptive direction.

In this descriptive scheme, third-order "mutations" are more or less identical with Richard Goldschmidt's "systemic mutations," which represent the major genetic transformations (or macroevolutionary changes) that have produced the different species throughout evolution, along with their major adaptive structures. In contrast, second-order "mutations" represent the relatively minor variations (microevolutionary changes) that have subsequently occurred around these major systemic changes. Third-order "mutations" (or macroevolutionary changes) would thus be responsible for creating the basic plant and animal forms themselves, whereas second-order "mutations" (or microevolutionary changes) would be responsible for producing the relatively minor variations on these basic themes.

On this view, the production of new species isn't necessarily limited to third-order "mutations." It is also distinctly possible that, depending on the degree of directedness displayed by second-order "mutations," a brand new species will eventually form through the gradual accumulation of second-order "mutations." If this turns out to be the case, then the only difference between second-and third-order "mutations" is in the overall quantity of the changes themselves, not in their individual quality.

In other words, both second- and third-order "mutations" appear to be different manifestations of the same underlying directional force in the genome. To the extent that this is actually the case, we now have at our disposal another way to distinguish between second- and third-order mutations that is based on their individual temporality. On this view, third-order "mutations" can be understood to represent the *initial appearance* of a given conglomeration of adaptive forms, while second-order "mutations" can be understood to represent all the *subsequent variations* around this basic form.

Another distinction between second- and third-order "mutations" concerns the degree of directionality they happen to display. Third-order "mutations" apparently need to be rather strongly predetermined, since they are responsible for generating the basic adaptive forms themselves. In contrast, second-order "mutations" seem to be much less firmly predetermined, since they merely produce the different variations that occur around each adaptive structure; indeed, it is this very diffuseness that *enables* them to vary as much as they do.

With all this talk about directionality in evolution, one might initially think that the role of natural selection in this evolutionary scheme would be reduced to a minimum. Such is not the case, however. For even with a strong element of directionality in the variations themselves, natural selection is still required to choose the fittest variations for continued survival.

The biggest difference, then, between the non-theistic evolutionist and the Deistic Evolutionist concerns the status of the variations themselves: the non-theistic evolutionist believes that variations do not display any directionality whatsoever, whereas the Deistic Evolutionist argues precisely the opposite. Both insist that natural selection is the force that chooses the fittest variants for continued survival. The Deistic Evolutionist simply believes that natural selection requires something coherent and functional to select *from*.

Darwin, of course, was fundamentally a deist, so he believed that the Creator was somehow responsible for guiding the direction of variations. Predictably, this is anathema to modern non-theistic evolutionists, who have little choice but to disown this part of Darwin's philisophico-theological background. Indeed, many of these individuals try to take up for Darwin's "misinformed opinion" by pointing out that Darwin had no knowledge of modern genetics. On this argument, Darwin had little choice but to resort to some form of theism because he didn't understand how genes behave during the evolutionary process; if he did, so the argument goes, he would have seen that there is no need for God at all to help explain the molecular nature of genetic variation.

While it is indeed true that Darwin had no knowledge of modern genetics, it is also true that the modern geneticist is just about as far from an adequate explanation of variations as Darwin was over a century ago. Sure, we know far more now about how genes behave at the molecular level than Darwin did, but this is at best irrelevant to the central question which is at issue here, because the present-day behavior of genes *assumes* the prior existence of beneficial variations; hence we can't use our knowledge of molecular genetics to explain variations without begging the ultimate question which is at issue here. This is a *non sequitur* pattern of reasoning that many scientists easily fall victim to, but it simply doesn't hold up under strict logical analysis. The mere fact that genes behave in a certain way today cannot properly be used as a sufficient explanation for how they originally came to possess this behavioral capacity to begin with. It is never correct to assume the validity of the very thing one is trying to prove!

The modern non-theistic evolutionist must thus resort to an irrelevant red herring in order to get around the need to adequately explain the ultimate source of heritable variations. Darwin surely would have seen the fallaciousness of this type of argument, but his modern-day counterparts apparently do not. But this is precisely what we have to expect as long as we insist on dividing the twin historical disciplines of science and philosophy into two separate fields of study. Not so long ago, science was just another branch of philosophy, which went under the name of "natural philosophy." All the scientists of that bygone era thus had the benefit of strict philosophical training, which enabled them to effectively navigate through all manner of causal interpretation. The vast majority of today's scientists, however, have been stripped of this capacity to think and reason philosophically, due to their extreme emphasis on scientific over-specialization. The assumption has been that philosophical expertise is unnecessary as long as good scientific data is available, but this prejudice has turned out to be incorrect time and time again. For what is science but the interpretation of evidence, and what is interpretation but philosophy fleshed out? Accordingly, science without philosophy is lame, because it can't always make sense out of its own evidence.

Getting back to our original discussion regarding the implications of directionality in the evolutionary process, it is still possible for natural selection to perform a positive role with the internally-directed variations in any population. These internally-directed variations, or second-order "mutations," would be comprised of an entire spectrum of pre-determined genetic variants, which would cluster around each major adaptive structure. It would then remain for natural selection to "choose" only the most well-adapted of these variants for continued survival. *"Randomness" in this sense would simply refer to the range and incidence of variation around the central morphogenetic structure in question, not to a true state of directionless genetic change per se.* Around this central morphogenetic theme, the variation would be "random," insofar as there would be no set pattern to the variations themselves. However, because these "random" variations would themselves be clustered around a coherent morphogenetic structure, they couldn't truly be considered random at all, since they would be strongly directed towards conformity around this central morphogenetic theme.

The non-theistic evolutionist thus errs insofar as he confuses these "random" variations around coherent structures for genuine randomness itself. That is to say, he correctly observes a "random" pattern of variation around a given morphogenetic theme, but he incorrectly extrapolates this randomness out to the nature of *all* variations. He fails to see that the "randomness" he is observing is only "random" with respect to the actual range and incidence of variations around a preexisting morphogenetic theme. He thus fails to see that these "random" variations are nevertheless very strongly directed towards conformity around the central morphogenetic structure in question, so he draws the false conclusion that all variations themselves must be random (i.e., undirected). However, the lack of a firm directional pattern in the actual incidence of variations around a preexisting structural focal point most definitely does *not* mean that there is no larger direction to the variations themselves, because they are clearly being directed towards conformity around the morphogenetic structure in question.

Let us take the range of variability around the beak of a certain species of finch for instance. In any given group of offspring, there might be dozens of slightly different variations on this basic beak theme. Some beaks might be a little longer, harder, and more pointed, while others might be a little shorter, softer, and more rounded, and there might be any number of combinations in between. Now, the actual incidence of these variations in any group of progeny would seem to be truly random, insofar as there would be no set pattern to them at all. Twenty percent might be long, hard, and pointed, thirty percent might be short, hard, and more rounded, twenty-five percent might be long, soft, and pointed, and twenty-five percent might be short, soft, and more rounded. In the next generation, however, these percentages might be totally different. Even so, it would be a profound mistake to extrapolate this small-scale randomness around the central beak theme to true mutational randomness in general, because the actual conformity of these variations around the central beak theme is anything *but* random. So we see that it is distinctly possible for there to be a lack of directionality in the small scale (in the actual incidence of variations around the central beak theme), but for there to be a strong presence of directionality in the large scale (in the conformity of all these variations to the central beak theme).

Second-order "mutations," then, are only "random" in the small scale, insofar as their actual incidence around a central morphogenetic theme is concerned. From a larger point of view, however, they are very strongly directional, and hence not random at all, because they conform so strongly to preexisting morphogenetic themes.

Speaking of these second-order "mutations," noted French biologist Pierre Grassé believes that they do not contribute significantly to the evolutionary process.[10] According to Grassé, second-order "mutations" (variations) are "merely hereditary fluctuations around a medium position; a swing to the right, a swing to the left, but no final evolutionary effect . . . they modify what pre-exists."[11] Since Grassé evidently does not believe that second-order "mutations" are responsible for the diversity of forms seen throughout the evolutionary record, it would seem that he must believe in the existence of third-order or systemic "mutations," which determine the various biological structures themselves, and not just the relatively minor variations around these basic structures.

Grassé seems to have a point. If second-order "mutations" were chiefly responsible for producing new species, one would think that artificial breeders—who routinely manipulate these variations for economic gain—would have been able to create at least one new species by now. The fact that they have not strongly suggests that second-order "mutations" are not responsible for producing the various species that have evolved over the millennia. This distinction would then fall on third-order "mutations" almost exclusively.

It would appear as though the chief shortcoming of modern neo-Darwinian theory has been its failure to distinguish between these three types of "mutations," preferring instead as it does to view them all as different manifestations of one and the same process. In light of the observational evidence, however, they most definitely do not *seem* to be examples of the same underlying process at all. The first type of mutation is the unintended result of a random genetic change—perhaps resulting from exposure to radiation or to a teratogenic chemical influence—which acts to destroy the preceding order of the genome; hence the deleteriousness that is almost always observed in this type of mutation. This is why these first-order mutations are truly random: because the mutagenic forces that impinge on the genome are *themselves* random. The second and third types of "mutations," on the other hand, aren't really unintended at all; they are "intended" genetic transformations that produce new levels of adaptive order in a given species (in conjunction, of course, with the "pruning" effects of natural selection). It is some combination of these latter two forms of "mutation" that is apparently responsible for producing the regularly observed "saltations," or evolutionary jumps, in the fossil record.

Interestingly enough, physicist David Bohm believes that the presumed randomness of the mutational process is *itself* largely the result of a mistaken generalization from the realm of quantum mechanics, insofar as he believes that quantum randomness might not be truly random after all:

> We see, then, that even in physics, quantum processes may not take place in a completely random order, especially as far as short intervals of time are concerned. But after all, molecules such as DNA are in a continual process of rapid exchange of quanta of energy with their surroundings, so the possibility clearly exists that the current laws of quantum theory (based on the assumption of randomness of *all* quantum processes, whether rapid or slow) may be leading to seriously wrong inferences when applied without limit to the field of biology . . . It is evidently possible to go further and to assume that, under certain special conditions prevailing in the development of living matter, the order could undergo a further change, so that certain of these non-random features would be continued indefinitely. Thus there would arise *a new order of process*. The changes in this new order would themselves tend to be ordered in yet a higher order. This would lead not merely to the indefinite continuation of life, but to its indefinite evolution to an everdeveloping hierarchy of higher orders of structure and function.[12]

If Bohm's ideas regarding the illusory nature of quantum-level randomness are true, then it could very well be the case that what passes for randomness in the biological realm may not truly be random after all. Bohm even proposes that such a refutation of biological randomness may be testable:

> One observation that could be relevant would be to trace a series of successive mutations to see if the order of changes is completely random. In the light of what has been said, it is possible that while a single change (or difference) may be essentially random relative to the previous state of a particular organism, there may be a tendency to establish a series of similar changes (or differences) that would constitute an *internally ordered* process of evolution.[13]

3.2 The Drosophilia Connection

Scientists have attempted to create a new species of the fruit fly *Drosophilia melanogaster* by using x-rays to artificially create a wide variety of spontaneous (first-order) mutations. The reasoning behind these experiments has been that if random mutations are in fact the ultimate cause of all genetic diversity in nature, then it should be possible to create at least one new species of fruit fly in the laboratory, especially considering the extremely short length of the fruit fly "generation" (12 days), and the power of x-rays to induce mutations.

The results of these experiments, however, were surprising. Although the scientists were able to artificially induce over 400 different genetic mutations with the x-rays, they were unable to create a single new species of *Drosophilia*.[14] These results have been taken to mean that random mutations alone are probably *not* the key to speciation in nature.[15]

Also working with *Drosophilia* (1948), world-renowned evolutionist Ernst Mayr attempted to see how many bristles he could obtain on fruit flies through selective breeding. Normally, the fruit fly has 36 bristles on its body, but through clever experimental manipulation Mayr was able to get the number down to 25; at this point, however, the line became sterile and died out. Aiming in the other direction, Mayr was able to get the number of bristles up to 56, but at that point the line became sterile as well.[16]

The point to be gleaned from these experiments is that there is only so much variation that you can induce in a given creature through x-ray induced mutations and selective breeding; beyond this point sterility intervenes and the line dies out. Thus, species apparently have a built-in mechanism that *prevents* them from getting transformed into a new species through selective breeding or artificially-induced mutations. But now comes the all-important question: If selective breeding and artificially-induced mutations are unable to create a new species in the laboratory, what basis is there for assuming that natural selection will be able to do so in the wild?

3.3 The Limits of Artificial Breeding

Darwin, of course, based his original idea of natural selection on the process of artificial breeding that he repeatedly observed in his native England. He reasoned that if humans could induce such large changes in plants and animals merely through selective breeding, then the selective hand of nature herself should be able to induce even more changes, since her criterion isn't economic gain but pure survival.

Again, Darwin turns out to have been severely mistaken. As any artificial breeder well knows, there is only so much variability that can be selectively bred into any given plant or animal species. When that extreme point is reached, no further change can be induced in the species.[17]

Indeed, it is a well-known fact amongst artificial breeders that new species *cannot* be created utilizing selective breeding techniques alone.[18] Although a wide variety of genetic variants can regularly be produced in this manner, these variants are still members of the same species. They are also not as hardy as their normally-bred counterparts. Indeed, the closer one gets to creating a new species by selective breeding, the weaker and less fit the resulting variant seems to get.[19]

That is to say, the concentration of a desired variation in organisms by selective breeding also has the effect of causing the resulting variants to become much weaker and less hardy. Based on this one example of artifical breeding alone, even if nature *could* selectively breed certain extreme characters into a given species by means of natural selection, the survival value of the "adaptation" would probably be more than offset by the resulting weakness of the variant. Artifical breeders know this to be true, because they see natural selection as a conservative force that *prevents* the kinds of large-scale variations that the breeders themselves like to encourage.

Another interesting characteristic of artificially bred plants and animals is that they tend to revert back to the original variation whenever they can. This intriguing phenomenon has even been given the status of a law in the community of artificial breeders: the Law of Reversion to the Average.[20] Thus, instead of there being a "pull" towards the creation of new species through the process of selective breeding, there is instead a "pull" in the opposite direction: namely, towards keeping each species *constant*. This agrees with the evidence contained in the fossil record, which shows long periods of species fixity, punctuated by relatively short periods of rapid change.

The "take-home" point here is that one of the chief real-world examples that Darwin used to base his theory of evolution on—artificial breeding— has never once produced a new species. The genomes of all artifically bred species clearly have an extremely limited capacity for change, which is typically set far below the amount of change that would be required to create a new species. While it is true that all domesticated dogs belong to the same species, despite their vast differences in appearance, this fact cannot be used to argue for a random process of speciation in nature, because all domesticated dogs do in fact belong to the same species. No artificial breeder has ever succeeded in creating anything more than another variation on the same old dog species, *Canus familiaris*. This striking fact in and of itself prevents us from drawing an analogy between artificial breeding and natural selection.

However, there is one additional point that also prevents us from drawing such an analogy. Artificial breeding is a very meticulous practice that is carefully controlled by *intelligent beings*, while evolution by natural selection is supposed to be a random, unguided process. On this one point alone neo-Darwinian evolution by natural selection cannot be considered to be analogous with artificial breeding, because the very question at issue here is whether or not evolution by natural selection *is in fact* able to mimic the efforts of artificial breeders.[21] It is, to be sure, a telling weakness of the neo-Darwinian paradigm that the closest Darwin was able to come to an effective analogy for natural selection happened to involve the intelligent activities of artificial breeders, who nevertheless haven't been able to create a viable new species by their own efforts.

In view of these two irrepressible realities, then, no basis for drawing an analogy between artificial breeding and evolution can rightfully be said to exist. Therefore, we can expect any conclusions that have been based on this mistaken premise to be equally in error.

3.4 Coordinated Mutations

One important aspect of favorable genetic change, already briefly mentioned, is the fact that several mutations must be coordinated together to produce a single new phenotypic characteristic (such as height or eye color). At one time, scientists used to think that single phenotypic characters were coded for by single genes. Today, however, it is a well-known fact that phenotypic characters are rarely if ever coded for by single genes. They are instead coded for by a complex *series* of genes that work together to produce a given phenotypic characteristic.

It is now known, for instance, that eye color in the fruit fly *Drosophilia melanogaster* is coded for by 13 different genes on several different chromosomes. As a consequence, in order for a coherent genetic transformation to occur that is capable of producing a single coherent phenotypic characteristic, a coordinated series of several point mutations must first occur. Isolated point mutations are thus of little or no value in producing coherent characters. This is why point mutations alone are almost always deleterious; because they usually represent a serious *disruption* of an already coherent and adaptive phenotypic character.

This relatively new genetic finding is absolutely devastating to the neo-Darwinian assertion that the mechanism of evolution involves nothing more than natural selection acting on random mutations alone. Given the number of coordinated point mutations that would first have to occur by chance in order to effect just a single phenotypic change in an organism, it is no longer credible to believe that such changes could have been truly random. It is improbable enough for a single beneficial point mutation to occur in a given organism, but it is next to impossible for ten or fifteen of them to *all* occur at the same time and in the same way as to produce the same coherent phenotypic change. Even staunch evolutionist George Gaylord Simpson has admitted that the simultaneous and coordinated mutation of just five genes would literally take forever.[22] Taylor agrees:

> That these sequences of coordinated reactions—and there are literally thousands of them in the human body—should all have arisen by chance mutation of single genes is in the highest degree unlikely.
>
> It is as if we expected the famous monkeys who inadvertently typed out the plays of Shakespeare, to produce the works of Dante, Racine, Confucius, Tom Wolfe, the *Bhagavad Gita* and the latest copy of *Punch* in rapid succession. Moreover, the curious bunching I have described under the term 'radiation' would suggest that they produced one of Shakespeare's plays, then waited a million years and produced the remaining nineteen in an almost continuous stream.[23]

Based on these observations, Pierre Grassé concludes that the evidence is so strong that it forces us "to deny any evolutionary value whatever to the mutations we observe in the existing fauna and flora."[24]

This radical conclusion is supported by the findings of modern comparative anatomy, which show that, due to the millions of complex structural and functional interrelationships in even the most "simple" of creatures, a single character cannot be changed without simultaneously changing the integrity of the whole. This of course would almost certainly spell doom for the mutating creature, because of the ruthless hand of natural selection. Clearly, then, change must transpire *in toto* in order for the creature to remain viable. William Coleman agrees:

> The organism, being a functionally integrated whole each part of which stood in close relation to every other part, could not, under pain of almost immediate extinction, depart significantly from the norms established for the species by this first anatomical rule.
>
> A major change, for example, a sharp increase in heart beat or the diminution by half of the kidney and thus a reduction in renal secretion, would by itself have wrought havoc with the general constitution of the animal. In order that an animal might persist after a change of this magnitude it would be necessary that the other organs of the body be also proportionally modified. In other words, an organism must change en bloc or not at all . . . Transmutation by the accumulation of alterations, great or small, would thus be impossible.[25]

This idea makes immediate intuitive sense, for it is a well-known fact that complex machines cannot be tampered with in any significant way without rendering them malfunctional. A single mechanical feature in the cockpit of a 747, for example, cannot safely be altered without simultaneously altering all the other features in the cockpit to keep up with it. This same principle undoubtedly holds true for living organisms as well. Before biological change can happen en bloc, though, there *must* be some sort of inner directionality in the genome.

3.5 Schrödinger and the Quantum Nature of Mutational Change

Erwin Schrödinger—one of the greatest physicists of all time and discoverer of the quantum wave function equation that still bears his name—once wrote a wonderful little book entitled *What is Life?* In it he explores the nature of genetic mutations, and comes to the striking conclusion that they are discontinuous, just as the various energy levels for an electron about the nucleus are also discontinuous.

In other words, Schrödinger believed that the vast majority of significant mutational events in the DNA molecule are "jump-like," as opposed to the small and continuous types of random changes envisioned by Darwin, and he cited known experimental results to support his case:

> We known definitely, today, that Darwin was mistaken in regarding the small, continuous, accidental variations, that are bound to occur even in the most homogeneous population, as the material on which natural selection works. For it has been proved that they are not inherited. The fact is important enough to be illustrated briefly. If you take a crop of pure-strain barley, and measure, ear by ear, the length of its awns and plot the results of your statistics, you will get a bell-shaped curve . . . where the number of ears with a definite length of awn is plotted against that length. In other words, a definite medium length prevails, and deviations in either direction occur with certain frequencies. Now pick out a group of ears . . . with awns noticeably beyond the average, but sufficient in number to be sown in a field by themselves and give a new crop. In making the same statistics for this, Darwin would have expected to find the corresponding curve shifted to the right. In other words, he would have expected to produce by selection an increase of the average length of the awns. That is not the case, if a truly pure-bred strain of barley has been used. The new statistical curve, obtained from the selected crop, is identical with the first one, and the same would be the case if ears with particularly short awns had been selected for seed. Selection has no effect—because the small, continous variations are not inherited. They are obviously not based on the structure of the hereditary substance, they are accidental. But about forty years ago the Dutchman de Vries discovered that in the offspring even of thoroughly pure-bred stocks, a very small number of individuals, say two or three in tens of thousands, turn up with small but 'jump-like' changes, the expression 'jump-like' not meaning that the change is so very considerable, but that there is a discontinuity inasmuch as there are no intermediate forms between the unchanged and the few changed. De Vries called that a mutation. The significant fact is the discontinuity. It reminds a physicist of

quantum theory—no intermediate energies occurring between two neigh-
boring energy levels. He would be inclined to call de Vries's mutation
theory, figuratively, the quantum theory of biology. . . . The mutations are
actually due to quantum jumps in the gene molecule.[26]

Though Schrödinger originally wrote his book in 1944, well before the
recent explosion in molecular genetics, his conclusions are nevertheless
astute and well in accordance with our modern knowledge of the mutational
process. Indeed, we shouldn't be surprised to learn that the DNA molecule
mutates on the same basic quantum principle that applies without exception
to the entire physical realm. DNA, after all, is itself *comprised* of subatomic
particles which unfailingly obey the quantum principle, so it is no wonder
that the gene also mutates on this same basic principle. We mustn't forget
that reality is a single unified whole, and that any universal principle that
applies without exception to its foundational level is bound to percolate up
to higher levels as well.

3.6   Microevolution vs. Macroevolution

The concept of *microevolution* is used to refer to the relatively minor
changes that take place within an overall kind, due primarily to the agency
of natural selection. This is also known as the "special theory" of evolution,
and it is so well-established that virtually everyone accepts its validity. Even
religious fundamentalists feel compelled to agree with it, because the Biblical story of Adam and Eve is based on the microevolutionary idea that all
the diverse races of the world have descended from a single ancestral pair.

The concept of *macroevolution*, on the other hand, is used to refer to
both the actual origin of life and to the full-scale changes that had to have
occurred on the way to the present diversity of species. Macroevolution is
thus fundamentally different from microevolution, because microevolution
depends on the prior existence of macroevolution in order to be possible.
For instance, the microevolution of one species of finch into another would
not be possible if a great deal of macroevolution hadn't already occurred in
the world.

In trying to account for the actual origin of species, though, Darwin got
things backward. He tried to explain macroevolution *in terms of* microevolution, in what has become known as the "general theory of evolution." In
other words, he tried to extrapolate from the reality of small-scale evolution
to the possibility of large-scale evolution. However, as Michael Denton has
pointed out:

It does not necessarily follow that, because a certain degree of evolution
has been shown to occur, therefore any degree of evolution is possible.

There is obviously an enormous difference between the evolution of a colour change in a moth's wing and the evolution of an organ like the human brain, and the differences among the fruit flies of Hawaii, for example, are utterly trivial compared with the differences between a mouse and an elephant, or an octopus and a bee.[27]

Philip Johnson agrees:

The point in dispute is not whether microevolution happens, but whether it tells us anything important about the processes responsible for creating birds, insects, and trees in the first place. Gould himself has written that even the first step toward macroevolution (speciation) requires more than the accumulation of micromutations.[28]

Denton goes so far as to conclude that macroevolutionary processes *necessarily* entail a major saltational change in the entire structure of an organism, which is something that a series of gradual microevolutionary changes simply could not accomplish. He bases his radical idea on a detailed analysis of the intrinsic necessities that surround change in complex systems, and concludes that, "in all such cases, the extrapolation from micro-to macroevolutionary change does not hold."[29]

But if microevolutionary trends cannot be extrapolated out to explain the existence of macroevolution, then another force capable of eliciting sudden major changes *en masse* must be found. Incredibly, the only other plausible alternative involves some form of Intelligent Design. Darwin was fully aware of this possibility, as he openly stated that the sudden appearance of a new adaptive structure or function would be tantamount to a miracle.[30]

It is important to note, however, that such a saltational miracle would not necessarily be confined to a direct Divine Intervention into the evolutionary process. It is also possible that these macroevolutionary changes could have been programmed into the genetic code of evolving organisms from the very beginning. In this case, macroevolutionary changes would not be directly due to the activity of an Intelligent Designer. They would, however, be *indirectly* due to Him, because He would have been the One who originally programmed these evolutionary sequences into the first living cell. Either way, then, Darwin was correct: sudden massive saltational changes *are* miraculous by their very nature.

Darwin, however, was firmly committed to the concept of gradualism because it was an integral part of his theory, and because he believed that enormous spans of time were capable of transmuting microevolutionary trends into huge macroevolutionary changes.

Natural selection can act only by the preservation and accumulation of infinitesimally small inherited modifications, each profitable to the preserved being; and as modern geology has almost banished such views as the excavation of a great valley by a single diluvial wave, so will natural selection, if it be a true principle, banish the belief of the continued creation of new organic beings, or of any great and sudden modification in their structure.[31]

T.H. Huxley, who has often been called "Darwin's bulldog" because of his many vigorous public arguments in Darwin's behalf, recognized that Darwin had gotten himself into quite a fix by committing himself so absolutely to the notion of gradualism. On the day before the publication of the *Origin*, Huxley went so far as to tell Darwin in a letter that, "You have loaded yourself with an unnecessary difficulty in adopting *natura non facit saltum* so unreservedly."[32]

Huxley's words proved to be prophetic, because in the years since 1859, virtually all of the scientific evidence has strongly supported some form of saltationism. In the words of Michael Denton:

Neither of the two fundamental axioms of Darwin's macroevolutionary theory—the concept of the continuity of nature, that is the idea of a functional continuum of all life forms linking all species together and ultimately leading back to a primeval cell, and the belief that all the adaptive design of life has resulted from a blind random process—have been validated by one single empirical discovery or scientific advance since 1859.[33]

Nevertheless, many scientists and philosophers are so firmly committed to the neo-Darwinian paradigm that they aren't even fazed by this extreme lack of empirical support for their ideas. They believe that there is simply no other rational alternative for modern evolutionary theory. As a consequence, they feel philosophically compelled to accept it as valid. Clearly, though, the lack of an acceptable theoretical alternative does *not* in itself guarantee the validity of any existing theory, especially if it seems to be in contradiction with the known scientific evidence.

The fact is, however, that there *is* a plausible alternative to the nontheistic evolutionary paradigm that is both rational and in full agreement with the observed facts. It is the doctrine of Deistic Evolutionism, which Darwin himself was a proponent of in his more clear-headed moments. As we have seen, Deistic Evolutionism does not require a person to sacrifice his belief in science or evolution at all. It simply requires a person to suspend belief in an *undirected* evolutionary process that takes place entirely by chance.

This isn't as scientifically unreasonable as it may superficially seem, because many of the most important scientists in the past have been openly sympathetic with this God-centered point of view. In fact, virtually all of the founding fathers of the modern scientific movement, including Newton,

Boyle, Kepler, and Copernicus, were devout theists themselves, and they used their belief in God to justify their search for intelligence and order in the universe. A Rational Creator, they believed, would have deliberately infused the universe with rationality and design, which could then be discovered by rational men. A chance-generated universe, on the other hand, was believed to be beyond the reach of human science, because chance processes alone are not compatible with the mathematical order and regularity that is demanded by the scientific method.

Indeed, an unbiased examination of the philosophical foundations behind the modern scientific movement reveals a most striking fact: *they are based, at their most fundamental level, on the same sort of theistic assumptions that the founding fathers of science themselves actually possessed.* Modern-day scientists possess an almost mystical belief in the orderliness and law-fulness of the entire universe, and for good reason: no science at all would be possible without it. However, natural law demands a natural Law-Giver, especially when the scope of natural law itself is acknowledged to date all the way back to the Big Bang, and to extend to the very borders of spacetime. It is therefore extremely doubtful whether the concept of natural law would make any sense whatsoever in the true absence of Intelligent Design. A randomly generated universe, on the other hand, would in all likelihood be characterized by random motions and relationships at all levels of physical reality, and these of course are the very antithesis of law and order.

Therefore, it simply isn't true that a plausible alternative to neo-Darwinism hasn't yet been found. The reality of the situation is that a plausible alternative has in fact been in existence all along, and has actually functioned as the invisible philosophical foundation for the entire edifice of the modern scientific movement. The upshot of this realization, of course, is that one can no longer honestly commit oneself to orthodox evolutionary theory for lack of a plausible alternative.

3.7 Is Chance the Creator of Us All?

Overall, there are five reasons for concluding that life is most probably the result of Intelligent Design: 1) the existence of order-prone atoms and molecules, 2) the existence of a stable universe and solar system, 3) the existence of a life-facilitating ecosystem, 4) the existence of functional genetic machinery within the cell, and 5) the existence of coordinated group-ings of individual genes, whose purpose is to produce coherent external characters.

It thus isn't enough for the non-theistic evolutionist to simply assume that the nucleic acids which comprise the genetic material just happened to evolve all by themselves, because such a "possibility" goes against all that we have come to know and expect from the scientific realm. It also isn't enough for the non-theistic evolutionist to simply assume that the millions of other conditions that are absolutely essential for the existence of life also just happened to come into being all by themselves, not the least of which is the unbelievable amount of coordinated organization that is found in even the "simplest" of living creatures. Having assumed all that, though, the non-theistic evolutionist then goes on to assume that it was random mutations alone that were responsible for creating all the profound genetic diversity that we now observe throughout the biosphere! In reference to these genetic mutations, Jacques Monod has written the following:

> We call these [genetic] events accidental; we say that they are random occurences. And since they are the *only* possible source of modifications in the genetic text, itself the *sole* repository of the organism's hereditary structures, it necessarily follows that chance *alone* is at the source of every innovation, of all creation in the biosphere. Pure chance, absolutely free but blind, at the very root of the stupendous edifice of evolution: this central concept of modern biology is no longer one among other possible or even conceivable hypotheses. It is today the *sole* conceivable hypothesis, the only one that squares with observed and tested fact. And nothing warrants the supposition—or the hope—that on this score our position is likely ever to be revised.[34]

Needless to say, the Deistic Evolutionist disagrees wholeheartedly with Monod's radical conclusion. While it is certainly true that many first-order (i.e., unintended) mutations occur in nature, it is clearly going too far to claim that they are the "only possible source of modifications in the genetic text." How could Monod possibly *know* that? It seems apparent that this type of wishful thinking is rooted in a firmly entrenched anti-theistic bias, because Monod won't even bring himself to *consider* the alternative. Having instantly dispelled with the possibility of directional change within the genome, Monod goes on to make the unsubstantiated assumption that first-order (i.e., directionless) mutations are the *only* possible source of genetic modification in evolution. Based on this overly dogmatic premise, Monod concludes that chance alone is ultimately responsible for creating the most complicated structures in the entire known universe.[35] And as if that weren't enough, he even has the audacity to claim that such a dismal conclusion will probably never be revised in the future.

Even if we give Monod the benefit of the doubt and agree with him on the central role of chance in the creation, we must nevertheless disagree with him on an even deeper score: that of his intrinsic capacity for reaching such grand conclusions. For if chance alone were ultimately responsible for creating everything in our present world, then it would have also been responsible for creating Monod himself. But if this were true, then Monod's conclusions would simply have been the result of an accidental and therefore totally meaningless series of biochemical processes, and no one would want to put their trust in that. So we see that Monod's appeal to chance as creator is undermined by his own desire to separate truth from falsehood.

Monod bases his "scientific" reasoning on the so-called Principle of Objectivity," which asserts that the only thing science can properly comment on is "objective reality" (which is comprised exclusively of that part of reality that can be objectively measured and verified). Now, since the creative activity of God cannot be measured in the laboratory, it follows that in order for the Principle of Objectivity to be followed, all technical considerations of God must be thrown away. This is a necessary prerequisite for any type of bona fide laboratory study, and is therefore not objectionable in and of itself, since religious matters cannot possibly figure into cut and dry experimental procedures. On this level, religion must of necessity be separated from experimental science if both are to experience their optimal value in society.[36]

It is only when scientists abandon the Principle of Objectivity *themselves* by considering the origin and meaning of life that the Deistic Evolutionist must voice an objection. For once they start considering questions which by their very nature lie outside the realm of verifiable science, they are automatically leaving the realm of objective science and entering the realm of philosophical interpretation, and once they do this, they no longer have the Principle of Objectivity to fall back on. Indeed, almost all of Monod's *Chance & Necessity* is centered around the non-objective search for the origin of living things. The fact that God isn't considered even in these non-objective circumstances shows beyond reasonable doubt that Monod was probably motivated by some form of anti-theistic bias.

Surprisingly, however, Monod is aware of the extreme contradiction between the Principle of Objectivity, on the one hand, and the obvious teleonomy[37] (purposefulness) of living things, on the other. He writes that:

> The postulate of objectivity is consubstantial with science; it has guided the whole of its prodigious development for three centuries. There is no way to be rid of it, even tentatively or in a limited area, without departing from the domain of science itself.

> Objectivity nevertheless obliges us to recognize the teleonomic character of living organisms, to admit that in their structure and performance they act projectively—realize and pursue a purpose. Here therefore, at least in appearance, lies a profound epistemological contradiction. In fact the central problem of biology lies with this very contradiction, which, if it is only apparent, must be resolved; or else proven to be utterly insoluble, if that should turn out indeed to be the case.[38]

As long as one steadfastly remains within the proper bounds of science, it would seem as though the problem of teleonomy would of necessity remain insoluble. The question of purpose is by its very nature beyond the realm of objective science altogether. It is only when one ventures outside the domain of science that the answer begins to reveal itself: teleonomy seems to have its origin in some sort of larger Cosmic Purpose. Monod thus errs because he attempts to reach a conclusion regarding the nature of teleonomy from within the domain of science, when such a conclusion can only be properly drawn from *outside* this domain. Within this strict limitation, Monod is correct—the only "scientific" explanation for the teleonomy in nature is chance. Such a statement, however, shouldn't be taken to describe the way things really are; it should only be taken to show how pointless it is to make philosophical statements about the origin of teleonomy from within the bounds of objective science alone. One cannot cross such fundamental methodological boundaries and still hope to retain any semblance of rationality in one's conclusions. The fact that so many people continue to neglect this fundamental rule reveals the serious (and profoundly mistaken) conviction of Western society that objective science can discover the true meaning of all things.

Objectivity does in fact oblige us to recognize the inherent teleonomy of all things, as Monod has pointed out. But what this statement really means is that the objectivity of science itself points *beyond* the scientific realm to the world of Divine Directedness. As a consequence, the dedicated scientist who refuses to go beyond the self-restricted realm of his profession cannot even *consider* the origin of teleonomy without first abandoning his purely scientific perspective. And abandon it he must, if he is to make any significant progress in his understanding of teleonomic phenomena.

The most serious mistake of all is thus to question the obvious teleonomy of life solely from within the bounds of objective science alone. Such behavior causes one to focus, not on the origin of teleonomy, but rather on the teleonomic object that is pointing *away* from itself and *towards* its teleonomic Creator. As C.S. Lewis once pointed out, it is rather like a dog who stares at his master's pointing finger, instead of where the finger itself is actually pointing. The message is clear: if we hope to make any progress at all towards understanding the ultimate origin of teleonomy, we must first abandon the Principle of Objectivity and begin looking in the appropriate intuitive direction.[39]

Ultimately speaking, the scientific realm is actually under the domain of religion, in the sense that the God of religion (if He exists at all) must be the true Author of natural science as well. This is why theology has been referred to as the "Queen of the sciences." It is only because of the strict limitations in our measuring capacity that we have had to separate science from its theological parent. In the end, though, there are no concrete divisions within reality; only a uni–verse that is connected together in a total and seamless whole.

It is surprising that such a gifted thinker as Monod was unable to remain true to his own fundamental distinction between science and religion. He was obviously unable to resist the temptation of speculating on the origin of teleonomy, but in so doing he should have ventured outside the self-restricted boundary of scientific conjecture. Since he did not, and instead insisted on explaining the origin of teleonomy from within the bounds of experimental science, he ended up with incoherence, not insight. Indeed, we can take his claim of being unable to "conceive" of any other possible hypothesis as *proof* that he was driven by some sort of deep-seated anti-theistic bias. This is an excellent example of the extreme power that one's personal beliefs can have on how one interprets the existing scientific evidence.

Monod claims that his hypothesis of random change is the only one that "squares with observed and tested fact." This "observed and tested fact" is actually comprised of two separate instances of "experimental confirmation," each of which ends up *detracting* from his overall point in the end.

The first fact Monod refers to concerns the randomness of first-order mutations, which has indeed been verified many times over. Monod errs, however, because he fails to distinguish between first-order mutations, which are genuinely random in nature, and second- and third-order "mutations," which are not. Since he takes first-order mutations to be the only form of genetic change in existence, he concludes that chance itself must be responsible for the origin of life, since first-order mutations are largely driven by chance. As we have seen, however, first-order mutations are no longer regarded as being the chief guiding force of evolution. Consequently, any statement that is true of first-order mutations cannot be applied to the evolution of life as a whole, as Monod cleverly tries to do. "A" (the randomness of first-order mutations) may equal "B" (the reality of first-order mutations), but because "B" does not equal "C" (i.e., because first-order mutations do not guide the evolution of life), it cannot be said that "A" equals "C" (i.e., it cannot be said that the evolution of life was a totally random event).

Monod clearly confuses first-order (i.e., random and unintended) mutations with second and third-order "mutations" in his overall view of the evolution of life. He correctly sees that a huge number of genetic changes have occurred throughout evolutionary history, but mistakenly assumes that they all must have been unintended first-order mutations, largely because his philosophical world view explicitly forbids any type of directionality in the evolutionary process. As a result, he is automatically compelled to reject the very existence of directional "mutations" in nature, in favor of unintended first-order mutations. This is why he can be so confident that the scientific evidence supports his idea that chance (along with necessity) is the creator of us all: because his internal anti-theistic bias prevents him from interpreting the evidence in any other way.

This leads us to consider the second "fact" that Monod uses to support his contention that chance is the creator of us all. Earlier in his book he asserts that because there is no discernible pattern in the various sequences of amino acids that have been decoded by geneticists, the proteins themselves must have therefore been formed through some type of chance-mediated process.[40] Such a momentous conclusion, however, does not follow from the observational evidence. The lack of any discernible pattern in a given sequence of amino acids has no necessary connection at all with how the original amino acid sequence was formed. While science may not yet be able to predict the actual sequence of amino acids in a protein, this is certainly no justification for concluding that proteins themselves are just random aggregations of meaningless atoms, and therefore that blind chance was originally responsible for creating them! To the contrary, there is obviously *some* higher degree of rationality in the sequence of amino acids in proteins, otherwise they would be unable to work together so beautifully to build the structural components of the human body.

Curiously enough, Monod seems to be aware of this fact, since earlier he concludes that "the quantity of information that would be needed to describe the entire three-dimensional structure of a protein is *far greater* than the amount of information defined by the sequence [of amino acids] itself."[41] This is an *ipso facto* admission of rationality concerning the order of amino acids in a protein. After all, this is how we define information in the first place: as highly-ordered data that transmits an intelligible message. It is for this reason that scientists are utterly unjustified in proclaiming the random origin of any given protein, just because they are still unable to figure out the level of order displayed by its constituent amino acids.

The biggest problem with Monod's conclusion, however, is that it utilizes an inappropriate reference point as far as the sequence of amino acids in proteins in concerned. The proper reference point for defining this order isn't to be found in the actual sequence itself; it is rather to be found in the functional three-dimensional structure of the larger protein.

We can better understand this distinction by means of an analogy. If one were looking for some sort of order in the sequence of letters that make up the word "sentimentality," it would be a mistake to concentrate only on the individual letters themselves, because no conceivable amount of order would then be capable of being discerned (apart from the individual gestalts or coherent syllables that make up the word). It is only when one looks at the entire word (or a good portion of it) that one can accurately predict the actual sequence of letters in it. In the same way, it seems doubtful that scientists will ever be able to discover any type of rationality in the order of amino acids in proteins merely by looking at the amino acids themselves; they need to look at the three-dimensional nature of the larger protein in order to be able to discern this order.

So we see that Monod has committed a deadly *faux pas* in his generalization from the apparent randomness in the structural format of proteins to the larger supposition that randomness itself must have been responsible for creating all things. Such a serious error in reasoning reveals a fundamental incongruency that pervades much of the scientific community these days: non-theistic scientists routinely believe that when they finally discover how a given system works, they will also simultaneously discover why it works and where it came from. Of course, these conclusions in no way follow from the available evidence; they simply reveal the arrogance of those who would presume to be capable of discovering the underlying meaning of life from within the bounds of objective science alone.

3.8 Information Theory

From the above discussion it is apparent that any supposition of a random origin for living systems is strongly disconfirmed by the existence of clearly-discernible *information* within the genetic code. Indeed, it has been said that the genetic information contained in the tiny one-celled *E. coli* would contain "the equivalent of 100 million pages of Encyclopedia Britannica."[42]

It is clear that the existence of such a prodigious amount of information in the genetic code counts against the prospect of a mindless origin to life, for the following reason. There are two informational systems in living cells, the sequence of nucleotides in DNA and the sequence of amino acids in proteins. These two systems are intimately related to one another, because it is the nucleotide sequence in DNA that ultimately determines the various amino acid sequences in proteins. These two sequences comprise an extremely complex molecular "language" that confers an incredible amount of highly specific information to the protein-synthesizing machinery of the cell. It thus cannot be denied that living systems are characterized by truly unbelievable amounts of information, the contents of which are far more complicated than anything human beings have ever made.

Even a cursory look at the astonishing nature of proteins shows why this must be so. There are three basic levels of structure in a protein molecule, two of which concern us here: the primary structure, which refers to the order of amino acids that comprise the protein, and the tertiary structure, which is comprised of the unique three-dimensional shape of the protein, and which results from a precise "folding" of the molecule in its incessant striving for the lowest possible energy state. It is this folded three-dimensional structure that determines the function of all biological proteins, since it is what enables them to interact with other types of biomolecules that are specifically designed to accomodate them.

What this means is that the order of the nitrogeneous bases in a cell's DNA is ultimately determined by the three-dimensional shape of the various proteins that it actually codes for. More incredible yet, all of these proteins somehow "know" how all the others are shaped, since they all work together to form a beautiful, seamless whole. In order for this to be possible, a truly stupendous amount of holistic genetic information is required. For many, the only intelligible source for this sophisticated information is none other than God Himself. Professor Chandra Wickramasinghe agrees:

> If you look at the structure of our living system, microorganisms or ourselves under the microscope . . . if you investigate a living system that is before us . . . one is driven to the conclusion, inescapably, that living systems could not have been generated by random processes, within a finite time-scale, in a finite universe. I think the evidence from life is very hard, a hard fact . . . The information content in the living system that we have on the earth is perhaps the hardest cosmological fact. You can't get away from that.[43]

In response to a question about the legitimacy of Monod's assertion that life is a grand accident, Wickramasinghe points out that Monod's conclusion is:

> . . . not borne out by the facts at all. There's not a shred of evidence for it . . . It is worse than that. It's a defiance of science. The scientific method should lead to quite the opposite result: that some miraculous property of life that's either explained in terms of a statistical miracle or in terms of an Intelligence intervening. It's one or the other . . . I think these people have no respect for facts at all. The facts are too disturbing, *so* they consider [them] irrelevant.[44]

3.9   Genetic Information and the Role of Chance

Recent advances in computer technology have brought with them similar advances in information theory. Scientists have learned that a great deal can be discerned through the detailed examination of an informational source, ranging from the complexity of the internal message to the message's actual content. By all accounts, the information in even the simplest living cell utterly dwarfs anything that man has ever been able to come up with in terms of complexity. Indeed, the information in DNA is so incredibly complex that it seems as if the only reasonable way to explain it is in terms of an Intelligence that is literally "out of this world." Even Monod assures us that "information presupposes a source."[45] Surprisingly, though, Monod fails to consider the most likely source of the cell's genetic information.

Monod's hidden agenda is plainly evident throughout *Chance & Necessity*: he wants to prove to himself and the reader once and for all that a supernatural Creator was not responsible for creating the vast array of life forms that are presently found on this planet. As we have seen, though, his arguments fail under the force of the evidence that he himself presents. But it isn't as if Monod is alone in this regard; the vast majority of nontheistic evolutionists also seem to be driven by an underlying need to prove theism wrong. It is precisely this underlying anti-theistic fervor that is apparently responsible for their extreme lack of objectivity when it comes to interpreting the known facts of science.

The point is that the prevailing scientific opinion regarding the origin of life is based on *faith*, not hard scientific evidence. As astrophysicist Robert Jastrow has pointed out:

Perhaps the appearance of life on the earth is a miracle. Scientists are reluctant to accept that view, but their choices are limited; *either* life was created on the earth by the will of a being outside the grasp of scientific understanding, *or* it evolved on our planet spontaneously, through chemical reactions occurring in non-living matter lying on the surface of the planet.
The first theory places the question of the origin of life beyond the realm of scientific inquiry. It is a statement of faith in the power of a Supreme Being not subject to the laws of science.
The second theory is also an act of faith. The act of faith consists in assuming that the scientific view of the origin of life is correct, without having concrete evidence to support that belief.[46]

There is perhaps no better summarization of the problem facing modern science than Nobel laureate Sir John Eccles' pronouncement at the end of *The Wonder of Being Human*:

Science has gone too far in breaking down man's belief in his spiritual greatness . . . [by giving] him the belief that he is merely an insignificant animal that has arisen by chance and necessity in an insignificant planet lost in the great cosmic immensity. This is the message given to us by Monod in *Chance & Necessity*. The principal trouble with mankind today is that the intellectual leaders are too arrogant in their self-sufficiency. We must realize the great unknowns in the material makeup and operation of our brains, in the relationship of brain to mind, in our creative imagination, and in the uniqueness of the psyche. *When we think of these unknowns as well as the unknown of how we come to be in the first place, we should be much more humble.*[47]

3.10 A Call for Reconciliation

With the extremely rapid proliferation of scientific knowledge in recent years, the time has now come for there to be an ideological reconciliation between science and religion. Although the Principle of Objectivity must necessarily remain in effect in the laboratory (i.e., religious matters should be left out of the internal procedures of experimental science), a new branch of science should begin to be employed where the religious and philosophical implications of our new scientific advances can be freely and openly discussed without fear of discrimination or censorship. This would represent a bold return to the type of "natural philosophy" employed by Aristotle, which was where the modern pursuit of scientific knowledge actually began.

Notes

1. It has been estimated that approximately 1 in 10,000 random mutations are beneficial, yet "it is doubtful that of all the mutations that have been seen to occur, a single one can definitely be said to have increased the viability of the affected plant or animal" (Duane Gish, *The Challenge of the Fossil Record* (San Diego: Creation-Life Publishers, 1985), p. 38.
2. Maurice Caullery, *Genetics and Heredity* (New York: Walker and Co., 1964), p. 10.
3. Hickman, *Integrated Principles of Zoology* (St. Louis: The C. V. Mosby Co., 1978, Sixth Edition), p. 872.
4. Ernst Mayr, *Animal Species and Evolution* (Cambridge: The Belknap Press of Harvard University Press, 1963), p. 7.
5. Maurice Caullery, *Genetics and Heredity*, p. 10.
6. Ernst Mayr, *Animal Species and Evolution*, p. 7.
7. Quoted in John Polkinghorne's *Science and Creation* (Boston: Shambhala, 1989), p. 57.
8. Ibid.
9. The word mutation usually refers to random and directionless genetic change. It is also used to refer to genetic change in general *for any reason*. The nontheistic evolutionist typically understands these two meanings to be synonymous, since the only type of genetic change that can be incorporated into his theory is the random and undirected variety. However, as soon as one postulates the existence of *directed* genetic change, a great deal of potential confusion is created, since the use of the word "mutation" in this sense only refers to genetic change in general, and not necessarily to random genetic change. It is for this reason that I enclose the word "mutation" in quotes whenever I use it to refer to those types of genetic changes that appear to be directed.
10. Although Grassé does not use this terminology in his writing, he seems to be referring to the same phenomenon.
11. Quoted in Rifkin's *Algeny*, p. 133.
12. David Bohm, 'Some Remarks on the Notion of Order,' in C.H. Waddington (ed.) *Towards a Theoretical Biology* (4 vols, Edinburgh University Press, 1969), vol. 2, p. 18.
13. Ibid.
14. Maurice Caullery, *Genetics and Heredity*, p. 119.
15. Ibid.
16. Norman Macbeth, "The Question: Darwinism Revisted," *Yale Review* (June 1967), pp. 622–623.

17. Rifkin, *Algeny*, p. 133.
18. Ibid., p. 131.
19. Ibid., p. 133.
20. Ibid., p. 132.
21. Even if we assume, for the sake of argument, that the analogy is appropriate, the fact that artificial breeding cannot create a new species, and indeed tends to produce less hardy creatures on the whole, doubly invalidates the neo-Darwinian theory.
22. Taylor, *The Great Evolution Mystery*, p. 230.
23. Ibid., pp. 183–184.
24. Pierre Grasse', *Evolution of Living Organisms: Evidence for a New Theory of Transformation* (New York: Academic Press, 1977), p. 202.
25. William Coleman, *Georges Cuvier: Zoologist* (Cambridge: Harvard University Press, 1964), pp. 172–173.
26. Erwin Schrodinger, *What is Life?* (Cambridge: Cambridge University Press, 1967), pp. 24–36.
27. Michael Denton, *Evolution: A Theory in Crisis*, p. 87.
28. Philip Johnson, *Darwin on Trial* (Washington, DC: Regnery Gateway, 1991), p. 68.
29. Michael Denton, p. 91.
30. Charles Darwin, *The Origin of Species*, p. 242.
31. Charles Darwin, quoted in Philip E. Johnson's *Darwin on Trial*, p. 33.
32. T.H. Huxley, letter to Darwin, dated November 23, 1859, in Huxley, L., *Life and Letters of T.H. Huxley* (New York: Macmillan and Co.), Vol. 2, p. 176.
33. Michael Denton, p. 345.
34. Jacques Monod, *Chance & Necessity*, (New York: Alfred A. Knopf, 1971), pp. 112–113.
35. It is ironic that some of the greatest minds in the history of science have been able to crown mindless chance, of all things, as the noble creator of us all. Such an observation is all the more incredible when one considers the fact that ordinary common sense tells us precisely the opposite, namely, that when things are left to themselves, they almost always tend to go wrong. There's even a name for this principle: Murphy's Law.
36. On a higher level, though, science can be directly influenced by religion, insofar as religion can, when it is used properly, specify important guidelines on *what* science should be studying, and *how* that study can best take place.
37. It is a testimony to the profound schism between science and religion that scientists have felt compelled to coin a new term (teleonomy) to describe the purposefulness of living things, just so they won't have to resort to the traditional concept of "teleology," because of its deep religious implications.
38. Ibid., pp. 21–22.
39. Of course, this isn't to say that we can't be reasonable, and even "objective" in a sense, in our metaphysical speculation; we obviously can. It is only to say that we can't be objective in a precise, experimental sense when we speculate on the origin of teleonomy, because this question intrinsically does not lend itself to empirical quantification.
40. Ibid., pp. 91–95.
41. Ibid., p. 93.
42. R.L. Wysong, *The Creation-Evolution Controversy* (Midland, Michigan: Inquiry Press, 1976), p. 195.

43. Chandra Wickramasinghe, in Roy Abraham Varghese, ed., *The Intellectuals Speak Out About God*, (Chicago: Regnery Gateway, Inc., 1984), p. 33.
44. Ibid., pp. 33–35.
45. Monod, *Chance & Necessity*, p. 12.
46. Robert Jastrow, *Until the Sun Dies* (New York: Warner Books, 1977), pp. 51–52.
47. Eccles and Robinson, *The Wonder of Being Human*, p. 178.

CHAPTER 4

Species and Speciation

Through the use and abuse of hidden postulates, of bold, often ill-founded extrapolations, a pseudoscience has been created. It is taking root in the very heart of biology and is leading astray many biochemists and biologists, who sincerely believe that the accuracy of fundamental concepts has been demonstrated, which is not the case.[1]

PIERRE GRASSÉ

One of the fundamental assumptions of non-theistic evolutionary theory is that all the different life forms on this planet had to have come from a single ancestral species with no internal guidance or direction. This biological requirement is a great problem for the evolutionist, because of the well-known fact that only like kinds can reproduce; indeed, the term "species" is defined as the ability to interbreed so as to be capable of producing viable offspring.

Evolutionist Gavin De Beer confirms this fact by explicitly stating that "one species does not grow from the seed of another species."[2] The Bible also confirms this genetic law by saying that "God made the beasts of the earth after their kind (species), and the cattle after their kind, and everything that creeps on the ground after its kind, and God saw that it was good" (Gen. 1:25, NAS).

Clearly, a particular species can only give rise to offspring of the same species—dogs only give rise to dogs, and fish only give rise to fish. Yet, this biological law totally contradicts the most fundamental tenet of non-theistic evolutionary theory, which says that the very first species on this planet *had* to have given rise to all other species in existence (through random mutation and natural selection), in order for the great diversity of life on this planet to be properly accounted for. Marshall and Sandra Hall sum up the evidence in the following manner:

No one, as far as we know, disagrees with this [genetic] law of nature. Yet for evolution to have occurred, this law had to be bent, broken, twisted, and finally discarded an absolute minimum of 1,200,000 times in order to account for the 1,200,000 species that have been classified.[3]

It seems that when non-theistic evolutionists no longer have a Creator to impart a sense of direction to the evolutionary process, they must resort to the ridiculous notion that the various species have accidentally grown out of one another entirely by chance, with no form of internal or external directedness. It thus isn't the idea that the various species have grown out of one another that the Deistic Evolutionist finds objectionable; it is that they could have done so without any need for internal or external direction. Indeed, the Deistic Evolutionist believes that, in all likelihood, the various species probably did grow out of one another, but *only* in response to some form of larger direction.

A viable compromise, then, between non-theistic evolutionism and special creationism is that God somehow programmed the capacity for natural speciation into the genetic material of the very first life form. This could have happened in two distinct ways: 1) He could have programmed each individual act of speciation into the first genome, thereby rigidly determining all of the instances of speciation that were to subsequently take place (perhaps in concert with some form of environmental feedback), or 2) He could have programmed the *capacity* for environmental adaptation into the genome of the very first living cell, thereby enabling it to program itself, as it were, during the course of evolutionary history, with the different species being produced whenever the surrounding conditions began to stimulate their appearance. In either of these ways, God's Creative Intentions would have automatically been realized during the entire process of evolution, yet all the species would nevertheless have grown out of the first primordial life form.

In other words, God could have naturalistically created the very first life form, complete with the inner capacity to speciate whenever appropriate. Having done this, He could have then left it alone to develop as best as it could according to natural "evolutionary" processes.

Indeed, this appears to have been just what God did with man. Psychospiritual man obviously was not created in his final form, so why should we expect the various members of the animal kingdom to have been created in *their* final form? Humans are born, at least in a certain epistemological sense, as immature "blank slates" (except for their inheritance of certain predispositions), but then they slowly grow and develop towards their ultimate goal of self-actualization, in accordance with the natural laws that govern human development. That is to say, they start out life as fertilized eggs and then gradually "evolve" into mature human beings. But, if this is true with humans, why shouldn't it also be true with the animal kingdom as a whole? If humans slowly evolve into their final form in accordance with natural law, then why shouldn't the various animal species have also done the same?

On this view, God gives both man and the animals all they need to exist, grow, and develop, and then He leaves them alone to be subject only to the law of natural selection. This is one way to partly reconcile non-theistic evolutionary theory with a more theistically-inclined perspective.

Contrary to popular belief, the Bible is supportive of this idea of one type of creature being directly created "out of" the flesh of another pre-existing creature. Although Eve was of the same species as Adam, we are nevertheless told in Gen 1:21–22 that Eve was created directly "out of" the rib of Adam. This mechanism of creation may not be an isolated phenomenon, as it could conceivably represent the fundamental creative paradigm that God may have used to create the entire animal kingdom. If so, then God would have somehow drawn all of the various species "out of" one another when the time was right.

4.1 The Discontinuity of Nature

Being gradualistic to the core, the neo-Darwinian theory assumes a fundamental continuity amongst the various species on earth, in which those species that accidentally gave rise to other species are considered ancestral to them.

The early morphologists and taxonomists, such as the Swedish botanist Carl Linnaeus, the French biologist Georges Cuvier, and the British anatomist Richard Owen, based their classification systems, not on the Darwinian concept of continuity in nature, but on precisely the opposite: a discontinuous, typological model of the natural world, in which there were-cut, irreconcilable differences between each major kind of organism. They based their conclusions primarily on the morphological and anatomical differences between plants and animals, and what they came up with was a circumferential arrangement in which no species was considered to be ancestral to any other.[4] Owen, for instance, saw absolutely no evidence for gradual transformations in the fossil record, and his conclusions were based, not on religious prejudice, but on a careful analysis of the plant and animal kingdoms. Indeed, as Denton points out, there is no necessary reason why theologians should demand any sort of discontinuity in nature, because the Principle of Plenitude—which states that God created all possible life forms from the very lowest to the very highest—was accepted as holy doctrine by a large number of prominent Christian theologians throughout recent history, even though it posited a continuous model of the living world.[5]

With Darwin's publication of the *Origin* in 1859, however, the early taxonomists' model of typological discontinuity in nature came under severe criticism, because it was clearly at odds with Darwin's theory of gradualism. In an effort to make the existing taxonomic system of classification consistent with the tenets of gradualism, Darwin's followers simply posited certain ancestral relationships between different classes of creatures in the "evolutionary tree of life." For instance, they concluded that amphibians must be ancestral to reptiles and that reptiles must be ancestral to mammals, even though there was no hint of this kind of evolutionary relationship in the existing taxonomic system of classification.

Remarkably, the discontinuous, typological views of the early taxonomists have recently been vindicated by the findings of modern molecular biology. In the process, the continuous, gradualistic views of the neo-Darwinians have been all but laid to rest.

Biologists now have at their disposal a fascinating new way to compare organisms at a deep molecular level. It involves a detailed comparison of the amino acid sequences in specific proteins that belong to different species. After years of comparing and contrasting these sequential differences in different species, a general principle of relationship has revealed itself. It states that the specific amino acid sequences between two species will typically differ in direct proportion to how closely related the two species happen to be.[6] Take the oxygen-carrying molecule hemoglobin for instance. Although it is utilized by a wide variety of different species, its internal amino acid sequence differs significantly from species to species. For example, the sequential divergence between two mammals, such as a dog and a man, is known to be around 20 percent, whereas the sequential divergence between a man and a fish is known to be 50 percent. This same pattern has held true for all the amino acid sequences that have ever been analyzed in the laboratory. We thus now have at our ready disposal a strictly quantitative means for assessing how closely related different species happen to be.

Incredibly enough, it was soon learned that the molecules themselves were not going to provide any evidence for a sequential, ancestral arrangement amongst the different species. To the contrary, they were validating the traditional view, which stated that "the system of nature conforms fundamentally to a highly ordered hierarchic scheme from which all direct evidence for evolution is emphatically absent."[7]

The respiratory protein cytochrome c provides a good case in point. If the gradualistic theory of evolution were true, we would expect there to be a continuous gradient in the sequential divergence of the amino acids that comprise cytochrome c as one ascends the evolutionary scale from procaryotic bacteria.[8] However, nothing of the kind has ever been observed to exist. Rather, the percent sequence difference between the bacterial cytochrome and the cytochromes of the horse, pigeon, tuna, silkmoth, wheat, and yeast cells are more or less identical.[9]

Given the radical structural differences between procaryotic bacteria and the eucaryotic cells of such widely varying species as yeasts and the horse, Denton rightly concludes that:

> . . . this must be considered one of the most astonishing findings of modern science.

It means that no eucaryotic cytochrome is intermediate between the bacterial cytochrome and other eucaryotic cytochromes. As far as the bacterium is concerned, all the eucaryotes are equally distant. All the eucaryotic cytochromes are as a class isolated and unique. No intermediate type of cytochrome exists to bridge the discontinuity which divides the living kingdom into these two fundamental types. The bacterial kingdom has no neighbor in any of the fantastically diverse eucaryotic types. The "missing links" are well and truly missing.[10]

The same conclusions are borne out when one diagrams the living world according to the sequential differences displayed by their respective cytochromes. The fundamental division is between the procaryotes and the eucaryotes. From this global division, the eucaryotes can be further subdivided into yeasts, plants, and animals, and from this, the animals can be further sub-divided into insects and vertebrates.[11] As Denton concludes:

Each class is isolated and unique. No classes are intermediate or partially inclusive of other classes. The isolation of each class becomes greater as the taxonomic hierarchy is ascended, but even relatively closely related classes such as insects and vertebrates are still clearly distinguished . . . In terms of their cytochromes, the three major eucaryotic kingdoms may be thought of as equidistant from a common hypothetical archetype, while within each group all the members are similarly equidistant from the hypothetical archetype of their group.[12]

The orthodox evolutionist tries to sidestep this conclusion by assuming that a uniform rate of mutation per unit of absolute time has occurred for all the homologous proteins that have been analyzed thus far. This has become known as the "molecular clock" hypothesis in modern molecular biology, and it assumes that intra-molecular mutations have occurred at a steady rate for all homologous proteins throughout evolutionary history.

However, as Denton has pointed out, no one has been able to show how such a time constant process could conceivably work for all the different families of proteins involved. Since each family of homologous proteins varies at a different (though equally precise) rate, the orthodox evolutionist must postulate a separate molecular clock for each of the several hundred protein families in nature.[13] This being the case, it is immensely difficult to see why all the various protein families in nature should have been capable of varying by such a precise rate in all of the species that have been studied thus far.

One possible explanation for this peculiar phenomenon has been forwarded in terms of neutral selection: as long as natural selection is presumed to be unable to act at the level of these intramolecular variations, it is possible to imagine that they could all mutate at approximately the same rate, through some elaborate set of internal functional constraints. And indeed, there is evidence that the mutation rate per generation in higher organisms is the same for a wide variety of different genes.[14]

The key word here, though, is "generation," for as long as the generation times for two different organisms are similar, we can expect similar rates of mutation to exist. But what about when the generation times between species are radically different? A tree, for instance, has a typical generation time of around 80 years, whereas the typical generation time for a bacterium is some 10^5 times *smaller.* How can we expect to find a similar mutation rate per unit of absolute time between two species with such radically different generation times? Obviously we cannot, and the experimental evidence corroborates this conclusion: vastly different mutation rates per unit of absolute time are now known to exist for different creatures, so "this effectively excludes drift as a mechanism for the generation of uniform rates of evolution."[15]

This being the case, the molecular clock hypothesis seems to reduce to a tautology, which amounts to "no more than a restatement of the fact that at a molecular level the representatives of any one class are equally isolated from the representatives of another class."[16]

If Denton is correct, the traditional neo-Darwinian scenario will have been dealt a severe—even fatal—blow. In response to such a finding, we would be compelled to reject gradualism altogether in favor of the discontinuous, typological model of the natural world that was originally worked out by Linnaeus and Cuvier, in which all species are related merely as sister groups. In this scenario, no species can be considered to be ancestral to any other, since all species are more or less equidistant from a postulated common ancestor.

It would seem to be no accident that the pattern displayed by the various cytochromes is more or less identical to the taxonomic pattern that was originally proposed by the nineteenth-century typologists. In all likelihood, this remarkable theoretical convergence can be taken to represent a mutual confirmation of the phenomenon of discontinuity in nature.

4.2 Typology and Essentialism

One of the chief tenets of the typological model of the natural world is that there is no such thing as a transitional form between an amphibian and a reptile, or between a reptile and a mammal (and this is apart from any consideration of a Divine Influence in the process of evolution). For if the Platonic notion of the *eidos* can be applied to the forms or essences that are instantiated in the living world, it may be that each species corresponds to a distinct essence that defines its basic features in a predetermined way. If this is true, there may be no such thing as transitional forms because there may be no larger essences for them to incoporate, i.e., the lack of transitional forms may reflect a deeper metaphysical reality, and not simply a local, evolutionary one. In his classic description of the essentialist position, Victorian scholar D'Arcy Wentworth Thompson wrote the following:

> An algebraic curve has its fundamental formula, which defines the family to which it belongs . . . We never think of "transforming" a helicoid into an ellipsoid, or a circle into a frequency curve. So it is with the forms of animals. We cannot transform an invertebrate into a vertebrate, nor a coelenterate into a worm, by any simple and legitimate deformation . . . Nature proceeds from one type to another . . . To seek for steppingstones across the gaps between is to seek in vain, forever.[17]

It is important to understand that just because we think we can visualize the appearance of any number of transitional forms, this doesn't necessarily mean that they could in fact exist in the real world. Many people think that they can visualize what a round square would look like, but such a "thing" is recognized by most mathematicians and philosophers as being manifestly impossible. The capacity to imagine a given state of affairs thus doesn't necessarily make it an actual possibility in the real world. Accordingly, the fact that a given biological form might seem to be logically possible doesn't necessarily mean that it could in fact obtain in the real world. It isn't logical possibility *per se* that is the issue here for the essentialist, but rather the availability of larger essences that can be instantiated in the real world. So, while a part-reptile/part-mammal may not represent a logically impossible state of affairs (like the round square), it *may* in fact represent a state of affairs that is no less impossible in the real world (because of the lack of functional essences to be incorporated).

Other areas of physical reality also reflect this characteristic "notchiness" between possible forms or energy states. The quantum nature of the atom provides a good case in point. There are only a certain number of discrete energy levels that a given electron can occupy in its orbiting about an atom. Any in-between states either appear to be non-existent, or, at the very least, totally non-realizable in fact. If these discrete quantum states can be used as a metaphysical model for the types of forms that can be realized in the biosphere, this would mean that there are only a certain number of discrete animal essences in existence. This in turn would mean that any in-between forms would be impossible to attain by definition.

The typologists of the nineteenth century based their theory of discontinuity in nature precisely on this type of supposition, which states that there is no such thing as evolutionary intermediates between different types of creatures. Such a belief, as we have seen, harks back to the centuries-old system of thought known as *essentialism*, which states that all possible objects possess a certain essential set of defining properties that give their respective objects their intrinsic nature. Between these possible essences there can be no intermediates, because there is no such thing as an intermediate between two successive forms or essences.

Take, for instance, the progression of geometric forms from the triangle through the hexagon, which are created by the successive addition of a single side to the preexisting form. Between a triangle and a rectangle there can be no intermediate form, because these two geometric shapes are part of a hierarchical succession of forms. Indeed, it is *logically impossible* for there to be a geometric intermediate between a triangle and a rectangle, because no such form could possibly exist (since there are no integers between three and four).

The nineteenth-century typologists simply transferred this kind of typological thinking to the natural world. They were of the opinion that each major demarcation of type in the living world was intrinsically necessary and distinct; they therefore believed that there could be no such thing as evolutionary intermediates, because no such creatures could possibly exist.

According to the typological model of nature all the variation exhibited by the individual members of a particular class was merely variation on an underlying theme or design which was fundamentally invariant and immutable. Each individual member of a class conformed absolutely in all essential details to the theme or archetype of its class. It followed from this that all the members of a class were equally representative and characteristic of their class and that no individual member could be considered in any fundamental sense any less characteristic of its class or any closer to any member of another class than any of the other members of its class. In other words, all the members of any defined class are equidistant from the members of other classes as well as being equirepresentative of the archetype of their class.

Such a model of biological classes completely excluded any sort of significant sequential order to the pattern of nature. Because no member of any defined class could stray beyond the confines of its type in terms of its basic characteristics, then no class could be led up to gradually or linked to another class through a sequence of intermediates. Further, within one class, because all the members conform absolutely to the same underlying design and are equidistant in terms of their fundamental characteristics from all other classes, it is impossible to arrange them in a sequence leading in any significant sense towards another class. Typology implied that intermediates were impossible, that there were complete discontinuities between each type.[18]

Georges Cuvier believed that intermediates were impossible because they represented "incoherent combinations" of characters that would have never been able to survive in the real world. He further believed that these incompatibilities were responsible for creating the gaps between major classes of organisms.

> Nature, inexhaustible in fecundity and omnipotent in its works . . . has been settled in the innumerable combinations of organic forms and functions which compose the animal kingdom by physiological incompatibilities alone. It has realized all those combinations which are not incoherent and it is these incompatibilities, this impossibility of the coexistence of one modification with another which establish between the diverse groups of organisms those separations, those gaps, which mark their necessary limits and which create the natural embranchments, classes, orders, and families.[19]

D. Dewar, a prominent anti-Darwinian in the 1930s, was also convinced by this typological train of thought, so much so that he actually challenged his colleagues to come up with blueprints of the supposed intermediate forms that led up to the whale.[20] The immense difficulty of the challenge mystified many of Dewar's opponents, and no one ever took up his challenge.

Dewar's chief point was that any genuine intermediate between land and sea mammals could not possibly survive, due to the radical differences between their respective modes of life:

> Let us notice what would be involved in the conversion of a land quadraped into, first a seal-like creature and then into a whale. The land animal would, while on land, have to cease using its hind legs for locomotion and to keep them permanently stretched out backwards on either side of the tail and to drag itself about by using its fore-legs. During its excursions in the water, it must have retained the hind legs in their rigid position and swim by moving them and the tail from side to side. As a result of this act of self-denial we must assume that the hind legs eventually became pinned to the tail by the growth of membrane. Thus the hind part of the body would have become like that of a seal. Having reached this stage, the creature, in anticipation of a time when it will give birth to its young under water, gradually develops apparatus by means of which the milk is forced into the mouth of the young one, and meanwhile a cap has to be formed round the nipple into which the snout of the young one fits tightly, the epiglottis and laryngeal cartilage become prolonged downwards so as tightly to embrace this tube, in order that the adult will be able to breathe while taking water into the mouth. . . . These changes must be effected completely before the calf can be born under water. Be it noted that there is no stage intermediate between being born and suckled under water and being born and suckled in the air. At the same time various other anatomical changes have to take place, the most important of which is the com-

plete transformation of the tail region. The hind part of the body must have begun to twist on the fore part, and this twisting must have continued until the sideways movement of the tail developed into an up-and-down movement. While this twisting went on the hind limbs and pelvis must have diminished in size, until the latter ceased to exist as external limbs in all, and completely disappeared in most, whales.[21]

More recently, Steven Stanley has made the excellent point that there simply wasn't enough time in the distant past to give all the transitional forms that would have led up to a modern-day mammal the chance to exist. In order to make his point, Stanley relies on the concept of a "chronospecies" to tell us which groups of fossils can be thought of as representing the same species over time and which cannot. This is important, because we don't know for sure which series of fossils actually represented a genuine species in the distant past and which did not, since we have no way to determine the actual degree of their reproductive isolation. We thus have little choice but to rely on their overall physical appearance to determine how long they constituted a single species. The term "chronospecies" is therefore used to refer to a particular segment of a given fossil lineage that is judged, by way of its external appearance of stasis, to have probably remained unchanged enough over a given period of time to be representative of a single species.

Let us suppose that we wish, hypothetically, to form a bat or a whale . . . by a process of gradual transformation of established species. If an average chronospecies lasts nearly a million years, or even longer, and we have at our disposal only ten million years, then we have only ten or fifteen chronospecies to align, end-to-end, to form a continuous lineage connecting our primitive little animal with a bat or a whale. This is clearly preposterous. Chronospecies, by definition, grade into each other, and each one encompasses very little change. A chain of ten or fifteen of these might move us from one small rodentlike form to a slightly different one, perhaps representing a new genus, but not to a bat or a whale![22]

There seems to be no way to reconcile this devastating criticism with the traditional evolutionary concept of slow, random change. There is simply no way to cover all the necessary intermediate forms in the relatively short time span available without some form of directional bias to move the process along in large, coherent steps.

4.3 The Possibility of Intermediate Forms on the Way to the Avian Lung

In order to explore the hypothetical possibility of intermediate forms, Michael Denton has conducted a detailed comparison between the avian and reptilian lung.[23] As Denton points out, it is immensely difficult to see how the avian lung, which is a continuous through-put type of structure in which the air flows in one direction only, could have evolved from the reptilian lung, which is a dead-end type of structure in which the air moves in and out through the same passage, because the structural and functional differences between them are so profound that any possible intermediate would have been totally nonfunctional, and therefore would have spelled instant doom for the hybrid creature.

Just how such a different respiratory system could have evolved gradually from the standard vertebrate design is fantastically difficult to envisage, especially bearing in mind that the maintenance of respiratory function is absolutely vital to the life of an organism to the extent that the slightest malfunction leads to death in minutes. Just as the feather cannot function as an organ of flight until the hooks and barbules are coadapted to fit together perfectly, so the avian lung cannot function as an organ of respiration until the parabronchi system which permeates it and the air sac system which guarantees the parabronchi their air supply are both highly developed and able to function together in a perfectly integrated manner.

In attempting to explain how such an intricate and highly developed system of correlated adaptations could have been achieved gradually through perfectly functional intermediates, one is faced with the problem of the feather magnified a thousand times. The suspicion inevitably arises that perhaps no functional intermediate exists between the dead-end and continuous through-put types of lung. The fact that the design of the avian respiratory system is essentially invariant in ALL birds merely increases one's suspicion that no fundamental variation of the system is compatible with the preservation of respiratory function. One is irresistibly reminded of Cuvier's view that the great divisions of nature are grounded in necessity and that intermediates cannot exist because such forms are incoherent and non-functional.[24]

Denton further notes that it is next to impossible to even *conceive* of a possible intermediate between the avian and reptilian lung, and concludes that this only serves to heighten the extreme discontinuity between birds and reptiles in nature.[25]

As far as the typological model itself is concerned, Denton notes that it cannot always be applied at the species level, because of the fact that species do actually evolve through a wide variety of intermediate forms. However,

. . . at levels above the species, the typological model holds almost universally. Indeed, the isolation and distinctness of different types of organisms and the existence of clear discontinuities in nature have been self-evident for centuries, even to non-biologists. No one, for example, has any difficulty in recognizing a bird, whether it is an eagle, an ostrich or a penguin;

or a cat, whether it is a domestic cat, a lynx or a tiger. Moreover, no one can name a bird or a cat which is in any sense not fully characteristic of its class. No bird is any less a bird than any other bird, nor is any cat any less a cat or any closer to a non-cat species than any other cat.

The reason for the distinctness of each class and the absence of sequential arrangements, whereby classes can be approached gradually through a series of transitional forms, is precisely as typology implied because each class of organism (just like a class of geometric figures) possesses a number of unique defining characteristics which occur in fundamentally invariant form in all the species of that class but which are not found even in a rudimentary form in any species outside that class.[26]

4.4   An Explanation for the Interrelatedness of Nature

A major reason why scientists believe in the theory of evolution is the profound interrelatedness of nature. They see how many of the same structures and biochemical processes are present in a wide variety of different species (the same digestive enzymes, for instance, are used throughout the animal kingdom, from amoeba to man), and this leads them to conclude that all of the species on earth physically evolved out of one another. Moreover, they consider this process of common descent with modification to be a sufficient explanation for why the various life forms on this planet are so closely related to one another.

The Deistic Evolutionist does not dispute this notion that the various plants and animals probably grew out of one another through a naturalistic process of descent with modification.[27] He does not, however, regard this as a sufficient explanation for the many commonalities of structure and function that are found throughout the living world. He simply regards it as the physical vehicle through which these commonalities were passed on from generation to generation, and from species to species. In order to identify a sufficient explanation for this phenomenon, he insists that we need to ask ourselves where the original structures and processes themselves came from, and how they came to be capable of evolving into the myriad of life forms that have existed throughout evolutionary history.

For the theist, it is the Mind of God that is ultimately responsible for the many unifying themes that are found throughout the living world. Within this broad theistic framework, two creative mechanisms are conceivable: 1) God directly created all the various species on earth *ex nihilo* according to a common plan, or 2) God directly created the *potentiality* for the unified evolution of life in the Big Bang itself. Thereafter, in the fulness of time, this potentiality could have revealed itself in the evolution of the first living cell, which somehow would have contained within itself the capacity for evolving into all the various species that have ever existed on this planet. On this latter view, God would still have created the entire living world according to a common plan, only instead of directly creating it in this manner, He would have directly created only the *potentiality* for it, thereby allowing the evolutionary process to subsequently unfold "on its own."

For the theist, then, it is the creative activity of a single Intelligence that is the sufficient explanation for the interrelatedness of nature, whether life arose through a long and drawn out evolutionary process or not. On this view, all species are interrelated because the entire living world mentally "evolved" in the Mind of God *before* it was ever instantiated in reality. Just as all of Shakespeare's works are interrelated because they originated in the same creative mind, so too are the various species of life on earth interrelated, because they also originated in the same Creative Mind.

4.5 God Used Adaptive Radiation to Create Closely-Related Species

The term *adaptive radiation* is often used in modern evolutionary theory to denote the expansion of a single species into a variety of different, but closely-related, species. The classic example of adaptive radiation was originally noted by Darwin during his expedition to the famous Galapagos islands.

Darwin observed that several closely-related species of finch had radiated into widely varying niches on the islands. He further observed that the type of niche that was actually chosen seemed to depend on the particular type of beak that each species possessed. Darwin reasoned that all thirteen varieties of finch must have had their origin in a single parent species that had flown over to the islands long ago. Over time, natural selection had apparently acted upon the natural variations in the progeny's beaks so as to eventually produce 13 different varieties of beak. These naturally-occurring variations gradually enabled the progeny to "radiate" into different niches, so that they could best exploit their own style of beak in the harsh island environment.

In other words, due to the natural variations that regularly occur in all species, the descendants of this original finch came to possess slightly different types of beaks. Because of this, some were naturally a little more adapted to feeding in trees, while others were slightly more adapted to feeding on the ground. Since there was only a limited amount of food in either area, the Galapagos finches couldn't all feed in the same place. Therefore, some of them naturally radiated to the trees while others radiated to the ground. In a relatively short period of time, this slight geographical separation caused some degree of reproductive isolation. Those finches with tree-feeding beaks gave rise to offspring with the same type of beak, while ground-feeding finches gave rise to offspring with their own type of beak. This process continued generation after generation until the various groups of finches had become so genetically separated that mating between them had become impossible.

The result of this process of adaptive radiation is that at least 13 different species of finch are now alleged to exist in the Galapagos islands. The important thing to note about this natural process of speciation is that it is entirely consistent with the doctrine of Intelligent Design. After all, speciation needs to take place in *some* fashion. What better way to have it occur than by connecting it to a fundamental linkage between the various environmental niches and the naturally-occurring variations in each species?

Even so, not all taxonomists are in agreement concerning the number of finch species in the Galapagos. Indeed, one taxonomist who originally classified these finches into over thirty species later said that they all might as well have been called one species.[28]

It is easy to see how there could be a great deal of confusion and uncertainty in such a delicate process of classification. The true definition of a species (which uses interfertility as its chief point of reference) is next to impossible for taxonomists to use in the field, because it is extremely difficult to ascertain whether or not two groups are actually interfertile. To be sure, just because two groups don't interbreed on a regular basis doesn't mean that they can't. But unless we know that they in fact cannot, we really have no absolute criterion for distinguishing two species, at least on the basis of this definition. Taxonomists tend to rely on appearance and behavior in making their classifications, but these variables alone aren't necessarily correlated with interfertility. Thus, it is indeed possible that using the ultimate criterion of interfertility, all the Galapagos finches could in fact be one species.

In speaking of individual species, it is easy to forget just how nebulous this taxonomic category really is. On this score, the Biblical word "kind" appears to be far more useful, as it refers to a unified constellation of many variations within a given genus, while the term "species" attempts to distinguish between the different variations themselves.

The ordinary dog *Canus familiaris* provides a good case in point. Although all domesticated dogs are members of the same species, and can therefore interbreed, there is such a tremendous variety among them that it is hard to see how we can distinguish between other species that are as closely related as the Galapagos finches. It may be that the majority of species that we have assumed were created through the process of adaptive radiation aren't really distinct species at all. If so, we can't attribute the creation of these new intraspecific varieties to adaptive radiation *per se*, but simply to the inwardly-produced variations that are a natural part of all coherent populations.

It is important to note that, as far as the Deistic Evolutionist position is concerned, it doesn't really matter whether the Galapagos finches are all members of the same species, or whether each basic form constitutes a separate species. The Deistic Evolutionist simply recognizes that there is a tremendous amount of genetic variability that is built into each species, such that, in the right circumstance, it is indeed possible for a single ancestor to give rise to many distinct varieties, which can then radiate to different niches.

Although the process of adaptive radiation seems to be capable of creating new species, these new species nevertheless seem to be largely confined to different varieties of a single overall genus or "kind." The point is that while the process of adaptive radiation itself may be capable of generating new species within a single basic kind, it does not seem to be capable of generating new species that are representative of a new kind altogether. This production of new kinds apparently requires a stronger and more directed form of genetic change than the relatively simple types of genetic variations (second-order "mutations") we have been discussing here.

If these stronger orthogenetic changes (third-order "mutations") have indeed occurred in the past, they certainly aren't occurring now with any appreciable frequency, except for the phenomenon of polyploidy in hermaphroditic plants.[29] As far as the apparent lack of these third-order "mutations" in the present-day animal kingdom is concerned, it may simply be that there is no longer any cause for them, since the major forms of life have all been in existence for some time now. On this view, the only thing that remains to be accomplished is for relatively minor instances of speciation to take place within each basic kind, presumably through some form of adaptive radiation.

The upshot of this discussion is that the production of several closely-related species from a single parent species though the naturalistic process of adaptive radiation can never be construed as being evidence against a Grand Designer. For as we have seen, God can use these naturally-occurring mechanisms to help Him produce new species in the world. This would explain why the genetic code of each animal contains such impressive adaptive powers. Presumably God doesn't want His creatures to be dependent on just one set of environmental conditions; He wants them to be flexible (within certain limits, of course), so that they can change when the environment does.

4.6 Vestigial Organs

If it is true that the entire animal kingdom has gradually evolved from a single common ancestor, then it would stand to reason that changing environmental conditions could possibly render certain organs unnecessary in various newly-evolved species. This would account for the so-called vestigial organs in the animal kingdom, organs which have atrophied because they are no longer being actively used by their particular owner. The presence of these seemingly unneeded organs is thus considered to be a "vestige" of an earlier, more functional version of the organ.

Once again, the question of whether or not vestigial organs actually exist has no bearing whatsoever on whether or not the world has been created by a supernatural Being, for as we have seen, the possibility remains that God may have allowed the whole biosphere to gradually evolve on its own, entirely in response to naturalistic forces within the world itself. This deistic scenario would seem to have entailed within it the possibility of vestigial organs in species that have changed to the point that they no longer require them.

Non-theistic evolutionists have used vestigial organs to argue against the possibility that God created all the animals in their final form by Divine Fiat. Since it is hard to see why God would have given a particular animal a useless organ, the conclusion seems to be that God didn't do so at all; the useless organ was simply retained as an inevitable result of continued evolutionary progress.

However, if one affirms, as the Deistic Evolutionist does, the idea that God may have allowed the entire animal kingdom to gradually evolve in sole response to natural evolutionary processes, then the existence of vestigial organs doesn't present a problem at all. Indeed, there is a psychological parallel to the possible existence of these vestigial organs in our own minds. For just as vestigial organs represent the historical remnants of earlier ancestral forms, there are also psychological vestiges of earlier developmental periods that remain in our minds throughout our lives, even though they no longer serve any useful purpose. They simply constitute left-over "baggage" from earlier developmental periods, which is something we would expect from a long and drawn-out developmental (i.e., evolutionary) process. In the same way, to the extent that physical vestigial organs actually exist, they may simply represent the left-over "baggage" from earlier evolutionary periods.

At the same time, though, not everyone is convinced that vestigial organs even exist in the first place. These individuals argue that "vestigial" organs only seem to be useless because we don't yet know their true function.

Take the human appendix, for example. It is often cited in the evolutionary literature as a vestigial organ that allegedly proves man's non-theistic origin. Recent evidence, however, suggests that the appendix isn't nearly as useless as it was once thought to be.[30] Today, for instance, we know that the appendix performs an important infection-fighting function in the body. And while we may be able to survive without it, this doesn't necessarily mean that it fails to serve an important bodily function. As Rifkin has adroitly pointed out, we can also survive quite well without our hands, eyes, or feet, but this doesn't mean that these structures don't serve a useful purpose! It thus may not be entirely accurate to brand the appendix as a genuine vestigial organ, but even if it is, it still cannot properly be used to argue against the doctrine of Intelligent Design, for the aforementioned reason.

4.7 Marine Mammals and the Problem of Adaptation

One of the biggest problems for the conventional neo-Darwinian paradigm concerns the huge transformation many species made during their radical changeover to different environments. The problem centers around how a creature can spontaneously move into a radically different environment, and yet still be well-enough adapted to it to be able to survive and to produce viable offspring.

The classic example of this remarkable process is the celebrated "return" of mammals to the sea in the form of whales and dolphins. According to traditional evolutionary dogma, the mammals grew out of a stock of creatures whose original ancestor was "that first brave fish who wandered out onto dry land in search of a new way of life." But if this is true, then why did the first whales and mammals "choose" to go back to the sea to begin with? Did they regret the initial "decision" of their revolutionary ancestors to move onto dry land? And even if they did, how were they able to adapt so quickly to such a radically new environment? Did they grow fins and tails overnight? If not, why weren't the very first dolphin-like creatures killed off immediately in their initial attempt to re-enter the sea before they were fully equipped for it?

Obviously we are dealing with a major conceptual farce here. There seems to be no rational way to explain the sudden appearance of marine mammals in the fossil record in the absence of some sort of weak orthogenetic program, because there doesn't seem to be any possible way that genuine functional intermediates could have ever survived. Are we to suppose: 1) that fishes initially turned into amphibians by accident, 2) that amphibians then turned into reptiles by accident, and 3) that reptiles accidentally turned into mammals, all with no Outside Help, and then, after such a long and tiring evolutionary journey, that 4) certain mammals accidentally opted to *return* to a life in the sea, already well-adapted to their new change in lifestyle?!

It is at this point that even die-hard Darwinist Ernst Mayr begins to concede that these evolutionary events "seem indeed as decisively directed towards perfect adaptation in the new medium . . . as if someone had directed the course of evolution."[31]

There doesn't seem to be any coherent way around this conclusion, because the traditional neo-Darwinian position is so profoundly unreasonable. This leaves the prospect of Intelligent Design as the only acceptable alternative.

4.8   A Possible Mechanism for Species Transmutation

As we have seen, it is entirely possible that God could have allowed the evolution of the entire animal kingdom to be programmed into the genome of the first living cell. This isn't as outrageous a scenario as it may initially seem, because we already know about one example of such an internally-directed process of self-transmutation in the world: the development of tadpoles, which are fish-like creatures, into frogs, which are air-breathing amphibians. Now, if such a large-scale transmutation can happen in this one instance, there is no *a priori* reason why it couldn't have happened in a similar manner to the entire living world. As far as the actual mechanism of transmutation is concerned, it doesn't really matter whether each new species was directly programmed into the genome from the very beginning, or whether the genome was simply programmed with the capacity to respond to changing environmental conditions in a pre-determined manner (neo-Lamarckism).

The existence of an evolutionary program within the genome would account for Darwin's observation of descent with modification in the living world, because the very existence of such a program would have enabled the various species to physically grow out of one another in a coherent, step-wise fashion.[32] It would also explain why certain structures in one species tend to get reused for other purposes in "later" species.[33]

But if this is true, we are then led to consider an even deeper question: why would God have created the biosphere in this evolutionary fashion to begin with, when He presumably could have done so instantaneously, and thereby avoided all the pain and suffering of the last few billion years? Part of the reason for this may be related to God's apparent tendency to delegate creative responsibility onto His creation whenever possible. But why would God have wanted to do this, especially when it is clear that this type of delegation has been responsible for so much misery and destruction over the years? The answer may ultimately be related to God's manner of dealing with the human race. For as we will see in the final section of this book, the larger ontological definition that human beings seem to be based upon requires that God do nothing for man that man can do for himself. To the extent that this is the case, it follows that God *must* delegate a certain amount of creative responsibility onto His human creatures whenever possible, not just because man is able to acquire his own development for himself, but because he apparently cannot be fully human *unless* he acquires it for himself, because his own unique psychospiritual identity seems to be *derived from* this sort of self-guided developmental process. If this is so, then we can expect God to have given the living world a similar ability for self-development through the gradual process of species transmutation.[34]

Of course, there are those who like to think that a God who delegates creative responsibility onto the physical universe itself is an inferior Creator. But who is the better creator, the one who must build all his creations directly by hand, or the one who can build machines that are so advanced that they can carry on the creative process *themselves* beyond a certain point? Obviously, it is the latter type of creator who is inherently superior. By this mode of reasoning, then, it follows that the more God is able to delegate creative responsibility onto His creation, the more impressive a Creator He actually is.

This being the case, it follows that a God who can delegate the responsibility for speciation onto the species themselves is a more impressive Creator, all things considered, than one who must directly assemble each species "by Hand." Thus, the fact that the scientific evidence itself indicates a naturalistic process of descent with modification from a common ancestor in no way invalidates the theistic hypothesis; it rather *supports it*.

Indeed, state-of-the-art computer engineers are currently designing intelligent computers that can learn from "experience," and that can apply their self-attained "knowledge" to design other computers that are more "intelligent" than themselves. Even so, would it be sensible for us to claim that this computerized ability is *itself* proof that these state-of-the-art computers had no original designer? Of course not. By the same token, we cannot properly use life's apparent ability to transmutate on its own as evidence against a Grand Designer.

Notes

1. Pierre Grassé, *Evolution of Living Organisms: Evidence for a New Theory of Transformation*, p. 6.
2. Gavin De Beer, *Charles Darwin* (Garden City, NY: Doubleday & Company, 1909), p. 1.
3. Marshall and Sandra Hall, *The Truth: God or Evolution?* (Grand Rapids: Baker Book House, 1975), p. 43.
4. Michael Denton, *Evolution: A Theory in Crisis*, p. 99.
5. Ibid., p. 101.
6. Ibid., pp. 275–306.
7. Ibid., p. 278.
8. Procaryotic cells do not contain a membrane-bounded nucleus, whereas eucaryotic cells do.
9. Ibid., p. 281.
10. Ibid.
11. Ibid., p. 282.
12. Ibid., p. 283.
13. Ibid., p. 296.
14. Ibid., p. 297.
15. Ibid., p. 298.
16. Ibid.
17. D'Arcy Wentworth Thompson, *On Growth and Form* (New York: MacMillan, 1942).

18. Michael Denton, *Evolution: A Theory in Crisis*, pp. 95–96.
19. Georges Cuvier (1835), quoted in Michael Denton's *Evolution: A Theory in Crisis*, p. 13.
20. D. Dewar, *More Difficulties of the Evolution Theory* (London: Thynne and Co., 1938), pp. 23–24.
21. Ibid.
22. Steven Stanley, *The New Evolutionary Timetable* (1981), pp. 93–95, quoted in Philip Johnson's *Darwin on Trial*, p. 51.
23. Michael Denton, *Evolution: A Theory in Crisis*, pp. 210–212.
24. Ibid., pp. 211–212.
25. Ibid., p. 213.
26. Ibid., p. 105.
27. Although he strongly affirms the reality of the evolutionary process throughout the history of life on earth, the Deistic Evolutionist does not rule out the possibility that God may have directly created the first species on this planet *ex nihilo*. In his way of thinking, the central issue with regard to evolution isn't how life arose *per se*, but whether God was ultimately responsible for creating it.
28. Taylor, *The Great Evolution Mystery*, p. 129.
29. Polyploidy refers to the fact that certain hermaphroditic species of plant can evolve into a new species in a single generation, through a doubling of the progeny's chromosomes.
30. It is thought that the appendix was originally involved in the digestion of large amounts of cellulose, which our ancestors supposedly ate. As the human race's diet moved away from cellulose over the millennia, the size of the appendix is thought to have shrunk as well. Today, it is a relatively small organ that often causes more trouble than it is worth.
31. Quoted in Taylor's *The Great Evolution Mystery*, p. 160.
32. Another possible explanation for the appearance of modified descent from a common ancestor is that the same Creator could have designed the various animals according to a common, unified Plan. In this case, the "common ancestor" would have been God Himself!
33. This reutilization of the same structures for other purposes can also be explained by appealing to a common Designer.
34. There are two other possible reasons why God may have given so much creative responsibility to the world. On the one hand, if God is genuinely omnipotent, and therefore had the original freedom to coerce His creation in any logically possible manner, then He could have elected to delegate a certain amount of creative responsibility onto His creation in order to give it a sense of freedom and self-determination that would have been impossible in an instantaneously created world. While these qualities may not seem to be important in and of themselves, they are apparently essential for *our own* freedom, because it is difficult to see how we could be genuinely free in a rigidly deterministic world where everything has been planned out ahead of time. On the other hand, if God is not omnipotent, and if He had no choice but to work with a pre-existing world of self-determining actualities, as the process theologians believe, then it would have been metaphysically impossible for God to have created the world instantaneously.

CHAPTER 5
Natural Selection

But then arises the doubt, can the mind of man, which has, as I fully believe, been developed from a mind as low as that possessed by the lowest animal, be trusted when it draws such grand conclusions?

CHARLES DARWIN

5.1 The Reality of Natural Selection

Once an organism's genetic material is somehow altered, neo-Darwinian evolutionary theory says that its existence will either be selected for or against by the environment, depending on how well it is able to adapt and survive. The fittest members of any given population will thus stand the best chance of surviving long enough to reproduce, thereby increasing the concentration of these favorable traits in the progeny. This is the concept of natural selection in a nutshell.

There is no question that this notion of the "survival of the fittest" is a very real phenomenon. We see it every day in almost every area of life. There is competition for survival all around us, from the tropical fish aquarium to the business community. Only the "fittest" members of any population can survive and proliferate *by definition*.

Natural selection even appears to be a major factor in the speciation process, as orthodox neo-Darwinian theory has long asserted. Zoologist Peter Grant of Princeton University has helped to demonstrate this fact through his extensive analysis of wild finch populations on Daphne Major, a small islet in the Galapagos archipelago. Grant observed significant morphological changes after the occurrence of a single drought, most notably a trend towards larger body and beak sizes.[1]

Grant estimates that as few as 20 such selection events would have to occur in order to transform the medium ground finch, *G. fortis*, into the large ground finch, *G. magnirostris*, which is 50% larger.[2] This is a remarkably small figure for the occurrence of true speciation, which in turn seems to validate the process of natural selection as an important mechanism in the evolution of the earth's flora and fauna.

For the Deistic Evolutionist, of course, findings like these are not threatening in the least, because he fully affirms the reality and importance of the selective process in nature. Indeed, as far as traditional theological doctrine is concerned, our entrance into heaven itself appears to be predicated on a spiritual version of the "survival of the fittest." Only the "fittest" members of the human race, judged in terms of their inner spiritual development and attitude towards God, are said to intrinsically be "worthy" enough to enter the kingdom of heaven.

As far as we're concerned in this book, though, the big question isn't whether natural selection occurs or not; it is whether it, in conjunction with random mutations of form, is capable of producing the millions of different species of life that have appeared on this planet. While structural and functional adaptations undoubtedly enable an organism to survive in its particular niche, and while natural selection clearly favors the continued existence of these beneficial adaptations, this is a far cry from saying that its adaptive suitability for the niche, and indeed its very character as a species, was originally *caused* by the selective action of a harsh and unforgiving environment (in conjunction with random genetic mutations).

The biggest problem with natural selection is that while it clearly tends to concentrate certain adaptive variations in a given species, and while it may indeed help to generate closely-related species in the same overall genus, it typically does *not* seem to be the chief creative force behind the production of new genera; it rather seems to operate to keep the larger classifications of form constant. Since each species, by virtue of its continued existence over time, is more or less well adapted to its own particular niche, any significant change in that species would tend to render it less adapted overall (barring any major change in the environment), and so would tend to cause it to be selected *against*.

Of course, phenotypic change in and of itself isn't always an occasion for negative selection; it can also represent an enterprising opportunity for the organism to move on to a new niche, where it will then hopefully be able to exploit its new characteristics to advantage. It all depends on the intrinsic nature of the phenotypic change itself: if the change is favorable (i.e., if it enables the creature to adapt to a new part of the environment), then the organism will be able to escape nature's selective hand; if it isn't, then adaptation will be impossible and death will result.

This is perhaps the chief reason why random mutations alone could not possibly have guided evolution. For as we have seen, the production of new adaptive characters typically takes more than one concurrent genetic change in order to be operative, and the odds for two or more coordinated and beneficial changes randomly taking place in the same overall area are exceedingly remote. But even if we assume that such a coordinated change could indeed occur, it doesn't automatically follow that the newly altered creature will simply be able to move on to take advantage of a new niche. In all likelihood there will be other long-established occupants of the new environment to be reckoned with, and since they have been there longer, they will typically be better adapted to it, and so will tend to force the newcomer to be selected *against*.

Natural history corroborates this point of view. The fact of extinction permeates the past history of life on earth. Indeed, it has been said that more species have died out in the history of our planet than now exist in the entire world![3] And since extinction directly implies a local failure[4] of adaptation, we see that natural selection has resulted in at least as much extinction as it has outright evolution.

A closer look at the extinction rate, however, shows that natural selection alone may not be the primary causative factor in the elimination of species, either. Leigh van Valen[5] of the University of Chicago, for instance, has shown that the rate at which species become extinct is largely the same no matter how long they've been alive.[6] But if natural selection were the primary determining factor in the survival of species, one would naturally suppose that those species that had been alive the longest would show the greatest resistance to extinction, since their persistence over time would be direct evidence of their fitness to the environment (excluding, of course, the impact of major catastrophes). But such is apparently not the case.

In fact, there is a great deal of paleontological evidence indicating that it is the most specialized animals that become extinct the fastest.[7] This is because the most specialized animals are also the most sensitive to changing environmental patterns and conditions. Thus, as Taylor points out, "it would seem that a high rate of evolution is undesirable. It is the creatures which evolve least which last longest."[8]

According to the neo-Darwinian evolutionist, however, the whole point of evolution is the development of specialization via natural selection, which in turn helps to adapt an animal to a particular niche. Moreover, traditional evolutionary doctrine says that the faster a species evolves, the more genetically-based variations it is likely to experience, which in turn means the more likely it is to develop successful adaptations to the local environment. At the same time, though, any such species must be careful not to become *too* successful in the specialization game, because this would tend to make it *less* flexible in the event of sudden environmental change. But even if the environment remains the same, overspecialization can cause a given species to become so successful at foraging for food that it inadvertently depletes its own niche of food. In these cases, the inadvertent victims of overspecialization become their own worst enemies.[9]

In order to have the best chance for survival, then, an organism must be "careful" not to become too successful with its particular mode of specialization. It must strike just the right balance between specialization and overspecialization, or be faced with the prospect of self-imposed extinction. Thus, at a certain point, it must back off from the tendency to specialize in its environment. At the same time, though, specialization via natural selection is the name of the game for the non-theistic evolutionist; hence, to avoid specialization is to:

> . . . avoid the process of natural selection. The evolutionist who condemns over-specialisation is thus in conflict with himself. Moreover, if non-specialisation is advantageous, there should have been selection for a mechanism which ensures it. In short, Simpson's throw-away line [stating that extinction occurs when an organism fails to adapt to a changing environment fast enough] doubly invalidates the Darwinian thesis.[10]

It is interesting to note how Edward Blythe, the man who originally conceived of the idea of natural selection some 20 years before Darwin:

> . . . used the theory . . . not to explain how species can arise from pre-existing species, but rather to explain how species remain constant. The action of selection, he [correctly] thought, would serve to eliminate not only monsters, but all deviants from the norm, all the abnormal types that arise in every population; and so it would make each species hold true to type, and stay fit to continue its existence within the given environment.[11]

It is a well-known biological fact that every organism in the world today is exquisitely well-adapted to its particular niche. Consequently, any random change in an organism's genetic material would clearly tend to make it *less* adaptable overall, and this would tend to render it far more susceptible to death instead of life. On the whole, then, natural selection doesn't seem to act to create new species nearly as much as it does to keep a given species constant. This observation correlates well with the extraordinary amount of stasis that pervades virtually the entire paleontological record.

The tremendous limitations of natural selection were recognized by T.H. Morgan and L.T. Hogben half a century ago, when they pointed out that if selection had never occurred, all the known forms of life would have still appeared, amidst untold numbers of other creatures that would have escaped extinction.[12] What are we to conclude from this startling realization? Namely, that "the present results of evolution owe nothing to natural selection . . . which has only had the effect of eliminating the less viable forms that would otherwise have persisted."[13]

It would seem, then, that natural selection is only able to govern the relative proliferation of species, not their ultimate origin. To the extent that this assertion is valid, the neo-Darwinian evolutionist errs when he assumes that the natural law that governs the proliferation of animals was also somehow responsible for their creation as well.

5.2 Altruism in the Natural World

For the neo-Darwinian, competition between species is the major theme that drives evolution forward. It is assumed that the various species will tend to compete for the available resources, so that only the most fit individuals will be able to survive to the point of being able to reproduce. Without competition, then, the neo-Darwinian theory is as good as dead.

When we look to the natural world, though, we find that things aren't nearly as ruthless as the neo-Darwinians would have us believe. Although there is a certain sense of "competition" between animals in the perennial struggle for survival, there is also a surprising amount of cooperation as well. In fact, there are so many separate instances of "altruism" in the wild that one begins to wonder just how valid the neo-Darwinian emphasis on competition really is.

Orthodox evolutionists attempt to account for this altruism by viewing it as a more advanced way to compete. Since animals that cooperate with one another are presumably able to survive longer than those who do not, cooperation both within a species (group selection) and between species would seem to be an expected result of natural selection. Yet, how could it possibly be the case that amoral creatures, who had evolved over millions of years through ruthless competition, could all of a sudden reverse their behavior and begin cooperating with one another for *whatever* reason? While such cooperative behavior may in fact favor the survival of the group, it is hard to see how any one animal could "know" this, and behave accordingly. Non-theistic evolutionary theory is predicated on the assumption that each animal acts directly for its *own* good. On this level, altruistic behavior is out of place, because there is no immediate survival-based reason to engage in it. The fact that it may foster the survival of more individuals in the end is immaterial on this level, because animals who are primarily interested in their own minute-to-minute survival would seem to be incapable of such long-range motivations.

Nevertheless, the entire non-theistic theory of evolution is predicated on the existence of natural selection "as a mindless process, as the impersonal operation of purely natural forces. If it is mindless, it cannot plan ahead; it cannot make sacrifices now to attain a distant goal, because it has no goals and no mind with which to conceive goals. Therefore every change must be justified by its own immediate advantages, not as leading to some desirable end."[14]

According to this conceptualization of natural selection, altruism should essentially be unknown in the wild, because there are few, if any, immediate advantages for it. Whatever other advantages that may exist for it are too remote and too "other-oriented" to be consistent with the fundamentally selfish character of natural selection. The notion of one individual risking his or her own life to help others is fine for human life, but it is very much out of place in a world where natural selection is the chief arbiter over what exists and what doesn't.

Of course, this isn't to say that cooperation between animals doesn't foster survival in the wild; it does. It is only to say that this long-range survival is intrinsically incapable of motivating cooperation in the here-and-now, because natural selection requires there to be an immediate advantage for all adaptations that happen to evolve. We mustn't confuse a beneficial *byproduct* of a certain type of behavior with being an antecedent *cause* of that behavior, i.e., just because altruistic behavior may enhance survival in the wild isn't a sufficient reason in and of itself for supposing that it was the prospect of increased survival that originally *caused* the altruistic behavior in the first place.

It thus comes as no surprise that the concept of altruism is a subject the non-theistic evolutionist would rather not discuss, since it is very much at odds with his belief system. Nevertheless, the phenomenon of altruism in the animal world is very real. Consider, if you will, the case of certain varieties of ant, who routinely use some of their own eggs to feed their queen and other workers. Or what about robins, thrushes and other birds who routinely warn other birds of approaching danger by emitting a kind of whistling alarm? One would think that if ruthless competition were such a strong force in the wild, an individual bird would never risk its own life by trying to warn its neighbors. While such behavior might end up fostering the survival of the group in the long run, one would think that the warning birds themselves would eventually get selected *against* by their highly conspicuous behavior. Yet, they continue to do very well in the wild. This very fact seems to speak of a larger organizing principle in nature, one which greatly transcends the limits of natural selection alone.

Perhaps the most stunning example of cooperation between species can be found in the sea, where small "cleaner fish" and certain varieties of "cleaner shrimp" are routinely allowed to remove parasites from within the mouths and gills of big predator fish. Many of these parasite-eaters perform an elaborate dance in order to advertise their services, in spite of the fact that such conspicuous behavior would seem to render them far more susceptible to hostile predators. Surprisingly, though, a long line of large predator fish can often be found waiting patiently for their turn to be cleaned of parasites.

Amazingly, these "friendly" predator fish allow the tiny cleaners to move in and out of their mouths at will. Then, when the cleaning session is over, each individual predator fish for some reason goes *against* its natural inclination and allows the cleaner fish to swim out of its mouth unharmed, even though the predator fish could easily swallow the cleaner with no untoward consequences whatever. This is an extreme type of mutualism known as *cleaning symbiosis*, where each species adopts a "friendly" attitude toward the other, because both derive benefit from the relationship.

A particularly interesting example of cleaning symbiosis involves a certain variety of shellfish known as Pedersen's shrimp. When the cleaner shrimp is approached by a "friendly" predator fish, the shrimp proceeds to wave:

> . . . its long antennae. The fish, if interested, presents its head and gill covers for cleaning. The shrimp climbs aboard and walks rapidly over the fish, checking irregularities, tugging at parasites with its claws, and cleaning injured areas. The fish remains almost motionless during this inspection and allows the shrimp to make minor incisions in order to get at subcutaneous parasites. As the shrimp approaches the gill covers, the fish opens each one in turn and allows the shrimp to enter and forage among the gills. The shrimp is even allowed to enter and leave the fish's mouth cavity. Local fishes quickly learn the location of these shrimp. They line up or crowd around for their turn and often wait to be cleaned when the shrimp has retired into the hole beside the anemone.[15]

Such altrustic behavior defies rational explanation by non-theistic evolutionists. While it may be possible to see how natural selection could be responsible for generating part of this mutualistic relationship, insofar as both the shrimp and the predator fish derive some degree of benefit from one another, there are two additional factors that cannot be explained in terms of natural selection. First, it is hard to see how there could be any adaptive advantage whatever in a given shrimp repeatedly risking its life by looking for food in the most dangerous of places; unless, of course, there was some *prior arrangement*, where the shrimp's safety could more or less be guaranteed. Secondly, while it may be in the predator fish's immediate interest to allow the cleaner shrimp to clean its mouth and gills of parasites, it is *not* in its best interest to allow the cleaner shrimp to swim away uneaten, unless it was somehow anticipating the need for the cleaner shrimp at some point in the future. But how could a predator fish that is only interested in its own immediate needs possibly know that it would need something in the future, unless it was given this instinctual knowledge by some prior arrangement?

As we have seen, the doctrine of natural selection only allows us to posit the development of structures and behaviors that confer an immediate advantage in the struggle for survival. Yet, there is no immediate survival advantage at all to be gained when a small shrimp enters the mouth of a much larger predator fish; there are certainly far safer places to look for nourishment than in the jaws of a hungry predator. One would think that the first creatures who first possessed such a suicidal impulse would have quickly been weeded out by natural selection. Similarly, there is no immediate survival advantage at all to be gained when a predator fish allows the cleaner shrimp to swim away unharmed. According to the "law of the jungle," we would expect the predator fish to eat the cleaner shrimp when the latter creature's job was over, because appetite satisfaction is the only immediate survival tactic that is applicable here. There are certainly no punitive laws in the natural world that facilitate the punishment of "law-breakers." Hence, the predator fish would have nothing to fear by eating all the cleaners that would be so stupid as to swim into its hungry jaws. And since it is presumably incapable of adjusting its present behavior in order to make allowances for a future need, we cannot argue that it chooses to allow the cleaner fish to swim away unharmed, due to its anticipation of a future need to have more parasites removed.

The non-theistic evolutionist, of course, sees things differently. He believes that cleaning symbiosis originally came into being when a group of parasite-hungry sea creatures happened to stumble upon a group of predators who just happened to be full of parasites (and who for some reason opted to not eat the cleaners when the cleaning session was over). Since both groups of creatures derived benefit, both were supposedly favored by natural selection.

This is an exceedingly unlikely state of affairs on two separate accounts: 1) By failing to explain where the original compulsions came from that made cleaning symbiosis possible, the traditional neo-Darwinian explanation begs the true question that is at issue here, and 2) One would never expect the cleaner fish to be so accurate in their choice of which predators to approach for a parasite feeding. Since all it would take is one mistake to eliminate a given cleaner fish, one would expect enough mistakes to have accumulated over the years to have eliminated the cleaners altogether; that is, unless some sort of hidden principle were really at work here.

Interestingly enough, there are a number of impostors in the seas that are camoflaged to look just like cleaner fish, but their intentions are hostile: they want to actually take a bite out of the parasite-ridden predators themselves. However, very few predator fish are actually deceived; they typically proceed to swallow the hostile pretenders whole.

Now, how are we to explain the existence of these hostile pretenders by natural selection? One would think that these suicidal fish would have been eliminated long ago in their futile attempt to impersonate the cleaner fish, yet they are doing very well today.[16]

It is hard to resist the impression that these impostors are, like the bona fide cleaners themselves, part of a much larger scheme that is able to coordinate the various forces of the biosphere together towards a common goal: that of the continued efficiency and survivability of the ecological whole. To this end, each of the individual forces in the natural world appears to be subordinated to the good of this larger goal.

Indeed, the deeper one looks, the harder it is to find even a single case of ruthless competition in nature that does not foster the good of the whole, either within a given species or even between species. While there is always the predator-prey dichotomy at work between certain species, one still would be hard-pressed to say that any true "competition" was taking place here. Kills are made for food only, with the beneficial side effect of keeping prey populations in check. Thus, even in the most "ruthless" of instances, a profound cooperation between species for the good of the whole nevertheless seems to exist. This is, of course, much more than can be said for human society. In fact, Darwin's original concept of "competition" in the natural world is said to have had its origin, not in the natural world *per se*, but rather in the severe economic competition that Darwin observed to be taking place in his native Victorian England. In an unconscious effort to rationalize and justify this ruthless economic competition, Darwin seems to have simply projected the human reality of competition out onto the natural realm itself.[17]

However, it is now a widely-recognized fact that the inherent cruelty of the animal kingdom doesn't even come close to rivaling the cruelty that is regularly seen in human society. Although we regularly chide each other for behaving "like animals," we would actually be doing very well to imitate them in much of their behavior.

Of course, this isn't to say that there isn't a constant struggle for survival going on in the natural world. There obviously is. This struggling, however, is largely restricted to each animal's relationship to its own local environment; other animals seem to play a decidedly minor role in the overall survival process (excluding, of course, the impact of roving predators). Quite clearly, then, an animal can struggle to stay alive without actually "competing" with other animals *per se*. In view of these considerations, it seems safe to conclude that Darwin's original idea of ruthless competition in the animal world actually says more about *human* society than it does about the animals themselves. John Thompson and Patrick Geddes agree:

> What has gotten into circulation is a caricature of Nature—an exaggeration of part of the truth. For while there is in wild Nature much stern sifting, great infantile and juvenile mortality, much redness of tooth and claw . . . there is much more. In face of limitations and difficulties, one organism intensifies competition, but another increases parental care; one sharpens its weapons, but another makes some experiment in mutual aid . . . The fact is that the struggle for existence need not be competitive at all; it is illustrated not only by ruthless self-assertiveness, but also by all the endeavors of parents for offspring, of mate for mate, of kin for kin. The world is not only the abode of the strong, it is also the home of the loving.[18]

The overall point is that some additional factor seems to be operative in the evolution of species besides the mere struggle for survival *per se*. It is this additional factor that has allowed a certain amount of altruism, which we otherwise would not have expected, to play a role in the day-to-day activities of the living world.

Actually, we should have been able to infer from the existence of suicidal behavior in certain species that the animal kingdom could never have been formed by natural selection alone (working, of course, in conjunction with randomly-occurring mutations). After all, survival is the very essence of natural selection—only those individuals who are fit enough to survive and reproduce are said to be capable of escaping nature's selective hand. But if this is true, how are we to explain the evolution and continued existence of bees, who routinely sacrifice their own lives when they sting other creatures? One would think that stinging bees would never have evolved in the first place, since their suicidal behavior runs directly counter to the traditional notion of the survival of the fittest. While it is certainly possible that they could reproduce before they would actually sting anything, one would nevertheless expect such suicidal behavior to have been completely selected *against* over the years, since, by hypothesis, those bees that would not sting would tend to leave behind more offspring than those that do, thereby increasing their relative incidence in the progeny. To the contrary, though, stinging bees are doing very well today, in spite of their suicidal behavior. The obvious implication of this fact is that natural selection alone cannot be responsible for the original evolution of the stinging bee.

5.3   Natural Selection and the Diversification of Species

We have seen that while it may be possible for natural selection, in conjunction with naturally-occurring variations, to act on a limited scale to transmute one species into another closely-related species, as may have happened with Darwin's finches in the Galapagos islands, these processes do not appear to be entirely responsible for the origin of species, or for the transmuting of one species into a wholly different species (i.e., a fish into a human), even if the transmutation occurs in gradual steps over billions of years. Natural selection only seems to be responsible for the proliferation of certain species into other closely-related species, and most importantly, for the extinction of species.

As Harvard botanist Asa Gray once pointed out, we understand natural selection to be:

> . . . a sort of personification or generalized expression for the processes and the results of the whole interplay of living things on the earth with their inorganic surroundings and with each other. *The hypothesis asserts that these may account, not for the introduction of life, but for its diversification into the forms and kinds which we now behold* . . . (emphasis mine).[19]

In other words, Gray is arguing that there seem to be two distinct stages in evolution: the original introduction of life, and the subsequent evolution of these species partially by means of natural selection. Taylor agrees with this basic contention:

> It looks as if evolution developed in two phases, an opening one in which certain major patterns were established and a second phase in which speciation worked within narrower and narrower set limits.[20]

In other words, natural selection implies something to select *from*. And since there was no living matter to select from before the actual origin of life (unless one believes that some form of natural selection was operative in pre-biotic, inorganic matter), natural selection alone could not have been solely responsible for the origin of species.

Neo-Darwinian evolutionary scientists are aware of this serious limitation to their theory, so in an effort to account for the origin of life by means of natural selection (through the chance recombination of molecules), they have hypothesized that the non-living matter which eventually evolved into life somehow perpetuated itself by means of natural selection. Such a notion is far from scientific in the strict experimental sense, as it cannot be proven to have happened in the past, nor can it be observed to be going on now to any significant extent. Even so, the non-theistic evolutionist opts to place his personal faith in the possibility that natural selection could have somehow operated on chance combinations of molecules (which are themselves unaccounted for) to give rise to the first primordial cell.

In order to operate, natural selection requires a constantly varying, as well as a persistently surging, class of substances to choose *from*. Normally, these substances are thought of as being alive, because only living matter seems to possess the variability, upward force, and reproductive capacity that are needed as raw materials for natural selection to work on. It is hard to see how anything inanimate could consistently possess these characteristics (apart from crystals perhaps).

To the extent, then, that natural selection requires living matter to act upon, it *presupposes* an already existing living population to select *from*. Within the organic realm, it thus seems to be a natural principle of diversification and proliferation, and not one of origination *per se*. Darwin himself realized this to a certain extent, as he did not attempt to explain the actual origin of life in *The Origin of Species*. His book would have thus been more appropriately called *The Proliferation of Species by Means of Natural Selection*, instead of *The Origin of Species by Means of Natural Selection*.

All in all, we can draw two major conclusions about the action of natural selection in the wild:

1. It requires an original stock of plants and animals to select from.
2. It acts as a merciless filter to eliminate all but the fittest genetic vari-

ants for continued survival. Concerning the spontaneous appearance of potentially advantageous variations, natural selection simply causes a concentration of these variations in later generations, which sometimes may lead to the creation of new, closely-related species.

Seen from this perspective, one possible explanation for the current diversity of living creatures is that God somehow created the original stock of plants and animals on this planet, either through a direct creation of each major type, or through a genetically preprogrammed sequential unfolding of the first living cell. Once created, each organism then automatically became subject to the law of natural selection, for better or for worse. Radical environmental changes would have thus had the effect of causing all but the most flexible and adaptable of animals to completely die off. On the other hand, whenever organisms would spontaneously develop potentially advantageous variations, natural selection would use these variations over time to produce new, but still closely-related, species.

5.4 Natural Selection and Random Variations of Form

According to the principle of natural selection, the only biological forms that can remain in existence are those that confer some sort of immediate survival advantage to the host organism. But if this is the case, then how are we to explain the existence of seemingly random variations of form that don't appear to have any direct survival value associated with them?

Some plants, for instance, have their leaves arranged in pairs on opposite sides of the stalk, while others have their leaves placed alternately. No clear selective advantage can be seen as existing in either arrangement, yet both types of plants flourish in the same environment.

Look closely at the turf of downland and there you will find a score of flowers, grasses, and mosses within inches of one another—quite different in form yet occupying the same habitat. In what sense are they all 'adapted' to it? There will be flowers with four petals or with five or six or even eight. Is there any advantage in having five petals rather than four? It does not seem so. There will be flowers with one stamen or several; leaves which are smoothly oval and leaves cut into lacy shapes. Is there any advantage in having a few additional hairs at the mouth of the corolla? We are forced to admit that some variations of form, at least, are quite random. That is, they are neutral as far as natural selection is concerned. So how did they arise and become stabilised?[21]

It seems apparent that some other force besides natural selection had to have been responsible for bringing certain selectively neutral biological forms into existence. To admit this, however, is to also admit that adaptive value alone cannot be the sole determining factor in what actually exists and what does not. Even if this other force is sheer randomness, it remains true that natural selection is not the sole arbiter of all that exists in the natural world.

5.5 Can Natural Selection Create Coherent Adaptations Out of Random Variations?

In orthodox evolutionary theory adaptations are thought to have arisen solely in response to natural selection acting upon random mutations. The cleverness of these adaptations is simply thought to have been due to the fact that cleverness is required for survival; hence, only those adaptations that are clever enough to contribute to the survival of the host species are thought to have been able to persist in a given population.

This idea is itself based on three critical assumptions: 1) that creatures are able to spontaneously produce a wide range of possible (e.g., random) variations, 2) that some of these variations happen to be coherent enough to form a functional adaptation, and 3) that natural selection will determine which of these coherent adaptations will continue surviving into the next generation.

There is, however, another way to explain the cleverness of biological adaptations. An intelligent Creator could have played a role in the design of these adaptations long before any life ever existed on this planet. Having done so, He then could have infused these partially directed adaptations into the genetic programs of the first living creatures, so that whenever the time was right for a given creature, the right adaptation would suddenly present itself, most probably in response to some type of environmental stimulation.[22] These variations, in turn, would tend to repeatedly express themselves in any given population, so that natural selection could then act to choose the most environmentally appropriate variations for continued survival.

As we have seen, it is this wide range of variations on a given basic theme that seems to have been mistaken by evolutionary scientists for genuine randomness. Since variations seem to randomly occur around a central morphogenetic structure or function, evolutionists have been duped into believing that the variations *themselves* must have been randomly produced as well. However, the very fact that they occur around a central basic theme proves that they are *not* being randomly produced; it is merely the numerical incidence and structural diversity of these variations around each basic theme that can be thought of as "randomly" occurring.

If these variations were truly random, the vast majority would be incoherent and so would not be able to function well enough to escape nature's selective hand. Hence, the very fact that coherent variations tend to occur over a certain range supports the idea that there is a certain degree of directedness to evolution. This directedness, however, isn't absolute, due to the fact that all the members of a given population do not simultaneously express an optimal set of variations for their local environment. Because these variations tend to occur over a certain predetermined range, only a relatively small percentage of the population will be fortunate enough to have inherited a set of variations that will be environmentally appropriate enough to give them the luxury of continued survival; the rest will be eliminated by natural selection.

The Creator's intention in producing these "random" variations around each basic theme is easy enough to deduce: since environments are always changing, He clearly would have wanted to design an optimal degree of adaptability into His creatures, and the best way to have done this was to design a certain amount of variability into them so that the selective force of the environment could then be allowed to choose those that are best adapted for continued survival. This would clearly have given them the best chance for survival through a wide range of possible environmental conditions. (This adaptability isn't infinite, though, which explains why there have been so many extinctions throughout evolutionary history.)

Actually, the traditional evolutionary picture isn't as far away from this limited degree of directedness as it may superficially seem. For by assuming that some variations will be coherent enough to give a creature the luxury of continued survival, the orthodox evolutionist is automatically assuming that these variations will be directed enough to represent coherent adaptations.[23]

Darwin himself was of the opinion that at least some of these variations had to have been coherent enough to pass nature's selective test, otherwise no variations at all would have been capable of existing. As Denton explains, in order to "account for the required number of simultaneous beneficial variations he was forced into an almost vitalistic Lamarckian position, having to toy with the idea of some sort of directional bias in the occurrence of variation and mutation."[24]

As we have seen, Darwin attributed the apparent directedness of evolution to a deistic sort of Creator, whom he thought would have allowed the entire biosphere to evolve in full accordance with natural law. He openly expressed this belief in the last paragraph of the *Origin*:

There is grandeur in this view of life, with its several powers, *having been originally bequeathed by the Creator into a few forms or into one*; and that, whilst this planet has gone cycling on according to the fixed law of gravity, from so simple a beginning endless forms most beautiful and most wonderful have been, and are being evolved (emphasis mine).[25]

In this one paragraph Darwin shows himself to be in full agreement with the central tenet of Deistic Evolutionism, insofar as he admits that the ultimate power behind the evolutionary process was "originally bequeathed by the Creator into a few forms or into one."[26] However, as we saw in the opening chapter, Darwin continued to be mystified by the question of *why* the Deity would have utilized such a painful and wasteful creative process to do His creating, when presumably a much more innocuous and efficient means was available to Him. As we will be seeing in more detail later on, a coherent and plausible rationale for this Divine choice *can* be forwarded, but it necessarily must transcend the limits of the biological sciences themselves, since it is essentially a theological issue. Darwin's mistake was that he sought an answer to this theological problem from within the ranks of the empirical sciences only.

5.6 Popular Examples of Evolution in Action

An often cited example of natural selection at work is the gradual change seen in the British peppered moth *Biston betularia*. Up until the mid 1800s, the dominant form of this moth was grey in color, which enabled it to camouflage itself from predators amidst the grey lichen on trees. Although a black variation of the moth was also found occasionally, it was easily spotted by birds and subsequently eaten. Around the turn of the century, however, enough soot from the Industrial Revolution had settled on the local trees to render the grey form more visible by birds and the black form more camouflaged. Consequently, within a few short years the black form grew to comprise approximately 99 percent of the entire peppered moth population in the sooty parts of England.

Although this is a classic case of natural selection at work, it is important to note that the black variant didn't turn into a new species. It remained *Biston betularia*; the black variant simply became more numerous because of changing environmental conditions. Jeremy Rifkin agrees:

> All the peppered moth example proves is that variety in a species—in this case black-and-white moths—ensures that when environmental conditions radically change, the species itself may be able to adapt with sufficient success to maintain its own perpetuation as a species. Far from being an example of evolution at work, the change from a white variety of moth to a black variety of the same moth is an example of species maintenance.[27]

Another often cited example of natural selection at work involves the evolution of the horse. Every introductory biology student has seen impressive photographs of the evolutionary rise of the once tiny *Eohippus* to its current size and prominence. What these texts usually leave out, however, is the fact that the horse fossils that were used to form this evolutionary series were found at different times and in different places, with the surprising result that there is no real line of descent among them at all. Norman Macbeth has clarified this important point on a recent Public Television documentary entitled "Did Darwin Get It Wrong?"

> About 1905 an exhibit was set up [in the American Museum of Natural History] showing all these horses . . . They were arranged in order of size. Everybody interpreted them as a geneological series. But they are not a geneological series; there is no descent among them. They were found at different times, in different places and they're merely arranged according to size.

> But it's impossible to get them out of the textbooks . . . As a matter of fact, many of the biologists themselves forget what they are. I had a radio debate with a paleontologist some years ago, and when I said there were no phylogenies, he told me I should go out to the Museum and look at the series of horses. I said, "But Professor, they are not a family tree; they are just a collection of sizes." He said, "I forgot that."[28]

Of course, a wide variety of horse fossils from different places and times in no way constitutes a genealogical series, for even today a wide variety of horse sizes can be obtained, from the very small to the very large, but this doesn't mean that one horse literally grew out of another (at least not in an entirely accidental manner). This is a clear example of how a desired but inaccurate meaning can be read into the fossil "evidence." Stanley confirms this conclusion by noting that:

> The known fossil record fails to document a single example of phyletic (gradual) evolution accomplishing a major morphological transition and hence offers no evidence that the gradualistic model can be valid.[29]

This type of fundamental misinterpretation of the existing fossil record appears to be extremely widespread in non-theistic evolutionary circles. As we will see in more detail later on, many of these individuals have apparently projected their own biased expectations onto the entire field of life's origins, with the result that they have unknowingly misinterpreted much of what has been learned in this important area.

Another famed example of accidental evolution at work involves the ancient bird *Archaeopteryx*. This paleontological marvel was supposed to be the long sought-after missing link between the reptiles and the birds, since it had both bird-like features, such as feathers, and reptilian features, such as teeth, vertebrae along the tail, and claw-like appendages on the outer part of its wings. However, as Rifkin and others have pointed out, these reptilian features are more cosmetic than structural, and have even been found in certain modern-day birds.[30]

Moreover, *Archaeopteryx* had feathers that were clearly designed for flight, even though it may have been unable to fly for a variety of structural reasons. But if it was unable to fly, how could such a creature have possibly evolved feathers that were designed for flight, when there was as yet nothing for natural selection to act upon? Although some have argued that *Archaeopteryx's* feathers first evolved to conserve heat, a deeper inspection shows that this could not have been so, since its feathers were of the stiff variety that is specifically designed for flight, and not of the downy kind designed for heat conservation. Anyway, one would think that if heat conservation were the primary issue, natural selection would have evolved a much simpler adaptation for conserving it: hair.

Another damaging piece of evidence against the possible "missing-link" status of *Archaeopteryx* was *Science News'* 1977 report describing how a fully-developed bird fossil had been found in the same geological period as *Archaeopteryx*, thus providing powerful evidence that *Archaeopteryx* wasn't a true "missing link" after all. It rather appears to have been a contemporary of true flying birds.[31]

But even if we assume, for the sake of argument, that *Archaeopteryx* was indeed the long sought-after "missing-link" between the reptiles and the birds, this still ends up proving absolutely nothing about the issue of Divine Creatorship *per se*. For as we have seen, it is possible that God could have allowed the entire animal kingdom to evolve itself entirely according to natural "evolutionary" processes. If this were indeed the case, we would then expect certain intermediate forms of creatures to have "evolved" (or appeared) over the years. The significant thing to note about these possible "missing-links" isn't that they occur midway between two major taxonomic classes (which is irrelevant as far as Divine Creatorship is concerned), but that they represent coherent animals who would have been sophisticated enough to survive the harsh demands of their local environment.

At most, then, so-called "missing-links," if they exist at all, only succeed in showing us that God probably did not create all the animals by instantaneous Fiat. This, however, says nothing at all about whether God created the living world through some other, more indirect means.

In view of the multitudinous amount of evidence that is currently piling up against non-theistic evolution, many scientists are just beginning to see the light. Consider, for example, what evolutionary biologist Jean Rostand has had to say about the current status of their theory:

No, decidedly I cannot make myself think that these slips of heredity [mutations] have been able, even with the cooperation of natural selection, even with the advantage of immense periods of time in which evolution works on life, to build the entire world, with its structural prodigality and refinements, its astounding adaptations.[32]

It is hard indeed to see how random mutation and natural selection alone could possibly have produced the astounding beauty and intricacy of, say, a peacock's feathers, even if it is conceded that the process only progressed in gradual stages, via cumulative selection. This point can be effectively demonstrated by looking at the mechanism by which colors manifest themselves in creatures like the peacock.

The color and physical dimensions of each of the peacock's feathers is determined by a complex series of biochemical steps that is coded for by an even more complex nucleotide arrangement in the peacock's genes. Hence, there is a precise informational correlate to this external color pattern that is encoded within the peacock's chromosomes.

This being the case, are we to suppose that the original genetic sequence for determining the color pattern of peacock feathers just happened to evolve by chance alone? Natural selection clearly needs something to select *from*, and since the traditional neo-Darwinian theory does not allow for any type of directionality in the evolutionary process, the original color pattern in the peacock's feathers must have therefore been randomly produced. But how could the original *capacity* for encoding color have gotten started to begin with? There had to have been a point before which any survival value at all would have existed in any such pigment pattern, so it doesn't seem possible that the very first color patterns could have originally been formed by survival value alone.

It seems, then, that the orthodox neo-Darwinian answer to this dilemma only begs the true question which is at issue here. Natural selection might favor the continued existence of certain patterns of color in peacock feathers, but where did the original colored patterns themselves come from? Saying that they spontaneously arose by chance mutation alone is tantamount to an indirect admission of ignorance, because there doesn't seem to be any way that: a) chance mutations alone could have possibly created the capacity for producing colored feathers, or b) that chance mutations could have ever produced such remarkably coordinated patterns of color, even over a long series of cumulatively-selected generations.

In other words, the non-theistic evolutionist is almost forced into concluding that the original capacity for encoding and producing complex color patterns had to have arisen by pure chance, with no prior design and without any immediate survival value as an original causative force (which by definition would not have yet existed). But it is very difficult to see how such an intrinsically complex series of steps could have begun "out of nowhere." Such an assertion amounts to little more than a belief in magic (where effects do not have sufficient precipitating causes), and as such, constitutes an actual *defiance* of everything science is supposed to stand for. To then take this unsubstantiated belief in scientific magic and then boldly proclaim that it is the *only* way it could possibly have happened, is to opt out of the scientific realm altogether, into the arena of irrational, self-serving prejudice, which is something scientists are supposed to be opposed to.

Natural selection, of course, can only encourage the development of adaptations that aid in the overall process of survival. Yet, the existence of the peacock's bulky and colorful fan is clearly a severe liability as far as the avoidance of predators is concerned, since it not only calls undue attention to itself, it also makes it more difficult for peacocks to escape from predators once they have been noticed. This being so, one would think that the peacock's outrageous plumage would never have evolved in the first place.

The orthodox evolutionist gets around this apparent impasse by claiming that the peacock's feathers evolved because they sexually stimulate female peahens. Therefore, the more colorful a peacock's feathers are, the more likely he is to create progeny that will carry the trait for his own bright plumage. This is known as sexual selection, but it simply isn't capable of explaining the evolution of the peacock's bright feathers, as Philip Johnson has pointed out:

> Why would natural selection, which supposedly formed all birds from lowly predecessors, produce a species whose females lust for males with life-threatening decorations? The peahen ought to have developed a preference for males with sharp talons and mighty wings. Perhaps the taste for fans is associated genetically with some absolutely vital trait like strong egg shells, but then why and how did natural selection encourage such an absurd genetic linkage?[33]

There seems to be no plausible way for the orthodox evolutionist to avoid this utterly damaging criticism of his theory. Interestingly enough, Darwin himself was aware of the immense difficulty of trying to account for the origin of variations by natural selection alone, so he never attempted to account for them. He simply took them as a given and concluded that natural selection must have acted upon them to create new species.[34] However, it is precisely here in the origin of the variations themselves that the entire debate between theistic and non-theistic evolutionism comes to a head. Hence, one cannot avoid the question of the origin of variations and then proclaim that one has explained the origin of species without need of an external Creator. Yet, this is precisely what many modern evolutionists continue to do.

Actually, Darwin did believe in a deistic Creator, as we have seen. This deistic God was thought by Darwin to have originally created the atoms and molecules themselves and then, having done so, Darwin believed that such a Creator would have left them alone to develop solely according to natural law. On this score, Darwin was far more progressive than his modern, non-theistic counterparts, since it is precisely here with the origin of self-organizing matter that God "fits into" the whole evolutionary scheme. Nevertheless, most neo-Darwinian evolutionists have lost sight of this Primordial Deistic Force, and have mistakenly concluded that a God who creates naturalistically is no God at all.

5.7 Natural Selection Unable to Account for Explosive Radiations

As we have seen, slow change is the *sine qua non* of neo-Darwinian evolutionary theory. Over eons of time, small genetic variations are thought to have been routinely selected for by constantly fluctuating environmental conditions, so that eventually, major morphological (structural) changes naturally resulted. These major changes are in turn thought to have eventually accumulated to the point that entirely new species were produced.

Within this orthodox neo-Darwinian scenario, rapid change is next to impossible to explain solely by means of chance mutation and natural selection, because such a haphazard process by definition can only operate gradually. Yet, as far as the fossil evidence is concerned, relatively rapid change has been the *rule* rather than the exception.[35] This fact alone has devastating consequences for the non-theistic evolutionist, because it is very much at odds with the underlying presupposition of his theory. This fundamental inconsistency becomes apparent when he attempts to explain rapid change in terms of the neo-Darwinian paradigm, because the orthodox explanation for rapid change—a high mutation rate, short generation span, and a large population—is actually more characteristic of *slow* change than rapid change! Humans, for instance, have evolved more than any other creature, yet the intrinsic qualities that have surrounded their evolution—a relatively low mutation rate, long generation span, and small population—are more characteristic of *slow* change than rapid change. Bacteria, on the other hand, have probably evolved less than any other known creature, yet they possess precisely the opposite set of developmental qualities: a high mutation rate, short generation span, and huge population!

Of course, one small segment of a population can rise to higher levels of complexity without the entire population having to do so. Indeed, this is precisely what the non-theistic evolutionist believes has actually happened in the world. A relatively small segment of microorganisms are thought to have followed a line of development that eventually led to human beings, while the vast majority are thought to have remained more or less the same over the eons. However, this possibility does not necessarily count against the possibility that the evolutionary process has been Divinely directed, because if God did somehow guide the process of evolution from the first living cell, then a certain segment of microorganisms had to have pursued a much more ambitious line of development. Thus, the ultimate question at issue here isn't whether or not certain primordial creatures left their fellow creatures behind to develop into more advanced creatures, but *why* they were able to do so. The non-theistic evolutionist believes that this process occurred entirely by chance, while the Deistic Evolutionist believes that it happened in response to some sort of Divinely-Inspired "loading" of the evolutionary "dice."

5.8 Natural Selection Cannot Account for the Rise of Man

Perhaps the greatest obstacle for the theory of evolution by random mutation and natural selection concerns the rise of man himself. According to the principle of natural selection, a given creature can only evolve within the relatively narrow limits defined by the survival demands of its environment (assuming, of course, the prior capacity of the organism to produce coherent variations for natural selection to act upon). Thus, a given characteristic can only be selected for if it contributes to the organism's immediate "struggle for survival" in a meaningful way. Qualities that are far out of proportion to any type of environmental need are therefore next to impossible to explain via this orthodox neo-Darwinian paradigm.

Alfred Russel Wallace, the man who is credited for co-discovering the theory of evolution with Darwin, was well aware of this difficulty. He wrote:

A brain one-half larger than that of the gorilla would . . . fully have sufficed for the limited mental development of the savage; and we must therefore admit that the large brain he actually possesses could never have been solely developed by any of those laws of evolution, whose essence is, that they lead to a degree of organization exactly proportionate to the wants of each species, never beyond those wants . . . Natural selection could only have endowed savage man with a brain a few degrees superior to that of an ape, whereas he actually possesses one very little inferior to that of a philosopher.[36]

Such a penetrating observation is utterly damaging to the non-theistic theory of evolution by natural selection, as Darwin fully realized when, after having read the above passage, he wrote to Wallace, "I hope you have not murdered too completely your own and my child."[37]

The miraculous[38] nature of human consciousness does indeed seem impossible to account for by means of natural selection and random mutation alone. As John Polkinghorne explains, "it seems incredible that, say, Einstein's ability to conceive of the General Theory of Relativity was just a spin-off from the struggle for survival. What survival value does such an ability possess?"[39]

While it may be possible to "explain" the origin of most adaptations in the animal world in terms of some sort of connection to the ongoing quest for survival,[40] it is *not* possible to do the same for the rise of human consciousness, since it far exceeds any of the survival demands that could possibly be found in the environment.

Human consciousness is also sufficiently different from the other adaptations found in nature to warrant an entirely separate causal explanation than that which is routinely applied to the non-human world. For instance, both man's unique sense of self and his remarkable capacity for rational forethought are qualitatively different from all the other adaptations that can be found in the animal kingdom. And since even these non-human qualities defy explanation by traditional means, how much more do the miraculous qualities of human consciousness warrant the supposition of an entirely different set of causative principles?

Indeed, there is such a huge ontological gap between human consciousness and the remainder of the adaptations found in the animal world that it is hard to see how human consciousness could have blindly evolved from animal consciousness through a completely natural (i.e., non-Divinely originated) process. We don't even know what the human self actually *is*, to even *consider* positing its origin through such a completely natural means. As a consequence, science today knows remarkably little about the evolutionary origins of the self, and of the capacity to represent oneself to oneself as a subjective self.[41]

While the more psychological aspects of human consciousness and intelligence are profoundly difficult to explain from within the neo-Darwinian paradigm, the purely physical aspects are *equally* problematic. As C.O. Lovejoy[42] has pointed out, not only does intelligence possess no *a priori* advantage, the physical concomitants of the evolution of intelligence in man actually constituted a dual *reproductive liability*, and *not* a survival advantage to be favored by natural selection. In the prenatal sphere, the evolution of intelligence was a reproductive liability because highly evolved nervous systems require an unusually long gestation period, and the longer the gestation period, the more danger that is naturally incurred by both the mother and fetus alike. In the postnatal sphere, the evolution of intelligence was a reproductive liability because intelligent creatures intrinsically require a longer period of time to raise and educate their young, and the longer it takes to produce viable adults, the more susceptible a population is to harmful influences, both from within the population and without. Taken together, these two factors constitute an unequivocal *reproductive hazard*. It is for this reason that Lovejoy concludes that intelligence will only be rarely selected for in the global community, even amongst the primates.[43]

In fact, Lovejoy believes that the implications surrounding the rise of human intelligence are so unusual and compelling that humans must be the product of "a completely unique evolutionary pathway." But even here, he can't seem to find a sufficient reason to explain the initial rise of human intelligence, since:

> It is evident that the evolution of cognition is neither the result of an evolutionary trend nor an event of even the lowest calcuable probability, but rather the result of a series of highly specific evolutionary events whose ultimate cause is traceable to selection for unrelated factors such as locomotion and diet.[44]

But if the rise of human intelligence isn't the result of an evolutionary trend, and isn't an event of the "lowest calcuable probability," how on earth could it have been produced by selection for such mundane factors as diet and locomotion? It certainly doesn't require a human amount of intelligence to eat well; the primates have been eating well since time immemorial,[45] and their intelligence doesn't even remotely approach ours. Similarly, it definitely doesn't require a human amount of intelligence to be able to get around effectively in the jungle.

In *The Panda's Thumb*, Stephen Jay Gould argues that the traditional neo-Darwinian explanation for the evolution of intelligence doesn't necessarily require the "hyper-selectionism" spoken of by Wallace, wherein the specific trait in question is directly selected for. Rather, it need only involve an indirect process of selection via the prior selection for a different characteristic, such as an increased capacity for food gathering. The end result of this indirect form of selection is alleged to be the incidental development of other, somewhat related traits that can eventually come to possess a positive survival value (purely by chance, of course). As Gould explains:

> Natural selection may build an organ "for" a specific function or group of functions. But this "purpose" need not fully specify the capacity of that organ. Objects designed for definite purposes can, as a result of their structural complexity, perform many other tasks as well. A factory may install a computer only to issue the monthly pay checks, but such a machine can also analyze the election returns or whip anyone's ass (or at least perpetually tie them) in tic-tack-toe. Our large brains may have originated "for" some set of necessary skills in gathering food, socializing, or whatever; but these skills do not exhaust the limits of what such a complex machine can do. Fortunately for us, those limits include, among other things, an ability to write, from shopping lists for all of us to a grand opera for a few.[46]

While at first glance Gould's "explanation" for the rise of intelligence may seem plausible, it fails to hold up on deeper analysis. For one thing, in claiming that intelligence could have arisen as a mere side effect to the selection of other traits, Gould begs the real question at issue here, which is this: how could the capacity or potential for intelligence have ever arisen in the first place, especially in a purely fortuitous universe? It is evident that this potentiality has existed for as long as there have been atoms and molecules (since these are the building blocks from which we are made), but where did this potential *itself* originally come from? Gould would have us believe that it had no discernible cause, apart from blind chance, and that its real-world actualization was the unforeseen and unintended byproduct of mindless selection for other traits. Such an "explanation," however, doesn't even attempt to account for the origin of this potentiality. It is simply treated as a mere given, even though this cleverly sidesteps the true question at issue here. It is clear that any genuine explanation must attempt to account for the *origin* of this potential for intelligence, and in so doing it must take into account the fundamental properties of the atoms and molecules themselves, because they are the building blocks from which everything in our world, including human intelligence, is derived.

Of course, one can argue, as Gould has done, that an inner potential for intelligence can somehow exist without intelligence being "intended" from the start. But is this a plausible scenario? Does it make sense to suppose that the potential for intelligence could have existed from the very beginning in the total absence of any larger Design or Purpose? Put another way, could the potential for intelligence have been merely the result of a random accident? It is hard to see how.

Even if we assume the prior, unexplained existence of self-organizing atoms and molecules, it is still very difficult to see how mindless selection for one trait could end up accidentally producing a second trait that it so much better than itself, i.e., how could selection for one trait initiate the formation of a completely different trait that ends up being so much more complex and sophisticated than itself? To suppose that the ability to fly to the moon was an accidental byproduct of the evolutionary acquisition of increasingly sophisticated food-gathering skills is tantamount to saying that the accidental formation of a crop-reaping mechanism (which is unlikely enough) could also by sheer chance have the marvelous capacity for computing complex spreadsheets.

Although such a preposterous notion is not logically impossible, it is nevertheless unlikely to the highest degree. Indeed, by drawing an analogy to pre-existing machines, Gould inadvertently admits that the biological mechanism that accidentally produced intelligence was *itself* a machine. Granted that most intelligently designed machines display a capacity for accomplishing other tasks for which they weren't directly designed, this nevertheless assumes the prior existence of intelligently designed machines!

Gould can't have it both ways: he can't argue that the evolution of intelligence was an accidental and unintended byproduct of another undesigned process, and then in the same breath compare it to the natural attributes of an intelligently designed, human-built machine. The very basis for the analogy undermines Gould's entire argument, since intelligently designed machines and undesigned natural processes cannot be considered to be analogous. In drawing the analogy nonetheless, Gould seems to be implicitly acknowledging the intelligently designed nature of natural evolutionary processes.

For Gould's argument to succeed, he must provide a plausible explanation for the underlying process that could have evolved intelligence as an unintended side effect, i.e., he must show how the living "machine" could have evolved its forward-moving characteristics in the absence of any form of Intelligent Design. Since this has not yet been accomplished in any sort of exhaustive fashion, we are compelled to reject Gould's argument as circular, and therefore not truly explanatory of anything.

A common-sense examination of the facts confirms our suspicion that human intelligence could never have been the unintended result of an immensely unlikely series of accidental events. For one thing, the very basis of the mind for drawing such grand conclusions is intrinsically undermined by its supposed accidental origin, as Darwin fully realized (see the epigraph to this chapter). Secondly, the very notion that human intelligence could have accidentally evolved in response to selection for other, more mundane factors, seems exceedingly unlikely (if not downright impossible) under *any* set of circumstances.

Gould would have us believe that Einstein's capacity for conceiving of the theory of relativity was, ultimately speaking, merely the accidental by-product of the evolution of other important traits, such as the capacity to find food or to move about more efficiently. But, as Polkinghorne has pointed out, is it credible to assume that the miracle of human intelligence could have been merely the accidental byproduct of these types of survival-enhancing skills alone? One might expect faster locomotion, or even an ingenious capacity to elude enemies, to result as an unintended side effect to the development of more efficient food-gathering skills, but certainly *not* the ability to write musical sonatas or 1000-page novels. We are only justified in positing potential explanatory scenarios that are *sufficient to the task*, and not ones that are so far-fetched as to be almost entirely beyond rational consideration. It simply does not seem to be possible that the most complicated mechanism in the entire known universe (the human brain) could have accidentally been formed via selection for other, much more mundane factors.

The point is simply that no one has been able to offer an adequate explanation for the evolution of human intelligence. In fact, most evolutionists consider intelligence to be such a rare commodity that they have quietly come to a remarkable consensus amongst themselves: namely, that the evolution of intelligent life is so intrinsically improbable that it is unlikely to be found anywhere else in the entire galaxy.[47] *The catch here, though, is that if the evolution of intelligence is so inherently unlikely that it probably doesn't exist anywhere else in the galaxy, then by all accounts it shouldn't have evolved here either.* The fact that it did, in spite of an almost infinite number of reasons why it *shouldn't* have, is exceedingly powerful evidence that something else must have been going on "behind the scenes" during the evolution of human intelligence. It is also powerful evidence in favor of a weak anthropocentric[48] view of cosmic reality, for if man is so special that he probably couldn't have evolved anywhere else in the galaxy, then he just might be special enough to be important in the overall scheme of things.

In *The Ethical Animal*, Professor C.H. Waddington, one of the most important biologists of the twentieth century, came to the similar conclusion that it is impossible to account for the miracle of human consciousness solely by means of physical processes alone:

> As soon as one places the problem of free will in juxta-position with that of consciousness, it becomes apparent that it cannot be solved . . . by manipulation of our existing physico-chemical concepts . . . We need ideas which depart more radically from those of the physical sciences.[49]

In *Darwin and the Spirit of Man*, Professor Alister Hardy of Oxford University agrees that it is impossible to account for the miracle of human creativity from within the realm of physico-chemical processses alone:

> No one could have greater admiration than I have for the marvelous work and discoveries of the contemporary molecular biologists, but to suppose that this is the whole explanation of life is nonsense. We cannot have it both ways. We must . . . regard man as the product of a long evolutionary process; yet equally no one in his senses can really believe that the great works of art, in literature, painting or music, or the love of natural beauty, are the result of physico-chemical processes as we know them today.[50]

Nobel laureate Sir John Eccles is yet another world famous scientist who is fully aware of the miraculous nature of human consciousness. In *The Wonder of Being Human*, Eccles argues that the remarkable nature of human consciousness is itself *ipso facto* proof against radical materialism and for a spiritual component to human evolution:

> In the context of Natural Theology, I believe that there is a Divine Providence operating over and above the materialist happenings of biological evolution . . . we must not dogmatically assert that biological evolution in its present form is the ultimate truth. Rather, we should believe that it is the main story and that in some mysterious way there is guidance in the evolutionary chain of contingency.[51]

But it isn't just the existence of self-consciousness that is so remarkable; it is also the unique selfhood of each individual person that defies a purely materialistic explanation. As Eccles points out, our entire social and legal system is based on the independent selfhood of all people, yet when we try to explain the origin of each individual's self-perceived uniqueness in terms of physiological machinery alone, we come up against a dead end. Genes cannot in and of themselves be the ultimate source of this self-perceived uniqueness, because identical twins have the same genetic complements, yet they are still two distinctly different personalities.[52] The individual's unique life history also cannot be the sole source of this self-perceived uniqueness either, because any number of extreme changes to that history could never have undone the individual's unique sense of self. Indeed, no amount of change could destroy one self and create another in the same person; he or she would simply be the same person in totally different circumstances.[53] In view of these considerations, Eccles concludes that:

Since materialist solutions fail to account for our experienced uniqueness, we are constrained to attribute the uniqueness of the psyche or soul to a supernatural spiritual creation. To give the explanation in theological terms: Each soul is a Divine creation, which is "attached" to the growing fetus at some time between conception and birth. It is the certainty of the inner core of unique individuality that necessitates the "Divine creation." We submit that no other explanation is tenable; neither the genetic uniqueness with its fanatastically impossible lottery nor the environmental differentiations, which do not determine one's uniquness but merely modify it.[54]

Richard Leakey, the famous paleoanthropologist, agrees:

Humans are more than just intelligent. Our sense of justice, our need for aesthetic pleasure, our imaginative flights, and our penetrating self-awareness, all combine to create an indefinable spirit which I believe is the 'soul.'[55]

5.9 Hyper-Selectionism and the Human Voice

The notion of hyper-selectionism spoken of in the previous section has been applied to other organs besides the brain. Wallace, for instance, assumed the validity of hyper-selectionism when he tried to explain the existence of highly-evolved vocal cords in savages, who make no use of them:

The habits of savages give no indication of how this faculty could have been developed by natural selection, because it is never required or used by them. The singing of savages is a more or less monotonous howling, and the females seldom sing at all. Savages certainly never choose their wives for fine voices, but for rude health, and strength, and physical beauty. Sexual selection could not therefore have developed this wonderful power, which only comes into play among civilized people. It seems as if the organ had been prepared in anticipation of the future progress in man, since it contains the latest capacities which are useless to him in his earlier condition.[56]

Even Gould is prepared to admit that "if our higher capacities arose before we used or needed them, then they cannot be the product of natural selection. And, if they originated in anticipation of a future need, then they must be the direct creation of a higher intelligence."[57]

Wallace himself was so persuaded by the evidence surrounding the evolution of intelligence and the human voice that he based his entire world view on it:

> The inference I would draw from this class of phenomena is, that a superior intelligence has guided the development of man in a definite direction, and for a special purpose.[58]

We mustn't forget that Wallace is also credited with discovering the theory of natural selection independently of Darwin. A gifted naturalist in his own right, Wallace saw no conflict whatsoever between the evidence of evolution and the creative activity of an Intelligent Designer. This is a strong indication in and of itself that there is no intrinsic enmity between evolution and the concept of Intelligent Design.

One further point deserves to be mentioned. If Gould's criticism of hyperselectionism were valid, one would expect to find these accidental but useful functions only rarely in the human organism. And to the extent that one did find them, one would expect to find *some* evidence of their incidental origin, i.e., one would never expect them to be so utterly successful in their incidental production of useful functions. Yet, precisely the opposite appears to be the case. Numerous examples of these "incidental" functions exist throughout the body, and insofar as they are integrated with the body's many other systems on a deep, cooperative level, they don't appear to be accidentally-derived at all. To the contrary, they are almost perfectly attuned to the highly-evolved functions we demand of them. Had the native intelligence of the brain, for instance, been merely an accidental byproduct of selection for another function, we might expect *some* incidental degree of intelligence, but not the ability to write sonatas or to design interplanetary space vehicles. Similarly, had the human capacity for advanced levels of singing been merely an accidental byproduct of selection for some other survival-enhancing function, we might expect some minimal amount of singing ability, but not the ability to sing opera.

My point is simply this. Functions that are accidentally derived tend to retain some residual evidence of their incidental origin. Yet, no part of the human body can be shown to display any significant evidence of this incidental character, least of all the brain or vocal cords. Furthermore, it is hard to see how natural selection could have refined these incidental characters out of the present population completely.

Given the available evidence, the most reasonable conclusion is precisely the one reached by Wallace himself; namely, that the existence of such advanced organs as the human brain and vocal cords, which came into existence far before their intrinsic capacities were ever used or needed, is more consistent with the creative activity of a Grand Designer than it is with blind chance.

5.9.1 Mathematics and the Conceptual Link Between Man and the Cosmos

Further support for the Divine origin of human consciousness can be found in the fact that our mathematical systems happen to explain, to a large degree of accuracy, how the entire physical universe seems to operate. This is a supreme mystery that isn't noticed nearly as much today as it used to be in times past, as most modern-day scientists seem to take it for granted that our mathematics should be able to describe the nature of the cosmos. But why should there be any connection at all between mathematics and physical reality? Indeed, why should the inner workings of the human mind correspond to the outer workings of the physical universe in *any* coherent way?

If we are only the result of a titanic universal accident, then it follows that our thinking processes should also be quite accidental. But if this is true, then we should never expect to find our accidental mode of thinking correlating so well with the underlying structure of the universe. It is unlikely to the highest degree that we should have accidentally evolved a mode of reasoning that just happens to correspond to the structural language used by the physical cosmos itself.

Of course, one might contend that we have evolved the same mathematical "language" that the physical universe uses because we are are made of the same "stuff" that the universe itself is made of. On this view, math is a kind of holographic image that we humans "emit" because we are integral parts of the larger cosmos.[59]

Such an "answer," however, is inadequate because it explains nothing. It doesn't tell us *how* we are able to think in this cosmic language, or *where* this mysterious ability ultimately came from. It just tells us what we already know, which is that we are able to speak the language of mathematics because we are part of the same physical universe that we are somehow able to describe.

A far better explanation for this mathematical ability is that we have been blessed with the same sort of reasoning ability that the Creator Himself originally used to create the universe. Such a view fits in nicely with the Biblical assertion that we were created in the spiritual image of God, which orthodox theological doctrine has long maintained. On this view, it is no coincidence that our mathematics are able to correspond so well to the underlying physical structure of the universe, because we were deliberately given this capacity to connect to the heart of the cosmos by the great Creator Himself.

5.9.2   The Role of Beauty in the Grand Design

One of humanity's most impressive defining characteristics is its capacity for aesthetic appreciation. Not coincidentally, our world, along with the larger cosmos of which it is part, is literally overflowing with beauty. Whether we are gazing at the Milky Way on a clear night or at the awesome majesty of the Grand Canyon, we can see and appreciate the tremendous beauty that is an inherent part of the creation.

Interestingly enough, this concept of beauty even extends to the underlying structure of physical reality. As it turns out, reality itself seems to be constructed out of symmetrical principles that scientists can only describe as "beautiful." Many researchers in the field of theoretical physics are keenly aware of this profound beauty at the heart of physical reality; indeed, it is precisely this sense of the overwhelming beauty in nature that has transformed many a physicist into a kind of modern-day mystic.

To the physicist, beauty is comprised largely of symmetry and of symmetrical relationships. Although science originally began as a way to better understand this symmetrical beauty, it began to move away from this type of view of the cosmos in the pre-relativistic era of the nineteenth century. Today, however, with the advent of modern superstring theory, which itself is based on a phenomenon known as "supersymmetry," science has returned to an appreciation of the underlying beauty of symmetrical relationships.

Briefly, superstring theory is an attempt to unify the four fundamental forces of nature into a single building block known as a "superstring." A superstring is an imperceptibly small entity (100 billion billion times smaller than a proton) that is capable of vibrating in different "frequencies." According to superstring theorists, the various particles and forces that we observe in the physical universe are simply different vibrational modes of these superstrings. Gravity, for instance, is seen as the lowest vibrational mode, while higher vibration frequencies are thought to produce the different forms of matter in the universe. In short, superstring theory sees the entire physical universe as a type of "music" that is being produced by these various vibrational modes![60]

Symmetrical relationships play a crucial role in superstring theory, just as they do in music theory. This is where the notion of beauty comes in: there appears to be something inherently beautiful about certain types of symmetrical relationships in nature. In fact, many physical theorists believe that nature's symmetrical patterns are so inherently beautiful that they feel compelled to let this aesthetic principle guide their mathematical theorizing. In a theistic view of the cosmos, of course, this relationship between truth and beauty isn't very surprising, since it is easy to see how God could have created the present universe as a kind of supreme "art project," in which beauty and symmetry would have been the chief underlying features.[61] It is only in an atheistic universe that this correlation between beauty and mathematical truth seems out of place.

Certainly the concept of natural selection doesn't seem capable of explaining this intriguing correlation. It is very difficult indeed to see how any such correlation between truth and beauty could have ever come into being through the mere struggle for survival. While it is possible that we would find any set of circumstances from which we evolved "beautiful" simply because we naturally descended from them, a much better explanation, and one that seems far more consistent with our universe's underlying character, is that beauty is the deliberate creation of a Higher Intelligence who specifically designed it into the creation.

5.10 Natural Selection as a Tautology

Perhaps the most devastating criticism of all that has been levied against the theory of natural selection is philosophical in nature. It basically says that the concept of the "survival of the fittest" is meaningless because it amounts to little more than a barren tautology: since the "fittest" members of any population are generally defined as those which actually survive, the concept of the "survival of the fittest" actually amounts to little more than the survival of those who do in fact survive.[62] C.H. Waddington agrees:

> To speak of an animal as "fittest" does not necessarily imply that it is strongest or most healthy, or would win a beauty competition. Essentially it denotes nothing more than leaving the most offspring. The general principle of natural selection, in fact, merely amounts to the statement that the individuals which leave the most offspring are those which leave the most offspring. It is a tautology.[63]

It is a well-known fact, however, that tautologous statements possess very little explanatory utility in the real world. Philip Johnson humorously illustrates this point in the following quote:

> When I want to know how a fish became a man, I am not enlightened by being told that the organisms that leave the most offspring are the ones that leave the most offspring.[64]

The tautologous nature of traditional selectionist thinking is greatly compounded by the fallacious reasoning that routinely goes along with it. While it may be true that the fittest members of any population will preferentially survive to pass their genes on to their offspring, this tautologous fact does nothing to explain *why* these creatures are fit enough to survive in the first place. Arguing that they are fit enough to survive because they have in fact survived is clearly of *no* explanatory value, because it begs the true question at issue here, which is this: why are the beneficiaries of natural selection fit enough to survive in the first place?

Gould has attempted to break out of this deadlock by arguing that the best definition of biological "fitness" is not in terms of mere survival *per se*, but rather in terms of "good design."[65] On Gould's view, the beneficiaries of natural selection are fit enough to survive because they are well-designed. But while this is certainly true, it still begs the ultimate question at issue here, which deals with the problem of where good biological designs *themselves* originally came from. They couldn't have come from an Intelligent Designer because Gould doesn't believe in one. They could only have come from the undesigned process of evolution itself, and from the ingenious creative powers of natural selection, which is believed to be capable of creating good designs entirely by accident. But of course this is just another way of saying that modern-day creatures are designed well enough to survive because their ancestors before them were also designed well enough to survive.

Now, such an "explanation" is clearly inadequate, because no attempt is made to explain *why* the original ancestors themselves were designed well enough to survive in the first place. Ultimately, this ancestral line of fitness must be pushed all the way back to the inanimate precursors of the first living cell, but this is clearly not a sufficient explanation for the evolution of life either. *One cannot beg a question all the way back to the very beginning of our planet's history and then expect to credit chance processes alone for conferring good design onto the first life form.* Nevertheless, millions of people still talk about natural selection as if it were a demonstrable method of generating biological complexity, when in point of fact natural selection is unable to do anything of the kind. At the very most, it can only preserve certain optimally adapted forms; it cannot under any circumstances generate the optimally adapted forms themselves.

It is precisely here in this distinction between the generation and the preservation of complexity that the fallacy of traditional selectionist reasoning presents itself: evolutionists are fooled into thinking that, just because natural selection can *preserve* certain forms of complexity, it can also *generate* them as well. Clearly, though, such an assumption does not logically follow, because the generation and subsequent preservation of complexity represent two ontologically distinct categories of explanation that cannot under any circumstances be collapsed into one another.

This fallacious brand of reasoning is compounded by the fact that coherent variations *do* routinely present themselves in nature. This fact seems to obviate any need to explain their origin, because they are plainly evident to everyone. But just because natural selection is able to choose the fittest variants of a given population for continued survival isn't to say that the ultimate reason for the variations themselves must be natural selection as well. We mustn't be fooled into thinking that certain events are beyond need of explanation just because they are already known to occur. Indeed, this is exactly what the evolutionist is ultimately trying to show in the first place: why the variations *themselves* occur as they do.

In conclusion, it is safe to say that a theory that is based on tautologous and fallacious reasoning cannot possibly render an accurate account of the way life actually evolved. What it *can* do, however, is protect the neo-Darwinian theory from any possibility of falsification. Since a tautologous and fallacious interpretation of natural selection is so broad and all-encompassing that it can indiscriminately explain everything, it automatically puts the neo-Darwinian theory beyond theoretical reproach; that is, until one realizes that tautologies and fallacious reasoning cannot properly explain *anything*. Moreover, as philosopher of science Karl Popper has aptly pointed out, theories that cannot be falsified under any reasonable set of circumstances cannot properly claim to be scientific in the first place. This observation in itself discredits modern evolutionary theory as a valid scientific hypothesis.

5.11 A Failure to Evolve

One of the greatest problems facing modern evolutionary biology today is the failure of a great many species to evolve, even when they've had millions and sometimes even billions of years to do so. Take bacteria for example. Although they are by far the most successful living creatures in the history of the world in terms of age and sheer numbers, they have nevertheless failed to evolve to any significant degree over billions of years of time, and this in spite of the fact that bacterial populations are characterized by a high mutation rate, short generation span, and a ferocious rate of reproduction.[66] Based only on these considerations, one would have expected bacteria to have evolved more than any other type of creature. Yet, fossilized remains of ancient bacteria over three and half billion years old have been found, and they are virtually identical to "modern" forms.

Such a profound failure to evolve is found throughout the animal kingdom. Well-preserved bees from the early Tertiary period, for instance, have been discovered in amber deposits, yet they are essentially identical with "modern" bees. Similarly, the coelacanth, a fish that was supposed to have died out some 130 million years ago, was found to be alive and well off the coast of South Africa back in 1938, in essentially the same form as its fossilized ancestors.

As far as the orthodox evolutionist is concerned, one of the greatest evolutionary advances ever seen was the development of bony jaws in fishes, since it greatly expanded the evolutionary potential of fish-like creatures and presumably led to the human jaw. But then why, Taylor asks, "do we still find lampreys, which are jawless fishes, doing very well today? If possessing jaws was such a wonderful advantage, why did not the jawless fishes realize how backward they were and succumb?"[67]

Of course, it could be asserted that certain ancient lines of creatures did in fact evolve into more complex forms, leaving behind their unchanged relatives, but such a possibility is hard to accept in the absence of a larger tendency to evolve that goes beyond the activity of purely random forces. After all, what would have been the chief difference between those creatures that did in fact evolve into higher forms, and those that did not? As far as the Deistic Evolutionist is concerned, this difference could very well have been an inner tendency to evolve that could have conceivably been present in certain lines of creatures; this would have explained why some individuals evolved into higher forms and others did not. On this view, certain lines of creatures may have indeed evolved into higher forms of life, but only because they possessed an inner tendency to do so in the first place.

Apart from this inner tendency, one would be hard pressed to explain why some creatures evolved into higher forms, and others did not. If blind evolutionary forces alone were the sole cause of this change, one would think that they would have had a much bigger effect on the population as a whole. Thus, the fact that so many species have remained essentially the same over huge stretches of time indicates that some other factor besides natural selection probably played a causative role in the advancement of new species.

5.12 Punctuated Equilibria

A related problem concerns the profound stability, or stasis, that is regularly observed in the fossil record. Niles Eldredge, Curator of the American Museum of Natural History, has centered much of his research around this very issue. Working with trilobites, ancient fish-like creatures that swam in waters that once covered modern-day North America, Eldredge was surprised to discover that they exhibited very little change in form, even over huge spans of time.

At first, Eldredge was disappointed with his findings, as he had been trained to believe in the existence of continuous, small gradations of change in the fossil record. Instead, he found multiple instances of relatively rapid change, followed by huge spans of almost complete stability, not just in trilobites, but in virtually all other species as well.

These findings eventually led Eldredge and his colleague Stephen Jay Gould to propose the idea of *punctuated equilibria* to explain the existing data. Briefly, this doctrine asserts that most species tend to form relatively rapidly (at least in terms of evolutionary timescales), and that once they are formed, they tend to remain more or less the same over vast stretches of time. For Eldredge and Gould, then, the fossil record is one of profound stability punctuated by relatively brief periods of rapid change.

These "punctuations" in the fossil record can be interpreted in two ways: as genuine "saltations" (sudden evolutionary jumps) between species, or as traditional neo-Darwinian examples of slow change that only *appear* to be saltations because of the inherent spottiness of the fossil record *vis-à-vis* the process of speciation.

Richard Dawkins argues for the latter interpretation in his popular book *The Blind Watchmaker.* Dawkins alleges that "the reason the 'transition' from ancestral species to descendant species appears to be abrupt and jerky is simply that, when we look at a series of fossils from any one place, we are probably not looking at an *evolutionary* event at all: we are looking at a *migrational* event, the arrival of a new species from another geographical area."[68]

Dawkins clearly believes that the traditional neo-Darwinian paradigm of slow phyletic change is still valid. On his view, the fossil record only *appears* to be jerky and abrupt because, according to the most widely-accepted theory of speciation, speciating animals must first be geographically isolated from the ancestral species for a significant length of time before a genuine new species can emerge. This geographical isolation allegedly translates into the appearance of rapid change in the fossil record, because the underlying conditions for speciation seem to demand that no other similar creatures be in the same immediate vicinity. Accordingly, we would expect the fossils of these new species to appear "suddenly" (i.e. without local precedent) in the fossil record, thus giving the appearance of a genuine saltation.

According to Dawkins, though, the process of speciation would have been going on all along at a relatively slow pace, via the painstaking process of natural selection acting on random mutations. It is only the migration of the evolving species into its new niche that makes it appear like an actual saltation in the fossil record. What Dawkins is asking us to believe, then, is that the apparent jerkiness of the fossil record is only an *illusion*, fostered by the presumed speciation requirement of geographical isolation.

Now, if this were in fact the case, we would still expect to find fossil evidence of a gradual speciating process *elsewhere*, in the form of widely disseminated "missing links" between species. Yet, nothing of the kind has ever been found. Indeed, if Dawkins' orthodox interpretation were actually correct, we would expect to find a geographical gradient of gradual morphological change in the fossil record, beginning at where the species in question had initiated the process of change and ending where the speciation process itself had been completed. Even if the speciating process didn't end until the new species had migrated to the other side of the world, we would *still* expect to find fossilized evidence of its slow change sprinkled around the globe. Surely the fact that nothing of the kind has ever been found strongly disconfirms Dawkins' contention that slow change has been disguised as rapid change in the fossil record.

In *Ever Since Darwin*, Gould proposes yet another possible way to interpret the appearance of rapid change in the fossil record in the overall context of orthodox gradualism. Writing of the "sudden" appearance of fully formed creatures in the Cambrian Explosion some 600 million years ago, Gould argues that the appearance of rapid change in this part of the fossil record is illusory, since the biological building blocks for the "sudden" appearance of these creatures had allegedly been slowly developing over millions of years (even though there is little or no evidence of this development in the fossil record). Finally, when this gradual process of development was completed, hoardes of fully formed creatures "suddenly" appeared, after which point they proceeded to multiply feverishly in order to fill the existing wide-open niches. When these niches came to be filled, this manic process of adaptive radiation ceased, and the existing species settled down to a comparatively stable form of existence.

There are two major problems with this interpretation of the fossil evidence. To begin with, even if the immediate pre-Cambrian precursors to the first fully-formed Cambrian creatures were very simple, we would still expect to find *some* evidence of their existence in the fossil record. While the earliest forms of these precursors may not have had enough of a bony skeleton to allow them to be fossilized, the immediate precursors to the first Cambrian creatures *would* undoubtedly have had such a skeleton, since they would have structurally been very similar to the first Cambrian creatures, which possessed fully formed skeletons. Yet, no such fossilized intermediates have ever been found.

The second problem with Gould's gradualistic interpretation of the Cambrian explosion is that the "sudden" appearance of these Cambrian creatures was most definitely *not* an isolated event. To the contrary, virtually all of the fossil record is characterized by a similar jerkiness, yet is hard to see how Gould's explanation could possibly cover these later apparent saltations as well, especially since these more advanced creatures possessed bony skeletons that could be fossilized. Not coincidentally, no fossilized intermediates leading up to these later bursts of speciation have been found yet, either.

Even plants are known to have made their appearance suddenly in the fossil record, without any identifiable precedent. The angiosperms, for instance, suddenly burst on the scene in the Cretaceous Period, fully formed and with no known precursors.[69] Darwin himself was well aware of this "anomaly," as he once wrote in a letter to Hooker, "Nothing is more extraordinary in the Vegetable Kingdom, as it seems to me, than the *apparently* very sudden or abrupt development of the higher plants . . . The rapid development, as far as we can judge, of all the higher plants within recent geological times is an abominable mystery."[70] More extraordinary still is the fact that since Darwin's time, no pre-Cretaceous intermediates have ever been found linking the angiosperms with any other known types of plants. Cambridge University botanist E. Corner even goes so far as to conclude that:

. . . to the unprejudiced, the fossil record of plants is in favor of special creation. If, however, another explanation could be found for this hierarchy of classification, it would be the knell of the theory of evolution. Can you imagine how an orchid, a duckweed, and a palm have come from the same ancestry, and have we any evidence for this assumption? The evolutionist must be prepared with an answer, but I think that most would break down before an inquisition.[71]

There thus seems to be no escaping the apparent fact that relatively rapid change is a characteristic feature of the fossil record. The challenge, then, is not to try to accommodate this realization within the confines of neo-Darwinian dogma, which obviously cannot account for it, but to devise a *new* explanation altogether, one that is more consistent with the facts as they are currently known to exist.

5.12.1 The Cambrian Explosion and Atmospheric Oxygen Levels

According to Harvard University's Andrew Knoll, the Cambrian explosion was made possible by a cumulative increase in atmospheric oxygen levels, due primarily to the effects photosynthetic plants and organisms.[72]

It is a well-known fact that metabolism by oxygen-dependent cells and architecturally simple animals requires a minimum atmospheric oxygen content of around 1 percent. However, as UCLA's Bruce Runnegar has pointed out, macroscopic animals require a much larger atmospheric oxygen content, due to such complex physiological functions as collagen synthesis, aerobic metabolism, and full oxygenation of the creature's tissues.[73] Knoll further points out that the first macroscopic animals probably lacked a sophisticated oxygen delivery system (since there probably hadn't been enough time for one to evolve yet). This would have substantially increased the amount of atmospheric oxygen that would have been required by these Cambrian animals. Geological evidence indicates that a sufficient amount of atmospheric oxygen for macroscopic aerobic metabolism accumulated near the beginning of the Cambrian explosion, some 800 million years ago.[74] This relative increase in atmospheric oxygen levels is thought to have been the primary reason why macroscopic animals took so long to begin their evolutionary ascent.

It is also thought to be a primary reason why the Cambrian explosion occurred in the first place. Microscopic invertebrates by the billions are thought to have been "waiting in the wings," so to speak, for enough oxygen to accumulate in the atmosphere to support their evolution into more complex vertebrate forms.

Such a conclusion appears to be legitimate, because the Cambrian explosion could never have occurred at all without sufficient quantities of oxygen in the atmosphere. However, it would be a mistake to conclude that this one climatological variable alone provides a sufficient explanation for why the Cambrian explosion occurred the way it did. For while a certain minimum amount of atmospheric oxygen may have been a necessary precondition for the Cambrian explosion, it doesn't at all seem to be capable of explaining the entire event. Something more substantial had to have been at work to create the rich diversity of organisms that suddenly appeared "out of nowhere" around 600 million years ago. For the Deistic Evolutionist, this "something more" was the strategic direction of God Himself, which probably manifested itself through a genetically-contained evolutionary program when the time was right.

5.13 Natural Selection and Behavior

Another damaging problem for the orthodox theory of natural selection concerns the role of behavior change in animals. Traditional evolutionary dogma sees a given animal as being almost hopelessly dependent on a given environmental niche. According to this view, when the local environment changes, the animal had better hurry up and change as well or else it will die off. For the neo-Darwinian evolutionist, then, the race not only goes to the swiftest, it also goes to the most flexible as well, since only the most flexible creatures are thought to be able to survive the rigors of changing environments.

The problem with this view is that it ignores the crucial behavioral component behind adaptation. The fact is, when a particular environmental niche becomes too threatening, *animals often move on to another one.* Indeed, virtually all of the major evolutionary changes in the animal kingdom are thought to have been initiated by a change in behavior: a fish "decides" it wants to live on land, so it grows a lung in response to its attempts to live out of water; a pre-dolphin mammal "decides" it wants to go back to the sea, so this desire somehow causes it to become re-adapted back to the sea when it goes for a swim. While this appears to be a faulty bit of reasoning, the alternative is equally strange (as long as the evolutionary process is considered to be totally undirected): that the most "progressive" animals who find themselves adapting to radically different environments never really "wanted" to do so in the first place; they were instead forced into their new surroundings by randomly occurring structural changes in their bodies. On this view, the first fish that moved onto dry land only did so because it had somehow grown a set of lungs that made it easier for it to breathe on land than in the sea.

The prevailing opinion, however, is that a change in behavior must precede a change in niche, because if a given creature didn't explore different types of environments, it would never "know" that it had a structural "adaptation" that would be of more use to it in another environment. As Erst Mayr explains, "A shift into a new niche or adaptive zone requires, almost without exception, a change in behaviour . . . to be followed by a change in structure."[75] Thus, traditional evolutionary dogma recognizes the profound importance of behavior in effecting major morphological change.

At the same time, though, the phenomenon of behavioral change is almost totally ignored when it comes to the selective pressure exerted by the environment. The accepted view is that environmental pressure will cause all but the most fit animals to die off, thus allowing for a concentration of those characteristics that produced the original fitness. The problem with this mode of reasoning is that it fails to consider the important role of behavioral change in determining a particular animal's level of fitness. If an animal isn't turning out to be very fit in terms of a particularly demanding environment, it typically doesn't just keep struggling until it falls over and dies; it usually moves on to explore another area in which it will probably be more fit. To some degree, then, an animal is able to select the selective pressures that will subsequently act upon it.

We humans do the same thing. If we aren't well-adapted to a given niche within a particular city, we don't just roll over and die; we move on to other niches where we might be better "adapted" for survival. For the most part, animals do the very same thing, and this is what seems to count against the non-theistic theory of evolution by natural selection. For if an animal opts to move on to another niche in order to escape rising environmental pressures within its existing niche, it will be attempting to *preserve* its particular genetic structure. Over many generations such behavioral change in response to environmental pressure will tend to result in species fixity, not change. And indeed, this is precisely what we find to be true throughout the fossil record: most species have remained more or less the same throughout the vast epochs of evolutionary history.

On the other hand, if a struggling animal explores as many different niches as possible without success, then it *will* eventually die off. Moreover, if the environmental pressure is sufficiently intense, it is likely that a good proportion of the local population of that particular species will also die off, possibly leading to extinction. And indeed, this is precisely what is observed in the fossil record: either stasis or outright extinction.

It would seem, then, that the only way natural selection could possibly be seen as contributing to evolutionary change in any meaningful way is if certain animals in a given population were able to come up with the necessary structural and behavioral changes that would have allowed them to adapt to new areas of the environment. But where would these changes have come from? It is very hard to see how they could have ever been the result of random forces alone.

A further point also deserves mentioning. If the selective pressure in any given instance is sufficiently intense to have killed off all the "less fit" individuals in a given population, is it credible to believe that other, slightly different, individuals in the same population will nevertheless be different *enough* to allow them to survive the same selective pressure? If so, is it likely that they will be able to find similarly fit mates who *also* just happen to accidentally possess the same lifesaving variations?

More importantly, if the selective pressure of the environment is going to be capable of choosing certain variants for continued survival, it can only act within certain very narrow limits. If the pressure is too great, *all* the individual members of the population in question will be wiped out, regardless of the number of variations they possess. Similarly, if the pressure is too small, there won't be enough selective power to separate the more fit from the less fit.

In other words, if natural selection is going to function as a potent speciating force in the wild, a very fine balance must be struck between the presenting degree of environmental stress, on the one hand, and the adaptive capacity of a given population, on the other, which would enable nature's selective hand to kill off just enough of a population to have a significant effect on later generations. It is in this manner that the characters that originally conferred a significant degree of fitness to the survivors will be able to become concentrated in the progeny.

Such environmental fine-tuning appears to have been quite rare throughout global history. It seems as though the various local environments have either remained essentially the same over vast periods of time, in which case a sizable proportion of "less fit" individuals would have been able to survive, or else they have changed so dramatically that *no* individuals at all would have been fit enough to survive. This of course would have had the effect of bringing the species in question that much closer to extinction. Again, the fossil record corroborates this conclusion, as it reveals either stasis or outright extinction in the vast majority of cases. It is at this point that the temptation to invoke a type of Lamarckian inheritance of acquired characteristics becomes particularly strong. For it is apparent that limiting an organism's structural variations to exclusively random changes greatly reduces the number of beneficial variations that can possibly result, because they can never be tailor-made for the environment, at least not directly. The orthodox evolutionist, to the contrary, maintains that natural selection *indirectly* tailors these random variations to the specific demands of the environment. Nevertheless, it is clear that if a given variation can't be directly tailor-made for an environment, the odds for a successful adaptation become very small indeed, regardless of the action of natural selection, because natural selection requires coherent adaptations to select *from*. It would seem, then, that an evolving organism must find a way to obtain some type of feedback from the environment in order to have a reasonably good chance of effecting a successful adaptation. As Professor Rupert Riedl of Vienna University has put it:

... the idea that a creature should be put in an environment to which it has to adapt but be totally deprived of information about that environment, is 'preposterous and indeed unbelievable and catastrophic.' That the creature should achieve the correct response by chance mutation is 'as unlikely as the enhancement of a good poem by a printer's error.'[76]

One particularly attractive solution to this problem, as we have seen, would be to have the very first genome programmed in such a way that it could produce the necessary adaptations automatically in direct response to environmental feedback. Such an "orthogenetic" sequence would gradually produce morphological changes in the various species, in direct response to selective pressures, while natural selection would then act to "fine-tune" these internally-generated changes to the immediate needs of the local environment. This would solve the problem of coordinating a given set of adaptations to the specific needs of the environment, since the adaptations themselves would be an intrinsic part of the internally-generated process of change.

5.14 The Origin of Adaptations

According to the orthodox evolutionary view, all that is needed to "explain" the existence of a given organ or appendage is the attribution of a survival-enhancing function to it. If a fin, for instance, aids in the survival of a given species of fish in the wild, then this survival-enhancing function *itself* is deemed to be a sufficient explanation for the evolution of the fin.

Implicit in such an idea, of course, is the assumption that the fish is capable of generating fin-like forms over a sequence of many generations, and that only those forms that serve some sort of useful function will be selected for. The end result of this slow evolutionary process is alleged to be an exquisitely "designed" fin. For the non-theistic evolutionist, however, this "design" isn't a genuine pre-conceived design; it is only the formation of a useful pattern in response to the selective pressure of the environment.

Is it credible, though, to assume that the necessary structures and substructures for each adaptation in the animal kingdom were able to make an accidental appearance in just the right place, and at just the right time, for each evolving species? Even if we assume that a gradual process of cumulative selection produced each of these micro-adaptations one step at a time, we are still assuming that the proper structures for each original instance of selection could only have been formed by blind chance alone. If we take this statement to be true, and if we further assume that the environment is incapable of directly determining the structures of the adaptations themselves (as in Lamarckism), then we are more or less forced into concluding that each part of the evolving organism was originally capable of generating the entire range of possible structures, and that only those structures that originally served a useful survival function in each position were naturally selected for.

But this couldn't possibly be true. For even if we assume that a single location on a given evolving organism is accidentally capable of generating the right structure (hence providing positive selection value), it is nevertheless overwhelmingly unlikely that the various other locations on the organism will *also* accidentally follow suit by generating *their own* positive adaptive structures as well. Indeed, for every correct structure that is produced at a single location on the organism, it would seem that many more incorrect ones would accidentally form elsewhere. This follows from the very definition of true randomness. But if this is true, it is immensely unlikely that any struggling organism would be able to survive long enough to reproduce itself, due to the fact that the many maladaptive structures would vastly outweigh the relatively few correct ones in the overall survival game, thus leading to an early death, both for the organism as a whole, as well as for those few structures that *were* accidentally able to hit upon the right form. And since the organism itself probably wouldn't have survived long enough to reproduce itself, the few correct structures that did happen to appear would most likely not be passed on to subsequent generations.

It is thus the multitude of different adaptive structures that are necessary for the survival of any given species that makes it exceedingly unlikely that the various adaptations found in nature were originally the result of chance alone. If only one or two loci of random variation were needed to evolve each species, there might be an outside chance that this could happen (assuming, of course, a pre-existing organism that is capable of generating random change). But since even the simplest organisms possess innumerable loci of structural variation, it seems next to impossible that a sufficient number of correct variations would have been able to occur by chance to ensure the continued survival of even the "simplest" species. It would be like waiting for all the slot machines in a given casino to hit their respective jackpots *simultaneously*. While such a thing might be statistically possible, no one in their right mind would *ever* expect it to happen, not even in a trillion years.

The process of cumulative selection—wherein each beneficial structure is retained in each successive round of selection—is itself irrelevant to the basic question at issue here. For while cumulative selection may significantly decrease the amount of time it takes for a given complex form to be produced in an otherwise viable organism, *this assumes the prior existence of a viable organism*. But even the "simplest" viable organism is itself comprised of innumerable adaptive structures, *each of which has to exist in the proper form and in the right place if continued survival—and hence continued selection—is to take place*. In short, the process of cumulative selection requires a baseline series of adaptive structures in order to operate, but it is precisely this adaptive baseline that seems to be beyond the range of possibility if random change alone at each locus of variation continues to be affirmed.

It is for this reason that some degree of directionality for the rise of adaptations seems to be a theoretical must. Given this initial directionality, it becomes *much* easier to see how natural selection could have acted to refine the many adaptations found in the living world.

In conclusion, the non-theistic evolutionist's appeal to survival-enhancing function alone to explain the origin of each adaptation is, in and of itself, inadequate to explain why the various adaptations have the forms they do. For although each adaptive form may in fact enhance survival by enabling the organism to pass through nature's selective filter, this does not explain the origin of the adaptation itself. *One simply cannot use a structure's usefulness in a given environment to explain its ultimate origin, because this only begs the question of where this usefulness originally came from.* And since it appears to be incoherent to assume that chance variations alone could have ever formed the many exquisite adaptations found in nature, the only remaining explanation cites some form of inner directedness as the most sensible cause of these original adaptations.

Once the existence of a Larger Plan in evolution is affirmed, we can then indirectly attribute the design of any given adaptation to its survival-enhancing function in the environment, not because natural selection alone is capable of forming it, but because a Higher Power would have deliberately designed each adaptation to serve this survival-enhancing function from the outset.

5.15 Natural Selection and the Malthusian Principle of Competition for Limited Resources

It is a well-known fact that Darwin borrowed heavily from Thomas Malthus' *Essay on Population* in his initial conception of natural selection. Malthus believed that the growth of human society tends to outstrip the quantity of available resources; hence, calamities such as war, disease, or famine tend to intervene to reduce the overall population to levels that can be supported by the available food supply. Darwin simply took this idea and projected it onto his conception of the natural world.

On this Malthusian view, the various animal species compete for limited resources in the wild. However, since there usually isn't enough food for all, there is generally a state of ruthless competition for the food that happens to be available, with the result that only the fittest members of each species is able to eat enough to survive. Those individuals who are less fit tend to die off, the immediate consequence of which is that they are less likely to reproduce overall. It is in this manner that those characters that confer the greatest survival value tend to be concentrated in the progeny. This is the essence of natural selection.

It must continually be borne in mind, though, that even if we assume the validity of this Malthusian principle, the process of natural selection at best can only be used to explain the relative *prevalence* of certain characters in the population. It cannot be used to explain their ultimate origin, because the selection process clearly does not generate the variations themselves; it only tends to choose the fittest varieties for continued survival.

According to C. Dyke, however, this Malthusian principle of limited resources in the wild may not be accurate after all.[77] While some natural populations may in fact be at or near true Malthusian limits with respect to a given resource, the vast majority of populations throughout history don't appear to have been anywhere near such a Malthusian limit, for to assume so "would be to assume that the earth is a thermodynamic plenum, a zero-sum game with respect to all [biological and ecological] accounting systems. But the earth is a thermodynamically open system as a whole, as are all ecological subsystems. . . . It seems probable to me that when Malthusian closure does occur it occurs not as a result of population expansion, but more often as a result of environment contraction as a consequence of climatological and geophysical events."[78]

But if true Malthusian closure isn't a reliable feature of life in the wild, how can we possibly believe in a view of natural selection that is based precisely on the presupposition that most populations are at or near this Malthusian limit? As Dyke explains:

> Every selectionist explanation based on the competition for scarce resources depends on the demonstration that resources are indeed limitingly scarce. Oftentimes this sort of closure is attempted by assuming that populations will naturally expand to the point of Malthusian closure. But this is a bizarre assumption. For in turn it assumes that there are no constraints in any other relevant dimension or at any other relevant level that keep the population below Malthusian limits in the dimension being focused on.
>
> We can accept selectionist explanations based on competition for scare resources only when Malthusian closure can reasonably be demonstrated. It seldom is. What usually happens is the reverse. We are told that when plausible selectionist explanations can be provided, then we can reasonably assume that Malthusian closure was present. This of course is totally question-begging unless we have an a priori commitment to the exclusiveness and ubiquity of such explanations. The so-called "Just-So Stories" that have become famous in the literature of evolutionary biology, and especially sociobiology (Gould and Lewontin, 1979) are usually explanation guesses without the necessary closure conditions having been established. Somewhere along the line it was apparently decided that Mother Nature is a good frugal bourgeois Hausfrau.[79]

This is a momentous conclusion indeed, for if the Malthusian limit with respect to food supply has not been a dominant feature of the evolutionary process throughout natural history, we can hardly credit natural selection alone for the rise of so many exquisitely adapted creatures in the wild. If a sufficient food supply has been available to the majority of evolving species in times past, then many "less fit" individuals, who would otherwise have been selected against if the food supply had been scarce enough, would have been able to survive long enough to reproduce. This alone would have severely diluted the concentration of significant structural changes in each evolving population, since the accidental appearance of a variation that would confer a greater amount of fitness in a harsher environment would tend to be cancelled by less fit varieties in the gene pool, which were themselves able to gain entrance because of the comparative abundance of the food supply.

Significant evolutionary change (of the random variety) would thus be immensely unlikely on two separate counts: 1) it would be exceedingly unlikely that two separate instances of the same beneficial variant would be randomly produced in a given population (one male and the other female), and 2) it would be more unlikely still for these two individuals to accidentally choose one another as mating partners, especially given the huge number of potential partners in most populations.[80] But if this is true, the odds are vanishingly small that significant numbers of randomly produced variations would be able to be survive intact into subsequent generations, since each beneficial variant would tend to be diluted in the progeny by its less beneficial counterpart. And since these less fit counterparts would presumably abound in the population, due to a more than adequate food supply, significant changes in overall form would be very unlikely indeed, even over many generations. The end result would be relative stasis, not change. The fossil record corroborates this theoretical expectation, as it too records long periods of species fixity, punctuated by relatively short periods of rapid change.

5.16   The Relationship Between Explanatory Closure and Biological Complexity

In order to draw reliable conclusions from a given body of data, one must limit one's explanatory alternatives and seal out interaction effects. According to Dyke,[81] if a state of closure doesn't exist in one's set of explanatory alternatives, the observed result could be due to any number of other competing alternatives. Consequently, since a state of explanatory closure has most definitely *not* been established with regard to the evolutionary rise of life on earth, it is impossible to state for a virtual certainty that a given explanation is in fact the correct one for a given observation. What this means in practical terms is that *other* competing explanations besides the orthodox neo-Darwinian one could very well turn out to be most accurate in the long run.

Dyke's point in "Complexity and Closure" is thus well taken. The real world is stupefyingly complex in terms of its actual structural features and interactive dynamics. Yet, the traditional neo-Darwinian paradigm tends to overlook this profound complexity by stressing a relatively simple, one-dimensional understanding of the evolutionary process. It is this tendency to oversimplify the way nature works that has led to severe problems in the way evolution has traditionally been conceived. As Dyke points out:

> . . . a good part of the reason [these] difficulties have arisen is that the complexity of evolutionary (and ecological) systems has not always been confronted with sufficient respect. In attempting to achieve explanatory closure in terms of simple, one-dimensional mechanical systems, orthodox neo-Darwinians have cut off access to a full understanding of the phenomena they study.[82]

This is a very important point. Any attempt to oversimplify an extremely complex natural process is bound to produce severe conceptual errors as a result. It would thus appear to be a truism that any attempt to achieve an accurate understanding of natural complexity requires, first and foremost, a full appreciation of the degree of complexity that is actually being studied. Given the traditional neo-Darwinian view of "a largely indifferent universe within which inherited chance variations occur among organisms that compete with one another for scarce resources,"[83] it is easy to see why there has been a long-standing tendency to oversimplify: if the universe really is a meaningless place where life has accidentally arisen in spite of the odds, it is almost inconceivable to see how such prodigious levels of complexity could have possibly resulted by themselves. How can a mindless process possibly produce an end product that is so complex that it continues to baffle even the most sophisticated scientific minds? It is hard to see how this could ever be the case. As a consequence, the tendency in the nontheistic evolutionary community has been to deny that such phenomenal levels of complexity exist at all. It is from this reality-denying starting point that the oversimplified neo-Darwinian view of evolution is largely based. In point of fact, however, biological and ecological reality almost infinitely outstrips our capacity to fully understand it. Accordingly, any attempt to achieve an even partially accurate view of evolution *must* use this affirmation of natural complexity as a starting point; otherwise, it is doomed to failure.

It is precisely here that the Deistic Evolutionist's perspective holds the most promise. For by affirming the overwhelming complexity of the natural world from the outset, it is in a far better position to grasp the larger meaning behind the evolutionary process. Indeed, the Deistic Evolutionist holds that living systems are so utterly complex that the only sensible way to explain them is in terms of an infinitely intelligent Designer.

On the other hand, many traditional neo-Darwinians will be quick to argue that the process of cumulative selection alone *is* able to produce these prodigious levels of complexity, by starting at levels that are simple enough to spontaneously appear by themselves, and then by subsequently building upon previous successes one step at a time, with each subsequent step preserving the advances in complexity that came before it. While this "explanation" for the rise of complexity may in fact describe the proximate physical mechanism that has governed the rise of complexity in the biosphere, it hardly amounts to a self-sufficient larger explanation, for the simple reason that it fails to explain where those clever little atoms and molecules originally came from that made this type of cumulative selection possible in the first place. It also fails to explain where a suitable environment for this type of cumulative selection came from as well. It follows from this realization that the use of cumulative selection to explain the rise of biological complexity amounts to little more than an elaborate exercise in question-begging. For while cumulative selection may be able to explain *how* biological complexity could have come about (in the presence of self-organizing atoms and molecules), it fails to explain *why* it was able to come about in the first place.

5.17 The Fallacy of Using Natural Selection as a Causal Explanation for Life's Origin

As we have seen, there is a strong tendency in the scientific community to regard the principle of natural selection as a sufficient explanation for the origin of life, and for species diversity in general. The fact is, however, that natural selection is, at most, only a sufficient explanation of species diversification and proliferation, and *not* one of origin.

Indeed, the use of natural selection to explain origins is inherently mistaken, as it is based on the fallacy of circular reasoning, or the positing of one's conclusion in one's beginning premise. We mustn't forget that the central question which is at issue here isn't concerned with the origin of this or that species or this or that adaptation. Rather, it is concerned with the ultimate origin of the reproductive drive itself, which fuels the forward-marching surge of evolution. There would be no evolution at all if it weren't for this inherent reproductive drive that is found in all species, yet non-theistic evolutionists take this drive to be a mere given. This clearly won't do, however, because it is inherently fallacious to assume the very thing that one is trying to demonstrate.

It is thus of no explanatory value whatsoever to merely note that better adapted forms will preferentially survive to produce more offspring; this is an obvious surmisal that follows tautologously from the very assumptions of the neo-Darwinian theory. The *real* question that is of interest to us here is *why* reproduction is such a fastidious goal in the first place. One cannot simply assume that it must be so and then conclude that one has explained evolution, because this amounts to little more than an elaborate exercise in question-begging.

A parallel situation exists in the realm of "anthropic cosmology," where it is termed the Weak Anthropic Principle (WAP). According to the WAP, we shouldn't be surprised that we exist, despite the vanishingly small odds for our own evolution, because we couldn't possibly be aware of our existence if things were otherwise.

It is clear, however, that this tautologous observation is of no value whatsoever in explaining *why* the universe is biocentric. It merely tells us what we already know; namely, that we couldn't possibly be aware of our own existence if the situation in the universe were significantly different. Thus, when it comes to the deeper question of *why* things are the way they are, and not otherwise, the WAP falls short. This is why it cannot be used as a sufficient explanation for the origin of life: because using it in this manner begs the true question at issue here, which concerns *why* things are the way they are. For a deeper explanation of this life-supporting feature, we must look beyond the Weak Anthropic Principle, to an explanatory tool that is sufficient to the task.[84]

This same critique also applies to the neo-Darwinian theory of evolution by natural selection. It is of absolutely no explanatory value to simply assume that, given the prior existence of a reproductive urge in living populations, certain better-adapted forms will preferentially survive to produce more offspring. We want to know *why* this reproductive urge exists to begin with, but modern selective theory cleverly avoids this deeper, more relevant question by pushing it endlessly back to earlier generations of self-replicating molecules. But this too is a logically fallacious maneuver, since one cannot justifiably assume the prior existence of an infinite series of self-replicating improvements. A genuine explanation must stop somewhere, or else it will fall victim to the ultimate fallacy of them all, that of the *reductio ad absurdum*.[85]

The upshot of this realization is that the phenomenon of natural selection cannot be used to explain its own existence. The same thing can also be said about the phenomenon of self-organization. One simply cannot use the prior fact of self-organization as a sufficient explanation for the origin of this sophisticated property. We want to know *where* matter originally got the capacity to organize itself into increasingly complex forms in the first place, but modern theorists make no attempt to answer this question. They simply *assume* the prior existence of this marvelous property, and that this prior existence somehow obviates any need for a deeper explanation. But this is a profoundly mistaken conclusion, because as we have already seen, one cannot assume the prior validity of the very thing one is trying to prove.

A good illustration of this basic principle is provided by recent attempts to account for the obvious trend towards greater complexity in the biosphere. Many scientists believe that this trend is "explained" by the fact that open systems can experience an increase in complexity without contradiction to the Second Law of Thermodynamics. This amounts to a nonexplanation, however, because freedom from the constraining influences of the Second Law cannot explain why this trend towards greater complexity occurs in the first place.

> Biosystems are not closed systems. They are characterized by their very openness, which enables them to export entropy into their environment to prevent degeneration. But the fact that they are able to evade the degenerative (pessimistic) arrow of time does not explain how they comply with the progressive (optimistic) arrow. Freeing a system from the strictures of one law does not prove that it follows another.

> Many biologists make this mistake. They assume because they have discovered the above loophole in the second law, the progressive nature of

biological evolution is explained. This is simply incorrect. It also confuses order with organization and complexity. Preventing a decrease in order might be a necessary condition for the growth of organization and complexity, but it is not a sufficient condition. We still have to find that elusive arrow of time.[86]

Davies attempts to locate this arrow of time in the self-ordering capacity of far-from-equilibrium systems. Thanks largely to the work of Belgian chemist Ilya Prigogine, it is now known that order can spontaneously arise out of chaos in these "dissipative structures," and this seems to be the origin of the trend towards greater complexity in the biosphere.

However, while this "explanation" may indeed be true, it still begs the ultimate question that is at issue here, which is this: where did matter originally get the capacity to build itself into far-from-equilibrium systems in the first place? As we have seen, there are two possible ways to answer this fundamental question. On the one hand, we can simply take the self-organizing capacity of matter to be a raw given. This view presumes that no Higher Power is necessary to explain the property of self-organization, since it is conceivable that it could have happened on its own for no discernible reason. On the other hand, we can consider matter's self-organizing capacity to be so intrinsically impressive as to necessitate some sort of larger Design. On this latter view, matter could *not* have developed the property of self-organization entirely on its own.

Prigogine's term for this self-organizing property is "active matter," which is defined as matter that seems to have a "will of its own." Prigogine appears to be correct on this issue—matter does indeed seem to possess the ability to organize itself into increasingly complex forms with no apparent external contrivance. However, it would be a mistake to conclude that this self-organizing capacity can itself be used as a sufficient explanation for the obvious trend towards greater complexity in the biosphere. Matter simply does not seem to contain within itself the ultimate reason for its own existence or for its own self-ordering capacity.

This is why all non-theistic evolutionary theories are ultimately unsatisfactory: because natural selection is only capable of explaining the process of differential survival amongst self-replicating species; it can't explain where the initial capacity for self-replication *itself* originally came from. Non-theistic evolutionists thus beg the true question at issue here when they try to explain our current existence by means of natural selection. For while the process of selection may help to explain why certain groups, and not others, have been able to survive the test of time, it doesn't tell us a thing about where the original survival capacities *themselves* originally came from. This is why we have to look somewhere else for the origin of these capacities.

Evolutionists are thus guilty of committing a severe *category mistake* when they credit natural selection for producing the phenomenon of life. They mistake one distinct category of explanation, that of differing rates of survival amongst self-replicating objects, for an entirely different category of explanation, that of the original generation of self-replicating properties. These two categories of explanation are both metaphysically and ontologically distinct, so there is very little, if any, realistic chance that the first category of explanation could ever substitute for the second. Nevertheless, many non-theistic evolutionists spend their entire careers trying to do this very thing.

Another way of understanding this basic fallacy is in terms of how the word "originate" is used in the modern evolutionary literature. Two very different meanings for this word are routinely employed. The first (strong) sense of "originate" is used to refer to the ultimate origin of space, matter, and energy, and to the inherent capacity of living organisms to exist and reproduce. The second (weak) sense of "originate" is used to refer to the immediate origin or presence of a given species in a particular generation.

It is clearly the second, weaker sense of the word "originate" that the non-theistic evolutionist uses in conjunction with the "creative capacity" of natural selection. Since natural selection determines which species persist (i.e., originate) in any given generation, it is understood to be the causal force that is responsible for this "origination."

It is thus only when the evolutionist confuses the two senses of the word "originate" that trouble arises, because these two senses pertain to vastly different referents. The strong sense of the word refers to the ultimate origination of matter and life, while the weaker sense simply refers to the appearance of any given species in a particular generation. It is apparent that these two senses cannot be collapsed into one another without severe problems resulting.

As we have seen, the non-theistic evolutionist tries to get around this problem by pushing it back beyond the rise of life to the origin of self-replicating molecules themselves. It is precisely here, though, that his attempted solution fails, because once again, the principle of natural selection itself cannot be used to explain its own origin. If such a thing were actually true, it would require natural selection to exist *before* it actually existed, and this is clearly impossible. It follows, then, that some other force had to have been responsible for giving rise to the process of natural selection. For the theist, this other force was none other than God Himself.[87]

This is an important point that can perhaps be better illustrated by means of an analogy. It is a well-known fact that certain car models are able to survive the test of time in the marketplace, while others are not. The models that happen to survive do so because they fulfill a dual criterion of fitness:

they are popular with the public and they are profitable for the parent company.

However, it would be ludicrous to suppose that this profitability and public popularity somehow explains the ultimate origin of the various car models themselves. For while it may be true that the corporate executives in the automobile industry are aiming for maximum profitability and public popularity when they initially choose to take certain car models to market, these dual intentions still do not explain how these models were originally made. For this we have to look beyond the dual intentions of popularity and profitability, to the tremendous ingenuity of the automobile designers and engineers themselves.

Similarly, the fact that certain groups of living creatures preferentially survive in the wild doesn't explain where this survival capacity itself originally came from. For this we have to look beyond the selective process, to the ultimate Creative Powers that rule the heavens.

Non-theistic evolutionists, however, do not believe this. They are instead convinced that the self-replicating process could have come into being by chance alone, in the form of a relatively simple primeval replicator. Over time, these simple chemical replicators are believed to have been accidentally capable of developing into increasingly complex forms, which the agency of natural selection would have then preserved for future generations of selection to act upon. Eventually, these chemical replicators are thought to have accidentally developed into living cells.

It isn't difficult to see that a replicator's ability to stand the test of time cannot in and of itself account for the gradual progression towards greater levels of organic complexity. For as Paul Davies has pointed out, just because a replicator's internal degree of complexity enables it to survive the test of time without contradiction to the Second Law of Thermodynamics, doesn't mean that its complexity is *explained* by its ability to survive.[88]

Indeed, Davies' identification of the arrow of time with this trend towards greater complexity elevates this trend to the level of a *fundamental cosmic principle*.[89] However, it just doesn't seem possible that this trend could have ever occupied the status of a universal cosmic principle if it were merely the result of the differential process of survival. Something more direct and fundamental seems to be necessary for that.

As far as Davies is concerned, traditional evolutionary theory is incapable of explaining the origin of this trend towards greater complexity, because it defines success solely in terms of differential reproduction; the more offspring a species leaves behind, the more successful it is thought to be. But this definition makes the myriad members of the microbial world the most successful species of them all, since they leave behind by far the most offspring. Even so, this unprecedented rate of reproductive success has *not* been accompanied by any significant increase in evolutionary complexity, since most microbes today remain unchanged from prehistoric times.

Now, if differential rates of survival alone were the key to the evolution of complexity, you'd think that the various bacterial lines would have developed the most complexity, but such has clearly not been the case. Evidently another mechanism, intrinsic to the organic replicators themselves, must have been at work fueling the rise towards progressively greater levels of organic complexity. Natural selection in this case would have functioned in a secondary capacity to this internal drive, amplifying and refining it, but in no case substituting for it.

Indeed, if natural selection alone were the sole arbiter of the trend towards greater complexity, life probably never would have evolved to begin with, because natural selection in all likelihood would have never had anything coherent to select *from*. We mustn't forget that the phenomenon of self-replication is itself a highly sophisticated property, which inherently requires a substantial level of complexity in order to be operative. But if there is no self-organizing drive internal to matter, then the property of self-replication probably never would have come into being, and we would not be here to discuss the fact.

In other words, natural selection *presupposes* a significant degree of self-organization in matter. This is due to the fact that the only objects that natural selection can act upon are self-replicators, and self-replication is a sophisticated form of complexity that requires the prior existence of self-organizing atoms and molecules. Hence, natural selection in all probability could *not* have been responsible for generating the property of self-replication, since natural selection could not possibly have taken place before self-replication ever existed.

It follows, then, that the twin properties of self-organization and self-replication are necessarily *prior to* the property of being subject to natural selection, which in turn means that there had to have been a sufficient cause for matter to have originally become self-replicating in the first place; otherwise, natural selection almost certainly would have never become operational at all. This sufficient cause was probably a self-organizing drive internal to matter, because chance processes alone do not seem to be capable of producing self-replicating atoms and molecules, even over immense stretches of time.

This argument can be summarized in the following manner:

1) Matter must be self-replicating before natural selection can act upon it.

2) Self-replication is a highly sophisticated property that requires an impressive level of material complexity in order to be operational.

3) If no tendency towards greater complexity levels is intrinsic to matter, then the property of self-replication probably never would have evolved,

which in turn means that matter would have probably remained in the simplest form possible.

4) The simplest forms of matter are not self-replicating, because of (2). Furthermore, the simplest forms of matter are known to be incapable of self-replication.

5) Therefore, even the simplest forms of self-replication require the prior existence of an impressive level of material complexity.

6) Natural selection can only act upon matter that possesses a certain minimum level of complexity, which is the level that would enable it to be self-replicating.

7) It is next to impossible for natural selection to have initially created this level of material complexity, because prior to this point, matter could not have been self-replicating by definition, so there would have been nothing for natural selection to select from (barring the existence of highly creative chance processes).

8) If no tendency towards greater levels of complexity exists in matter, and if natural selection can only operate upon substantially complex self-replicators, then it follows that matter should exist in its simplest form only, which by virtue of its very simplicity, is not subject to natural selection, because it is not self-replicating.

9) Natural selection, however, is a fact.

10) Therefore, something internal to matter must have caused it to become complex enough to become self-replicating, because chance processes alone do not seem to be capable of producing self-replicating atoms and molecules.

The only way the evolutionist can escape from this bind is to assert that matter could have *accidentally* acquired the property of self-replication with no outside help. However, it is very hard to see how this could have ever been the case, especially if it is asserted that no natural tendency towards self-organization exists in matter (apart from the action of natural selection), and if it is acknowledged that natural selection is inoperative in a positive sense at this relatively simple level of organization. Davies agrees:

> Since the work of Boltzmann, physicists have appreciated that microscopic random shuffling does not alone possess the power to generate an arrow of time, because of the underlying time symmetry of the microscopic laws of motion. On its own, random shuffling merely produces what might be called stochastic drift with no coherent directionality. (The biological significance of this has recently been recognized by the Japanese biologist Kumura who has coined the phrase 'neutral evolution' to describe such directionless drift.)[90]

In order for matter to have accidentally acquired the property of self-replication, it had to have first discovered a means of becoming stable at the subatomic level. But as any particle physicist will immediately attest, this is a very tall order indeed, because subatomic stability is an *exceedingly* complex phenomenon that is only just beginning to be understood by theorists. For one thing, stable atoms must follow the Pauli Exclusion Principle, which explicitly forbids two subatomic particles from occupying the same quantum state at the same time. If this Exclusion Principle did not apply, all electrons would occupy the lowest possible quantum state, since it is the orbital with the lowest energy. This would cause the spontaneous rearrangement of the various positively and negatively charged particles in an atom, so that interactions between their nearest neighbors would predominate. This in turn would result in the spontaneous collapse of the entire atomic structure into a single particle of enormous density, thereby destroying any further possibility for life.

As Barrow and Tipler point out, it is possible to imagine a world in which the Pauli Exclusion Principle did not apply, but it would be a very different world containing superdense objects that would possess no capacity at all for complex organization.[91] Our very lives thus depend on the existence of the Pauli Exclusion Principle, yet we have no idea where it comes from or why it works the way it does. All we know is that it does indeed work, and that it is this very functionality that has enabled life to form.

The second stabilizing force at the subatomic level is the quantization of electronic energy levels. As Bohr originally showed in 1913, electrons can only exist at discrete levels about the nucleus, which amount to multiples of Planck's universal quantum of energy. The great benefit of this quantum nature of the atom is that it allows for all atoms of a particular atomic number and weight to be both identical and stable in the face of a continual bombardment of energy from without. In a non-quantum atom, electrons could possess all possible energy states, and therefore all possible orbital distances from the nucleus. This of course would render all atoms different from one another, and would allow electrons to continually change their energy levels in response to the slightest amount of incoming energy, be it in the form of photons, cosmic rays, or whatever. This in turn would make a given atom's chemical properties subject to change at a moment's notice, thereby making any stable form of chemical interaction impossible. Fortunately, the existence of discrete quantum states greatly stabilizes each individual atom, because an entire quantum of energy is needed to alter a given electron's particular energy level.[92]

Even so, physicists still have absolutely no idea where the phenomenon of quantization comes from, or why it operates the way it does. All they know is that it is a strict prerequisite for atomic stability, and hence for the existence of life.

In order for matter to have accidentally stumbled upon the property of self-replication, then, the atom had to have first discovered a reliable means of employing the Pauli Exclusion Principle within itself, and secondly, it had to have discovered a means of operating in a quantum fashion only. It is unlikely to the highest degree that matter could have accidentally stumbled upon these two discoveries by chance alone, again because of their overwhelmingly complicated nature. Indeed, these stabilization mechanisms are so profoundly complex that we humans haven't even begun to understand how they actually operate at the subatomic level.

Now, if these two properties are so complex that our best minds continue to be baffled by them, it is exceedingly unlikely that matter could have discovered a means of employing them purely by accident, which in turn means that matter in all likelihood did not acquire the twin properties of self-organization and self-replication by chance alone.

5.18   Historical Antecedents

Other thinkers throughout the history of evolutionary thought have shared this basic sentiment regarding the limits of natural selection. These individuals have also concluded that, at most, natural selection can only account for the proliferation of species, and not for their origin.

E.D. Cope, an American paleontologist and evolutionary theoretician working in the late nineteenth century, also was convinced that natural selection could only preserve adaptive traits that had come into existence through some other means. His book *The Origin of the Fittest*, reflected this radical belief.

The British zoologist George Mivart shared Cope's rejection of traditional Darwinism. His classic book, *On the Genesis of Species* (1871), was very influential in its day, and laid the groundwork for all subsequent critiques of Darwinian theory. Even Darwin himself begrudgingly acknowledged the force of Mivart's argument.

Mivart also believed that natural selection was incapable of explaining the origin of adaptive traits. In order to prove his point, he went straight for the Darwinian "jugular," so to speak, which is the rapid and mysterious appearance of complex organs such as the eye and ear. Mivart appreciated the profound complexity of these "organs of extreme perfection," and realized that their incipient stages could only have been useful in their final form. He therefore concluded that natural selection could not have formed them. Generalizing this belief into an overall view of the origin of species, Mivart reached the tantalizing conclusion that "new species have from time to time manifested themselves with suddenness, and by modifications appearing at once."[93]

Other noteworthy theorists working in the nineteenth century also shared this basic mistrust of Darwin's theory of natural selection. The Duke of Argyll, for instance, repeatedly argued that the mere struggle for existence could never adequately explain the richness and diversity of the living world.[94] Robert Chambers, Richard Owen, and Asa Gray were also in agreement on this score as well. These men appear to have been on the right track. For just because certain natural processes (such as the survival of the fittest) hold true in the present, doesn't necessarily mean that they were true in the past, or were in fact responsible for their own origin. Indeed, it is nothing less than "evolutionary whiggery" to conclude otherwise, because we cannot properly interpret the zoological past in terms of events and processes that are known to be true in the present only. While we know for a tautological fact that natural selection is able to preserve the fittest members of any population, it doesn't necessarily follow from this that natural selection itself was primarily responsible for creating this original fitness.

5.19 The Nature and Origin of the Selective Process

In *The Blind Watchmaker*, Richard Dawkins attempts to defend Darwin's concept of natural selection from attack by arguing that it is anything *but* a random natural process. He correctly points out that only random mutations can be said to be truly random. Natural selection, on the other hand, is the very opposite of random, insofar as it chooses from among these random mutations those that are fit enough for continued survival. Dawkins therefore concludes that it is fallacious to call natural selection "random."[95]

The error in Dawkin's argument is easy enough to spot. Natural selection may not be random, but it cannot manufacture functional levels of order out of gibberish either. That is to say, if the only things that are ever presented to nature's selective hand are incoherent mutations, it is naïve to think that any coherent traits at all will ever result, even with the help of cumulative selection over huge spans of time. Natural selection simply cannot be counted on to produce order out of true chaos, because there will never be anything coherent to choose from.

Everything turns on whether one believes that the genome is capable of producing mutations that are coherent enough to be chosen for continued survival by natural selection. Since natural selection obviously can only choose traits that are coherent enough to contribute a minimum amount of survival value to the organism in question, it must be conceded that these "random" mutations necessarily have *some* degree of coherence to them. If this is true, though, then the mutations cannot *truly* be random, because genuinely random mutations would not be cohesive enough to form a coherent trait, since virtually all traits are comprised of a number of separate, yet coordinated, genetic components.[96]

In response to this assertion, Dawkins has counterargued that it is cumulative selection, as opposed to single-step selection, that makes these extremely complicated traits and adaptations possible. Cumulative selection refers to the process wherein entire constellations of characters, which have already passed through prior selective filters, are subjected to further rounds of selection. Single-step selection, on the other hand, refers to a one-time selective process where each characteristic is chosen independently of all the others. On a purely mechanistic level, Dawkins is correct—cumulative selection *is* capable of generating impressive levels of order over many generations. It would be a mistake, however, to think that this is the whole story behind life's phenomenal complexity.

To begin with, Dawkins fails to give a coherent account either of the origination of the selection process itself, or of the curious capacity of inanimate molecules to spontaneously order themselves over time. Instead, he takes these crucial factors as mere "givens," which only begs the true question at issue here: where did atoms and molecules originally get *their* marvelous capacity to create order via the self-driven process of cumulative selection?

Dawkins chooses to answer this question by simply asserting that "each successive change in the gradual evolutionary process was simple enough, *relative to its predecessor*, to have arisen by chance."[97] This is undoubtedly true enough, but *only* in a pre-existing material realm where the selective process is already taking place. Within these constraints, it *is* possible for a given degree of change in the evolutionary process to be so small that it could happen by "chance" alone.

Dawkins, however, takes this assumption one step further and argues that if the *original* building block that initiated the process of cumulative selection was simple enough, *it too* could have come into existence by chance alone. This of course translates into the conclusion that the entire evolutionary process leading to humans could have been due to chance alone if the starting point was simple enough.

In order to achieve his goal, Dawkins relies on the process of inorganic selection to get the biological process of cumulative selection going. The problem with this reliance, though, is that it simply isn't rudimentary enough to get the job done. Inorganic crystals are only able to exist and "reproduce" because of the unique properties of atoms and molecules, which themselves result from the complex interplay of a huge number of distinct structures, forces, and subatomic principles. Thus, the only way Dawkins' argument can work is if he takes the existence of atoms and molecules for granted, because there isn't any possible way to explain *their* structure and design in terms of natural selection. Indeed, as Barrow and Tipler have pointed out, the fundamental constants themselves, which are the ultimate constituents of everything in the physical realm, have *not* slowly developed through a process of natural selection to possess their current life-supporting values. They were instead "born" with the correct values from the very beginning.[98]

This momentous fact instantly short-circuits Dawkins' argument and thereby renders it false.

Put another way, the cogency of Dawkins' argument rests on his ability to explain two things: 1) how the fundamental constants themselves were able to adopt the right life-supporting values from the very beginning, and 2) how self-organizing atoms and molecules could have ever formed at all, given their profoundly complicated inner structure. Since he cannot do so without appealing to the non-explanation of blind chance, he is forced to take the fundamental constants and the existence of self-organizing atoms and molecules for granted. In so doing, however, his entire argument is undermined, because the only way he can avoid the accusation of question-begging is by providing a suitable *explanation* for the values of the constants and for the existence of self-organizing atoms and molecules, since this is what the process of cumulative selection ultimately comes down to. It is highly significant to note that, given their almost unbelievable degree[99] of inner complexity, these foundational elements are essentially impossible to explain in the absence of an Intelligent Designer.

In other words, Dawkins' argument is only persuasive if we grant him the validity of his premises, because his conclusion is directly implied in his assumptions. However, there is no good reason to accept the validity of his premises. In order to reach his conclusion, Dawkins utilizes an extremely subtle "sleight of hand," insofar as his argument contains two hidden assumptions that are far too grandiose to simply be taken for granted. To begin with, Dawkins believes that it is indeed possible for a subatomic particle to be sufficiently simple to enable it to come into existence by pure chance. This assertion, as we have seen, is far from obvious, since even the "simplest" known subatomic particle contains an intrinsic level of complexity that vastly exceeds our ability to fully understand it. If the truth could be completely known, the metaphysical requirements for *any* type of concrete existence are probably far too elaborate to have *ever* been satisfied by chance alone. Indeed, the original Big Bang explosion, which set the stage for the existence of all subsequent particles, appears to have been *anything but* a chance event.[100] As cosmologists have recently learned, the initial conditions surrounding this primordial explosion were so exquisitely "fine-tuned" with respect to the conditions necessary for the evolution of life that the only reasonable way to explain it is in terms of some sort of Intelligent Contrivance. Dawkins, however, fails to consider the ultimate birthplace of the subatomic realm. He simply assumes that it is possible for a self-repro-ducing particle to have been so simple that it could have come about purely by chance. But since all subatomic particles had their ultimate origin in the Big Bang, Dawkins is only justified in making his claim if he is *also* prepared to say that the entire Big Bang itself was simple enough to have come about by pure chance. Since all present indications are that this does *not* appear to be the case, we must reject Dawkins' first assumption as assuming far too much.

But even if we grant, for the sake of argument, that a viable material realm is for some reason already in existence, it is still far from obvious that a self-replicating structure could ever be simple enough to have arisen purely by chance. Self-replication is an extremely elaborate property that is based on a multitude of complex preconditions, each of which is, in all likelihood, far too elaborate to have been able to come into existence by pure chance. The Pauli Exclusion Principle, for instance—which is the subatomic law that says that two particles of a particular kind and spin cannot occupy the same quantum state—is the single most important ingredient[101] in determining the stability of all matter, and is therefore an essential prerequisite for the existence of *any* type of coherent chemistry, yet no one knows how it works or where it comes from. Similarly, the fact of quantization in the subatomic realm—which restricts electron orbitals about the nucleus to certain discrete energy values—is an essential prerequisite for enabling atoms of the same atomic number and weight to be identical with one another, and for protecting atoms from the disorganizing influences of small environmental[102] perturbations, yet no one knows how it works or where it comes from either. Based on these observations, we are compelled to conclude, with Barrow and Tipler, that "despite its traditional reputation as the harbinger of chance and indeterminism, quantum theory is the basis for the fidelity and large-scale stability of Nature."[103]

In asserting, however, that it is possible for a self-replicating particle to come into existence by chance alone, Dawkins clearly shows himself to be unaware of the many extraordinarily complex factors that go into the making of a single coherent atom, not the least of which are the many precise conditions that surrounded the birth of the universe in the Big Bang. It is unreasonable to the highest degree to simply assume that these factors could have come about by pure chance. As a consequence, it is even *more* unreasonable to simply assume that a self-replicating molecule could have been simple enough to come into existence by pure chance. This is why we can feel safe in concluding that the fact of self-replication in the material realm is *itself* powerful evidence for Intelligent Design.

In order to cover these two glaring weaknesses in his argument, Dawkins uses the fact that it *is* possible for one cumulatively-selected degree of order to spontaneously move up to the next higher degree of order by "chance" alone. While this may be true, it is again only true within a pre-existing realm of self-replicating atoms and molecules. It simply is not possible to use this type of chance-mediated increase in complexity to argue that matter itself, as well as the process of self-replication, could have come into existence by a similar chance-mediated process. The first chance-mediated process occurs in a pre-existing world where stable, self-replicating molecules are known to exist, whereas the second chance-mediated process entails both the creation of matter *and* the creation of the self-replicating process out of virtual nothingness. To thus argue that chance must be equally facile in bringing about the desired level of complexity in *both* realms is clearly fallacious. Dawkins is aware of this severe shortcoming in his theory:

> [The process of] cumulative selection cannot work unless there is some minimal machinery of replication and replicator power, and the only machinery of replication that we know seems too complicated to have come into existence by means of anything less than many generations of cumulative selection! Some see this as a fundamental flaw in the whole theory of the blind watchmaker. They see it as the ultimate proof that there must originally have been a designer, not a *blind* watchmaker but a far-sighted supernatural watchmaker. Maybe, it is argued, the Creator does not control the day-to-day succession of evolutionary events; maybe he did not frame the tiger and the lamb, maybe he did not make a tree, but he *did* set up the original machinery of replication and replicator power, the original machinery of DNA and protein that made cumulative selection, and hence all of evolution, possible.[104]

Despite the power and simplicity of this type of argument for the origin of cumulative selection, Dawkins nevertheless chooses to reject it as being "transparently feeble," for the following reason: Since we have no choice but to posit *some* primordial form of organized complexity in order to account for the phenomenon of replication, we're more justified in positing the self-existence of a relatively simple replicator molecule than we are in positing the self-existence of a Supreme Deity, since the latter is infinitely more complex than the most sophisticated inanimate molecule, and we would naturally expect the simplest possible entity to have been the most likely cause of its own existence. As Dawkins explains:

> Any God capable of intelligently designing something as complex as the DNA/protein replicating machinery must have been at least as complex and organized as that machine itself. Far more so if we suppose him *additionally* capable of such advanced functions as listening to prayers and forgiving sins. To explain the origin of the DNA/protein machine by invoking a supernatural Designer is to explain precisely nothing, for it leaves unexplained the origin of the Designer. You have to say something like 'God was always there,' and if you allow yourself that kind of lazy way out, you might as well just say 'DNA was always there,' or 'Life was always there,' and be done with it.[105]

The problem with this type of argument is that it fails to consider the intrinsic definitions of those entities with which it is concerned. God, of course, is *defined* as the self-caused Being who created the worlds. Nothing else can be defined this way *by definition*. It is therefore fallacious to even *attempt* to attribute this property of self-causation to the DNA/protein replicating machine, or even to non-Divine life itself. The ancients were well aware of this necessity, but many moderns seem to have forgotten what they had to say.

Indeed, this is where the Cosmological Argument for the existence of God gets its primary impetus: it recognizes that a First Cause is intrinsically required if we are to obtain a coherent understanding of universal origins. And since an infinite progression of causes does not contain within itself a First Cause, and since there is, by all accounts, only one possible type of Self-Caused Entity in the universe *by definition* (which we understand to be God), it follows that God had to have been the First Cause of our present universe.

In his attempt to discover the ultimate origin of replicator power, Dawkins has inadvertently come up against the full force of the Cosmological Argument. However, instead of abdicating to its demand for a Self-Caused Deity as the only appropriate first cause of replicating matter, Dawkins cleverly attempts to side-step this need by arguing that such a first cause doesn't necessarily have to be Divine at all. And since it doesn't have to be Divine, it might just as well be DNA, or whatever.

This "transparently feeble argument" fails because it commits the most serious fallacy of all: the fallacy of trying to substitute a *de dicto* explanation of an object's fundamental properties for a *de re* explanation. The *de dicto* mode of necessity refers to what we *say* about the real world; it is the form necessity associated with propositions. The *de re* mode of necessity, on the other hand, refers to the essential properties of objects which necessarily surround the things themselves. Thus, when we speak of *de re* necessity, we are referring to the essential definitions of things as they are found in themselves; when we speak of *de dicto* necessity, we are only referring to what we *say* about these fundamental objects.

It follows, then, that whenever we attempt to characterize the identity of the universal first cause, or the essential properties that are possessed by that cause, we are talking about *de re* necessity, not *de dicto* necessity. This means that the identity and properties of this first cause are *already fixed*, and so cannot be changed by our mere theorizing about them. Thus, if we want to discover the true identity of this first cause, we need to concentrate on the thing itself, and not simply on what we have to say about it.

In other words, we simply cannot conjure up our own gratuitous propositions about this first cause and then expect them to be true, just because we came up with them. *Things are what they intrinsically are no matter what we say about them.* Therefore, we cannot hope to alter the essential properties of things in our minds and then expect these new definitions to necessarily be true, because this would be tantamount to altering the the natural definitions of objects to fit our own idiosyncratic needs. The *most* we can do is to attempt to learn what these natural definitions are in and of themselves, so we can then base our philosophical and metaphysical arguments on them.

Continuing on, we mustn't forget that a universal first cause is *itself* an object, complete with its own set of essential defining properties. One of the essential properties of this first cause, as Aquinas, Plantinga, and a whole host of other thinkers have realized over the years, is self-causation. But self-causation is a property that can only be attributed to some form of Infinite Deity, since it is inherently impossible for *any* finite material object to be the true cause of its own existence. Self-causation means the capacity to cause one's own existence out of one's *own* being. But this is clearly impossible for any non-eternal entity, because in order to be able to cause its own existence, it must somehow exist *before* it actually exists, i.e., it must exist as a causative agent before it exists as a created product. This is why only God Himself is capable of true self-causation: because only God's *eternal* lifespan enables Him to generate His own existence out of His timeless Being. This is why it is logically impossible for any non-eternal object or process to cause its own existence: because no such finite entity could possibly exist before it ever existed.

In response to this charge, it could be retorted that it is possible that matter itself could be eternal, and so could be responsible for its own origin. There are two severe problems, however, with this counterargument. First, the most recent cosmological evidence indicates that matter is most definitely *not* eternal. It is a well-known fact today that matter had its beginning in the Big Bang some 15 billion years ago, and while it is possible that some form of matter could have predated the Big Bang, thermodynamic considerations have effectively ruled out this possiblity.[106] Secondly, the traditional definition of matter has never been understood to include self-causation. If it did, then matter itself would be God, and this is clearly absurd. Therefore, matter in all likelihood is not eternal, and the Cosmological Argument stands.

The upshot of this realization is that one cannot gratuitously attribute self-causation to a non-Divine material object. Or put another way, one cannot flippantly change the intrinsic definition of a universal first cause to fit one's own personal agenda. But this is precisely what Dawkins has done by arguing that we can just as easily attribute self-causation to an inanimate replicator as we can to a Divine Creator. Therefore, Dawkins' argument fails, and we find that God *had* to have been the First Cause to our present universe after all.

Another weakness in Dawkins' thesis revolves around its insistence that explaining how a complexity-building process works in terms of natural cause-and-effect processes automatically does away with the need for a Grand Designer. As we have seen, the only place where this premise can possibly be valid is in terms of an instantaneous creation by Divine Fiat. God obviously could not have created the various animals instantly by Miraculous Fiat and still have had them gradually construct themselves according to the principle of cumulative selection. As far as a more remote Creator is concerned, who chooses to create entirely by natural cause-and-effect processes, Dawkins' premise becomes thoroughly invalidated. For such a naturalistic Creator, the step-by-step process of cumulative selection is simply one of His world-based "tools" for the gradual assembly of progressively more complicated biological structures.

It is possible, then, to affirm the complexity-building power of cumulative selection without giving up theism. On this view, *how* biological structures are ultimately produced is largely irrelevant in the face of the final *product* that eventually obtains, since it is distinctly possible for a Divine Creator to use any and all conceivable means for producing a given mechanism. In terms of Paley's watch, it doesn't really matter *how* it is put together, since there are any number of ways a watch can be assembled. What matters is the final product that is produced, not the means by which that product has been created. To thus infer that a self-driven, naturalistic process of cumulative selection somehow obviates the need for a Larger Designer is clearly fallacious, because there is no necessary, or even likely, connection between how a given item is made, and the ultimate origin of its basic structure.

Dawkins has apparently been misled by the self-driven character of the evolutionary process into believing that it is somehow *self-explanatory*. In other words, since no Creator appears to be responsible for making our world operate, Dawkins seems to conclude that none must actually exist. Appearances, however, can be deceiving. For if God is truly as skilled a Creator as His definition directly implies, we would expect His Creative Prowess to be so acute that there would be *no* direct evidence of contrivance in *any* of His created objects. To thus conclude that the creation is so perfect that it doesn't need a Creator is, as Marcel Proust has pointed out, the greatest compliment an atheist can give the Supreme Being.

In short, Dawkins errs when he projects an anthropomorphic view of the creative process onto God Himself, as if God were somehow limited to the creative restrictions that are an inherent part of human life. Just because humans cannot fail to leave behind evidence of contrivance in any of their created objects is no justification for assuming that God must do the same. Indeed, since the appearance of contrivance in any created object is largely an indication of how well it has been assembled, it would be amiss to expect to see *any* evidence of contrivance in a Divine Creation, since *a priori* we would expect God—by virtue of His Supreme Creative Capacity—to create in so natural a means that it would probably escape our notice.

The essence of Dawkins' argument, as we have seen, is that the gradual, step-by-step evolution of a complex form based on previous successes somehow eliminates the need for an Intelligent Designer. But isn't this essentially the same process humans use in building complex mechanical devices? Let us take watches for example. They aren't built instantaneously; they are rather built in a gradual, stepwise manner that is *also* based on previous successes. That is to say, given the successful completion of the first step, the watchmaker goes on to the next step; when this step is successfully completed, he goes on to the next step, and so on. In a very real sense, then, the watchmaker also uses the process of cumulative selection to build a watch: each successful stage of assembly is selected by the watchmaker to advance to the next step, which adds onto it, and so forth.

From this point of view, there are three major differences between the deliberate building of a watch and the natural evolution of a complex biological design: 1) The watch has a plainly evident designer right in front of it, while no Designer is immediately apparent in the natural world. 2) The same watch typically makes it through each successive stage of "selection" in the assembly process, whereas in the natural world, many generations of progeny are utilized in perfecting a given form, and 3) In human watchmaking, a functional design is immediately forthcoming, whereas the process of biological evolution seems to operate solely in a trial-and-error fashion, in which the final design isn't produced for many generations.

Interestingly enough, none of the above differences are sufficiently great to allow us to postulate a major difference in kind between the two types of creative processes under consideration. To begin with, a Designer clearly doesn't have to be visible in order to exist or be ascertained. Similarly, a Designer is under no obligation to use the same biological organism to perfect a given form in a single generation; He can just as easily spread the creative process out over many generations, so as to take maximal advantage of environmental change, genetic variation in the progeny, and the like. Indeed, if the evolutionary production of new biological forms is dependent on genetic variation (as almost all are agreed that it is), then such a spreading out of the creative process over many generations is logically required.

Finally, while the process of evolution does indeed seem to have an unmistakable trial-and-error character to it, this doesn't have to represent the lack of Intelligent Design *per se. It can simply represent the Divine Intention to have evolving life forms opportunistically interact with a constantly changing environment.* On this view, what would seem like a blind, trial-and-error process would actually represent a critical opportunistic linking between evolving life forms, on the one hand, and constantly fluctuating environmental demands, on the other. Although we would still have to explain why God would want to create the world in this fashion[107] in order to make this viewpoint more plausible, it isn't absolutely necessary, as there is no logical contradiction between the observed fact of opportunism, on the one hand, and the creative activity of a Grand Designer, on the other.

We can conclude from these observations that there are no major differences in kind between the human process of watch assembly and the Divine process of biological evolution (assuming, of course, the prior existence of a viable material realm). Both processes produce intelligent functional designs, using a step-by-step method of gradual assembly based upon previous successes. As a consequence, Paley's original argument holds, and we are left, not with a blind watchmaker, but with a Watchmaker who has 20/20 vision!

5.20   Could Natural Selection Have Formed the Eye?

In *The Blind Watchmaker* Dawkins also vigorously defends the orthodox idea that natural selection could have formed "organs of extreme perfection," like the eye. The classic argument against this position charges that half an eye confers no positive survival value at all to the host creature; therefore, natural selection could never have formed the eye. Dawkins counters this assertion by pointing out that half an eye does indeed possess a certain amount of survival value, because half an eye "is better than none at all."[108]

The fallacy in Dawkin's counterargument is that the rudimentary capacity for vision (as found in a light-sensitive spot) has nothing at all to do with the development of *new* structures which themselves must all be present in good working order before they can be capable of functioning. Even if we assume the prior existence of a light-sensitive spot, there is no reason at all to assume that an iris, pupil, lens, and retina (along with the many other necessary parts of an eye) will also start forming by chance alone. For one thing, there is no reason to assume that the genome is capable of randomly producing the barest building blocks of these important structures without some form of inner guidance.

But even if we assume that these structural building blocks are capable of appearing randomly, there is no reason to believe that they would ever be chosen for continued survival by natural selection. For unless these randomly generated characters are capable of improving vision in some way, they are incapable of being selected for (unless by the wildest stroke of luck they happen to serve *other* important survival-enhancing functions). But how could the incipient stages of a pupil or optic nerve act to improve vision? Not only must these structures be fully formed (or close to it) in order to be capable of performing their function even minimally, the other structures that they cooperate with to produce vision must *also* be more or less operational before vision can be improved even the slightest bit.

So, even if we assume the prior existence of a light-sensitive spot, and the prior capacity of the genome to produce the barest building blocks that comprise the various structures of the eye, there is no reason at all for assuming that any of them would pass the ruthless test of natural selection, since vision can only be improved upon by the *simultaneous* interplay of a large number of separate, yet highly complicated, structures. So, even though half an eye may be better than none at all (assuming, of course, that such a thing is functional in the first place), this still does not explain how the first half of the eye originally came about, or how the remainder proceeded to develop. Errol Harris agrees:

. . . although complex organs, like the human or the cephalopod eye, could be shown to have developed in stages, from a pigment spot to a light-concentrating, image-forming photoreceptor, this could not have been simply by successive additions of fortuitous and random variations, because such variations would be favourable, even when of the right sort, only if they occurred in the right order, and only if modifications in the structure and function of other organs, required to ensure that the developing eye worked more efficiently, were made concomitantly. It is not just that the eye is a highly complex organ, but that its effective use is not possible without the coordinated functioning of associated muscles, glands, neural engrams, and behavioral dispositions, involving numerous other organs and parts of the body (for instance, the reflex turning of the head to bring and to keep moving objects in focus). If all these factors were to be supplied piecemeal, by chance mutations, they must occur in the proper sequence and mutual association, which is not only stupendously improbable, but, if the mutations occurred in the wrong order, they would be disadvantageous and selection would eliminate them.[109]

We can see, then, that Dawkins' assertion that half an eye is better than none at all is correct only if we first assume that it will indeed be functional in the first place, *but this is precisely the point that Dawkins is trying to demonstrate.* And while it is indeed true that a light-sensitive spot confers more survival value onto a host creature than no light-sensitive organ at all, it doesn't follow from this assertion that half the present structure of the eye will be also functional. A light-sensitive spot does *not* constitute 5 percent of a mammalian eye; it constitutes 100 percent of an eye for those creatures which possess it. The modern mammalian eye, on the other hand, is a radically different structure, with vastly more interlocking structures and biochemical processes in support of the faculty of vision.

This being the case, it would be absurd to the highest degree to conclude that, just because a light-sensitive spot confers some survival value onto a creature, that half of a modern mammalian eye will also be more functional than no eye at all. We mustn't forget that before *any* biological structure can offer survival value, it must be optimally constructed with respect to its underlying pattern of design. And since the underlying pattern of design of the modern mammalian eye is vastly different from a mere light-sensitive spot, it is clearly fallacious to regard a light-sensitive spot as 5 percent of a modern mammalian eye. Carried one step further, this means that anything less than a fully functional modern eye will never be able to offer any significant survival value to its host, because it typically takes 100 percent of an existing biological structure before it can be functional. Just as it takes 100 percent of a computer's underlying design before it will be capable of working properly, it also takes 100 percent of a biological design before the particular structure in question will be capable of working properly. And since a given structure must be capable of working properly before it can offer survival value to its host, it follows that nothing less than 100 percent of a modern mammalian eye will *ever* be able to work well enough to confer survival value in the ongoing struggle for existence.

The point is simply that natural selection, working in conjunction with random mutations, could never have formed the mammalian eye without some inner form of directedness. Even the principal instigator of modern selectionist thinking, Charles Darwin, found himself in agreement with this conclusion:

> To suppose that the eye with all its inimitable contrivances for adjusting the focus to different distances, for admitting different amounts of light, and for the correction of spherical and chromatic aberration, could have been formed by natural selection, seems, I freely confess, *absurd in the highest degree* (emphasis mine).[110]

Notes

1. Peter R. Grant, "Natural Selection and Darwin's Finches," *Scientific American*, Vol. 265, No. 4, Oct. 1991, pp. 82–87.
2. Ibid., p. 86.
3. Sadly, extinctions are occurring in our modern world at the unbelievable pace of one a minute, due to the aversive effect our advancing "civilization" is having on the natural world. In Brazil, for instance, thousands of acres of tropical rain forest—said to be the natural "lungs" of the earth—are being deliberately burned down each and every day, because of local financial considerations. However, there is much more at stake now than simple financial well-being: the ecological stability of the entire world is currently in mortal danger because of this relentless deforestation, and indeed, for all we know, it is already too late. Clearly, if something isn't done soon, there *won't be* any future for us to fight about.
4. A given case of extinction can only be considered a "failure" in terms of the immediate species itself, because from a larger point of view it could very well be advantageous. For instance, had the dinosaurs not died out, it is doubtful whether humanity could have arisen at all.
5. Taylor, *The Great Evolution Mystery*, p. 160.

6. It must be continually borne in mind that slow change is the *sine qua non* of neo-Darwinian evolutionary theory. It is, therefore, a major prediction of the theory that species should gradually be replaced as better adapted creatures slowly evolve. However, the fossil record is characterized by anything but a gradual rate of extinction. It is, to the contrary, characterized by a number of worldwide mass extinctions, in which the difference between survival and extinction seems to have been purely arbitrary.

7. Ibid., p. 87.

8. Ibid.

9. Ibid.

10. Ibid.

11. Henry L. Plaine, ed., *Darwin, Marx, and Wagner: A Symposium* (Columbus: Ohio State University Press, 1962), pp. 38–39.

12. T.H. Morgan, *The Scientific Basis of Evolution* (London: Faber and Faber, 1932), p. 130, and L.T. Hogben, *The Nature of Living Matter* (London: Routledge and Kegan Paul, 1931), p. 181.

13. Harris, *Cosmos and Anthropos*, p. 80.

14. Norman Macbeth, *Darwin Retried: An Appeal to Reason* (Boston: Gambit Press, 1971), pp. 99–100.

15. Taken from Taylor's *The Great Evolution Mystery*, p. 225.

16. It may be that these impostors don't choose to engage in their suicidal behavior until after they have engaged in a species-maintaining act of reproduction.

17. Rifkin, *Algeny*, pp. 72–98.

18. John Arthur Thompson and Patrick Geddes, *Life: Outlines of General Biology* (London: Williams & Norgate, 1931), vol. II, p. 1317.

19. Asa Gray, "Natural Science and Religion," *Is God a Creationist?* Roland Mushat Frye, ed., (New York: Charles Scribner's Sons, 1983), p. 111.

20. Taylor, *The Great Evolution Mystery*, p. 83.

21. Ibid., p. 30.

22. I say "partially directed adaptations" because as we saw in the earlier chapter on mutations, there are numerous variations on each basic adaptational theme. To the extent that these variations cluster around a major morphogenetic structure or function, they can be considered to be partially directed towards a given level of adaptation.

23. The possibility that these variations could have derived their coherence from cumulative selection effects in the past does not significantly enter into this discussion, because at some point in time these variations had to have been coherent enough in a single generation to promote the luxury of continued survival; and given the outrageous complexity of even the simplest living creature, it is inconceivable that a set of truly random variations could have accidentally struck upon any such coherent theme. Indeed, the very act of replication assumes the prior existence of variations that are coherent enough to allow the process of replication to occur. Hence, without the prior existence of coherent variations, cell replication itself could never occur. But the capacity for an organism to self-replicate is *itself* based on a large number of coherent variations which *themselves* could never have been formed through cellular reproduction. Therefore, the non-theistic evolutionist is forced into assuming that the extremely complex process of cellular reproduction had to have been spontaneously produced by the random aggregation of atoms and molecules, which themselves had to have been produced by the random aggregation of subatomic particles into coherent atoms, all of which seem to be manifestly impossible.

24. Michael Denton, *Evolution: A Theory in Crisis*, p. 64.
25. Taken from Michael Denton's *Evolution: A Theory in Crisis*, p. 37.
26. This isn't so surprising when we recall that Darwin's professional training was in theology, not biology.
27. Jeremy Rifkin, *Algeny*, p. 134.
28. Taken from Jeremy Rifkin's quote in *Algeny*, p. 129, of the PBS Television show, "Did Darwin Get It Wrong?" Originally broadcast on November 1, 1981.
29. S. Stanley, *Macroevolution* (San Francisco: Hutchinson Publishing Co., 1979), p. 39.
30. Jeremy Rifkin, *Algeny*, p. 128.
31. Although contemporariness between two species doesn't necessarily mean that one species did not originate from the original stock of the other, it nevertheless makes it less likely.
32. Quoted in Marshall and Sandra Hall's *The Truth: God or Evolution?*, p. 37.
33. Philip E. Johnson, *Darwin on Trial*, pp. 30–31.
34. See F.R. Tennant's "Cosmic Teleology," in *Philosophical Theology*, Vol. II, Chapter IV (New York: Cambridge University Press, 1930), pp. 79–93.
35. Stephen Jay Gould, *Hen's Teeth and Horse's Toes* (New York: W.W. Norton and Company, 1980), pp. 259–260.
36. Alfred Russel Wallace, *Natural Selection and Tropical Nature* (London: Macmillan, 1895), p. 202.
37. Quoted in Rifkin's *Algeny*, p. 141.
38. I understand human consciousness to be miraculous for two reasons: 1) because we have absolutely no idea what it really is or how it actually works, and 2) because in point of fact it is by far the most complex and sophisticated thing yet discovered in the entire universe.
39. John Polkinghorne, *Science and Creation* (Boston: New Science Library, 1988), p. 21.
40. The traditional evolutionist seeks to explain the existence of beneficial adaptations in terms of the positive survival value they confer on the host species. That is to say, since the only variations that could have ever survived are the ones that confer positive survival value, these are the only ones we are capable of observing today. The problem with this "explanation," as we have seen, is that it assumes the prior existence of coherent variations. *But it is precisely these variations we are trying to explain.* Thus, this neo-Darwinian "explanation" amounts to little more than a question-begging circular argument. It therefore cannot serve as a legitimate causal explanation for the existence of adaptations.
41. Alister Hardy, *Darwin and the Spirit of Man* (London: Collins Press, 1984), p. 156.
42. C.O. Lovejoy, *Life in the Universe*, ed. J. Billingham (Cambridge: MIT Press, 1981), p. 326.
43. Ibid.
44. Ibid.
45. In fact, their diet is vastly *superior* to our own in terms of its overall healthfulness.
46. Stephen Jay Gould, *The Panda's Thumb* (New York: W.W. Norton & Company, 1980), p. 57.
47. Barrow and Tipler, *The Anthropic Cosmological Principle*, p. 133.
48. Weak anthropocentrism refers to the view that man is one of the most important

entities in the entire universe. This is contradistinction to strong anthropocentrism, which sees man as the single most important part of creation.

49. Quoted in Alister Hardy's *Darwin and the Spirit of Man*, p. 156.
50. Ibid., p. 23.
51. Sir John Eccles & Daniel N. Robinson, *The Wonder of Being Human*, p. 18.
52. Ibid., p. 43.
53. Ibid.
54. Ibid.
55. Richard Leakey, *The Making of Mankind* (New York: E.P. Dutton, 1981), p. 20.
56. Taken from Gould's *The Panda's Thumb*, p. 56.
57. Ibid.
58. Ibid.
59. In holographic theory, each individual part somehow contains or reflects all the information of the whole.
60. See F. David Peat's *Superstrings and the Search for the Theory of Everything* (Chicago: Contemporary Books, 1988), as well as Michio Kaku and Jennifer Trainer's *Beyond Einstein: The Cosmic Quest for the Theory of the Universe* (New York: Bantam Books, 1987).
61. The universe itself is not perfectly symmetrical. If it were, there would be nothing at all in existence, because the introduction of the very first bit of matter would have necessarily disrupted the perfect symmetry of cosmic nothingness (assuming, of course, that matter was first created *ex nihilo*). Even within the current universe, it is impossible for life to exist in a realm of perfect physical symmetry, because asymmetrical entities such as galaxies and solar systems could then never exist. Life can only exist in a universe where there is a very fine balance between symmetry and asymmetry. Not surprisingly, this is the same type of universe that we presently inhabit.
62. A tautology is simply a way of saying the same thing twice.
63. C.H. Waddington, *The Strategy of the Genes* (London: Allen & Unwin, 1957), pp. 64–65.
64. Philip E. Johnson, *Darwin on Trial*, p. 22.
65. Stephen Jay Gould, "Darwin's Untimely Burial—Again!" in *Scientists Confront Creationism*, Laurie R. Godfrey, ed. (New York: W.W. Norton & Co., 1983), p. 143.
66. It is said that if bacteria were allowed to multiply unchecked, they would cover the entire earth 4 feet deep in less than 24 hours.
67. Gordon Rattray Taylor, *The Great Evolution Mystery*, p. 26.
68. Richard Dawkins, *The Blind Watchmaker* (New York: W.W. Norton, 1987), p. 240.
69. Michael Denton, *Evolution: A Theory in Crisis*, p. 191.
70. Letter from Charles Darwin to Hooker, quoted in Michael Denton's *Evolution: A Theory in Crisis*, p. 163.
71. E. Corner, "Evolution," in *Contemporary Biological Thought*, McLeod and Colby, eds., 1961, pp. 95–97.
72. Andrew H. Knoll, "End of the Proterozoic Eon," *Scientific American*, Vol. 265, No. 4, Oct. 1991, pp. 64–73.
73. Ibid., p. 70.
74. Ibid., pp. 72–73.
75. Quoted in Taylor, *The Great Evolution Mystery*, p. 163.
76. Ibid., p. 234.

77. C. Dyke, "Complexity and Closure," *Evolution at a Crossroads*, David J. Depew and Bruce Weber, eds. (Cambridge: The MIT Press, 1985).
78. Ibid., pp. 124–125.
79. Ibid.
80. This is of course assuming that most species do not deliberately choose their mating partners in accordance with their perceived morphological similarity to one another.
81. Ibid.
82. Ibid., p. 108.
83. Ibid., p. 98.
84. The WAP thus amounts to a form of natural selection writ large. According to the WAP, our universe consists of a large number of distinct compartments, each differing significantly from the other. Over time, at least one of these compartments is believed to have accidentally evolved the ability of producing intelligent life. The WAP thus alleges that it is our own self-consciousness that selects out the particular subsection of the universe that we presently inhabit.
85. Some thinkers have tried to argue that this same sort of criticism applies to God. This isn't so, however, because God's very definition presumably includes the property of eternal self-existence. Now, if God has been in existence for all eternity, and if He intrinsically contains within Himself the reason for His own existence, then the theist is not guilty of basing his belief on the fallacy of the *reductio ad absurdum*. Matter, on the other hand, is presumably *not* self-replicating by its very nature, so we are compelled to try to discover the origin of this curious property.
86. Paul Davies, *The Cosmic Blueprint*, p, 113.
87. This is just another version of the old Cosmological Argument for the existence of God that was initiated by Plato, and was later given a stamp of approval by Augustine, Aquinas, and a number of other important thinkers. Indeed, there is no doubt that a Divine Primordial Power (assuming that one exists) can itself function as a sufficient explanation for the origin of the twin capacities of self-organization and self-replication found throughout the biosphere. The Deistic Evolutionist is thus in full possession of a potentially sufficient explanation for the origin of these twin properties, provided only that his Divine Creator actually exists. In order for the non-theistic evolutionist's paradigm to be similarly coherent, he too must find an *equally* sufficient explanation for the origin of these twin properties, and not merely a necessary one. It doesn't matter whether this sufficient explanation is only a potentiality, or whether it is an observed reality. The important thing is whether his proposed explanation, if true, would genuinely qualify as a sufficient explanation for these properties.
88. Ibid.
89. Ibid.
90. Ibid.
91. Barrow and Tipler, *The Anthropic Cosmological Principle*, p. 303.
92. Ibid., p. 305.
93. Quoted in Stephen Jay Gould's *Bully for Brontosaurus* (New York: W.W. Norton, 1992), p. 141.
94. Duke of Argyll, *The Reign of Law* (New York: Lovell, n.d.), p. 136.
95. Dawkins, *The Blind Watchmaker*, p. 41.
96. As we have seen, most non-theistic evolutionists understand the word "random," as found in the phrase "random mutation," to refer to the *direction* of adaptive change, not to the actual quality of the changes themselves. Mutations

are random in this sense only if the direction they take is not directly related to prevailing environmental conditions. This of course is a very weak sense of the word "random," as it assumes that the mutations themselves will be "directed" enough to form coherent characters. Thus, the word "random" in this weaker sense doesn't refer to variations that are *totally* unrelated to local environmental conditions.

97. Dawkins, *The Blind Watchmaker*, p. 43.
98. Barrow and Tipler, *The Anthropic Cosmological Principle*, p. 288.
99. Ibid., pp. 302–305.
100. See my *God and the New Cosmology* (Lanham, MD: Rowman and Littlefield, 1993), pp. 42–72.
101. Barrow and Tipler, pp. 302–303.
102. Ibid., p. 305.
103. Ibid.
104. Dawkins, *The Blind Watchmaker*, p. 141.
105. Ibid.
106. See my *God and the New Cosmology*, pp. 37–38.
107. Please refer to Part IV for a suggested explanation as to why God would have chosen to create an opportunistic natural realm, when He presumably could have done otherwise.
108. Dawkins, *The Blind Watchmaker*, p. 41.
109. Errol Harris, *Cosmos and Anthropos*, pp. 81–82.
110. Charles Darwin, *The Origin of Species*, p. 190.

CHAPTER 6

God and the Nature of Perfection

God is a mathematician of a very high order, and He used very advanced mathematics in constructing the universe.

P.A.M. DIRAC

6.1 The Irish Elk

To the neo-Darwinian, virtually every structure and behavior in the biosphere is currently in existence because it has conferred some type of adaptive advantage to its possessor. But if this is indeed the case, how are we to explain the existence of "adaptations" that are obviously detrimental to their possessor?

The classic example of this type of "selection gone mad" is the Irish elk, *Cervas megaceras* (which really wasn't an elk at all, but a deer). For some strange reason, it grew antlers that were a full 12 feet across and weighed nearly a quarter of a ton!

How are we to explain the development of such obviously non-adaptive antlers by the theory of natural selection alone? Overspecialization cannot be accounted for by natural selection *by definition*, since non-adaptive characters would presumably be weeded out by environmental pressures long before they had a chance to grow to the point of threatening the survival of the species. Yet, the orthodox neo-Darwinian theorist has little choice but to credit natural selection for the development of these same non-adaptive characters. But he can't have it both ways: he can't argue that beneficial adaptations are ultimately formed in response to the selective pressures of the environment, and then in the same breath say that these *same* selective pressures can produce structures that are obviously detrimental to survival.

The traditional explanation for the Irish Elk's huge antlers is that it isn't the antlers that are actually selected for; it is increased body size, which is presumably advantageous because it offers greater access to females for mating.[1] Thus, as bigger body sizes were gradually getting favored by natural selection, so were bigger antlers. In fact, as Julian Huxley initially proposed and Stephen Jay Gould has subsequently confirmed, antlers don't increase in size in direct proportion to increased body size. Rather, they increase *allometrically*, meaning they increase at a proportionally faster rate than the body itself does.[2] Hence, a deer that has twice the body size of another deer will have antlers that are significantly *more* than twice as big. This would seem to explain how the Irish Elk's antlers could have gotten to be so gigantic: because it was their increasing body size that was the primary object of natural selection. As their bodies got bigger, their antlers got bigger faster.

Yet, one wonders how natural selection could have allowed the Irish Elk's body and antlers to get so big in the first place, because a significantly smaller deer with much smaller antlers would seem to possess much greater survival value than a larger deer with huge antlers, even though the larger deer might have somewhat greater access to females. Hence, one would expect that as antler size got to be a serious burden, smaller antlers, along with a smaller overall body size, would start to become selected for. Yet, smaller versions of the Irish Elk never took hold, so they eventually died out. This leads us to postulate that perhaps they were *unable* to revert back to smaller overall body sizes, even in response to natural selection. Being thus overburdened with vastly oversized antlers that could not be gotten rid of, the Irish Elk eventually died out.

According to Gould, a possible reason why natural selection may have allowed the Irish Elk's antlers to grow so big is because they were somehow adaptive. Gould conjectures that perhaps they were used for some form of ritualized combat in males. Hence, their function would be "to prevent actual battle (with consequent injuries and loss of life) by establishing hierarchies of dominance that males can easily recognize and obey." And since large antlers "confer high status and access to females, . . . selection pressures for large antlers must often be intense."[3]

Because he sees the Irish Elk's antlers as being primarily adaptive, Gould attributes the extinction of the elk to its inability to adapt to severe climatic changes. Most authors who have considered the fate of the Irish Elk, however, have cited their huge antler size as the reason for their demise, and for good reason: it is hard to see how a set of antlers that spanned 12 feet and weighed several hundred pounds could be unrelated to their extinction, especially since other species of deer *were* able to survive the same climatic changes. It is also hard to see how these oversized antlers could have evolved solely out of selection pressures surrounding ritualized combat and access to females, because one would then expect other species of deer to experience a similar type of overactive antler growth as well. One would also expect there to come a time when hindrance to overall survival would begin to take selective precedence over sexual and ritualistic functions.

That is to say, if natural selection alone is the final arbiter over which structures evolve and which do not, there *had* to have come a point when the advantages conferred by large body size were more than compensated for by the huge antlers. Accordingly, the fact that antler size increases allometrically in relation to body size is immaterial to the basic question at issue here, because it is hard to see how natural selection would allow such maladaptive structures to grow through *any* mechanism, because it is supposed to weed out harmful characters long before they reach such a destructive point. Cambridge zoologist G.S. Carter agrees:

> . . . the enormous size of the antlers of the elk make it difficult to believe that they were evolved by the processes of natural selection. At this size they must have interfered seriously with the activity of the animal, and therefore, one would have thought, have been disadvantageous and removed by selection.[4]

It would seem, then, that any sort of appeal to the doctrine of the "survival of the fanciest" as an explanation for the Irish Elk's huge antler size (in terms of being more appealing to females and hence being reproductively favored) simply won't do in the end, because there is a certain critical point where the overall practicality of large antlers in terms of survival will begin to outweigh their appeal to females. And given the extreme handicap to their everyday level of functioning that seems to have been produced by these huge antlers, this critical point was apparently greatly surpassed by the time the elk became extinct.

With these considerations in mind, perhaps antler size in the Irish Elk *was* in fact an example of an orthogenetic trend that got "out of hand." Of course, we will probably never know for sure, but we can say one thing with confidence: regardless of what actually went "wrong" with the Irish Elk, natural selection was obviously unable to correct the problem, even by encouraging the existence of smaller-bodied animals.

But if the Irish elk's antlers were probably not evolved by natural selection alone, where did they come from? On the surface, it would seem that we cannot appeal to the creative activity of a Grand Designer, because it is hard to imagine why He would create (even indirectly) such obviously detrimental things in the first place. However, we mustn't eliminate the possibility that there may in fact be another purpose to the creation besides mere survival or perfect adaptation *per se*. If we assume that this world was never meant to be a hedonistic paradise, where all humans are supposed to be completely happy all the time, it may be the case that this type of "imperfection" also extends to the animal world as well. If so, then perfect adaptation in and of itself cannot be used as a yardstick for judging whether or not the world has in fact been created (either directly or indirectly) by a Supreme Being.

6.2 The Nature of Perfection

In *Time Frames*, Niles Eldredge examines this so-called "imperfection" in the natural world and comes to the conclusion that it constitutes *ipso facto* evidence that a perfect Creator could not have designed the animal kingdom. Gould shares this basic sentiment, arguing that "the theory of natural selection would never have replaced the doctrine of divine creation if evident, admirable design pervaded all organisms."[5]

Indeed, this is perhaps the greatest single problem most non-theistic scientists have with the prospect that life may have been Intelligently Designed. It is, on the face of it, hard to see how or why an infinitely powerful and intelligent Being would have created such an "imperfect" world, when He presumably could have created a perfect one.

As far as the reality of imperfection in the natural world is concerned, Eldredge and Gould certainly have a point. The world is *full* of examples of practical trade-offs on many different levels. Each extinction, for instance, can be viewed as a type of design "failure," while the reality of death for all creatures seems to constitute the final defeat for any sort of positive Divine Intention in the world. Since this profound degree of imperfection seems to be inconsistent with the notion of an all-knowing and all-powerful Designer, it is tempting to conclude that such a Designer probably does not actually exist.

The problem with this conclusion is that it is based on a very weak premise; namely, that such a Creator would *want* to create a "perfect" world from the start. This assumption is by no means obvious, because a great deal turns on precisely what is meant by the word "perfect." All we can safely assert *a priori* is that such a Being would want to implement His overall Purpose perfectly in the creation. This, of course, is a long way from saying that He would want to create a world that would be perceived as being "perfect" by some of its inhabitants.

As a consequence, we cannot properly conclude that, just because God would want to perfectly implement His Divine Purpose in the world, He would therefore want to create a "perfect" world by our own myopic standards. Such a conclusion doesn't necessarily follow at all. In order to ascertain, then, whether a supernatural Being could have been responsible for the creation of our world, we must first consider the possible nature of God's Purpose in creating the world.

It would be naïve to just blindly assume that this Purpose would have to necessarily entail perfection on all levels of worldly reality, for such an assumption reduces to the expectation that our world should be some sort of hedonistic paradise. As John Hick has aptly pointed out, it is much more reasonable to view our world in terms of its suitability for person-making, not only because such a purpose intrinsically seems more desirable, but also because it seems to be more in line with the basic character of our everyday experience.[6]

If we take Hick's suggestion to heart and substitute "person-making" for "hedonistic paradise" in our conceptualization of a possible Divine Purpose, we find that the only thing God would have wanted to do perfectly in our world is create an environment that is *perfectly suited* towards facilitating this goal of person-making, and this doesn't at all entail the need for each creature to be perfectly designed in and of itself. It only entails that each aspect of the person-making process be perfectly designed *in terms of the larger person-making process itself.* To the extent, then, that imperfectly designed creatures are able to fit perfectly into this larger person-making scheme, they can be considered perfect on a higher level.

On this view, perfection isn't always an absolute property that resides exclusively within any given object or process. It is a relative or relational property that is determined by how well a given object or process serves its intended function in the overall context of its existence. It follows, then, that what may seem like "imperfection" on one level of reality can actually turn out to be perfection on a higher level, when it is viewed in relation to its intended underlying purpose.

My point is simply that we cannot use the fact of "imperfection" in the world as *prima facie* evidence against a Grand Designer. At the most, it can only be used as *prima facie* evidence against a God whose underlying purpose was to create a hedonistic paradise. Assuming, however, the existence of a God whose purpose was to create a world that was optimally designed for person-making, the fact of "imperfection" in the world can instead be used as evidence *for*, and not against, Intelligent Design, because this "imperfection" can be shown to facilitate the person-making process in a wide variety of ways.[7]

Three additional factors help to confirm our suspicion that true perfection in the natural realm encompasses far more than mere survivability *per se*:

1) For animals to be "perfect" in terms of their structural design, they would have to be virtually indestructable and not subject to disease. This would, for all practical intents and purposes, render them immortal, and this in turn would seriously jeapordize our own continued survival on this planet. For if all creatures (including ourselves) were so "well designed" that they never died, animal populations would quickly expand to the point that we would be buried by their sheer numbers. While God could conceivably have made the world larger, or designed the reproductive process to be more self-limiting, it isn't at all clear that the reproductive process could have been any more self-limiting than it already is and still have been functional. Moreover, if these "perfectly designed" creatures had a growth rate that was even slightly positive, they would quickly fill up *any* planet of finite size due to exponential growth patterns. It would seem, then, that the only way a world of "perfect" (i.e., immortal) animals could possibly be maintained is if reproduction itself were eliminated. But this would not only do away with the evolutionary process itself, it would also produce a nightmar-

ish world where humans would live forever, and yet would still be incapable of reproducing. It is hard to see how this could possibly constitute a coherent world at all.

2) Apart from certain "imperfect" biological designs in the world, the overall ecological (and indeed cosmic) order is replete with a level of perfection that we have yet to even approximate in our own engineering.

3) The specific examples used by non-theistic evolutionists to illustrate "imperfection" in the world are themselves too trivial to be taken seriously. For example, Gould cites two circumstances that would be out of place in a world created by a Perfect Designer: a) the fact that marsupials (such as kangaroos) only live in Australia, where they fill the same roles that other placental mammals occupy on the other continents, and b) the fact that the structures used in orchids to ensure fertilization by insects are "jerry-built of available parts used by ancestors for other purposes. Orchids are Rube Goldberg machines; a perfect engineer would certainly have come up with something better."[8]

Concerning the first point, Gould seems to believe that the only rational way to explain the restriction of marsupials to Australia is in terms of an original continental drift, which would have functioned to separate the ancient marsupial ancestors from their mammalian cousins by purely natural means. The Deistic Evolutionist, of course, is fully prepared to accept the validity of this naturalistic explanation, since he also believes that evolution took place through natural cause-and-effect processes. At most, then, the exclusive residence of marsupials in Australia is irrelevant to the question of Intelligent Design in the world, especially if one accepts the Deistic Evolutionist's fundamental premise.

Gould apparently believes that a Grand Designer would have had no persuasive reason to allow marsupials to evolve exclusively on the continent of Australia. Since he can think of no good reason for God to have done so, and since there is a ready-made naturalistic explanation for the phenomenon in terms of continental drift, Gould concludes that a Grand Designer mustn't exist.

The problem with this sort of reasoning is that it places unnecessary restrictions on the possible creative mechanisms God might have used to bring the world into being. For instance, why couldn't God have actually *used* the phenomenon of continental drift as one of his naturalistic tools to separate and distribute the various animals on this planet? There is certainly nothing inherently wrong or contradictory about such an assumption. And as far as God's choice to allow marsupials to evolve only on the continent of Australia is concerned, what consequence does such a Decision ultimately come to? For all we know, there might be something endemic to Australia exclusively that is vital for marsupial well-being. Or, for that matter, the choice of Australia as the marsupials' home could have been purely arbitrary. Either way, the argument for Intelligent Design is not damaged one bit. Gould's charge thus turns out to be yet another red herring, which is designed to distract us from the reality of design that is evident throughout the world.

What this type of "scientific" objection comes down to isn't a criticism of the fact of design *per se*, but rather the *type* of design that is actually observed in the world. It is hard for materialistic scientists to see why a supernatural God would have resorted to a long and drawn-out evolutionary process to create the world, when presumably He could have created the whole thing instantaneously. But surely this lack of scientific comprehension cannot be used to argue that such a God does not exist, because the possibility remains that our conception of how a Supreme Being should create could *itself* be in error. On this latter view, it is Gould's conception of how an omnipotent God should have created the world that is in need of revision; not the question of Intelligent Design *per se*.

As far as orchids are concerned, what ultimate difference does it make whether orchids are "jerry-built" out of parts that were used by their ancestors for other purposes? Perhaps God found these basic designs to be so practical and efficient that He opted to use them for other purposes in later generations of orchids. To be sure, versatility of structural design is almost always an indication of intelligent contrivance and ingenuity, not fortuitous self-assembly. For instance, we use the wheel in a wide variety of functional applications because it is an extremely useful structure that can serve a wide variety of purposes. It would be foolish to the highest degree to try to use a different structure for each of these purposes, when a standard wheel would do the job just as good, or better. There is thus no *a priori* reason to believe that an Intelligent Designer would have used different structures to serve different purposes in the orchid; that is, as long as previously-used structures would have sufficed.

If anything, we would expect *a priori* that an Intelligent Designer would have wanted to *reuse* pre-existing structures to serve other functions in His creatures, in the interest of maintaining the structural integrity of the overall biological gestalt. Even the simplest organism is comprised of a profoundly complicated interplay of many different interconnecting structures, none of which can be significantly altered without seriously altering the cohesiveness of the biological whole. For all we know, God would have had to have completely redesigned each organism if any given structure were to have been totally replaced by an entirely different structure. This of course would have had the effect of *preventing* a given species from naturally evolving into another species, because it would have destroyed the natural cohesiveness of the evolutionary process itself.

It appears, then, that the naturalistic process of evolution from a common ancestor *requires* that the same structures be used over and over again as much as possible, so that the structural distance between evolutionary "jumps" can be as short as possible. If new structures were to be used each time a novel function is indicated in a new creature, this naturalistic process of common descent would be impossible because the damage to the cohesiveness of each organism would be sufficient to require a separate creation for each species.

Once again Gould appears to be projecting his own preconceived ideas concerning a possible creation onto his interpretation of the available evidence. If all Gould intends to show is that the various species were not all created instantaneously by Divine Fiat, he has largely succeeded (although a God creating in this manner could still have used the same structures over and over again because of their intrinsic usefulness). But this says nothing at all about whether God chose to create the biosphere through natural evolutionary pathways.

Gould claims that if an Intelligent Designer were to have actually been responsible for the creation, He "almost surely would have come up with a better design." This assertion is far from obvious, however, because the only relevant criterion for reaching a conclusion on this matter—the success of the organism as a whole—argues *against* Gould's position, because all the organisms Gould discusses have been extremely successful in the wild. The most, then, that Gould has succeeded in doing is rediscovering God's preference for using natural evolutionary processes in His creation.

When compared to the scores of brilliant innovations found throughout the living world, Gould's objections to the prospect of Intelligent Design pale away into insignificance. Why concentrate on the pointless question of marsupial isolation in Australia when there are so many instances of Intelligent Design in kangaroos? Why concentrate on the origin of the various structures in orchids when there are so many other impressive instances of Intelligent Design to be found in them? These "flaws" in the design of the natural world are trivial indeed, and therefore amount to little more than red herrings, whose function is to distract us from the much weightier considerations favoring the prospect of Intelligent Design in the world.

Gould asserts that orchids are "Rube Goldberg machines," and that a Perfect Engineer would almost certainly have come up with a better design. This is a very large assertion indeed, but one that seems to have little or no basis in fact. By what possible criterion could one make such a strong value judgment? By the non-theistic evolutionist's own yardstick of success—ongoing survival through many generations—orchids have been very successful indeed. It would seem, then, that Gould's value judgment boils down to a single issue that has nothing at all to do with success *per se*: he doesn't believe that the evolutionary history of orchids is consistent with the creative activity of a Grand Designer, or, more accurately, with *his* conception of how a Grand Designer would in fact operate. God does indeed work in mysterious ways, as the old saying goes, and apparently one of these mysterious ways has been His choice to create the world through gradual evolutionary pathways. But surely this choice in and of itself does not constitute sufficient reason for concluding that the design of the orchid could possibly be improved upon. If the orchid has been successful enough to survive for hundreds of thousands of years, then what ultimate difference does it make whether it was created directly *ex nihilo*, or indirectly, through a gradual process of self-driven evolution?

Concerning Gould's designation of orchids as Rube Goldberg machines, he apparently means to say that they utilize a needlessly complex apparatus to accomplish a relatively simple end result. Again, this is a strong value judgment that seems to have little or no basis in fact. While it is possible that orchids could have achieved the same result in a much simpler way, it is also possible that they could *not* have. We need to be very careful when we second-guess nature's creative hand; more often than not, human-inspired "improvements," if they could be enacted at all, would end up being detrimental to the world system in the long run, because in our finitude we are simply not aware of the tens of thousands of variables that constantly impinge on the botanic world. For all we know, orchids *need* to be this elaborate in order to achieve their particular function in the world. With these things in mind, prudence suggests that we reserve critical judgment on the orchid until all the facts are in.

By calling orchids Rube Goldberg machines, Gould also seems to be implying that they end up accomplishing a relatively simple or trivial purpose. But what trivial purpose could possibly be ascribed to them? Not only do they serve their ecological function in the environment in impeccable fashion, they also help to increase the overall beauty content of the world as well. But even if we concede, for the sake of argument, that orchids *are* Rube Goldberg machines, they are nevertheless machines that accomplish a clear purpose, and purposeful machines *require* an intelligent engineer for their design.

It would seem, then, that the very designation of the orchid as a Rube Goldberg machine contains the hidden assumption that, whatever else the orchid may be, it is *still* an intelligently designed machine. Certainly no one would want to assert that Rube Goldberg's actual machines were not themselves intelligently designed! But if this is true, and if orchids are similar to Rube Goldberg machines, then it follows that *they too* must be intelligently designed as well, whether or not one actually agrees with the content of their design.

It should further be pointed out that while there may in fact be a good deal of "imperfection" in the natural world, living systems are still the most complex (i.e., perfect) things in the entire known universe. While Eldredge may assert that living creatures are for the most part "relatively inefficient machines," the fact is, they are by far the most efficient energy-harvesting machines we know of! All things considered, living systems are able to harvest energy from glucose at approximately a 40 percent level of efficiency, compared with a figure of around 25 percent for the most efficient man-made systems known. Even more impressive is the fact that there are no unrecyclable waste products generated by the biosphere at all. The toxins that are produced by living creatures are totally recycled back into the environment by other living systems, and this is certainly far more than can be said for any of the factories that man has ever made. *This fact in and of itself constitutes clear evidence of Intelligent Design.* If perfection is the issue, the level of perfection regularly seen in living systems *vastly exceeds* our limited ability to fully comprehend it. Accordingly, Eldredge's assertion that that living systems are "relatively inefficient machines" must be dismissed as mere wishful thinking.[9]

As E.M. Namay has pointed out, one cannot properly accuse *anything* of imperfection unless one first has an idea of what perfection actually is. Presumably Gould and Eldredge have in mind some idea of what perfection in the animal world might theoretically consist of, but if we exclude individual and species immortality as being unreasonable, and if we assume the prior existence of the evolutionary process in the overall cosmic scheme, it is hard to even *imagine* what form this "perfection" might take. In the end, Gould and Eldredge's criticisms seem to boil down to the simple observation that the facts surrounding the evolution of life do not seem to be consistent with the way they think an omnipotent God would have created the world (assuming, of course, the prior existence of such a God). But surely this cannot suffice as a legitimate criticism of God's alleged choice to create the world in this evolutionary manner, because it is certain that we are *not* aware of all the factors that were involved in God's decision to create the world the way He did.[10]

In the final analysis, we must agree with Philip Johnson's comment that:

> The task of science is not to speculate about why God might have done things this way, but to see if a material cause can be established by empirical investigation. If evolutionary biology is to be a science rather than a branch of philosophy, its theorists have to be willing to ask the scientific question: *How can Darwin's hypothesis of descent with modification be confirmed or falsified?*[11]

Significantly, this question has never been seriously addressed in the scientific community, because it has been a foregone conclusion since the days of Darwin that (non-theistic) evolutionary theory is itself a *fact*.

6.3   Could God Have Done Better?

It is ironic that Gould has chosen to attack the various levels of design found throughout the animal kingdom, because elsewhere[12] he has argued that the best definition of biological "fitness" is in terms of "good design," and not in terms of mere survival *per se*. This distinction is critical, because as we have seen, if biological fitness is defined as "those creatures who in fact survive," natural selection reduces to a meaningless tautology (the survival of those who survive).

But surely it is the height of inconsistency to define fitness in terms of good design, and then in the same breath to say that an Intelligent Designer would have been able to do a better job in creating the world. Gould even goes so far as to argue for a definition of fitness that parallels "an engineer's criterion of good design."[13] But if one believes that certain creatures are designed well enough from an engineering point of view to survive the rigors of natural selection (as Gould clearly does), how can it possibly be asserted that an Intelligent Designer would have been able to do a better job? The only way this accusation could possibly be true is if *all* creatures were designed well enough to survive nature's selective hand, but if this were in fact the case, there wouldn't be any evolution at all in the higher sense, since there wouldn't be any preferred survival of the most well-adapted creatures.

Worse yet, this type of "good design" would quickly result, as we have seen, in the earth being overrun with these "perfectly designed" creatures, so much so, in fact, that there wouldn't be any more room for new creatures (like humans) to evolve and grow. A larger planet wouldn't solve the problem, because these "well-designed" creatures would quickly fill up *any* planet of finite size (due to exponential growth patterns). This wouldn't be evidence of better design; it would be *hell*.

It doesn't appear, then, that an Intelligent Designer could have done a better job of creating the biosphere at all and still have had a world where there was room for individual existence and growth. The most, then, that can coherently be meant by Gould's accusation is that our world isn't yet perfect on all conceivable levels, and this is something the Deistic Evolutionist is fully prepared to admit (because he believes that the world is "imperfect" for a Higher Reason.)

6.4   More on the True Nature of Perfection

As we have seen, perfection is not always a static commodity to be understood only in relation to itself. It is, rather, a holistic concept. That is to say, a thing can be perfect, not in terms of its own structure, but in terms of its contribution to a larger whole. It follows from this definition that what appears to be "imperfect" on one level of reality can often turn out to be perfect when it is viewed from a higher level.

To illustrate, consider the example of a father who disciplines his young son for violent behavior. The son will undoubtedly view his father's behavior as being grossly imperfect. From our larger perspective, though, we realize that the father's behavior is actually quite justifiable, and is even "perfect" in a way, because it will hopefully end up making the son a better person in the long run. The higher purpose of facilitating the boy's growth is thus the appropriate point of reference for judging perfection in this case.

In the same way, much of the imperfection that we see in our world is actually justifiable (and therefore perfect in this sense) when it is viewed from the Higher Perspective of God's presumed Purpose in creating the world: that of providing an optimal environment for human growth. Unfortunately, due to the intrinsic limitations of the Human Definition, it doesn't appear as though this purpose could have been achieved without a certain amount of apparent imperfection in the world. On this view, our world is "imperfect" only when it is viewed up close, in terms of its own self. This imperfection vanishes, though, when the world is viewed from the Higher Perspective of God's Developmental Intentions for man. From this perspective, our world is indeed the very pinnacle of perfection, because it perfectly accomplishes God's Higher Purpose for man.

Actually, this issue of a less-than-perfect creation is just another manifestation of the age-old problem of evil, which humans have been grappling with for centuries. Although an in-depth discussion of this problem is beyond the scope of this book, it should be pointed out that the existence of evil has been probed by some of the most logically rigorous minds in the history of the planet, and has been shown to be logically compatible with the existence of a good and all-powerful God.[14] Notre Dame's Alvin Plantinga, for instance, has analyzed the problem of evil in mind-numbing detail utilizing the rigors of modal logic, and has concluded that the apparent existence of evil is *not* logically incompatible with the existence of a good and all-powerful God.[15]

Indeed, as John Hick has pointed out, the problem of evil (represented in this case by malformed adaptations) is irreconcilable with the goodness of God only as long as one insists on viewing this world as a would-be hedonistic paradise. Scottish philosopher David Hume made this same mistake long ago; he saw the earth as simply a home for humans, and nothing more, and concluded that a good God would never have created such a poorly designed house (in the sense of all the evil in contains). Again, though, such a conclusion contains the prior assumption that the purpose of the world is to be a perfect paradise. But what if the purpose of the world isn't pleasure at any cost, but *instruction*? What if we're all here, not to languish in a perfect paradise, but to learn through the painful process of trial and error, so that we can grow into a more mature state of being? If this is the case, then we need to take another look at presumed "evils" like the flu or even cancer, because the fact is, suffering is the most potent motivating factor of all in human life. Indeed, the prospect of suffering seems to be implicit in the very process of self-directed growth from humble beginnings. Immaturity implies the lack of full character assembly, and a lack of full character assembly seems to be subjectively unpleasant in and of itself, insofar it is represents a critical diminution of our own innermost being. This unpleasantness in turn has the power to motivate us on to higher and higher levels of development, through a process of negative reinforcement: the more we grow, the more pain and suffering that is removed from our innermost lives, and the better we feel as a consequence. On this view, necessity is not only the mother of invention; it is also the mother of character growth as well, because people typically grow only when they *have* to.

A brief perusal of the various aspects of human life reveals that most day-to-day experiences can be understood to possess some degree of growth-facilitating functionality by their very nature. Take the human body for instance. It certainly needs to be functional enough to enable most individuals to live a relatively normal life, yet it mustn't be so functional as to take away one's consciousness from the more important things in life, such as one's psychospiritual development vis-à-vis the Kingdom of God. On this view, if the body was made *too* well, we would stand in danger of becoming complacent about those issues that ultimately matter in our lives. The body's imperfections, then, can be understood as serving the higher purpose of not allowing us to be too content in our present sinful condition, and this encourages us to make a greater effort towards effecting our own maximal development. It is in this larger growth-facilitating sense that the "imperfections" of the body can nevertheless be considered to be "perfect." The vast majority of other "evils" in life can be shown to intrinsically possess a similar growth-facilitating function.

But if such presumably negative things as pain and suffering can be thought of in a positive light, then perhaps the apparent "failures" of the animal kingdom, like the gigantic antlers of the Irish elk, can be thought of differently as well. It is possible that the many extinctions of the past could simply be the evolutionary "price" that must be paid in any type of naturalistic evolutionary process; for every species that survives, it may be the case that a certain number of others must be sacrificed.

It is also possible that the fundamental dynamics surrounding the evolution of the various animal forms have a deeper sense of importance or meaning, in terms of God's original Purpose for creating the world. If we grant that this Purpose may have something to do with human beings, then it could be that the animals evolved the way they did, and currently are the way they are, in order to fulfill this weak anthropocentric Purpose.[16]

6.5 The Democracy of Extinction

According to David M. Raup, a statistical paleontologist at the University of Chicago, approximately 99.9 percent of all the species that have ever lived on this planet are now extinct.[17] This is an astounding figure that clearly illustrates the tremendous scope of extinction in the overall evolutionary process.

For many people, however, this overwhelming incidence of extinction is somehow equated with failure—the failure of millions of species to survive throughout the millennia. This in turn is taken to be evidence that an all-powerful God could not have been responsible for creating our world, because such a prodigious Being presumably would never have created so many design "failures" to begin with.

Such a belief, of course, is based on the prior assumption that long life, or even species immortality, was God's primary purpose in creating the world. It is clear, however, that such an assumption doesn't necessarily follow from the mere positing of an Intelligent Designer. It doesn't even seem to be a plausible assumption, because there are a number of severe problems associated with a world where the various species are immortal. The most important of these problems has to do with the total number of species that can introduced into the world over a certain length of time. If species were immortal, then this total would necessarily be restricted to the maximum number of species that could inhabit the earth at any one time. This would in all likelihood have been catastrophic for us, because our evolution was apparently contingent on the prior extinction of the dinosaurs.

In light of this consideration, is it reasonable to view the extinction of the dinosaurs as a failure of God's Creative Design? Is it really evidence of failure when one species is allowed to die out so that another can take its place? To a certain extent, this can be considered to be a natural form of "democracy" in action.[18]

This raises one final point: what possible right do we have to accuse God of failing on behalf of all the extinctions in the past when right now, we humans are wiping out species from the face of the earth at the unprecedented rate of one a minute?! It is therefore incumbent upon us that we solve *our own* problem of species-murdering *before* we accuse God of being a species-murderer as well.[19]

6.6 On the Compatibility Between the Natural and the Supernatural

As we have seen, the vast majority of apparent imperfections in the world seem to be directly tied to God's choice of evolution as His chief creative tool. On this level, it is possible to see how a Grand Designer can co-exist with these "imperfections," which seem to speak of "a natural process, based on environmental complexities and the limitations on just how much can be achieved starting with a given species, rather than the design of a perfect system by a supernatural Designer."[20]

However, while we may be able to affirm the exclusive use of natural cause-and-effect processes in the creation, it does not follow from this affirmation that a naturalistic universe intrinsically *precludes* the existence of a supernatural Creator. To think that it does is to fail to consider the distinct possibility that a supernatural Creator might have created such a naturalistic universe for a Higher Purpose. It is for this reason that the terms "God" and "natural cause-and-effect universe" cannot be considered to be mutually exclusive alternatives.

For some reason, though, the "supernatural" nature of God's Being has been confused with the type of universe He would (or should) have created. It is commonly assumed, for instance, that a supernatural Being would have created a universe in which all events would have had a clearly discernible supernatural cause. But if this were actually the case, how would we ever be capable of *knowing* that these causes were in fact supernatural? A universe of exclusively supernatural causes would lack any identifiable referent for the accurate perception of their true underlying nature. Like the proverbial fish that would be the last creature on earth to discover water, if we ever lived in an exclusively supernatural universe we would probably be too inundated by supernatural events to be able to recognize their true nature.

It is thus possible that our universe could in fact consist entirely of supernatural causes without our being directly aware of it. Moreover, since we are most definitely not all wise, we would necessarily require some sort of perceptual contrast in order to be able to eventually detect this supernatural background.

A two-tiered metaphysical structure, where both the natural and the supernatural could intermingle on a variety of different levels, could conceivably provide this needed contrast.[21] The purpose of this two-tiered structure would be to allow for the perceptual identification of the natural in terms of the supernatural, and vice versa.

To the extent, then, that the natural aspects of physical reality necessarily entail a degree of imperfection to them (in comparison to the more perfect supernatural aspects), it follows that an entirely supernatural universe would intrinsically require a significant degree of imperfection in it if it is to ever be capable of being identified as supernatural by creatures such as ourselves.

A parallel situation exists with the word "good." As Ninian Smart[22] has pointed out, we are only justified in calling people "good" in the overall context of a world in which it is possible to be bad. On this level, goodness presupposes the prior existence of badness. Similarly, the word "supernatural" only seems to have meaning in a universe where the natural exists as well. In this sense, we can't even speak about the supernatural without presupposing the prior existence of some sort of naturalistic cause-and-effect realm.

Now, if we assume the existence of a two-tiered metaphysical structure, where both the natural and the supernatural coexist beside and within one another, it follows that an exclusively naturalistic science would be unable to detect the existence of this supernatural realm, since it would ultimately consist of everything in reality. Its detection, then, would require an *attitudinal* or *perceptual* shift towards the very things that exist all around us, and not the physical discovery of an elusive supernatural realm *per se*. This is why it is a profound mistake for scientists to conclude that a supernatural Creator does not exist, simply because their naturalistic instruments are unable to detect Him! Given the very nature of God's supernaturalness, we should never expect otherwise.

It is one thing for God to be supernatural, but it is quite another to expect the whole of universal reality to openly display this same level of supernaturalness. It would therefore be fallacious to conclude, on the basis of a lack of empirical evidence for God's supernaturalness, that a supernatural God mustn't exist. The supernaturalness of God only refers to God's *own* Being; it makes no necessary reference to the type of universe that such a Being might have created. It is thus entirely possible that a supernatural Being might have created a purely natural universe that operates solely according to natural cause-and-effect processes. Such a creation would be natural, while its Creator would be supernatural.[23] While this type of natural creation might ultimately be comprised of elements that are entirely supernatural, these same elements could easily be put together in such a way that their underlying supernatural nature would not be immediately apparent.

Even so, modern science seems to have stumbled upon the supernatural in several different areas of inquiry. For example, the advent of quantum mechanics has shown that our ordinary conceptions of causality tend to break down at the atomic and subatomic level. Regardless of how hard they try, scientists cannot predict the behavior of quantum particles. Moreover, physicists have learned that the most fundamental building blocks of matter don't seem to have a concrete existence at all. Instead, they seem to have a shadowy, ghost-like reality that only comes into concrete form when they are actually observed by an observer. And yet, despite the seemingly ghost-like, random nature of the subatomic realm, the larger world that we inhabit is both concrete and predictable. How are we to explain this huge discrepancy?

The traditional explanation is that while the activity of a single particle may be random and ghost-like, the activities of trillions of particles *are* predictable to a large extent, because they follow the laws of probability.

But where do the laws of probability themselves come from? And, where do the sub-atomic events *themselves* that the laws of probability describe come from? Science itself has no answer to these fundamental questions, yet any viable explanation of the universe *must* take them into account. To simply accept them as "givens" is to thus avoid the deeper, foundational questions of physical existence that are ultimately at issue here.

For the theist, God Himself is the One who is supporting the activity of subatomic particles, not in the sense of determining their every motion, but in the larger sense of giving them a metaphysical foundation for their existence. This could conceivably explain why their motions seem so random to us: because we can't actually observe how or when He is bringing them into existence (in response to causes that are initiated in our own world). It would also explain how the entire universe is capable of existing, in spite of the apparent fact that an observer needs to be present in order to collapse the all-inclusive universal wave function: in this case God Himself would be the "Ultimate Observer" who would perpetually observe the entire universe into being.

The cause-and-effect nature of the natural world can thus be explained by the postulation that God Himself is supporting quantum reality in such a way as to make all causes result in their own corresponding effects. This was the opinion expressed by the ancient Stoic philosophers, who believed that if God existed at all, He *had* to be the Logical Mediator between cause and effect. They even had a name for such a Mediator: the Logos, or Logical Mediator, whom they thought functioned to create a coherent causal realm. Seen from this perspective, the natural world only has its present cause-and-effect character because a supernatural God is acting "behind the scenes" as the Logical Mediator between every world-based cause and its corresponding effect. To the extent that this hypothesis is true, it would explain why the major religious traditions have consistently urged humans to mend their destructive ways: because each time humans engage in destructive behaviors, they "force" God as Logos to bring about the corresponding logical effect of their actions.[24]

We can now bridge the gap between a supernatural Creator and a natural cause-and-effect world in four separate ways: 1) By suggesting that God Himself is supporting the existence of the entire universe at the subatomic, quantum level, 2) By suggesting that God is using His Universal Observership to bring the shadowy quantum world into existence, 3) By suggesting that one way to understand God's relationship to natural causality in the world is in terms of the Divine Logos, or Logical Mediator, between cause and effect, and 4) By suggesting that in a very real sense, the entire universe may ultimately be supernatural in nature.

This proposed relationship between a supernatural God and a natural world itself raises a further question: Why would a supernatural God deliberately choose to limit His creation to this exclusively naturalistic level, especially given the fact that it has obviously caused a great deal of pain and suffering in the world over the years? According to the Deistic Evolutionist, the answer to this question gets back to the primacy of the human developmental pattern in determining the character of the entire universal order. As we have seen, a world of natural cause-and-effect processes is the optimal type of environment for human psychospiritual development. There are a variety of important reasons for this, many of which will be discussed in the final section of this book. Another reason can be added here: If we humans could invoke the supernatural powers of the universe whenever we desired, so as to overcome the intrinsic limitations of naturalism, this world would be an inconceivably chaotic place where very little, if anything, constructive could ever take place. People only grow when they are forced to struggle against a strong opposing force. Not surprisingly, a physical cause-and-effect world seems to provide an ideal amount of this opposing force.

So we see that a naturalistic world not only has the advantage of facilitating the human developmental process in an optimal fashion; it also has the advantage of preventing irresponsible people from abusing their would-be supernatural powers. It would appear, then, that the underlying structure of the world is eminently reasonable after all, but only when it is viewed from the larger perspective of the human developmental process. On this view, God has created a world that seems to fall short of perfection, but only because it perfectly serves His Purpose on a higher level.

It all boils down to the realization that God's criteria for perfection are not man's (usual) criteria, so we cannot make global accusations concerning these imperfections until these Higher Criteria are duly considered. If anything, our feeble accusations of imperfection in the world are more a reflection of *our own* imperfection than they are of any true imperfection in the natural realm *per se*.

According to the Deistic Evolutionist, everything in our world is "perfect," insofar as all things work together for the good of the entire biosphere, including the human developmental process. It is for this reason that we can join Leibniz in asserting that our world is about as perfect as it's ever going to get, within the larger limitations delineated by God's all-encompassing Cosmic Plan.

Notes

1. Stephen Jay Gould, *Ever Since Darwin* (New York: W.W. Norton and Co., 1977), p. 85.
2. Ibid.
3. Ibid., p. 89.
4. Quoted in Taylor's *The Great Evolution Mystery*, p. 27.
5. Gould, *Ever Since Darwin*, p. 91.

6. See John Hick, *Evil and the God of Love* (New York: Harper and Row, 1977).

7. See John Hick's *Evil and the God of Love*, as well as my own forthcoming *Evil and the Essence of Man* for a fuller discussion of this important subject.

8. Gould, *Ever Since Darwin*, p. 91.

9. If living systems were as inefficient as Eldredge implies they are, it is doubtful that we could have evolved to our present state of complexity in the first place.

10. It is ironic that the most complex things in the entire known universe can be criticized by the very people who are (or should be) most aware of this complexity.

11. Philip Johnson, *Darwin on Trial*, p. 71.

12. Stephen Jay Gould, "Darwin's Untimely Burial—Again!" in *Scientists Confront Creationism*, Laurie R. Godfrey, ed. (New York: W.W. Norton & Co., 1983), p. 143.

13. Ibid.

14. According to David Ray Griffin, logical compatibility alone between God and evil is not enough; what is needed is a theodicy (a defense of God's goodness in the face of evil) that is *plausible*. I would agree wholeheartedly, and plan to devote my entire next work to this all-important issue.

15. See Alvin Plantinga's *The Nature of Necessity* (New York: Oxford University Press, 1974) and *God, Freedom, and Evil* (Grand Rapids: William B. Eerdmanns Publishing Company, 1974).

16. I don't mean to imply that the *only* value the animals might possess is in terms of how they can be used or exploited by humans. To the contrary, it would seem that all living things have their own *intrinsic* value. But this doesn't necessarily negate the possibility that the primary purpose for the animals would be to serve man. Indeed, it would only be by some sort of addition to, or subtraction from, their intrinsic value that humans could be stimulated to feel love or compassion for any given creature. In this sense, the intrinsic value possessed by the animals would be *synergistic* with the value they serve in relation to human beings.

17. David M. Raup, *Extinction: Bad Genes or Bad Luck?* (New York: W.W. Norton & Co., 1991), pp. 3–4.

18. Hopefully, there are no more species on the way that will end up displacing the human species! But even if there are, we will probably beat them to the task by displacing *ourselves* first, either through a self-induced ecological catastrophe or through an all-out nuclear holocaust.

19. Although God must ultimately be responsible for creating man in his present sinful condition, He still cannot be blamed for it, under the assumption that there was simply no other way to create a human-like being besides the way He chose. Had God created us in such a way that we would have been guaranteed not to sin, we would have been little more than pre-programmed robots, with no spontaneity of spirit and no capacity for moral goodness. By all accounts this would have been far worse for us overall. Thus, the only possible object for blame concerning the origin of human sinfulness turns out to be the eternal realm of Platonic Possibilities, which seems to have played the largest role in dictating the type of world that we could realistically inhabit.

20. Niles Eldredge, *Time Frames*, p. 148.

21. The Deistic Evolutionist believes that all of reality is ultimately supernatural in nature. He further believes that it is only within God's deliberate contrivance of a natural cause-and-effect world that this supernatural nature becomes obscured.

22. Ninian Smart, "Omnipotence, Evil, and Supermen," *Philosophy*, Vol. XXXVI, No. 137 (1961), pp. 190–191.

23. As David Ray Griffin has pointed out, this type of creation would only be natural in the sense of operating according to natural cause-and-effect processes, not in the sense of *existing* naturally, apart from the creative fiat of God Himself.

24. It isn't as if humans are capable of "forcing" God to do something against His Will. Rather, as a direct consequence of God's free election to impart a certain amount of theological freedom to humankind, we by hypothesis have the capacity for initiating destructive causes in the world, and if God as Logos is the Logical Mediator between cause and effect, we find that free-willed humans are indeed capable—by virtue of the power God has freely given them—of indirectly "forcing" God as Logos to produce the resulting effect. This would explain how the God of the Old Testament claims to cause so much death and destruction in the world. He wouldn't *directly* be acting to bring about these destructive events; He would simply be responding to the destructive causes that are initiated by human beings, by *indirectly* bringing about their corresponding natural effects.

CHAPTER 7

The Fossil Record

If the [evolutionary] theory be true, it is indisputable that before the lowest Cambrian stratum was deposited long periods elapsed, as long as, or probably far longer than, the whole interval from the Cambrian age to the present day; and that during these vast periods the world swarmed with living creatures. . . . To the question why we do not find rich fossiliferous deposits belonging to these assumed earliest periods prior to the Cambrian system, I can give no satisfactory answer. . . . The difficulty of assigning any good reason for the absence of vast piles of strata rich in fossils beneath the Cambrian system is very great.

CHARLES DARWIN

7.1 The Nature of the Paleontological Evidence

When most people think of scientific proof for the non-theistic theory of evolution, they think of the "indisputable" fossil record. They see fabulously reconstructed dinosaurs in science museums and then somehow deduce that everything the evolutionists say must be correct. Indeed, Mosby's zoology textbook goes so far as to say that "it would be difficult to make sense out of the evolutionary patterns or classification of organisms without the support of the fossil record. The documentary evidence for evolution as a general process, the progressive changes in life from one geologic era to another, the past distribution of lands and seas, and the environmental conditions of the past . . . are all dependent on what fossils teach us."[1] If fossils are so important, then, what do they *really* teach us about evolution?

To begin with, we need to reiterate the two basic assumptions of non-theistic evolutionism:

1. That every life form that has ever existed on this planet has descended from a common biological ancestor.
2. That widely-differing species ultimately arose directly "out of" other pre-existing species in an entirely unplanned fashion, due solely to the effects of natural selection acting on random micromutations.

As we have seen, there is nothing inherently antitheistic about the assertion that all species are descended from a single common ancestor. Indeed, the weak form of orthogenesis that will be discussed in the next chapter *assumes* such a descent with modification from a common ancestor. The chief problem with non-theistic evolutionism is rather to be found in the actual *mechanism* through which these evolutionary changes took place: non-theistic evolutionists say that these changes were genuinely random in origin, and conclude that they were therefore unplanned in every sense of the word, while the Deistic Evolutionist asserts that there was indeed some form of directionality to the overall evolutionary process.

The main difference between these two basic paradigms is thus to be found in the proposed mechanism of new species production. The orthodox evolutionary view is that new species gradually arose through the cumulative effects of natural selection acting on micromutations. In order for this hypothesis to be true, however, there would have to be an immense variety of transitional fossils to document this slow change. The weak orthogenetic view, on the other hand, proposes that no truly intermediate fossils will ever be found, because of its direct postulation of saltationism in the process of new species production.

The stunning fact of the matter is that very few, if any, transitional fossils have *ever* been found. This is an extremely damaging piece of evidence that renders the entire neo-Darwinian paradigm of slow change obsolete. Even Darwin himself was greatly concerned by this conspicuous lack of transitional fossils in his own day. He was able to overcome this serious threat to his theory by resorting to the presumed incompleteness of the fossil record. His hope was that someday in the future, when a better grasp of fossilized history would be obtained, these critical transitional fossils would eventually turn up.

Today, however, we know otherwise. Not only have no new transitional fossils turned up in the fossil record, we actually seem to have fewer now than we did back in Darwin's time.[2] Although a few evolutionists believe that the fossil record is still incomplete enough to account for this lack of transitional fossils, this belief is effectively disproved by the fact that each new batch of unearthed fossils generally yields specimens that have *already* been catalogued; true intermediate forms are thus almost never obtained with new excavations. This pattern in the fossil record was plainly evident even in Darwin's time, as the following quote by paleontologist Francois Jules Pictet well illustrates:

> Why don't we find these gradations in the fossil record, and why, instead of collecting thousands of identical individuals, do we not find more intermediary forms? To this Mr. Darwin replies that we have only a few incomplete pages in the great book of nature and the transitions have been in the pages which we lack. But why then and by what peculiar rules of probability does it happen that the species which we find most frequently and most abundantly in all the newly discovered beds are in the immense majority of the cases species which we already have in our collections?[3]

As if this weren't enough, the vast preponderance of transitional fossils that *have* presumably been found have been located between minor taxonomic divisions; virtually none have been found between major divisions, such as that between a primitive land mammal and a whale. This pattern holds up throughout the entire living kingdom, yet it is precisely the *opposite* of what orthodox evolutionary theory predicts.[4]

One of the ways in which traditional evolutionists have tried to dismiss this conspicuous lack of transitional fossils is by pointing out that in the immense Precambrian period some 800 million years ago, the vast majority of life forms were non-skeletal in nature, and so could not be expected to have left behind any fossilized remains. Though this "explanation" at first appears to be quite plausible, a deeper inspection reveals a fatal flaw: although the very first intermediate creatures may have been unable to leave fossilized remains, more complex creatures appearing later *should* have been able to leave them. Indeed, if there truly were intermediate life forms during the initial part of evolution, then there *had* to have been creatures that, for example, were "almost" fish but hadn't quite made it yet. These creatures would easily have had bones or shells that could have been fossilized (otherwise they wouldn't have been "almost" fish), and, being intermediate creatures, they would have existed before and during the Cambrian Explosion. But not even one such transitional fossil has *ever* been found.[5] Instead, all of the "missing links" are said to have occurred in the many so-called "gaps" in the fossil record.

Thus, the sudden appearance of complex phylogenies during the "Cambrian Explosion" some 600 million years ago remains a complete mystery to the orthodox evolutionist. He simply cannot explain the sudden appearance of so many complex life forms seemingly "out of nowhere," fully formed and ready for life, within the confines of his existing theory.

George Gaylord Simpson has called this sudden Cambrian appearance "the major mystery in the history of life."[6] He has even gone so far as to claim that two-thirds of evolution was over by the time the first fossils were deposited.[7]

The 1977 discovery of fully developed heterostracan vertebrate fish in the Upper Cambrian rock deposits of Wyoming has only made the situation worse for the traditional neo-Darwinian picture. Prior to this discovery, which was reported in the May 5, 1978 issue of *Science* magazine, it was believed that the vertebrates did not make their initial appearance in the fossil record until the Lower Ordovician, some 450 to 500 million years ago. Now that they have been officially placed in the Upper Cambrian, the startling fact of the matter is that *every major phylum is now represented in the Cambrian stata.*[8]

What we have, then, is a three-pronged evolutionary process that is the exact opposite of what traditional neo-Darwinian theory would predict.

First, all the basic body plans that were to ever exist on this planet are known to have suddenly appeared at the beginning of the Cambrian Period. These were followed by long periods of stasis and large numbers of extinctions. Most importantly, all subsequent instances of evolutionary diversification are known to have taken place *within these pre-existing phyla*. No new phyla are thought to have evolved after this point, even though over 600 million years were available for them to develop in. The historical record is thus one of sudden appearance, followed by relatively minor structure and function changes.

At one time it was argued that the crucial Precambrian strata, which would have contained the intermediate fossils leading up to the fully-formed Cambrian creatures, had somehow eroded or metamorphosized away, causing all traces of the Precambrian fossils to vanish as well. This was originally called the "Laplalian Interval," and it was used to make the doctrine of gradualism more consistent with the sudden appearance of the various Cambrian phyla. Today, however, we know that there are no such geological intervals spoiling the fossil record, as there are several known instances where up to 5000 feet of Precambrian strata continuously grade into the Cambrian, with no evidence at all of erosion or geological metamorphosis.[9]

It is for this reason that even Gould himself, one of the most heroic supporters of the neo-Darwinian dogma, has publicly stated that "the failure to find a clear 'vector of progress' in life's history . . . [is] . . . the most puzzling fact of the fossil record."[10]

Evolutionists have been telling us for years that there are untold numbers of "missing links" in the fossil record, which supposedly document the gradual change of one species into another, and which are just waiting to be found. The fact is, though, that "the fossil record does not convincingly document a single transition from one species to another."[11]

It is at this point that we can begin to see evidence of an obvious theoretical contrivance in neo-Darwinian thought that has deliberately been designed to accommodate these "missing links" in the fossil record. Since, according to their theory, there *must* be missing links in the fossil record, evolutionists have been forced to conclude that there must be gaps in the fossil record as well, otherwise the missing links would surely have been found by now. But what if there *never were* any missing links? This would explain why there appear to be so many "gaps" in the fossil record: because evolutionists would have been looking in vain for something that never existed to begin with! On this view, paleontology's modern "gap" theory is nothing more than an *ad hoc* revision of the basic neo-Darwinian thesis, whose function has been to simply accommodate the puzzling lack of missing links within the existing theory.

In retort, the traditional evolutionist will typically argue that missing links are rare in the fossil record because the transitional species themselves are extremely rare. But why should transitional species themselves be rare? One would think that precisely the opposite would be the case, since a significant number of transitional forms would have to exist in order to produce each concrete species observed in the fossil record.

But even if we assume, for the sake of argument, that transitional species were themselves rare, this "explanation" amounts to little more than an empty tautology, which is designed to save the evolutionary theory from empirical disconfirmation:

> If evolution is true then indeed the intermediates must be very rare. But unfortunately we can only know that evolution is true *after* we have found the transitional types! The explanation relies on belief in evolution in the first place. . . . We save evolution because we believed in it in the first place.[12]

Darwin, as we have seen, relied upon the presumed incompleteness of the fossil record to explain why no transitional fossils had yet been discovered. Yet, even he felt compelled to admit in the *Origin* that "the case at present must remain inexplicable and may be truly argued as a valid argument against the views here entertained."[13]

Judging from their profound lack of success thus far, it seems likely that paleontologists will *never* be able to find their much sought-after missing links. Indeed, by many modern accounts, the fossil record is *already* more or less complete in its present format.[14] Yet, we have even fewer transitional fossils today that we did in Darwin's time, because a number of fossils that were once thought to be genuine intermediates have turned out not to be. But if neo-Darwinism were actually true, we would have expected the fossil evidence for evolution to have continually increased in direct proportion to the number of specimens that were collected. Significantly, precisely the opposite has turned out to be the case.

The evolutionary faithful have chosen to deal with this fatal exposé of their theory by proposing a new theory based on overall stasis, or species stability, punctuated by relatively brief periods of rapid change. Appropriately dubbed the theory of "punctuated equilibria," this new view attempts to accommodate gradualism within the apparent confines of punctuationalism by asserting that each change in species was only rapid in terms of geological time. For instance, the punctuationalists are saying that it may have only taken a few hundred thousand years for a given species to evolve, instead of several million, and this turns out to be a mere tick of the earth's geologic clock. But even if this were true, there would nevertheless have been millions of intermediate creatures throughout evolutionary history that would have left behind a large number of transitional fossils. Yet, no such transitional fossils have ever been found. Based on this hard, inescapable fact, it would appear as though the *ad hoc* attempt to accomodate gradualism within the confines of punctuationalism is doomed to failure. Not all species, however, originated during the Cambrian Explosion. In fact, a great many species, including our own *Homo sapiens*, did not originate until much later, so how did *they* develop? According to the non-theistic evolutionist, one species gradually grew out of another solely through the action of natural selection working on random genetic mutations, until eventually all the species, including *Homo sapiens*, were created. But if this really happened, where are the transitional fossils to prove it?

These mandatory transitional fossils have been called the "missing links" to non-theistic evolutionary theory, as we have seen. They are missing links because they are supposed to represent the intermediate fossils between species that have never been found, and they are mandatory because without them non-theistic evolutionary theory is as good as dead. Consider what evolutionary scientist John Moore[15] has to say about the importance of these transitional fossils:

> The very essence of evolutionary thinking is slow change. Therefore a major prediction from the General Theory of Evolution would be that researchers would expect to find a record of *gradual transition* from the least complex to the complex. This is the major prediction from the general theory. In fact, if the General Theory of Evolution ever has any empirical basis, such a gradual transition of fossils *must* be found.
>
> In other words, systematic or regular gaps must be *absent* from the fossil record, and transitional forms at some stage between all phyla, orders, families, genera, and species must be found. Such transitional forms must be found if the General Theory of Evolution, defined already as amoeba to man, has occurred. Of course, to be fair, one must admit that some sporadic gaps might be expected in the fossil record. The geological record is not complete. However, there must be *no regular or systematic gaps* in the fossil record.[16]

Indeed, as we saw in the epigraph to this chapter, not even Darwin himself could understand why the fossil record didn't support his theory. He simply thought that the existing record of his time was incomplete; he therefore believed that his theory could survive on the hope that one day in the future these transitional fossils would eventually be found. Today, however, there are even *fewer* fossil specimens supporting the neo-Darwinian concept of slow change than existed in Darwin's time.[17]

Even the New York Times has acknowledged this persistent lack of missing links in the fossil record:

> The chief puzzle in the record of life's history on earth . . . [is] . . . the sudden appearance, some 600 million years ago, of most basic divisions of

the plant and animal kingdoms. There is virtually no record of how these divisions came about. Thus the entire first part of evolutionary history is missing.[18]

What are we to conclude from all of this? Namely, that "where there should be hundreds of millions of transitional links, *there are none.* . . . This fact cannot be overemphasized. There are clear-cut distinctions from specie to specie, both in the fossil record and in the study of contemporary species. If evolution occurred [in the traditionally conceived manner], there would be no such clear-cut distinctions. There would instead be a gradual connection more or less among all life. There would have to be billions and billions of fossil records of these gradual connections [links], and there would have to be millions upon millions of observable living links today. The truth is, however, that there is not one single fossil or one living example of a gradual connection. There is no missing link. Evolutionists lie or don't know the truth if they say otherwise."[19]

In view of these facts, Denton goes so far as to conclude that it is the anti-evolutionists who are actually more empirically-based than their traditional evolutionary colleagues, because their ideas are in full agreement with virtually all the scientific evidence that has been discovered thus far.

Whatever the initial source of its appeal, the concept of the continuity of nature has always suffered the enormous drawback in that at no time throughout the whole history of Western thought, from the first glimmerings of the idea on Ionia, through its theological phase in the eighteenth century, right up to its latest manifestation in twentieth-century Darwinian thought, has it been possible to provide any direct observation or empirical evidence in its support. Put simply, no one has ever observed the interconnecting continuum of functional forms linking all known past and present species of life. The concept of the continuity of nature has existed in the mind of man, *never* in the facts of nature. In a very real sense, therefore, advocacy of the doctrine of continuity has always necessitated a retreat from pure empiricism, and contrary to what is widely assumed by evolutionary biologists today, it has always been the anti-evolutionists, not the evolutionists, in the scientific community who have stuck rigidly to the facts and adhered to a more strictly empirical approach.

The idea that it was the opponents of evolution who were blinded by the error of *a priorism* is one of the greatest myths of twentieth-century biology. If anyone was blinded, it was the seekers after the phantom of continuity. How could it be otherwise when they admitted as did Darwin himself that the crucial evidence in the form of connecting links was emphatically absent? Can we accuse anti-evolutionists like Agassiz of "looking down the wrong road," a phrase used recently by Mayr, when the evolutionists themselves conceded that in the last analysis nature provided no direct empirical support for their views? If the evolutionists were "looking down the right road" it was certainly not a road derived directly from the facts of nature.[20]

7.2 Punctuated Equilibria and the Cambrian Explosion

In *Ever Since Darwin*, Stephen Jay Gould discusses the story of Roderick Murchison, who is said to have given up fox hunting to become a scientist. When Murchison learned that the first major stocking of the earth's oceans took place abruptly, and not through the gradual transformation of one marine species into another, he was pleased, because he was a creationist, and he interpreted this "Cambrian explosion" as direct evidence for an Intelligent Creator.

Darwin was aware of this seeming discrepancy in the fossil record, but he simply attributed it to an inherent imperfection with the fossils themselves, speculating that perhaps the various continents collected no sediments during Precambrian times. Gould in turn assures us that Darwin has since been vindicated in his beliefs, since "Cambrian life did arise from organic antecedents, not from the hand of God."[21]

But why does there have to be such a mutually exclusive dichotomy between: a) the idea that Cambrian life may have arisen from "organic antecedents," and b) the idea that Cambrian life may have directly arisen from the "Hand of God"? Why can't the Hand of God *Itself* create life from organic antecedents? Indeed, in its proclamation that the earth "brought forth" living creatures (Gen. 1:24), the Bible itself seems to directly acknowledge the possibility that God may have regularly used organic antecedents to do His creating.[22]

In reference to the existing fossil record, though, Gould reassures us that "we would have no science without the foundation that these data provide."[23] Yet, a bit later, he admits that "we haven't the slightest idea why the eukaryotic cell arose when it did more than 2 billion years after the evolution of [its] prokaryotic ancestors . . . Speculation may be intriguing, but we have little concrete to say about the [initial cause for the] increase."[24]

The fact of the matter is that scientists have no concrete evidence whatsoever supporting their claim that the Cambrian explosion was not due, either directly or indirectly, to the "Hand of God." How then can they make such bold anti-theistic assertions in the holy name of science? It is one thing to see how the Principle of Objectivity might require that all references to God, both positive and negative, be left out of science altogether, but it is equally clear that many members of the non-theistic evolutionary community are *not* abiding by this fundamental rule. To the contrary, these individuals are claiming to know for a fact that life did *not* arise from the Hand of God. This direct violation of the Principle of Objectivity directly invites confrontation and criticism by both theists and deists, and only functions to deepen the existing schism between science and religion.

Non-theistic scientists should try to be more careful with their sweeping claims about God, especially when these claims aren't supported by the least bit of genuine scientific evidence. Indeed, as Karl Popper has pointed out, assertions that are not falsifiable in principle cannot even claim to be legitimately scientific. Popper goes so far as to argue that Darwinism can, at best, only be considered to be a "metaphysical framework" for the establishment of other genuinely testable theories.[25]

Gould errs when he assumes that God would never have used "organic antecedents" to do His creating. There is certainly nothing in the Bible to support such a belief. Indeed, as we have seen, there is evidence to the contrary, since in the first chapter of Genesis both the earth and the seas are commanded to "bring forth" living creatures. This can be taken to mean that the natural processes that are inherent in both the earth and the seas somehow worked together to "bring forth" living creatures. And as we have already seen, there is good reason for believing that God creates through natural "evolutionary" pathways whenever He possibly can. Hence, it is quite probable that God really did use organic antecedents to generate the Cambrian Explosion.

In order to bring his neo-Darwinist way of thinking more in line with the fossil record, Gould has proposed an S-shaped sigmoidal curve to explain the "sudden" nature of the Cambrian Explosion (see Fig. 7.1). He argues that the building blocks for the Cambrian Explosion were actually in the making for a substantial length of time before the explosion actually took place, but because they were still in the process of getting formed, they were unable to immediately become translated into hoardes of creatures. But then, once everything was set in place, the explosion took off, creating the vertical part of the sigmoidal curve that describes the natural population growth of the various Cambrian species.

Taken by itself, Gould's employment of a sigmoidal curve to represent the events of the Cambrian Explosion appears to be an appropriate depiction of the known facts. It is important to note, however, that a sudden Divinely-Inspired Event (which could have occurred either through a sudden creation by Divine Fiat or through the spontaneous unmasking of pre-existing genetic information) could have had precisely the same effect that Gould describes with his sigmoidal curve. In this case, the slow "lag" phase of the curve would correspond either to direct Divine Intervention, or to the sudden unmasking of the appropriate evolutionary sequences, and this, in turn, would have resulted in the original stock of Cambrian sea creatures. The fast "log" phase of the curve, on the other hand, would correspond to the rapid proliferation of these creatures to fill the wide open niches in the earth's primordial seas. Then, after these creatures would have reproduced

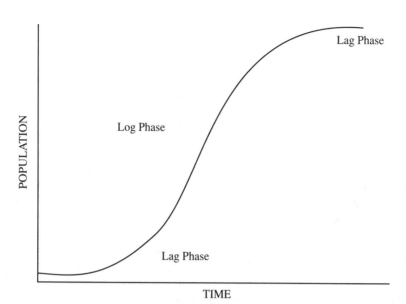

Fig. 7.1: A Sigmoidal Curve Representing a Typical Growth Pattern

to the point of filling most of these available niches, the explosion would have tapered off into the final lag phase of the curve.

According to the Deistic Evolutionist, Gould goes wrong, not in his use of the sigmoidal curve *per se* to represent the dynamics of the Cambrian explosion, but rather in his explanation of *how* this relatively sudden event took place. Even Gould himself admits that though "we may deny the Cambrian problem by casting it back upon an earlier event, . . . the nature and cause of this earlier episode remains as the enigma of paleontological enigmas."[26]

Gould tries to maneuver around this dilemma by claiming that new species arose rapidly in small, peripherally isolated populations; hence, our chances of finding significant numbers of transitional fossils are clearly not good. For Gould, this is a sufficient explanation for why there are so many gaps between species in the fossil record.[27]

From a microevolutionary point of view, Gould's hypothesis seems quite reasonable. It is only when it is extended to include the major systematic gaps *between* different classes of organisms that the hypothesis seems implausible. As Denton explains:

The gaps which separate species: dog/fox, rat/mouse, etc. are utterly trivial compared with, say, that between a primitive terrestrial mammal and a whale or a primitive terrestrial reptile and an Ichthyosaur; and even these relatively major discontinuities are trivial alongside those which divide major phyla such as molluscs and arthropods. Such major discontinuities could not, unless we are to believe in miracles, have been crossed in geologically short periods of time through one or two transitional species occupying restricted geographical areas. Surely, such transitions must have involved long lineages including many collateral lines of hundreds or probably thousands of transitional species. . . . To suggest that the hundreds, thousands or possibly even millions of transitional species which must have existed in the interval between vastly dissimilar types were all unsuccessful species occupying isolated areas and having very small population numbers is verging on the incredible.[28]

Philip Johnson agrees that the "important question is not whether rapid speciation in peripheral isolates has occurred . . . but whether this mechanism can explain more than a relatively narrow range of modifications which cross the species boundary but do not involve major changes in bodily characteristics."[29]

While it may be possible to view certain types of fossilized species, such as *Archeopteryx* or the rhipidistian fishes, as limited forms of fossil intermediates, "there is no evidence that they are any more intermediate than groups such as the living lungfish or monotremes which . . . are not only tremendously isolated from their nearest cousins, but which have individual organ systems that are not strictly transitional at all. As evidence for the existence of natural links between the great divisions of nature, they are only convincing to someone already convinced of the reality of organic evolution."[30]

With such an overwhelming amount of empirical information legislating against them, one wonders why the non-theistic evolutionary community doesn't just "bite the bullet" and agree that the evidence is most consistent with a providentially designed evolutionary process. Arguing that there is no scientific evidence supporting this claim simply will not do, because as we have seen, there is *even less* evidence supporting the non-theistic evolutionist's position.

The big fear here seems to be that once God is credited with the initial creation, true science will become impossible, since everything in nature will then supposedly be explainable by the simple declaration that it is merely part of the Divine Plan. This fear is unnecessary and inappropriate, however, because crediting God with the initial creation won't be the end of science at all. It will rather be the *beginning* of true science, since it will involve a fundamental acknowledgement of the actual Author of the natural world.[31] Philip Johnson agrees:

Why not consider the possibility that life is what it so evidently seems to be, the product of creative intelligence? Science would not come to an end, because the task would remain of deciphering the languages in which genetic information is communicated, and in general finding out how the whole system *works*. What scientists would lose is not an inspiring research program, but the illusion of total mastery of nature. They would have to face the possibility that beyond the natural world there is a further reality which transcends science.[32]

Many informed individuals are just beginning to see the light concerning the obvious inner directedness of the evolutionary process. As Taylor points out, acknowledging the inner directedness of nature doesn't do away with science at all, for "a degree of directedness is [entirely] compatible with the body of scientific theory as it [now] exists. After all, we know of one excellent example already. The fertilized egg is clearly programmed to produce an adult organism. The coordination of parts in a living creature is not achieved by chance but by precisely controlled development. We should not, *a priori*, exclude the possibility that there are programmes in evolutionary development too."[33]

One thing cannot be denied, even by the staunchest evolutionist: If God really exists and is therefore actually responsible for creating the natural world (through whatever means He found most appropriate), biologists will *never* be able to achieve a full scientific understanding of life until they first acknowledge the existence and identity of the Creator. This possibility becomes all the more important when we consider the fact that the various problems in evolutionary biology make much more sense when God is included into the larger theoretical scheme. The notion of Divine Creatorship thus isn't just an *ad hoc* answer to the various problems of evolutionary biology. It is rather the critical missing link to a coherent and unified theory of life's origins.

7.3 Transformed Cladism

One of the most recent attacks upon traditional neo-Darwinist thinking has originated from within the ranks of evolutionary biology itself. It is called *cladism*, and it was initiated by Willi Hennig in 1966 in an attempt to show that the ordinary evolutionary trees used by orthodox evolutionists are inaccurate, since they do not concentrate exclusively on the process of branching in the formation of species. Hennig argued that evolutionary trees are taxonomically inaccurate when they are used to link present-day classification with evolution.[34]

In recent years an even more radical group has sprung up from within the ranks of the cladists. These individuals are known as "transformed cladists," and they have argued that the traditional Darwinian practice of reconstructing the entire past history of life on earth solely from the evidence of present-day relationships is a farce, because lines of evolutionary descent allegedly cannot be deduced from present-day relationships. Instead, they argue that the only accurate form of taxonomic classification must rely solely on the phenomenon of branching in the process of speciation.[35] In order to depict known taxonomic relationships using only this branching technique, "cladograms" have been constructed that show known relationships, but which do not attempt to deduce the evolutionary path by which these relationships have originated.[36]

It would appear as though the "cladist" movement is onto something significant here, because there would seem to be nothing intrinsic to a series of related creatures that would conclusively show the pattern of their evolutionary descent. As Michael Denton has put it, "in the final analysis nature's order is not sequential."[37]

To be sure, shared characteristics in and of themselves cannot be considered to be sufficient criteria for establishing the course of evolutionary descent. Given this observation, it would appear as though much of what has been inferred about the course of evolutionary descent based on present-day relationships is based on wishful thinking as much as it is on anything else. Indeed, the existence of present-day relationships may very well have provided evolutionists with a fertile breeding ground for the projection of *their own* scientific biases and expectations onto the various taxonomic categories, with the result that there may in fact be no causal relation whatsoever between taxonomy and evolutionary descent.[38]

These serious objections from within the ranks of the scientific community itself reveal an even deeper criticism of non-theistic evolutionary theory that we have already briefly touched on: namely, that modern evolutionism cannot lay claim to being a genuine science, since it is inherently untestable, and is therefore unfalsifiable. Deistic Evolutionism, on the other hand, doesn't claim to be a true science in the first place (in the sense of dealing directly with objectively measurable data). It is, to the contrary, a philosophical method of interpretation that tries to find the most plausible explanation for the known scientific evidence.

7.4 Homologous Resemblances

Hickman's *Zoology* text describes the concept of *homology* as referring to "structurally similar organs or functions that become adapted for different environmental conditions. It is best explained by common ancestral types that have become variously adapted."[39]

In other words, homology refers to a basic similarity in biological structure or function between two species which, though they may have had a common origin, have since become adapted to different environmental conditions. For example, there is a homologous resemblance between a bat's wing, a whale's fin, and a human forearm.

Evolutionists claim that these remarkable similarities in appendage structure and function among different species provide convincing evidence for the evolutionary claim that all species have grown out of one another purely by chance. They figure that if a bat's wing is so similar to a human forearm, then the human forearm had to have accidentally grown out of the bat's wing at some point during its supposed evolution, not by any direct intention, but totally by chance.

Two entirely different questions are really at issue here: 1) the possibility that homologous organs may have grown out of one another, and 2) the possibility that they would have done so entirely by chance. Clearly, an affirmation of 1) does not necessarily entail an affirmation of 2). It is also entirely possible that homologous organs could have grown out of one another by some sort of physically mediated Divine Intention. Consequently, homology cannot be considered to be irrefutable proof that a chance evolution of the various life forms on this planet has occurred.

To the contrary, this type of homologous similarity in structure could very well have been the deliberate creative intention of a common Designer, who plausibly could have found certain designs to be so effective and efficient that He subsequently used them on a wide variety of different organisms.

Take the pentadactyl design of the human hand and whale flipper for instance. Though both are based on the same pattern of design, this does *not* necessarily mean that they both evolved by chance from a common ancestor. The fact that the same pentadactyl design can be found in the limbs of *all* terrestrial vertebrates does not strengthen the non-theistic evolutionist's case at all, because the possibility remains that the pentadactyl design could be the best one for the job, which in turn would explain why an Intelligent Creator would have repeatedly used it in different creatures.

Human engineers do the same thing all the time. They deliberately use the same sort of steering apparatus (a steering wheel) in a wide variety of different vehicles, ranging from cars and trucks to planes, boats, and spacecraft. This basic similarity in design, though, doesn't at all mean that these homologous structures have accidentally grown out of one another. It simply means that a series of intelligent human designers have repeatedly found the wheel to be the most efficient design for the job of steering a moving vehicle. In the same way, God could have found many different types of biological structures to be particularly efficient at what they do, so He could have used them in a wide variety of different species.

As we have seen, though, the question of whether or not all species have actually grown out of an original, primordial species is immaterial when it comes to the existence of a Grand Designer. For if there really was some form of inner directedness to the evolutionary process, then all species could very well have originally grown out of one another *by prior design,* and hence without contradiction to the existence of a Grand Designer. The take-home point here is that a common descent alone doesn't fully explain the existence of homologous organs. It isn't the method of manufacturing in and of itself that determines whether certain structures are used over and over again in different humanly-contrived mechanisms; it is the underlying *plan* that the manufacturing process follows that makes this determination. Similarly, the fact that so many similar structures exist in the animal kingdom cannot be explained solely by appealing to the physical method by which they were produced. Rather, one must look to their underlying genetic blueprints to explain the existence of these similarities. This clearly leaves open the possibility that an Intelligent Designer could have been behind the development of homologous structures.

7.4.1 A Critique of Homology

The whole concept of homology in modern evolutionary thought is based on the assumption that homologous organs imply a common pattern of descent. This assumption, however, is by no means obvious, because the surprising fact of the matter is that the vast majority of homologous structures in the various vertebrate species are now known to originate in completely different parts of the embryo. As a consequence, "correspondance between homologous structures cannot be pressed back to similarity of position of the cells of the embryo or the parts of the egg out of which these structures are ultimately differentiated."[40] Based on this radical difference in their embryological origins, it could well be argued that homologous organs "aren't strictly homologous at all."[41]

But the entire concept of homology in orthodox evolutionary theory is *based* on a "relationship between parts which results from their development from corresponding embryonic parts."[42] Evidently, then, the traditional interpretation of homology as representing a common pattern of random descent must be false. It seems much more likely that these homologous structures represent a common pattern of design in the DNA itself, which subsequently uses different embryological pathways in the different species to express itself.

Furthermore, the fact that homologous structures in different species are coded for by completely different genes puts the traditional interpretation of homology even more in doubt. As Michael Denton points out, this "can only mean that non-homologous genes are involved to some extent in the specification of homologous structures."[43] But if the phenomenon of homology is actually indicative of biological descent, then it *ought* to be able to be traced back to similar embryonic parts and homologous genes, as Darwin originally assumed. The fact that this cannot be done in a great many instances strongly disconfirms the traditional neo-Darwinian interpretation of homologous structures.

Indeed, it is possible to show on other grounds that certain apparently homologous structures *cannot* be explained solely in terms of a common pattern of descent. Take the pentadactyl design of the vertebrate forelimb for instance. As we have seen, the orthodox evolutionist tries to explain this basic pentadactyl design in terms of a common pattern of descent amongst the various vertebrate species, but as Denton shrewdly points out, the vertebrate hindlimbs are *also* based on this basic pentadactyl design, yet no one doubts that vertebrate forelimbs and hindlimbs evolved independently from one another—the forelimb from the pectoral fins of a fish, and the hindlimb from the pelvic fins of a fish.[44]

How this complex and seemingly arbitrary pattern was arrived at twice independently in the course of evolution is mystifying. The question is bound to arise: perhaps the analogy between fore-and hindlimbs, the exact adherence to the same pentadactyl plan, is satisfying some, as yet unknown, necessities in the construction of tetrapod limbs? Perhaps only the pentadactyl pattern is, in Cuvier's terms, "compatible" with the vertebrate type. In the context of this unsolved question, it is obviously premature to interpret the occurrence of the pentadactyl pattern in verterate forelimbs to descent from a common ancestor. It may in the end reflect a necessity deeply embedded in the developmental logic of vertebrates. Whatever the ultimate explanation for this remarkable pattern turns out to be, there seems little intellectual satisfaction in attributing one case of correspondence to evolution while refusing it in the other.[45]

The fact is, though, that we already know why this same basic pentadactyl pattern was arrived at twice in the course of evolution: the genome of the host species coded for it both times. This explains one aspect of the developmental necessity that seems to be behind the evolutionary development of vertebrate forelimbs and hindlimbs. However, this only pushes the ultimate question at issue here one step backwards: why did the genome of the host species originally code for this same pentadactyl design in both the forelimbs and hindlimbs? Since a common pattern of random descent does not seem to be capable of explaining this apparently arbitrary pattern, we are left with the possibility that an Intelligent Creator could have designed this necessity into the vertebrate genome from the very beginning. If so, the only explanation for this Divine Choice would be that the Creator found this basic pentadactyl pattern to be the best design for *all* vertebrate forelimbs and hindlimbs.

Given the steering wheel analogy mentioned above, this doesn't seem to be as far-fetched as we might superficially expect, especially when we consider the fact that this pentadactyl pattern has been spectacularly successful in *all* the vertebrate species that have ever possessed it. Hence, the question of why a Creator would be restricted to this same pentadactyl pattern in His design of all vertebrate species turns out to be a moot point, because the fact of the matter is that it has been extremely successful in all of the cases that have ever been studied. Such a criticism of the Creator would only be appropriate if this pentadactyl pattern had proved to be clearly maladaptive in some of the species that had utilized it. However, nothing of the kind has ever been demonstrated. Hence, we are forced to conclude, by the sheer weight of the evidence, that this pentadactyl choice has been eminently justified in all of the creatures that have ever utilized it, since it has clearly been more than good enough in terms of serving its intended function in the animal kingdom.

With these ideas in mind, what are we to make of the relationship between homology and evolutionary theory? To be sure, if a common pattern of descent cannot be used to explain homologous similarities in the animal kingdom, then the traditional neo-Darwinian scenario seems to be doomed, because "homologous resemblance is the very *raison d'etre* of evolution theory. Without the phenomenon of homology—the modification of similar structures to different ends—there would be little need for a theory of descent with modification."[46]

In the final analysis, the phenomenon of homology can only be considered to be evidence for some type of theory of descent. It cannot tell us, though, whether this descent was sudden or gradual, or whether the causal mechanism behind it was "Darwinian, Lamarckian, vitalistic or even creationist. Such a theory of descent is therefore devoid of any significant meaning and equally compatible with almost any philosophy of nature."[47]

7.5 Convergent Evolution

Evolutionists use the term *convergent evolution* to describe how two unrelated species are able to "evolve" strikingly similar appendages and other bodily structures in the course of their development. An example of this idea would be how dolphins, which are mammals, have fins just like fish do. Clearly there is a great deal of "evolutionary" distance between fish and mammals, so these separate stocks are said to have "converged" together over time in the production of fins. As John Casti has pointed out:

> Whenever Nature has had a problem to solve, whether it be the optimal design for a sense organ to process visible light or an efficient way to tear food apart into bite-sized pieces, there has been a tendency for the problem to be solved in a very similar manner across a wide variety of species.[48]

The non-theistic theory of evolution has been unable to give a good explanation of convergent evolution. It simply says that animals "adapt" to their surroundings as best as they can. And since in many instances a particular appendage is valuable to all the creatures of a given niche, all surviving species eventually come to develop that appendage.

Such an "explanation," though, does little to explain the actual *origin* of these convergent organs. It only affirms the statement that the particular form that was originally chosen for these structures had to have been optimal in relation to each creature's particular environmental niche. However, are we to suppose that both dolphins and fish *accidentally* developed structures that just happened to look almost exactly like one another? The fact that both structures are remarkably efficient at what they do does not enter significantly into this discussion, because the primary question at issue here concerns the *origin* of these similar structures, not their utility in the environment once they are already evolved.

The odds for such an accidental convergence of structure clearly seem to be astronomical, even though both have occurred in the same environment. The traditional evolutionary explanation is that similar environments form similar shapes, but such an explanation only begs the true question at issue here, which concerns *how* the environment is able to repeatedly form the same adaptive shapes in unrelated species. It is difficult enough to explain how the environment forms a *single* adaptive shape in a given species through natural selection acting on random mutations, but it is next to impossible to explain how the same adaptive shape keeps popping up over and over again in large numbers of phylogenetically distinct species; that is, unless there is a common directional source for the appearance of these adaptations. The Deistic Evolutionist's explanation for convergent evolution thus seems to be far more persuasive than the neo-Darwinian explanation: the Creator knew that certain adaptive forms would be useful to a wide variety of different creatures, so He programmed the genome in such a way as to enable these similar forms to spontaneously appear whenever they were needed.

Perhaps the most unnerving example of convergent evolution is the development of the eye. Incredibly enough, we now know that the eye was reinvented a bare minimum of 40 different times in widely varying classes of species. While orthodox evolutionists openly acknowledge this fact, they don't even attempt to explain *how* so many different versions of the eye could have been built in more or less the same way. (Of course, the reason they don't tell us is that they don't know themselves.)

It is exceedingly difficult to see how the same structural format for the eye could have been formed over 40 separate times without some form of communication taking place between the evolving structures. Again, the fact that each incarnation of the eye was supposedly formed over millions of years in similar environments is immaterial to the fundamental problem that is at issue here, because it doesn't address the question of *how* a given adaptation is able to repeatedly appear in numerous unrelated species. Just because a particular adaptive design well suits a given environment does *not* necessarily mean that the environment *per se* (in conjunction with random mutations) is capable of forming the design all by itself. Such an assumption confuses the *object* of the design (adaptation to a particular environment) with the actual *production* of the design itself.

This is a glaring category mistake which severely undermines the traditional neo-Darwinian explanation for convergent evolution. The functional objective of a given adaptation represents one category of explanation, while the actual production of the adaptation itself represents an entirely *different* category of explanation. Although functional objectives (such as adapting to certain environments) have everything to do with the inherent design of a given object (since they represent the central task around which the design adheres), they are inherently incapable of producing the actual adaptations themselves. To assume otherwise is thus to confuse the formal cause of a given adaptation (its intrinsic design) with its efficient cause (the actual production of the adaptation itself).

To borrow an example from the automotive world, consider the process of producing a new off-road vehicle from scratch. Before the vehicle can actually be produced, all its functional objectives need to be carefully sketched out in the form of a blueprint. Since the chief functional objective of the new vehicle would be to adapt to off-road conditions as well as possible, the proper structural "adaptations" would have to be designed into the vehicle's conceptual blueprint from the very beginning. Then, once the designing process was completed, the vehicle could actually be manufactured.

The functional objective in the above example is clearly the production of a vehicle that is well-suited to off-road driving conditions, and it is taken into account at all stages of the designing process. However, the functional objective of the vehicle is obviously incapable of actually *producing* the 4-wheel drive "adaptations" themselves. A separate manufacturing mechanism is needed for that.[49]

In the same way, the functional objective of a fin, for instance, is to enable a sea creature to be well-adapted to an aqueous environment. Although it clearly plays an important role in the structural design of the fin itself, it would be a severe category mistake to assume that the fin's functional objective was *itself* capable of actually generating the fin, even in cooperation with local environmental pressures. A separate manufacturing mechanism is clearly needed for that.

It is for the above reasons that the traditional neo-Darwinian paradigm fails to give a realistic explanation of convergent evolution. Natural selection is simply incapable of forming the same complex structures time after time in phylogenetically distinct creatures, even in the same environment, unless the same sorts of raw materials (adaptive variations) present themselves repeatedly. Indeed, natural selection is incapable of forming *anything* unless it has something to select *from*, and it is unlikely to the highest degree that the same complex structures could be formed over and over again unless the same basic adaptive variations happened to repeatedly present themselves. Thus, the *most* that natural selection is capable of doing is fine-tuning a pre-existing variational pattern; it isn't capable of producing (albeit indirectly) the variational pattern itself.[50]

No other alternatives to the above view seem to make any sense at all. Indeed, it is precisely *because* there doesn't seem to be any other rational alternative to choose from that our appeal to a Divine Creator doesn't represent an issue of religious faith *per se*; it represents an issue of ordinary *common sense*. I don't believe that God is responsible for convergent evolution merely because I am religious; I believe that God is responsible for it simply because there doesn't seem to be any other rational alternative. Being religious, then, doesn't always have to be a matter of faith alone. If one is truly open to the various realities of being alive in the world, being religious can also be a matter of good old-fashioned common sense as well.

7.5.1 Convergence and Evolutionary Relationships

As we have seen, a major assumption of orthodox evolutionary theory is that certain fossilized types of creatures are intermediates in the long historical line of evolutionary descent with modification. However, the very concept of convergent evolution—which states that morphologically similar creatures can have radically dissimilar backgrounds—acts to undermine the whole evolutionary interpretation of a presumed fossil intermediate. For while the fossil may superficially appear to represent a certain intermediate type of creature, its internal organs could turn out to be part of a radically different type of creature.

Such was the case with the famous coelacanth. Prior to 1938, it was thought that the coelacanth was an extinct member of the ancient rhipidistian fishes, which, because of their amphibian-like bone structures, were themselves thought to be fossilized intermediates between fishes and amphibians. However, in 1938, a living coelacanth was caught off the coast of South Africa, so scientists finally had a living specimen to examine to see where it actually stood on the evolutionary scale of development. To their ultimate chagrin, they discovered that the coelacanth was actually a fully-formed fish in all of its relevant internal details; absolutely no evidence was found for any type of preadaptation for terrestrial life. It was thus concluded that the coelacanth could *not* have been an intermediate between the fishes and amphibians. This was particularly devastating to the evolutionary community, because no other fossilized fish species have been identified as plausible amphibian ancestors, and there are no other intermediate candidates in the offing.

As far as the presumed transition between amphibians and reptiles is concerned, no satisfactory fossilized intermediates currently exist to document this transition.[51] Some have called the fossil amphibian *Seymouria* a possible intermediate, since it seems to have possessed a few reptilian skeletal features, but recent evidence indicates that they were true amphibians.[52]

We also mustn't forget that there are several species in the world today that seem to truly be intermediate between two major types of organisms, such as the duck-billed platypus and the lungfish, but on the deepest possible level they invariably turn out to be specimens of their own class only.[53]

The same thing could be said of *Archaeopteryx*. While it may have possessed certain superficial reptilian features that were preserved in the fossil record, its soft biology and pattern of feather construction were probably all avian in nature, since it could allegedly fly. This casts severe doubt on the possibility that *Archaeopteryx* could have been an actual intermediate between reptiles and birds.

But if we can't rely on skeletal remains alone to tell us about the overall biology of organisms, then this makes any kind of paleontological evidence for traditional evolutionary theory extremely tenuous at best.[54]

The facts of convergent evolution further cast doubt on the neo-Darwinian paradigm, as they tell us that similar structures can evolve in phylogenetically distant creatures. This indicates that the agency which is responsible for generating this structural similarity is *not* dependent on a close evolutionary pattern of descent. And this, in turn, stands in direct contradiction to standard evolutionary theory, which states that similar structures were passed on from generation to generation as one species randomly evolved into another.

7.6 Weak Orthogenesis as a Compromise Position

The postulation of an inwardly-directed process of evolution represents an important compromise between both the existing fossil record and the insistence of science that the various species literally grew out of one another. According to this orthogenetic scenario, one species *really did* grow out of another, but because of the existence of this inner genetic program, these new species "evolved" so quickly (in perhaps as little as one generation) that very few, if any, transitional creatures were ever produced.

This perspective also represents an important compromise with the creation scientists as well, since the content of this orthogenetic program could only have been created by God Himself. And finally, it agrees very nicely with the existence of evolution's most impressive achievement: *ourselves*.

Notes

1. Hickman, Hickman, & Hickman, *Integrated Principles of Zoology* (St. Louis: The C. V. Mosby Company, Fifth Edition, 1974.), p. 817.
2. David M. Raup, "Conflicts Between Darwinism and Paleontology," *Field Museum of Natural History Bulletin*, Vol. 50, No. 1 (January, 1979), pp. 22–29.
3. Quoted in Michael Denton's *Evolution: A Theory in Crisis*, p. 104.
4. Ibid., pp. 191–192.
5. Taylor, *The Great Evolution Mystery*, p. 78.
6. George Gaylord Simpson, *The Meaning of Evolution* (New Haven: Yale University Press, 1953), p. 18.
7. Ibid.
8. John Repetski, "A Fish from the Upper Cambrian of North America," *Science*, Vol. 200, No. 4341, May 5, 1978, pp. 529–531.
9. Luther Sutherland, *Darwin's Enigma*, p. 45.
10. Stephen Jay Gould, "The Ediacaran Experiment," *Natural History*, Vol. 93, No. 2, February, 1984, pp. 14–23.
11. Steven Stanley, *The New Evolutionary Timetable*, p. 71, quoted in Philip E. Johnson's *Darwin on Trial*, p. 51.
12. Michael Denton, *Evolution: A Theory in Crisis*, p. 296.
13. Charles Darwin, *The Origin of Species*, p. 332.
14. Michael Denton, *Evolution: A Theory in Crisis*, pp. 189–190.
15. Although I do not agree with the traditional creationist position, which claims that no substantial form of evolution has ever occurred, it is still possible to accept some of their criticisms without accepting all of their conclusions. There is one thing, however, that both the traditional creationist and the Deistic Evolutionist will always have in common: both believe that the existence of life is unintelligible in the absence of a Divine Creator.
16. John N. Moore, *Should Evolution be Taught?* (San Diego: Institute for Creation Research, 1971), p. 6.
17. David M. Raup, "Conflicts Between Darwinism and Paleontology," *Field Museum of Natural History Bulletin* Vol. 50, No. 1, January, 1979, pp. 22–29.
18. Walter Sullivan, "Evolution: A New Concept," *The New York Times* (October 25, 1964), p. 8 E.
19. Marshall and Sandra Hall, *The Truth: God or Evolution*, p. 57.
20. Michael Denton, *Evolution: A Theory in Crisis*, pp. 353–355.
21. Stephen Jay Gould, *Ever Since Darwin*, (New York: W.W. Norton and Company, 1977), p. 126.
22. It would seem that Gould's framing of the problem in mutually exclusive terms actually represents a deep, underlying desire of the non-theistic evolutionary community to do away with the "problem of God" completely. It is equally clear, though, that God (if He exists at all) won't simply go away, just because some of us have deliberately chosen to leave Him out of our scientific theories.
23. Ibid., p. 128.
24. Ibid., p. 130.
25. Karl Popper, *Unended Quest* (Glasgow: Fontana Books of Collins, Sons and Co., Ltd., 1976).
26. Ibid., p. 130.
27. Stephen Jay Gould, *The Panda's Thumb*, p. 184.
28. Michael Denton, *Evolution: A Theory in Crisis*, pp. 193–194.
29. Philip Johnson, *Darwin on Trial*, p. 53.
30. Michael Denton, *Evolution: A Theory in Crisis*, p. 195.

31. We need to distinguish between two forms of science: "hard" experimental science, and philosophically-oriented scientific conjecture. In keeping with the Principle of Objectivity, God must be left out of the former type of science. In the latter type, however, objective measurement is impossible; therefore, God can be included in the overall theoretical framework.
32. Philip E. Johnson, *Darwin on Trial*, p. 110.
33. Taylor, *The Great Evolution Mystery*, p. 6.
34. Peter J. Bowler, *Evolution: The History of an Idea*, p. 345.
35. Ibid., p. 346.
36. Ibid., pp. 346–347.
37. Michael Denton, *Evolution: A Theory in Crisis*, p. 140.
38. Of course, what is at issue here isn't whether or not all species have descended from a common ancestor (the Deistic Evolutionist is fully prepared to accept this notion), but whether or not this descent was intended by a Higher Power. My point in this section has simply been to show that the non-theistic evolutionist cannot use present-day relationships to show that all species have descended in an accidental, and therefore unintended, fashion from a common ancestor.
39. Hickman, et. al., p. 823.
40. Gavin de Beer, *Homology: An Unresolved Problem* (London: Oxford University Press, 1971), p. 8.
41. Michael Denton: *Evolution: A Theory in Crisis*, p. 146.
42. Charles Darwin, *The Origin of Species*, p. 492.
43. Michael Denton, *Evolution: A Theory in Crisis*, p. 149.
44. Ibid., pp. 151–152.
45. Ibid., pp. 152–153.
46. Ibid., p. 154.
47. Ibid., pp. 154–155.
48. John L. Casti, *Paradigms Lost* (New York: William Morrow and Company, 1989), p. 392.
49. The fact that living creatures are self-reproducing, while automotive vehicles are not, is immaterial to the point being made here, which is that functional objectives themselves are incapable of producing structural adaptations in *all* types of things, including self-reproducing life forms. Self-reproduction in and of itself has nothing to do with transforming the functional objective of a design into a real world structural adaptation.
50. According to non-theistic evolutionary theory, natural selection in and of itself does not directly produce the variations it selects from; random genetic mutations do. But once these randomly occurring variations are produced, though, natural selection acts to concentrate them into various functional adaptations. Thus, natural selection is *indirectly* credited with forming the functional patterns themselves, out of the randomly-occurring mutations that occurred in the past. In relation to this bit of orthodoxy, I am simply arguing that, given the enormous amount of cooperative complexity found in even the "simplest" adaptations, this is a highly implausible notion in the absence of some form of inner directedness.
51. Philip Johnson, *Darwin on Trial*, p. 75.
52. Ibid.
53. The most important distinction between amphibians and reptiles is their mode of reproduction. Amphibians lay their eggs in the water and their progeny experience a complex metamorphosis on the way to adulthood, while reptiles lay hard-shelled amniotic eggs that produce miniature replicas of the adults upon hatching. Significantly, no plausible explanation has yet been forwarded for how

the reptilian process of reproduction could have accidentally evolved via traditional neo-Darwinian means. (For an excellent discussion of the vast differences between the amphibian and reptilian modes of reproduction, see Michael Denton's *Evolution: A Theory in Crisis*, pp. 218–219.)

54. Michael Denton, *Evolution: A Theory in Crisis*, p. 180.

PART II

Directed Evolution

CHAPTER 8

Weak Orthogenesis, Opportunism, and Lamarckism

God, the creator of the universe, can never be against learning the laws of what he has created.

MUSTAFA MAHMOUD

We have seen how the scientific task of accounting for the origin and proliferation of so many well-adapted species is prodigious indeed. This is why there are so many competing theories about how the process of speciation takes place: because as yet, no one knows exactly how or why it occurs.

Part of this problem has to do with deciding what actually constitutes a species. The very concept of a "species" implies the existence of a morphological type that is stable enough to be repeatedly identified over many generations; yet, at the same time, evolutionists tell us that the various species were fluid enough to have accidentally arisen out of one another. This raises an important question: if a given species is capable of steadily modifying its body structure over successive generations in order to meet the demands of the environment, why is there such thing as a stable and clearly definable species at all? Indeed, why "is the world not full of intermediate forms of every kind?"[1]

The orthodox answer to this question traces the basic format of each species to the surrounding environment. Since natural selection purportedly drives each species to adapt to the environment in whatever way it can, a stable species implies a stable environment. But it is a well-known fact that the various environmental niches throughout the world have *not* remained stable over the millennia. One geological or climatological upheaval after another is known to have taken place throughout the ages, and indeed, these are routinely credited for causing the massive number of extinctions in our planet's history. Even so, many species have remained more or less the same in spite of these upheavals, and this can only be explained by one of two possibilities; either: 1) certain environmental niches have remained stable in spite of the earth's major upheavals, in which case the stasis of each species would be directly tied to the stability of these niches, or 2) species stasis in these instances is not directly caused by environmental stability *per se*.

A corrollary to this latter alternative further states that the speciation process itself is not exclusively tied to the environment *per se*, but is rather driven primarily from within. To the extent that this corrollary is true, it means that the various species are more in control of their own fate, and less at the mercy of environmental change, than has traditionally been believed. Support for this position can be found in the fact that species aren't nearly as malleable as most orthodox evolutionists would like to believe. To the contrary, because of the profound stability exhibited by the DNA molecule when it reproduces itself, the resultant organism is able to maintain a relatively stable morphology over many generations. In fact, the phenotype (external structure) is generally *more* stable than the already stable genotype (structure of the genes), because of the fact that several *different* genotypes can code for the same overall phenotype. This affords each species an even greater degree of stability than would otherwise be expected. The fossil record, showing species fixity to be the norm throughout evolutionary history, corroborates this conclusion. So does the fact that artificial breeders have never been able to create a new species, despite truly heroic efforts to the contrary.

On the other hand, when speciation has taken place in the past, it has occurred so rapidly that virtually no intermediate forms have ever been found in the fossil record. Taylor finds such a phenomenon to be inexplicable in terms of the random, gradual change proposed by conventional neo-Darwinian thinking. Instead, he has suggested that perhaps all the phyletic changes that have occurred throughout evolutionary history were somehow programmed into the genetic code from the very beginning.[2] He has termed this notion *masking theory*, since only a particular set of genes would tend to become expressed or unmasked at any given time; the rest would remain masked in the genome until the appropriate time. Whenever this appropriate time would present itself, though, the resultant "evolution" would take place almost overnight.

One of the major appeals of Taylor's masking theory is that it provides a satisfactory explanation for the many apparent jumps or saltations found in the fossil record. It also provides a plausible explanation for how so many "organs of extreme perfection," like the eye, could have spontaneously arisen in the wild.

In many ways, Taylor's masking theory is just a variation on the old *orthogenetic* idea that once life originated in the primordial seas, it began a more or less straightline evolution into more complex forms, until the present level of complexity was finally attained.[3] Orthogenetic theories have been attractive to many because they seem to account for the fact that, to a large extent, evolution *really has* unfolded with a surprising amount of directedness. Indeed, perhaps the only place where orthogenetic theories run into difficulty is in the area of natural selection: they do not seem to account for the many random natural forces that appear to have had such a profound effect on the actual evolutionary trajectories taken by most developing forms of life. Modern neo-Darwinian theorists believe that the evolution of life on earth was "opportunistic," in the sense that the various species arose only when the surrounding environmental opportunity was sufficient for them to do so, i.e., they see life as responding to totally unforeseen environmental changes, with little or no inner impetus of its own, except for the ever-present will to survive.

But why must we be limited to only these two theoretical extremes? Why can't the truth consist of *both* alternatives operating at the same time? Why can't the evolution of life on earth have been both opportunistic *and* directed from within simultaneously?

A major reason for the exclusion of this possibility in traditional evolutionary thought has been the impression that these two theoretical extremes are mutually incompatible with one another; hence, to postulate opportunism in evolution meant that any type of directedness was impossible. There is nothing *a priori*, however, that makes these two explanations incompatible with one another. Rather, it is the larger *metaphysical implications* of these two positions that appear to be mutually exclusive. That is to say, the very idea of natural selection working on random variations seems to imply an atheistic universe with no overall direction, whereas the notion of genetic "foresight" seems to imply a deliberate creation by a larger Being. Since a mindless universe is logically incompatible with a God-centered one, it is concluded that an opportunistic view of evolution is incompatible with any degree of genetic foresight.

This is a faulty argument for two reasons. First, it assumes that the above-mentioned metaphysical implications are themselves accurate, and this is not at all apparent. The existence of opportunism in evolution doesn't necessarily imply a mindless creative process, since a larger Creator could have used these same opportunistic mechanisms as part of His overall Creative Plan. Secondly, it is inappropriate to let the perceived incompatibility of these metaphysical implications retroactively affect our conclusions regarding the facts themselves, for the distinct possibility remains that the metaphysical implications *themselves* may be in error. The existing scientific facts thus need to be carefully examined entirely on their *own* terms, without any metaphysically-inspired polluting effects being allowed to enter into the picture.

When this is done, it soon becomes apparent that there could very well be a dynamic creative collaboration going on in the world between diffuse orthogenetic tendencies, on the one hand, and the selective effects of specific environmental influences, on the other. Indeed, it is distinctly possible that there could be a much higher level of evolutionary organization in existence than we are currently able to perceive, which could bring the many apparently random forces in evolutionary history together into an intimate cooperation with this presumed orthogenetic tendency.

Therefore, it isn't necessarily contradictory to assert that life could have arisen with some degree of diffuse orthogenetic foresight, but that it *also* could have been opportunistic at the same time, in the sense of responding to the pruning effects of natural selection. In order to effect this conceptual synthesis, though, we must first distinguish between two types of orthogenesis: a strong form, in which all the unmasked structures are more or less perfectly appropriate for the local environment at hand, and a weak form, in which an *entire spectrum* of structural variations is unmasked, ranging from those that are intrinsically well-suited to the local environment, to those that are not.

It is the weak form of orthogenesis that most interests us here, because it allows evolution to be opportunistic, insofar as it gives natural selection the power to choose the best-adapted variants in any population from the wide variety that is naturally produced. The advantage of this weak type of orthogenetic evolution is that it affords a maximal amount of flexibility to evolving life forms, since it allows them to adapt to a wide variety of possible environmental conditions. Opportunism in this sense refers to the ability of some variants to take maximal advantage of a given set of environmental conditions.

The "cost" of this adaptive flexibility, of course, is the overproduction of genetic variants, many of which are wiped out by natural selection. Although this gives us the heartless opportunism we are looking for (in order to be consistent with a multitude of scientific observations), it comes at a relatively high price: that of the dying off of all those creatures whose adaptations to the local environment are less than optimal.

This weak version of orthogenesis thus accounts for all the observed evidence in the natural world: 1) the "ruthless" opportunism in the wild that is mediated by natural selection, 2) the overproduction of genetic variants, a few of which are functional enough to be chosen by natural selection, and 3) the almost complete lack of transitional fossils, since this inner orthogenetic striving, though diffuse, nevertheless produces fully formed adaptive structures whenever it becomes unmasked. Thus, the only feature that truly distinguishes this weak form of orthogenesis from orthodox evolutionary theory is the postulation of a diffuse inner directedness to the variations themselves.

If we take this weak form of orthogenesis to be true, we can see how evolutionists could have been thrown off track by a fundamental confusion between genuine mutational randomness (first-order mutations), on the one hand, and the extreme amount of genetic variation that naturally occurs in our weak orthogenetic paradigm, on the other. The primary difference, of course, is between unrelated mutations taking place entirely at random, and a group of *related* changes taking place through the spontaneous production of fully formed adaptations over a wide range of possible forms. *It is thus the extremely broad range of adaptive variability which the non-theistic evolutionist confuses for true randomness.* He assumes that every instance of a Divinely-created adaptation would be "perfect" from the very beginning; hence, he takes it for granted that the production of any inappropriate adaptations—which get mercilessly weeded out by natural selection—must be the result of genuine randomness instead of Divine directedness.

Such a narrow view, however, neglects to consider the larger adaptive value that such a broad range of adaptations would have on the various species themselves. A wide range of adaptive variability ensures that each species will be able to survive in as many different types of environments as possible, for it is clear that what counts as an appropriate adaptation in one environment can also be considered deadly in another. Indeed, given the extremely wide range of environmental conditions found on this planet, it follows that the only way to ensure maximal species flexibility is by designing a large amount of variation into the genome.[4]

It is thus the extremely wide range covered by most variations that seems to indicate the existence of a random and undirected evolutionary process in nature. According to the Deistic Evolutionist, however, it isn't the generic pattern or design of each adaptation that randomly occurs; it is the actual *distribution* of variations on this basic structural theme that is random.

For instance, if the adaptation under consideration is the beak of a certain species of bird, the Deistic Evolutionist believes that some form of beak, pertaining to a certain generic pattern or design, will be forthcoming in all generations. This adaptive pattern in and of itself is not random, because it has somehow been determined beforehand. However, given the extreme variability of the genome with respect to most phenotypic characteristics, a large number of variations on this basic "beak theme" will spontaneously appear in any given population. It is the actual distribution of these variations in any one population that seems to be "random," *not* the generic design of the adaptation itself. This type of "randomness" obviously has nothing to do with the lack of direction that is usually understood as being synonymous with the word "random." It is simply "randomness" under the overall rubric of an internally-directed evolutionary unfolding.

Now we can see why non-theistic evolutionists have been misled into thinking that it is the variations themselves that are truly random. *They have confused the random distribution of variations around a single, non-random form with the random appearance of the form itself.* This confusion is further exacerbated by the fact that natural selection operates in both the directed and the undirected evolutionary models, with the end result in both cases being the continued survival of only the most well-adapted forms.

8.1 Orthogenesis and Opportunism

It is much more difficult than one might initially think trying to figure out how and why species transmutate in the wild. From our limited perspective, we can only see the seemingly random forces of the environment acting on constantly changing life forms. Therefore, when we see a morphological change in a given species, we tend to assume that it is merely taking opportunistic advantage of a surrounding environmental change that was entirely unforeseen. But what if there is a genetic sub-program in the DNA of this species that causes a group of previously unexpressed genes to suddenly become unmasked in response to certain types of environmental change, leading to the spontaneous development of new adaptations or even a new species? In this case, the orthogenetic evolutionary program inside the genome would *itself* be the reason that the evolving life form was able to take opportunistic advantage of the changing environment. It is thus possible that evolving life forms are both opportunistic *and* endowed with a certain amount of genetic "foresight," the latter property of which enables them to respond with opportunistic action when the time is right, through the production of a broad range of adaptive variations.[5]

As we have seen, this orthogenetic force wouldn't necessarily have to represent an infallible, straightline evolutionary course to the present day. Rather, it might only represent an inner *tendency* for a given organism to evolve in a certain way, given the proper environmental conditions. Indeed, environmental pressures could, in this way of thinking, act as a type of stimulating agent that is designed to "coax" a certain degree of change out of the organism. Once such an environmentally-induced transformation would take place, however, the newly-evolved organism would then be "on its own," as it were, to deal with the selective pressures of the environment in the best way possible. If it found itself well enough equipped to survive nature's selective hand, it would then be able to reproduce, so as to be able to pass its genes on to future generations. On the other hand, if it did not find itself well enough equipped to deal with these environmental pressures, it probably would *not* survive long enough to be able to reproduce.

In short, it is possible for there to be a degree of orthogenetic foresight in evolving life forms, and yet for these same individuals to be largely at the mercy of their environment, both in terms of their internal structure and in terms of their prospects for immediate survival. While this inner orthogenetic tendency would still be ultimately responsible for the evolution of increasingly complex life forms, the actual evolutionary process itself would only occur over against the constraining effects of natural selection, through the sacrifice of the many other creatures that failed to meet the challenges of the harsh environment. In this sense, any type of orthogenetic force[6] would only represent an inner *tendency* to evolve in certain directions, given the proper environmental conditions.

In this quasi-orthogenetic mode of thinking, the success of each particular evolving individual would not be guaranteed; only the final end product would more or less be guaranteed. This is analogous to the quantum path that is taken by an electron when it travels from Point A to Point B. There is no way to predict which path the electron will actually follow during its brief journey; thus, there can be no guarantee that it will follow any particular path. What *can* be guaranteed, though, is that it will eventually end up at Point B.

In the same way, the success of any incipient member of an orthogenetically evolving species would never be guaranteed, because of the multitude of variables that would constantly be impinging upon it. The final end product (a stable species), however, *would* be more or less guaranteed, for two reasons: 1) it would be built on the sacrifices of many preceding creatures, and 2) it would represent the final inner "urging" of the orthogenetic program.

French moral philosopher Henri Bergson was also of the opinion that the evolution of life could be vaguely progressive in nature. As Peter Bowler explains in his book *Evolution: The History of an Idea*, Bergson was of the opinion that:

> The history of life has been progressive but only in a very irregular way. This could be accounted for, however, if we assumed a constant state of tension between the original creative life-force, the elan-vital, and the resistance of the inert matter from which that force must construct living bodies. Creation is thus a constant striving upward of the life-force, divided and redivided into a host of separate branches by the practical necessity of coping with the material world. The creative impulse impels life to always try to reach higher levels, yet it always has to fall back, unable to overcome completely the resistance of matter.[7]

The natural world is full of opposing forces which, by virtue of their tension with one another, produce a desirable result. This dialectical process appears to permeate the whole of physical reality, down to the subatomic particles themselves, which exist in balance with one another through a variety of electromagnetic and nuclear forces. But if this paradigm of the dialectic can regulate the structure and function of the physical world, why can't it also be applicable to the field of evolutionary development as well? On the one hand, there could be an orthogenetic tendency, arising from within the genome of a given species, that produces a certain group of coherent variations, while on the other hand, there could be the "pruning" effects of natural selection to "weed out" all but the most fit organisms. This suggestion appears to be quite reasonable, since before the process of natural selection can hope to act, it must first have something to select *from*. A general type of orthogenetic tendency or "yearning" could be the force that gives natural selection coherent items (second and third-order "mutations") from which to choose. This doctrine of opportunistic orthogenesis would account both for the irregular, branching nature of evolution, as well as for the final types of species that are eventually produced.

Salthe and Eldredge (1985) have proposed a similar process of evolution consisting of two interacting hierarchies: the *genealogical hierarchy* and the *ecological hierarchy*. The genealogical hierarchy refers to the genetically-controlled rise of species "forcing" themselves onto the environment, whereas the ecological hierarchy refers to the environmental constraints that are imposed on incipient life forms. It is thus the complex interaction of these two hierarchies that produces the specific results of evolution.[8]

The Deistic Evolutionist agrees wholeheartedly with this hierarchical view of evolution. He simply believes that the genealogical hierarchy contains some degree of inner directedness, whereas Salthe and Eldredge do not.

8.2   Why Lamarckism Has Been So Appealing Over the Years

The French biologist Jean Pierre Antoine de Monet (1744–1829), or the Chevalier de Lamarck as he is more popularly known, is credited for introducing the doctrine of the inheritance of acquired characteristics to the field of evolutionary biology. Although Lamarck's theory is said to have been experimentally disconfirmed many different times over the years, it still has its devotees, especially in France.

Actually, Lamarck was correct insofar as he noticed that there is a connection between the environment and a given animal's physical structure. Animals are in fact shaped the way they are so they can adapt to their surroundings as best as they can. The question thus isn't *whether* there is a connection between the environment and an animal's shape, but *how* this connection comes to exist in the first place. By noting that the environment seemed to dictate the exact nature of a given adaptation, Lamarck concluded that it somehow led to the inheritance of needed structures (i.e., acquired characteristics).

Modern day geneticists have largely proven, however, that there is no such thing as the inheritance of acquired characteristics *per se*. If a man loses both arms in an accident, for instance, and then impregnates a woman, his baby will in fact possess two arms.[9] Even so, the explanation that most orthodox evolutionists give for the connection between the environment and bodily structure is even more absurd than Lamarck's: they argue that chance mutations alone produce all sorts of random variations, and that natural selection subsequently chooses only those that happen to enhance survival.

There is, however, a third alternative from which we can choose that has largely been ignored by the orthodox community; namely, that each organism's basic morphology and adaptive format could have been specifically designed in advance, and subsequently programmed into the DNA of all life forms. Each species would thus express only those general adaptive characteristics that would be appropriate for it alone.

There are two mechanisms that could possibly mediate this type of inner directedness. On the one hand, each organism's basic structure could have been directly designed in advance, and then subsequently programmed into the genome. In this case, the environment would stimulate the expression of these pre-formed characters whenever the time would be right. On the other hand, the environment could play a more direct role in stimulating and designing these characters, insofar as the genome may have the ability to create the "proper" adaptations in direct response to environmental need. In this latter case, the genome would be programmed with the capacity to design and build the right adaptations in direct response to environmental pressure.

The chief difference between these two mechanisms concerns the dual roles that are played by the genome and by the environment. In the former mechanism, both the environment and the genome play a comparatively passive role in the production of these adaptive characters, insofar as the environment merely stimulates the genome to express the pre-designed characters that are already contained within it. In the latter mechanism, both the environment and the genome play a much more active role in the production of these characters, insofar as the environment directly stimulates the genome to design and build the proper adaptive forms.

In either case, there would be a definite inner directedness to the evolutionary process, and this in turn would explain many things. To begin with, it would explain why there is such a strong connection between the structure of adaptations and the nature of the environment. This sort of connection would exist because it would have been deliberately designed to be that way long ago. Secondly, it would explain why animals seem to inherit certain types of responses to their environment—what would seem like the inheritance of an acquired characteristic would simply be the unmasking of a genetic program that had existed all along. Thirdly, it would explain why adaptations typically appear not only *when* they're needed, but also *where* they're needed as well. Fourthly, it would also explain why almost all adaptations are either all or none: either they are very well designed on the whole or else they don't exist at all. Traditional evolutionists argue that imperfectly configured adaptations aren't selected for, but as Taylor points out, "this is not altogether true: an eye on the side of the head would be of *some* survival value even if it were not so immediately useful as an eye on top of the head. While chance *could* perhaps explain such modifications, response to need explains them much better. In the absence of decisive evidence, the probabilities point to Lamarck rather than Darwin."[10]

8.3   Weak Orthogenesis and Lamarckism

As we have seen, there are two possible ways in which a weak process of orthogenesis can produce pre-formed characters: 1) through the direct unfolding of a pre-existing genetic program that already contains the genetic determinants of the various adaptations themselves, or 2) through an indirect process of self-programming by the genome, where the genome responds to environmental demands by constructing its own adaptations to further its survival.

To the extent that either of these weak orthogenetic mechanisms turn out to be true, it is easy to see how such a phenomenon could be interpreted as being the inheritance of acquired characters. Suppose, for instance, that midway in its growth to adulthood, a given organism spontaneously grows a useful appendage in response to the unfolding of its internal orthogenetic program. Suppose further that this appendage appears not just anywhere, but precisely in the position where it would be most useful. To the external observer, the organism would seem to have mysteriously acquired the appendage in response to local environmental demands, when in reality these same environmental demands would have been anticipated to some extent all along by the inner orthogenetic program. Moreover, since genes for the appendage would automatically be passed on to all later progeny, it would appear as though a Lamarckian inheritance of an acquired character had taken place. In reality, though, this characteristic would have been acquired, not from the organism's strivings within the environment *per se*, but from its own internally-based orthogenetic program, which had anticipated the general features of the local environment from the very beginning.

In order for this weak form of orthogenesis to be true, however, the pre-formed variations themselves don't have to already be coded into the genome. It is possible, as we have seen, that certain environmental demands could trigger a variety of pre-determined *responses* that would themselves result in the self-programming of the genome for the character in question. In this case, it would be the *capacity* for self-programming in response to certain environmental demands that would *itself* be programmed into the genome.

8.4   Two Types of "Acquired Characters"

A major reason why Lamarckism is now discredited in the scientific community is because it has been very difficult to demonstrate conclusively any type of inheritance of acquired characters. Part of the reason for this difficulty may be due to a deep-seated confusion over which types of characters are heritable and which are not.

It has traditionally been assumed that a valid Lamarckian theory would mean that *all* characters that are acquired during an individual's lifetime would automatically be passed on to its offspring. On this view, a salamander whose tail is cut off before mating would be expected to produce progeny without tails. Such a thing, of course, was never demonstrated in the laboratory, so it was assumed that Lamarckism must be false.

There is a subtle fallacy, however, at the center of this mode of reasoning, as it doesn't necessarily follow that *all* acquired characters cannot be inherited, just because *some* cannot. It could very well be the case that only a certain type of acquired character can be inherited, while others cannot. If such a possibility turns out to be true, this would revive a qualified version of Lamarck's theory in the minds of many open-minded people.

It may be that the only acquired characters that are truly heritable are those that are "acquired" from *within* an organism's genome, in response to outer pressure from the environment. This type of "acquired character" is to be sharply distinguished from the kind that is externally imposed upon an organism from without, because the former kind seems to flow naturally from within the organism itself, whereas the latter type is impressed upon it by outside forces. Of these two types of acquired characters, it is much easier to see how only the former kind can be inherited by an organism's progeny.

This would explain why scientists have been unable to demonstrate the Lamarckian mode of inheritance experimentally: the very act of performing an experiment on a passive group of creatures automatically entails the imposition of an externally-originated "acquired character," which is precisely the type that we are presuming to be non-heritable.

If this view is correct, the only type of acquired character that could conclusively be demonstrated to be heritable would be that which is acquired *naturally* by the organism itself in response to normal environmental pressures. The reason for this gets back to the evolutionary program that may exist within the genome itself: only those "acquired characters" that are produced by this evolutionary program would be able to be passed on to subsequent generations, because they would *already* be contained within the organism's chromosomes; on the other hand, those "acquired characters" that are externally imposed upon the organism would probably not be incorporated within the organism's DNA content, which would explain why they are not able to be transmitted to future generations.

Admittedly, there is a very subtle distinction between *internally* generated changes that are made *in response* to certain outer pressures and *externally* imposed changes that are subsequently forced onto an organism's body. The chief difference between these two types of acquired characters has to do with *where* they are ultimately initiated: if they are initiated from within the genome itself, in response to pressure from without, they will presumably be inherited, whereas if they are initiated from without (and are thus externally imposed upon the organism), they will probably *not* be inherited. On this view, the genome itself must freely choose to initiate change of its own accord before changes will be heritable; it cannot be forced to change from without, except through the clever duplication of natural environmental conditions, which are *themselves* able to coax the genome to change of its own accord.

8.5   Preadaptation vs. Postadaptation and the Return to Lamarckism: An Experimental Verdict

As we have seen, the central issue separating the Deistic Evolutionist's position from the traditional neo-Darwinian position concerns the directionality of the variations themselves. The Deistic Evolutionist affirms the existence of a significant degree of directionality in the many variations that inevitably arise in any population, whereas the orthodox evolutionist does not. The orthodox evolutionist, of course, has a hidden reason for wanting to deny this directionality: if variations are assumed to be non-random in origin, then there must be a higher source for this directionality, which is usually taken to be God Himself.

One way to affirm the existence of some form of directionality in the evolutionary process is to revert back to the Lamarckian view, in which species are able to adapt to changing environmental conditions by adjusting their genomes accordingly. Since these altered genomes are then passed on to subsequent generations, a gradual process of species-based evolutionary change occurs. Long-term directionality can thus be seen in each subsequent generation's inherited variational pattern, which in turn can be attributed to the genome's purported ability to adapt to changing environmental conditions.

Needless to say, this Lamarckian view of the inheritance of "acquired" characters has been thoroughly discredited by the neo-Darwinian evolutionary community. Remarkably, however, it has been making a strong comeback in recent years. This resurgence is all the more impressive because it is based on hard scientific evidence, and not mere philosophical speculation.

Biologists have known for years that certain types of acquired characteristics are in fact heritable. Take the protozoan *Oxytricha* for instance. Every once in a while, it accidentally produces a "double monster," which consists of two whole individuals fused together.[11] If such a double monster is cut in two equal portions lengthwise, two "singlet" individuals are produced that give rise to normal offspring. However, if a double monster is cut in half crosswise, two more double monsters are produced that subsequently give rise to more double monsters. Clearly an acquired characteristic can be inherited through a single slice made by the experimenter.

Similarly, if the cell wall of a reproducing bacterium is completely removed in the laboratory, its progeny will not possess cell walls, despite the fact that this characteristic is clearly contained in the parent's DNA.[12] Along the same lines, if the chloroplasts of the protozoan *Euglena* are experimentally eliminated via treatment with the antibiotic streptomycin, its descendants will not possess chloroplasts.[13]

Other types of characteristics can be "horizontally" acquired, and subsequently inherited, through the incorporation of viral DNA into the host species' genome. This process of acquiring genetic material through viral infection is thought to have been a fairly frequent occurrence throughout evolution, and indeed, according to Georgetown University biologist Otto Landman, it may have even been responsible for speeding up the evolutionary process.[14] The basic idea here is that as long as organisms are able to incorporate the genetic skills of other organisms into their own DNA, they won't have to go through the long and arduous task of evolving these skills on their own.

In his *Scientific American* essay, Landman points out that one of the main reasons why modern biologists are so prejudiced against the inheritance of acquired characteristics can be traced to the spectacular failure of the Soviet plant breeder Trofim Lysenko, who believed that favorable traits can be transmitted to plants by training them.[15] Needless to say, Lysenko turned out to be dead wrong, and the Soviet state was forced to pay dearly for it. Unfortunately, modern biologists "have thrown an important baby out with the Lysenkoist bathwater."[16] They have generalized this one specific failure to all types of acquired characters, but clearly such a pattern of generalization doesn't necessarily follow at all. Just because one instance of this type of inheritance turns out to be false doesn't necessarily mean that all other forms will also be false. To the contrary, the experimental evidence clearly indicates that some types of acquired characteristics are indeed heritable.

On the other hand, experimental support for the random appearance of new evolutionary traits—a central feature of the neo-Darwinian paradigm—is far less convincing. According to G.Z. Opadia-Kadima, an extensive review of the biological literature reveals only two such instances of support for the neo-Darwinian view.

The first took place in 1943 when, after watching a few of his colleagues try their hand on a slot machine, Salvador Luria became enamored by what blind chance could do for the lucky gambler. Wondering if a similar sort of luck could have resulted in beneficial evolutionary effects in nature, he and his friend Max Delbrück soon devised an elaborate experiment that was designed to test whether or not randomly-produced evolutionary change could be demonstrated in the laboratory.

What they found was that a certain strain of *E. coli* could acquire resistance to the T1 bacteriophage without ever coming into direct contact with it.[17]. This finding was taken to mean that adaptive mutations can occur entirely by chance in nature, without any direct prodding by the environment taking place. Other experimenters were soon able to replicate these findings, so the downfall of Lamarckism seemed guaranteed. The prevailing scientific opinion was that if an organism could develop an adaptive mutation in the absence of an environmental stimulus that might trigger its appearance, then contact with the environment is probably not an essential requirement for the development of at least some adaptive mutations.

However, it does not follow from these findings that mutations are genuinely random in the strong sense of the word; only that direct contact with the environment is not a necessary prerequisite for all adaptations. *Where* these adaptations come from, of course, is another matter entirely. The Deistic Evolutionist, of course, believes that these adaptations arise spontaneously in response to some type of evolutionary program within the genome. Indeed, such a conclusion seems to be evident in the very fact that adaptive traits, such as the one cited above, are spontaneously able to appear fully formed and "ready for action," with no interim process of selection and development being necessary.

Of course, this isn't to say that adaptations which are themselves already fully formed in the genome cannot make a random appearance in the life of any given species. They obviously can, but this is a far cry from the orthodox neo-Darwinian belief that the *adaptations themselves* were originally *created* by a purely random process.

In other words, while the appearance of a certain adaptation may be random with regard to which members of a particular population will turn out to possess it, this does *not* mean that the origin of the adaptation *itself* must be random as well. On this view, it is the evolutionary program within the genome that would ultimately be responsible for producing the adaptations themselves, while the distribution of these adaptations within any given population *would* be limited to chance factors.

It follows from this distinction that it would be a serious category mistake to confuse the random *appearance* of a certain adaptation with the random *origin* of the adaptation itself. The first category is the one that determines the distribution of a certain adaptation in a given population. The second category is the one that concerns the ultimate origin of the adaptation itself. *While the distribution of a particular adaptation within a population may be random, this is no reason to conclude that the origin of the adaptation itself must be random as well. To conclude otherwise is to pervert the scientific evidence into saying something it does not.*

Getting back to our original discussion, Luria and Delbruck's finding concerning the unprovoked resistance of a certain strain of *E. coli* to the T1 bacteriophage stood in direct opposition to the well-known fact that bacteria could become trained to be resistant to a variety of drugs.[18] However, since this resistance was not absolute, but rather tended to occur in a gradual, step-wise fashion, in direct proportion to the concentration of drug used, it was taken to mean that the mutation was *postadaptive* in nature, meaning that it occurred in direct response to environmental challenge.[19]

A second experiment, conducted by J. and E.M. Lederberg in 1952, also showed that bacteria could become resistant to a drug (in this case streptomycin) without being directly exposed to it. This apparent confirmation of the neo-Darwinian thesis spelled the end for Lamarckism in the academic community, in spite of the fact that these two experimental findings didn't even come close to showing that *all* adaptive mutations in nature similarly occur in a random, unprovoked fashion. The neo-Darwinians, as Opadia-Kadima points out, were quick to develop an entire cosmology around these two very limited findings, in which "everything that evolved was designated the lucky beneficiary of chance. Enzymes, proteins, and even man himself, were held to be the products of mere chance. In short, the biologist's belief in the creative power of chance soon equalled or surpassed the Christian belief in the creative power of God."[20]

Opadia-Kadima goes on to show how Luria's original analogy relating "evolutionary chance" with "gambling chance" was unrealistic, and therefore mistaken. The reason for this is that while an individual gambler may continue playing on a slot machine until he eventually wins, his winnings rarely end up outweighing his losses. In order to obtain a "chance-win," then, a gambler has to make a significant investment that is rarely regained when the "chance-win" is finally made. Opadia-Kadima concludes that a "chance-win" in nature is also equally costly. For while a given adaptive mutation can be shown to "randomly" occur in the laboratory, the benefit conferred is largely confined to the unnatural environment imposed by the experimenter. In the natural world, these same mutations are an adaptive liability, and so typically lead to an early death.[21]

Interestingly enough, the preadaptive mutations which Luria, Delbruck, and the Lederbergs purportedly discovered fall precisely into this category. Whereas these mutations may be selected for in the artificial conditions of the laboratory, they are invariably selected *against* under natural conditions.[22] As a consequence, "they furnish false guidance about the types of adaptive mutations which were preserved in the evolutionary process."[23]

In other words, the artificial selection imposed by the experimenter in the laboratory amounts to a "survival of the less fit," which are then eliminated when the conditions revert back to normal.

In contrast to the severity of this type of artificial selection, natural selection isn't always lethal. Rather, it tends to impose hardship on the species in question.[24] This lack of extreme severity in the selective force gives much of the population in question a sufficient amount of time for generating evolutionary responses to it.

Opadia-Kadima goes on to note how most evolutionary responses in the wild typically involve two or more genes making a simultaneous and coordinated change, as we have seen.[25] This simple fact effectively rules out blind chance as the cause of such coordinated mutations, since the resultant probabilities are so low as to be beyond rational consideration. For instance, the probability of two coordinated mutations producing the ability to hydrolyze lactose in *E. coli*—the first in a structural gene and the second in a regulatory gene—is calculated to be no greater than 1 in 10^{14}. These odds are sufficiently remote to effectively rule out chance as a possible cause of the adaptive mutation.[26]

The climax of Opadia-Kadima's paper comes when he describes a series of experiments that clearly show how "genomic stress" can lead to adaptive mutations in *E. coli*. In the first of these experiments, J.H. Campbell in 1973 devised an experiment which targeted a strain of *E. coli* that was unable to utilize the sugar lactose, due to the deletion of a gene for the enzyme B-galactosidase, which ordinarily enables the organism to process the sugar. Once this B-galactosidase-deficient strain was obtained and cultured over many generations, it was never able to regain its ability to process lactose through a spontaneous genetic mutation, that is, as long as it was not allowed to come into contact with the sugar. When the sugar was introduced into the culture medium, however, the adaptive mutation soon appeared. The appearance of this adaptive mutation clearly was dependent on a Lamarckian type of contact with the relevant environmental stimulus.[27]

In order to confirm this important finding, Campbell introduced a second set of conditions that left the resulting conclusion unmistakable. Upon introducing this same strain of B-galactosidase-deficient organisms into a broth that contained both lactose and another carbon-based food source, the organisms were observed to thrive on the non-lactose food source without developing a single mutation that would have enabled them to regain their lost capacity to utilize lactose. Once the non-lactose food source was depleted, however, a specific "genomic stress" was initiated that resulted in the subsequent development of *two separate mutations*—one for a structural gene and the other for a regulatory gene—which together enabled the organisms to utilize the lactose for food. Clearly, a food-related environmental stress was able to stimulate a series of mutations that would not have otherwise occurred.[28] Opadia-Kadima concludes that "it was only when individual organisms were starved, in the presence of lactose, that mutation aimed at conferring the ability to utilize it occurred. In other words, it was 'genomic stress,' caused by the need to hydrolyze lactose, that set in motion the mutational events."[29] Interestingly enough, when the newly-produced enzyme was subsequently analyzed, it was *not* found to be the expected B-galactosidase. Rather, an entirely *new* enzyme with twice the molecular weight of B-galactosidase had evolved in response to the experimental challenge. In 1974, Hall and Hartl performed a similar series of experiments, with the intention of learning whether or not these new lactose-processing organisms constituted a single strain. They discovered a total of 34 different strains, all of which had the remarkable feature of possessing the *same* lactose-processing enzyme that Campbell had produced in his own experiments! Clearly there was nothing random about the evolution of this "new" enzyme. The capacity for synthesizing it had apparently existed all along, but only as a potentiality within the genome. Before this potentiality could be expressed, however, a specific type of "genomic stress" was required. Upon being exposed to this stress, the genome was able to do the rest.[30]

In response to these amazing discoveries, Opadia-Kadima draws the following conclusion:

> It appears that biologists have no option but to concede that the slot machine analogy led them astray. The fact that the new enzyme evolved in response to starvation, in the presence of lactose, suggests that *E. coli* are equipped with a mechanism for causing *new* enzymes to come into being when the need arises. The possibility that postadaptive mutation plays a major role in the evolution of *new* enzymes appears to be fairly strong.[31]

Similar findings have also been reported in recent years by two other investigators. In 1988, cancer researcher John Cairns, working at the Harvard School of Public Health, conducted an intriguing experiment that was designed to test whether genomic stress could induce the occurrence of favorable mutations.[32] Cairns cultured a strain of bacteria and then fed them a diet consisting primarily of lactose, a sugar they were unable to metabolize due to a long-standing genetic defect. Remarkably, a significant proportion of the starving organisms spontaneously acquired the ability to metabolize their new food source by mutating in a favorable direction.

Several months later Barry Hall, a University of Rochester mutation researcher, obtained even more convincing evidence of stress-induced mutational change.[33] He fed starving bacteria a novel food source that could not be digested without the occurrence of two separate mutations, neither of which carried any positive survival value in themselves. Amazingly, a significant percentage of the bacteria actually evolved to fit their surroundings by producing the two required mutations *simultaneously*. The odds for two such favorable mutations happening at random are vanishingly small, so Hall has ruled out the possibility that they could have been due to chance. He believes instead that his results signify a genuine case of selection-induced mutational change.

Hall's findings have been confirmed by several other researchers working with bacteria, and Hall himself has obtained similar results with yeast.[34] These findings indicate that the forces of selection can indeed steer mutations in a favorable direction, contrary to the predictions of neo-Darwinian theory.

8.6 Genomic Stress and Extinction

This relationship between genomic stress and favorable mutational change correlates with an intriguing historical fact. Each of the five major extinctions in our evolutionary past, and to a lesser extent all of the other "background extinctions" that have also taken place, have been followed by substantial increases in biodiversity and complexity after the initial dying.[35] We can account for these remarkable increases by referring back to the stress-mediated model of mutational change discussed above. If genomic stress is indeed capable of inducing an increased rate of favorable mutations, then one would expect a great deal of positive evolutionary change to have followed each of the major extinctions of the past, because these great dyings were in all likelihood precipitated by an extreme amount of environmental stress. Such a profound degree of ecological disruption would have overwhelmed the adaptive capacities of most species, and extinction would have been the typical result in these cases. However, in those instances where organisms were able to mount a sufficient response to these environmental cataclysms, an extremely rapid period of favorable mutational change could have easily been provoked.

This appears to have been precisely the case with the dinosaurs. Prior to the dinosaurs' extinction, mammals comprised a relatively tiny and insignificant part of the animal world. Following the huge K-T Mass Extinction that did in the dinosaurs, however, mammals rapidly flourished, and one line eventually evolved into *Homo sapiens*. This remarkable conjunction between the demise of one dominant species and the rise of another has traditionally been explained in terms of habitat availability.[36] On this view, mammals were unable to rise to prominence before the extinction of the dinosaurs because the dinosaurs were physically blocking their upward ascent. Once the dinosaurs were gone, though, there was suddenly room for mammals to flourish, so they did.

While there is undoubtedly some degree of truth to this standard teaching, an alternative explanation is much more enticing. It has to do with the phenomenon of stress-induced mutational change discussed above. In this conceptualization, the mammalian rise to prominence was precipitated, not by the physical removal of the dinosaurs *per se*, but rather by the severe genomic stress that the mammals experienced in response to the environmental upheaval that polished off the dinosaurs. This genomic stress could very well have induced a sufficient number of favorable mutations in the incipient mammalian population to eventually propel them into worldwide dominance.

A parallel situation exists in the field of human growth and development. It is a well-known fact that the most significant strides in individual psychospiritual growth are typically precipitated by major personal catastrophes. In an effort to cope with these heightened stress levels, people often find it necessary to rise to the occasion by growing more mature and responsible. This same "no pain, no gain" relation holds true for the body as well. Adults physically grow stronger when their muscles are first stressed to the point of exhaustion. This being the case, it is curious to note that the biosphere seems to have followed the same sort of principle in growing more diverse and complex over the millennia.

8.7   Protein Synthesis and Evolution

Protein synthesis is another area in which the environment may be capable of influencing the inner dynamics of the cell, thereby enabling the host organism to better adapt to its surroundings. Until recently, geneticists believed that protein synthesis was a relatively straightforward process, in which genetic information[37] in the nucleus was believed to be carried by messenger RNA (mRNA) molecules out to the ribosomes in the cytoplasm, where the proteins themselves are actually assembled. Today, however, we know that this is a gross oversimplification that doesn't do justice to the profound complexity of the cell's protein synthesizing machinery.

To the contrary, geneticists now recognize protein synthesis to be an *extremely* complicated procedure, in which mRNA molecules must typically undergo several stages of elaborate biochemical processing before they are ready to specify the structure of protein molecules.[38] Part of this biochemical processing is performed by the RNA molecule itself, as it employs its own cut-and-splice enzymes to edit out introns, or the nitrogenous bases that do not code for proteins.

At this point a second stage of editing takes place, in which information that is not directly contained in the DNA is actually added to the mRNA molecule itself by little "guide RNAs."[39] It isn't yet known how this process is actually mediated, or which factors determine the precise sequence of bases to be added. It could be something as straightforward as a series a base ommissions in the DNA, or it could be something much more elaborate. It could even represent the metabolic pathway through which the environment is able to influence the course of protein synthesis, thereby making it possible for the host organism to evolve in direct response to environmental pressures.

The final stage of mRNA processing occurs at the ribosomal level, and it involves a fundamental reinterpretation of the mRNA base sequence by the ribsomes.[40] This is called "RNA recoding," and it takes place through a complex series of frame-shifting events in the ribosomes themselves, in which they actually skip forward or backward over a series of bases in their search for a particular codon. In one instance, reported by University of Utah researcher Wai Mun Huang, a ribosome ignored a sequence of 50 bases in the mRNA molecule before it found the codon it wanted.[41] This process of RNA recoding provides yet another possible avenue through which feedback from the environment can influence the future course of protein synthesis, once again making it possible for organisms to better adapt to their surroundings in a variety of ways.

To the extent that this Lamarckian scenario is accurate, it would have the effect of greatly accelerating the rate of evolution in the wild, because it would enable organisms to play a direct role in their own adaptation. This could account, at least in part, for the punctuated nature of the evolutionary process that is observed throughout the fossil record. On this view, species would have evolved rapidly because they would have possessed the inner ability to respond to environmental change.

8.8 Discussion

What we seem to be uncovering here is a vast and utterly ingenious informational network at the molecular level that is designed to give organisms the capacity for dealing with a wide range of environmental stressors. It may have even been partly responsible for generating the various species themselves, again through an elaborate feedback process with the environment. While researchers have yet to elucidate all of the genetic mechanisms that are operative at the molecular level, it is significant for our purposes to note that we have *already* discovered enough to substantially bolster the Deistic Evolutionist's vision of an inwardly-directed evolutionary process.

While many of these genetic mechanisms seem to confirm some form of Lamarckian inheritance, this doesn't necessarily mean that those characters that were acquired in this manner were completely non-existent (i.e., absent from the genome) before they made their appearance. It is quite possible that they could have existed all along in a suppesed state in the genome, waiting only for the proper environmental trigger to become expressed. The findings of modern molecular biology strongly support this latter interpretation, as they show that the vast majority of adaptive variants that appear in different populations were *already contained* within the genetic material of the parent populations.[42]

Immunologists have discovered a similar property in the immune system's remarkable capacity to anticipate the appearance of a wide range of antigens (allergy-provoking substances) *before* it ever comes into contact with them. What this means is that the immune system doesn't have to actually be exposed to a given antigen before it can manufacture the appropriate antibody to deal with it, since the immune system apparently has had the marvelous capacity to produce all possible antibodies to all possible antigens from the very beginning, before any significant contact with the environment has ever been made. This is all the more amazing in light of the plethora of new chemicals that have been created by modern technology in recent years; even though these substances have never existed before, the immune system nevertheless "knows" how to deal with them, in the sense that it can somehow produce the appropriate antibodies to deal with each one.

The work of Nobel laureate Barbara Mclintock also corroborates these findings. In the 1930s Mclintock demonstrated that stress can induce transposon activity within the genome. Transposons, or "jumping genes," are highly portable genetic fragments that move around in a very precise fashion within the genome.

Now, if stress can induce transposon activity, and if transposon activity can reorganize the entire genome, then it follows that stress can induce genomic reorganization. Going one step further, if genomic reorganization can result in the spontaneous production of new characters and even new species, then it also follows that external stress must be potentially capable of inducing major changes in the evolutionary descent of organisms. This is very much in line with the view of the Deistic Evolutionist, who believes that the entire living world also arose in response to stress-induced changes within the genomes of the first living creatures. On this view, the genome is so ingenious and versatile that it can respond to stress by evolving itself into a plethora of new forms and structures whenever the need arises (to a point, of course).

In other words, the genome seems to possess within itself the capacity to produce all the relevant variations in any given species, long before any significant environmental contact has been made. Such an *a priori* adaptive capacity, however, only makes sense if it were somehow programmed into the genome all along, since environmental effects would by definition not be available at the very beginning to condition the genome in a certain direction. While it is possible to imagine that the genome somehow acquired these latent adaptive capacities by random selective effects in the distant past, this would not be possible for the many new adaptive variants that have recently been elicited by man, in response to substances and situations that have never existed before. This would seem to directly rule out any significant environmental role in the ultimate origin of this adaptive capacity. What this means in terms of how evolution probably took place is also quite clear: the genome was probably never as passive during the evolutionary process as was once thought. Indeed, given the fact that the genome obviously has the *a priori* capacity to evolve new structures and new enzymes in response to specific environmental stressors, it would seem that the genome was probably *directly* responsible for initiating many of the evolutionary changes that took place in the distant past.

The question ultimately boils down to how far back one is willing to take this genomic capacity for producing pre-formed characters in response to specific environmental needs. There is no reason to believe that this capacity is a recent phenomenon, because many creatures are essentially the same now as they were millions of years ago. It follows from the paleontological fact that the genomes of these creatures were probably equally similar to their modern counterparts. If so, it stands to reason that the genome was just as instrumental in producing pre-formed characters back then as it is today. This would seem to constitute powerful evidence for the existence of an evolutionary-type program within the primordial genomic structure itself, which would have been responsible for directing the evolutionary process all along.

Such a possibility would explain many things. It would explain why life was so quick to evolve into the many complex forms found in the Cambrian Explosion. It would explain why no genuine evolutionary intermediates have ever been found, and why the fossil record is one of remarkable stasis, punctuated by relatively brief periods of rapid change. It would explain how the eye in all its complexity could have evolved, not just once, but at least 40 separate times in distinct lineages.[43] Finally, it would explain the incredible degree of complexity found in all living creatures, including man.[44]

To the extent that this self-programming capacity of the genome is genuine, the question we now need to ask ourselves is this: where did the genome originally get this amazing capacity to begin with? Given the likelihood that this ability probably dates back to Precambrian times and even beyond, it is hard to see how it could have ever evolved as an accidental byproduct of the mere struggle for survival. For if the function of this genomic self-programming capacity is to make evolutionary change possible, and if Precambrian animals, many of which were virtually identical to their modern-day counterparts, also possessed this capability, it would seem that this capacity was directly involved in making the evolutionary process possible, and *not* the other way around. Indeed, how could the evolutionary process have bestowed this self-programming capacity upon the genome if this capacity was in existence *before* most evolutionary changes had taken place? While it is possible to assert that this self-programming capacity evolved shortly after life itself did, it is hard to see how this could have ever happened in response to the mere struggle for survival.

Perhaps this is why the neo-Darwinists have been so opposed to Lamarckism all these years: because of the many religious implications it seems to bring with it. To be sure, if the many adaptations that have occurred throughout evolutionary history were due solely to chance, it is possible to believe that the rise of life itself may have also been a chance event as well. However, if these adaptations were the result of the ingenious capacity of the genome to spontaneously adapt itself to changing environmental conditions, a Higher Intelligence seems to have been necessary to make this possible.

As far as the Deistic Evolutionist's position is concerned, however, it doesn't matter who ends up being right in the end—the Lamarckians or the neo-Darwinians—since the Deistic Evolutionist's position can be affirmed in both instances. If the neo-Darwinian insistence on "chance" variation turns out to be true, the Deistic Evolutionist can simply assert that adaptive mutations are the result of a predetermined genetic program that makes a random appearance in any given population. If, however, the Lamarckian insistence on the adaptability of the genome turns out to be true, the Deistic Evolutionist can simply assert that it was God Who originally gave the genome this miraculous ability to begin with, and that the Lamarckian inheritance of acquired characters is simply the naturalistic mechanism that God ordained to make evolution possible. Either way, God's ultimate Authorship over the evolutionary process is preserved.

Notes

1. Taylor, *The Great Evolution Mystery*, p. 141.
2. Although Taylor doesn't explicitly credit God for this initial genetic programming, it is hard to see how it could have ever happened in the absence of a Creator.
3. The term "orthogenesis," as I am using it here, differs significantly from the original meaning intended by Theodor Eimer, the chief popularizer of orthogenesis. Eimer used the term to refer to a straightline evolutionary course, with *nonadaptive* trends originating from within the organism itself, and with no role at all being played by environmental adaptation. I am using the term, however, to refer *only* to some degree of internal directedness to the evolutionary process. In this more limited sense, I do not see orthogenesis as being incompatible with environmental opportunism and adaptation. For even if we assume that nonadaptive trends actually exist (which may or may not be the case), this belief nevertheless entails a deeper affirmation of a general, inwardly-guided trend forward. In addition, it is also true that what is non-adaptive in one environment may be adaptive in another, so the whole question of orthogenetic maladaptation becomes subordinated to the overall push upward on the phylogenetic ladder. On the way up, any number of inwardly-driven trends can be rejected by natural selection, leaving behind only the best-adapted variants for continued survival.

Furthermore, this general push upward needn't be isolated from any significant degree of environmental input. To the contrary, it is possible for this general trend forward to work in tandem with the environment, but only in a general, diffuse sense. The environment can thus stimulate the organism to throw up certain types of variations, but it would still remain for natural selection to choose the best-adapted variants for continued survival.

4. In response to the accusation that an omnipotent God could have come up with a better means of ensuring the optimal adaptability of the creatures, we can only say that given all the other considerations that figured into God's Creative Plan, a better means was simply not available. While an omnipotent God could conceivably have designed perfect adaptability into each species from the very beginning, He could only have done so if this were the *only* creative task He was trying to accomplish. However, as soon as other creative goals, such as the instantiation of the Human Essence, are inserted into the picture, only certain combinations of creative mechanisms become *compossible* with one another. In conjunction with this law of compossibility, it was by hypothesis impossible for God to have designed perfect adaptability into the creatures, on the one hand, and to have instantiated the Human Essence, on the other, since, as we will see in Part IV, the Human Essence seems to necessarily entail an opportunistic evolutionary world which directly parallels the necessary nature of human development.

5. As we have seen, there is a tendency in the scientific community to side with only one alternative when two competing explanatory alternatives are faced. This tendency seems to have its origin in the actual mechanisms that mediate physical and chemical reactions, since at the foundational level of physical reality only one competing alternative is usually correct. For instance, although amino acids exist in both left-handed and right-handed forms, only the left-handed forms are used in living organisms. It would be a mistake, however, to generalize this "either-or" mentality indiscriminately to the realm of philosophical explanation, because oftentimes two competing philosophical alternatives, which seem to be mutually exclusive of one another, are not actually so in reality. In these cases, the apparent exclusivity of the alternatives turns out to be an illusion that is based on our fundamental ignorance of nature's higher degree of unity. Such appears to be the case with the ongoing battle between creation and evolution; it isn't one alternative or the other that is correct, but *both*, since both alternatives find expression in the natural world.

6. The use of the word "force" here applies only to an inner tendency, not a true force that would co-exist alongside the four primary forces of physics. Thus, I am not advocating a return to any type of dualistic vitalism, as there is no evidence that there are any other physical forces in living organisms besides those known to modern physics. I am rather suggesting a radical type of *emergentism*, where a certain level of molecular complexity automatically produces the "force" of life, through a fundamental manipulation of the basic laws of chemistry and physics.

7. Peter J. Bowler, *Evolution* (Los Angeles: The University of California Press, 1989), p. 241.

8. It should be pointed out that neither Salthe nor Eldredge directly supports any degree of orthogenesis in evolution. My purpose has been simply to show that their hierarchical view of evolution is nevertheless consistent with the weak orthogenetic view we have been discussing in this chapter.

9. This isn't a valid test of Lamarckism, however, because the role of the environ-

ment in this case is only a crude caricature of the way the environment may actually influence evolutionary development in the wild. The Lamarkian hypothesis is that certain forms of *appropriate* environmental stimuli will lead to genetically inspired changes in an organism's adaptive format, which are then passed on to its progeny.

10. Taylor, *The Great Evolution Mystery*, p. 53.
11. Otto E. Landman, "Inheritance of Acquired Characteristics," *Scientific American*, Vol. 266, No. 3, Mar., 1993, p. 150.
12. Ibid.
13. Ibid.
14. Ibid.
15. Ibid.
16. Ibid.
17. G.Z. Opadia-Kadima, "How the Slot Machine Led Biologists Astray," *The Journal of Theoretical Biology* (1987) *124*, p. 128.
18. Ibid., p. 129.
19. Ibid.
20. Ibid.
21. Ibid., p. 130.
22. Ibid.
23. Ibid., p. 131.
24. Ibid.
25. Ibid.
26. Ibid., p. 132.
27. Ibid.
28. Ibid., pp. 132–133.
29. Ibid., p. 133.
30. Ibid., p. 134.
31. Ibid.
32. John Rennie, "DNA's New Twists," *Scientific American*, Vol. 266, No. 3, March, 1993, p. 131.
33. Ibid.
34. Ibid.
35. David M. Raup, *Extinction: Bad Genes or Bad Luck?*, pp. 187–188.
36. Ibid., pp. 19–20, 187.
37. The genetic code contains the actual information for the assembly of the proteins themselves. Proteins are the structural and metabolic molecules of the body. They are comprised of long sequences of amino acids, which are themselves specified in the genetic code by unique three-base sequences called codons. Each codon specifies a particular amino acid, so a long string of codons is required to produce even the simplest protein.
38. Ibid., pp. 131–132.
39. Ibid., p. 132.
40. Ibid.
41. Ibid.
42. Gerald L. Schroeder, *Genesis and the Big Bang* (New York: Bantam, 1990), p. 137.
43. Letter from Ernst Mayr to FJT dated December 23, 1982.
44. If the Lamarckian inheritance of acquired characters turns out to have been responsible for the majority of evolutionary changes that have occurred in the past, the orthogenetic programming we have been discussing in this chapter will

then consist of two overall types. The first type is the orthogenetic programming of the genome's *capacity* to respond to external environmental input. The second type is the resulting programming changes that are subsequently acquired in *response* to this environmental input. Stated another way, the Lamarckian hypothesis requires a baseline capacity of the genome to *program itself* in response to changing environmental conditions.

CHAPTER 9

Evolution and the New Genetics

A universe predisposed to create life seems a more likely product of divine design than a universe in which life was a fluke.

ROBERT WRIGHT

According to the Deistic Evolutionist's weak orthogenetic view of the evolutionary process, genetic variations are coordinated to some degree with the environmental forces of selection in nature, so that a coordinated product—a useful adaptation—is eventually produced. But what exactly *is* this orthogenetic tendency, or does it even exist at all?

As Taylor and others have pointed out, given the many stupendous feats of creation that have been attributed to the evolutionary process, the evidence for the existence of an orthogenetic force appears to be overwhelming. After all, how could the eye in all its stunning complexity possibly have been invented[1] a bare minimum of 40 separate times, when even the *single* random occurrence of an eye, even over many generations of cumulative selection, would qualify as a miracle of the highest order? This fact, along with countless other similar ones, seems to indicate that some type of orthogenetic law or force has been operative throughout evolutionary history, and has in fact been responsible for bringing the pinnacle of evolution—human beings—into existence.

Actually, careful thinkers dating back to Aristotle have realized that some sort of vital force *had* to have been operative in living organisms, otherwise they would be no different than the inanimate matter of which they are comprised. This "life force" came to be known by various names (including the vis viva, elan vital, Lebenskraft, and Entelechie), and those who believed in its existence came to be known as vitalists.

As Ernst Mayr[2] has pointed out, however, a careful reading of Aristotle reveals that he didn't believe in an otherworldly life force *per se*. Rather, he seems to have believed in a kind of "genetic program" which turns out to be surprisingly similar to the masking theory proposed by Taylor. Johannes Muller's concept of the *Lebenskraft* appears to be a similar reference to such a genetic program.

In the last forty to fifty years, however, the spectre of vitalism has fallen into severe disrepute in the biological community, largely because no one has been able to demonstrate the existence of a vital life force in living tissue that transcends the laws of physics and chemistry. However, the primary reason why vitalism was proposed in the first place was simply to differentiate living matter from non-living matter. In order to be able to properly address the vitalist issue, then, we need to ask ourselves the following question: What exactly is present in the physical realm that separates all living matter from non-living matter?

As Mayr points out in the above-cited article, the one absolute difference between living and non-living matter is that the former contains "a historically evolved genetic program, coded in the DNA of the nucleus of the zygote (or in RNA in some viruses). Nothing comparable exists in the inanimate world, except for manmade computers."[3]

Now we are in a position to understand why the behavior of living matter is so different from the behavior of inanimate matter, even though both contain the same types of atoms and both follow the same set of physical laws. *Living organisms behave differently because they have been organized to an exceedingly high degree via the information contained in the DNA.* As a direct consequence of this fact, we don't have to resort to non-material forces *per se* to explain the unique behavior of living matter; we can simply attribute it to the enormously sophisticated genetic information contained within the DNA molecule itself.

Going one step futher, since the existence of DNA in living cells does in fact appear to be the only absolute difference between living and non-living matter (except for the extreme amount of order in living matter, which is largely a function of DNA[4]), it now becomes sensible for us to posit a second question: Could the existence of DNA *itself* somehow be responsible for the vital orthogenetic force that has brought living matter to its present state of order? The answer to this question appears to be "yes."

DNA's main purpose in the cellular economy is to provide detailed biochemical instructions for an organism's ontological development, as well as for its day-to-day metabolic functioning. Hence, the larger significance of the DNA molecule can be expressed in a single word: *information*, and lots of it. The DNA in a human cell, for instance, contains enough high-level information to fill over 1000 volumes of Encyclopedia Britannica.[5] Approximately two per cent of this information is used to code directly for the many structural and regulatory proteins (enzymes) that go into making up the body.

But what if the genetic code contains more information than this? What if, in addition to the instructions for the assembly and maintenance of a given organism, it also contains detailed instructions for the evolutionary development of the entire living world? This is certainly a very real possibility, since geneticists have only unraveled a very small percentage of the information that is actually contained in the DNA molecule. As a consequence, it is distinctly possible that an entirely different class of genetic instructions could actually exist within the genome.

There is good reason for believing that the genome is capable of encoding a great deal more information than that which is required by an organism's immediate needs. For instance, it is now known that the DNA of each cell in the body contains the genetic information—not just for the individual cell that happens to contain it—but also for the rest of the body as well. The DNA of bone cells, for example, not only contains vital genetic information pertaining to bone structure and development; it also contains the genetic information that pertains to all the *other* organ systems of the body.

Now, if each DNA molecule can contain all the genetic information for the entire body, there doesn't appear to be any *a priori* reason why it can't also contain the genetic instructions for the evolutionary development of all life on earth. In fact, if the same relationship holds true between each cell's genetic control of the entire body and the each individual species' relationship to the larger evolutionary process, then each individual species will also contain the genetic information for the evolutionary development of all life on earth.

Physicist David Bohm's theory of the *implicate order* supports this radical contention. Bohm believes, with good empirical[6] reason, that all the information of the entire universe is holistically enfolded into each of its constituent parts. Clearly, if this same principle of the implicate order can also be applied to the genome, then any DNA molecule in any given species will also contain the genetic information for the evolutionary development of all life on earth.

Indeed, given the fact that only two percent of the DNA molecule actually codes for structural proteins in the body, it is quite reasonable to suppose that the other 98 percent might be serving some other larger function in the evolutionary process. It is thus possible, then, that we have not yet fully realized the true scope of the DNA molecule's informational content.[7]

9.1 Homeotic Genes: A Model of Centralized Holistic Developmental Regulation

The existence of a centralized genetic program regulating evolutionary development isn't as far fetched as it may initially seem. A variation on this basic theme in the process of embryogenesis, called the *homeobox*, is already known to exist, and there is good reason to believe that this developmental precedent may extend to other areas of the evolutionary process as well.

The homeobox consists of a stretch of genetic material in the DNA molecule that codes for body-part formation.[8] Remarkably, these "homeotic genes" are arranged in a very precise sequence on the chromosome that directly mimics the order of body parts in a particular organism.[9] For instance, one cluster of homeotic genes in the fruit fly is known to control the development of the fly's head, while other clusters are known to control the development of other key body parts.[10]

Significantly, researchers have noted that the homeobox in all of these body-forming genes is identical, regardless of which particular body part is being coded for.[11] That is, the same group of homeotic genes are known to control the development of all key body parts.[12] This is the first instance in which the homeobox exerts global control over the developmental process.

The second instance of the homeobox's global control network is more astonishing still. Researchers have discovered that the same group of homeotic genes can be found throughout much of the living world, where they regulate the embryological development of species as diverse as the flatworm and the human. It doesn't matter whether the species under consideration is the nematode, the cow, or the human—the same sequence of homeotic, body-forming genes can be found in them all.[13] Yale University microbiologist William McGinnis has conclusively demonstrated the universality of the homeobox by effectively transplanting it from mice and humans to fruit flies: despite the huge phylogenetic jump between species, the transplanted homeotic genes were nevertheless able to accurately code for each stage of the fruit flies' embryological development.[14]

The implications of this genetic finding are truly enormous. It is nothing short of amazing to realize that the same group of homeotic genes is capable of coding for the embryological development of such radically different species as horses, bears, ringworms, and humans. This is clear evidence that the homeobox knows how to direct the embryological development of all the different creatures in the animal kingdom. But what is evolution but the sequential embryological development of a series of different creatures? This being the case, it is possible that an analog of the homeobox could indeed have been responsible for directing the evolution of all life on earth.

Prior to the discovery of the homeobox, the existence of a central genetic program directing evolutionary development seemed to many to be unlikely and even outrageous. But now that we know for a fact that the embryological development of all animal species is controlled by a single group of homeotic genes, it is no longer unreasonable to assert the further existence of an orthogenetic evolutionary program in all forms of life.

In other words, the discovery of the homeobox has automatically set a major biological precedent, insofar as it tells us that it is technically feasible for a single group of genes to preside over the development of all animal species. This being the case, the existence of the homeobox makes the existence of a larger orthogenetic evolutionary program more likely overall, because these two types of regulatory centers are fundamentally similar to one another. Both function holistically, for instance, and both are located within the genome. Both act across species lines to control development, and both are able to switch the appropriate biochemical cascades on and off to produce the "desired" end product. Finally, both are extremely elaborate teleological processes that far outstrip our current understanding of how developmental biology works.

At first it was believed that the existence of the homeobox was confined to segmented animals only. Recent ground-breaking research, however, has discovered homeotic genes in non-segmented organisms such as the nematode, leech, sea urchin, and even in higher plants.[15] This extends the homeobox's possible control of the evolutionary process over a much larger territory, and thereby increases the likelihood that it contains part or all of a hypothetical "master plan" governing evolution.

Indeed, the fact that the same homeobox exists throughout so much of the living world clearly illustrates that a single genetic regulatory center can in fact control the development of a wide range of different creatures. It would appear, then, that the sole difference between the homeobox and the larger orthogenetic program postulated by the Deistic Evolutionist lies in the actual *sequence* of species that is actually coded for. The homeobox controls the embryological development of each animal species within each species' rigid boundary lines. An orthogenetic program, on the other hand, would extend this trans-specific developmental control to an entire *line* of evolving creatures that physically grow out of one another. It is thus presumably able to code for the sequential evolution of a wide variety of different species whenever the surrounding conditions are appropriate.

The many similarities between the homeobox and a possible orthogenetic program within the genome suggests that these two genetic regulatory centers may in fact be related to one another, or perhaps even be identical. Indeed, if the homeobox could ever be demonstrated to control the sequential development of several different species out of a single line of evolving organisms, it would be indistinguishable from the type of orthogenetic evolutionary program I am postulating.

With these ideas in mind, the elucidation of the homeobox in 1984 undoubtedly ranks as one of the most important biological discoveries of all time, because it links the embryological development of the entire animal kingdom to a single set of trans-specific regulatory genes. The homeobox thus qualifies as an integral part of the larger evolutionary process, because evolution itself can only take place within a coherent line of developing creatures. Indeed, since the homeobox has survived intact[16] for a half a billion years, we can conclude that it has probably functioned in an extremely important capacity during much of life's evolutionary history on this planet.

Although homeobox researchers are not yet prepared to state that the homeobox has played an important role in the larger evolutionary process, they are nevertheless beginning to see a deeper connection between the two.[17] Schughart, Kappen,[18] and Ruddle, for instance, have conducted an extremely elaborate analysis of the phylogenetic relationships between 21 murine *Antennapedia*-class homeobox genes in the fruit fly, and have concluded that these regulatory genes were themselves ultimately derived from duplications of extensive genomic regions in a common ancestor. These duplications suggest a possible relationship between homeobox genes and the introduction of new species, as the following quote well illustrates:

> The homeobox gene system respresents an excellent system to study the evolution of vertebrate genomes. The extremely high conservation of both the nucleotide sequence of the homeobox and the structural organization of genes within clusters provides valuable tools to identify homologous sequences in different species and to analyze phylogenetic relationships of genes within this gene family. It will be challenging to investigate whether the expansion of the ancestral gene cluster is accompanied by the appearance of new structural elements and whether the duplication of homeobox gene clusters in vertebrates might have contributed to the establishment of new body plans.[19]

This is an intriguing passage that clearly seems to anticipate the discovery of a major relationship between ancestral homeobox duplication and the introduction of new species. As we have seen, this isn't as far-fetched as it may sound, since the same group of homeotic genes knows how to specify the embryological development of *all* segmented animals. The fact that the same homeobox sequence has been conserved for over a half a billion years strongly supports us in this contention, since we would expect any evolutionary regulatory center to persist unchanged throughout most of the evolutionary process.

9.2   "Junk" DNA

Another part of the genome that could possibly contain part or all of the orthogenetic regulatory center we are postulating is the so-called "junk" portion. Technically known as "introns," these long repeating segments comprise an astounding 98 percent of the DNA molecule's total base-pair content. They were discovered in 1977 and were originally believed to serve no useful purpose at all within the genome because they do not code for any structural proteins; hence their designation as "junk." (It is the remaining 2 percent of the genome that codes for the various proteins that make up the host species.)

With the advent of modern molecular genetics, however, it is now known that several classes of introns can actually code for proteins. Group I introns, for instance, can code for proteins that enable them to transpose at the DNA level; these introns are also self-splicing as well.[20] Group II introns can encode a large protein that is similar to reverse transcriptase, whose function is apparently to promote the loss of other introns through a process of reverse transcription in mitochondria.[21] Introns are thus turning out to possess a significant regulatory function within the genome, and many researchers are now openly discussing the role that introns may have played in genetic evolution itself.

The initial confusion concerning the possible role of introns in the cellular economy seems to have been exacerbated by the apparent fact that they do not code for any structural proteins at all within the host species. This realization seems to have led to the premature conclusion that introns are nothing more than useless "junk" within the genome. However, it clearly doesn't follow that, just because introns don't code for any structural proteins in the host creature, they are therefore useless junk. The possibility always remains that they could be serving *other* useful functions within the cell, such as gene regulation. And indeed, recent research is bearing this latter possibility out.

Nevertheless, some researchers have come to the conclusion that much of this "excess" DNA in the genome is simply there by chance. Others, utilizing complex computer models that attempt to simulate the many rules that are known to control DNA replication, have come to the conclusion that these "useless" segments may simply be needed to stabilize the genome.[22] While this hypothesis may in fact turn out to be true, this wouldn't necessarily be the only important role served by introns. The possibility always remains that they could also be serving a higher evolutionary function in the genome as well.

The one thing that seems almost certain about introns is that they are probably not nearly as useless as many researchers would like to believe. While they may not serve a direct function in structural protein synthesis, they could very well end up playing other important roles within the overall evolutionary process.

The very notion that "junk" DNA might be useless directly contradicts almost everything we have learned about the cell up until the present. For one thing, uselessness in general is utterly uncharacteristic of the cellular economy, as virtually everything that has been learned in the field of molecular biology has revealed the cell to be a miraculously efficient entity that wastes little or no unnecessary energy in accomplishing its goals. When compared to this spartan utilitarian background, the very thought that 98 per cent of the genetic code may ultimately be useless stands out like a sore thumb. It simply does not fit in.

The existence of nuclear editing enzymes supports us in this conclusion, as it shows that the nuclear apparatus is fully "aware" of these "junk" sequences, to the point that it finds it necessary to remove them before allowing the process of protein synthesis to continue. While this "awareness" in and of itself doesn't necessarily require "junk" DNA to serve a useful purpose (i.e., the "junk" sequences themselves could conceivably be edited out precisely *because* of their uselessness), it would seem to be more reasonable to suspect that the cell would only go to the trouble of editing out these sequences if their existence was important and necessary in the first place.

9.2.1 A Possible Role for Introns in Evolution

In order to get a feel for the possible functions that might be served by "junk" DNA, it will be useful to reiterate what is already known about the functions served by the DNA molecule. It has been known for some time now that one purpose of DNA is to code for the specific physical characters that are seen in a given organism (the phenotype). Another related purpose of DNA is to code for the specific developmental (i.e., ontological) sequences in the host organism, from conception to physical adulthood. Finally, it is further known that each DNA molecule contains the genetic instructions for the *whole* organism, and not just for the cell it happens to reside in.

Now, there is a principle of economy in the field of scientific inquiry known as Occam's Razor, or the Principle of Radical Conservatism. This principle says that, in order to explain new phenomena, one must ruthlessly pursue known explanations to the fullest *before* postulating new assumptions. Although the use of this principle is by no means failsafe, in the past it has proven to be of great value in leading to important new discoveries. It played an important role, for instance, in the discovery of the planet Neptune, as well as in Einstein's development of the theory of relativity.

In order to remain consistent with Occam's Razor, though, we must attempt to account for "junk" DNA's role in the cellular economy in terms of what is *already* known about the genome, before moving on to the postulation of bold new assumptions (namely, that "junk" DNA is superfluous and therefore unnecessary).

One way to do this is by extrapolating a possible function for "junk" DNA in terms of what is already known about the genome. For instance, since we know that the DNA of a single cell contains the genetic information for the development of the entire host organism, we can extend this relation one step further and assert that the DNA of a single organism might *also* contain the genetic information for the evolutionary development of the entire living world.

The discovery of the homeobox in 1984 has partially confirmed this hypothesis, as it is now known that the same group of homeotic genes is capable of coding for the embryological development of the entire realm of segmented animals. It would be just one step further for the genome to also contain the instructions for the evolutionary development of the entire living world.

If this latter hypothesis turns out to be true, it would explain several important things. First, insofar as this evolutionary regulatory center could be housed in a series of introns, it would explain why these seemingly superfluous DNA segments exist in the first place. Secondly, it would explain the vast size of these segments, relative to present-day protein synthesis needs. This is significant because it would seem to require far more genetic "space" to code for the evolutionary development of the entire animal kingdom than it would to code for the proteins of a single species. Thirdly, it would explain the existence of nuclear editing enzymes, whose chief purpose in this theoretical formulation would be to cut out these evolutionary sequences so that the present-day process of protein synthesis can take place. Fourthly, it would explain the purposeful, orthogenetic quality seen throughout much of evolution. Fifthly, it would have the effect of promoting the overall structural stability of the genome (at least to the extent that a large molecular size is necessary for the structural stability of the DNA molecule). Lastly, it would remain consistent with the known efficiency and goal-directedness of the cellular economy, since not a single one of these repetitive sequences would have ever existed without serving a useful function.

The routine occurrence of metamorphic transformations from one basic animal type to another in nature would seem to add to the likelihood that some form of orthogenetic sequence actually exists in the genome. It is easy enough to forget, but fish regularly turn into amphibians in the life cycle of frogs: tadpoles begin life more or less as gill-bearing fish, but then gradually develop into lung-bearing amphibians. Similarly, non-flying insects, in the form of caterpillars, regularly turn into flying butterflies.

Obviously, then, the genome is capable of coding for the immediate transformation of one major species type into another. But if the genome can direct the transformation of fish-like creatures into amphibians and crawling insects into flying ones in a single generation, why can't it also code for the development of reptiles from amphibians and mammals from reptiles? There is obviously no *a priori* reason why it can't be so. If anything, there is good reason to suppose that evolution did indeed happen this way, because apart from the external infusion of a genetic program into the genome from some sort of cosmic field, there doesn't seem to be any other plausible way to account for the extraordinary evolutionary transformations that have regularly occurred in the past.

Apparently, then, we have two overall choices: 1) to reject the constraints imposed by the Principle of Radical Conservatism by postulating the existence of a new, superfluous quality to the vast majority of nucleotide sequences within the genome, or 2) to remain in line with the Principle of Radical Conservatism by attributing some sort of useful function to "junk"

DNA, which could either be in terms of present-day gene regulation, or in terms of the orchestration of major evolutionary changes in the past (or both). If the history of scientific achievement can be used as any indication at all, choice (2) will probably turn out to be the correct one, since the Principle of Radical Conservatism has apparently led to more discoveries in the past than it has to failures. If this actually turns out to be the case, there is a substantial likelihood that these repetitive sequences will have actually served some important function in the evolutionary rise of life on earth.

Of course, as long as we blindly assume that the mysterious portions of the genetic code are useless, we'll effectively prevent ourselves from *ever* discovering their true underlying purpose, through a process of self-fulfilling prophecy. After all, it's hard to look for a purpose in something that is believed to have no purpose!

The chief reason why "junk" DNA is assumed to be useless is because it is largely comprised of long strands of repeating nucleotides that do not seem to code for anything in particular, since it is known that they do not code for any amino acids. However, there is no *a priori* reason why these repeating strands can't use *another* informational language to code for something else besides amino acids. A good candidate for this type of "on/off" informational system is the binary language used by modern-day computers. A given nucleotide repetition could itself represent either an "on" or an "off" in this type of informational system, so that the long repeating sequences in "junk" DNA could in fact be utilizing a binary informational system to code for major evolutionary changes.

Indeed, theoretically speaking, the evolutionary transformation of one species into another wouldn't necessarily require a significant amount of new genetic information at all, since a *single command* could conceivably alter each pre-existing genetic specification in a certain direction, which in this case would be the production of a new species. Modern-day computer programmers are well aware of this radical type of reprogramming efficiency, since they can also utilize a single command line of a program to change all the other commands of the program in a certain direction.

One possible way to ascertain the possible underlying purpose of these "junk" DNA strands is to compare the repeating sequences of several related species in order to see if there is any overlap or pattern between them, especially as relates to known evolutionary relationships. If these "junk" strands have actually coded for either part, or all, of the biosphere's evolutionary development, there is a substantial likelihood that certain patterns will be found amongst the repeating sequences of different species.

Remarkably, a similarity has indeed been found between the repeating base sequences of the toad *Xenopus laevis* and the sea urchin *Strongylocentrotus purpuratus*.[23] Although these two species are evolutionarily quite distant from one another, this similarity in their repetitive sequences could very well indicate a common genetic heritage, at least with regards to the hypothetical existence of an evolutionary program common to the entire living world.

In his discussion of this phenomenon, Gould goes so far as to argue that this similarity in repetitive sequences between the two species refutes Dawkins' "selfish" DNA concept, which sees the genes themselves as playing Darwin's game of maximal reproduction on the level of intra-genomic duplication. Since natural selection cannot directly "see" the effects of this duplication within the genome, it is supposedly allowed to continue unhindered.

To the contrary, Gould argues that this similarity of repetitive sequences between *Xenopus laevis* and *Strongylocentrotus purpuratus* "points to [a] common function, since wandering transposons [jumping genes] beholden only to their own level, should disperse more randomly among chromosomes."[24] It is distinctly possible that this common function could in fact relate back to the existence of an evolutionary program in each species' respective genomes.

In addition, differing strains of yeast and of the fruit fly *Drosophilia melanogaster* have been found to possess an important transposable element that is represented in the same number of copies of repetitive DNA, but which are themselves dispersed throughout the genome on different chromosomes.[25] Could this variable position represent some way of coding for the evolution of different strains of a given species? If so, then the number of copies of a given repetitive sequence might represent the type of species being coded for, while the actual position of the copies on the chromosomes might represent the specific variety or strain being coded for.

Further confirmation of a possible evolutionary function for "junk" DNA can be found in a molecular analysis of the three globin chains that comprise the oxygen-carrying hemoglobin and myoglobin molecules (hemoglobin is comprised of two pairs of two identical chains, named alpha and beta, while myoglobin is comprised of a single chain). The tremendous structural similarity between these molecules, and between the genetic sequences that code for them, strongly suggests a common evolutionary origin over a billion years ago.[26] More interesting still is the fact that each of the three globin genes is comprised of three exons[27], and two introns. These introns occur in the same part of the gene in each case, and even appear to have been preserved in their original form during the billion or so years of their existence.

Alec Jeffreys has performed a detailed analysis of the genetic sequences that code for the beta chain of the hemoglobin molecule in both humans and primates, and his results are nothing short of remarkable.[28] Jeffreys discovered that the nonsense segments in these different species are surprisingly similar, even though they have been separate for millions and millions of years. This suggests that these nonsense segements—which have obviously been conserved during the entire evolutionary history of each species—probably served some sort of valuable function, most likely in relation to some aspect of the evolutionary process itself.

9.2.2 Discussion

Now that certain evolutionary-type patterns may have already been found in the "junk" DNA of several different species, the next step—that of an actual laboratory demonstration of these orthogenetic sequences—will undoubtedly be much more difficult, since these sequences presumably have already served much of their purpose throughout the past history of life on earth. Nevertheless, given the phenomenal progress of genetic engineering in recent years, it is possible that a molecular means could eventually be found for cloning or unmasking these evolutionary genetic sequences. If this could ever be accomplished, it is conceivable that we could observe the evolutionary transformation of one species into another *in the laboratory*. We shouldn't, however, be too optimistic about any future success in this area, since it is unlikely that we will be able to simulate the unique biological unmasking cues and the extremely long time-frames in the laboratory that were regularly seen in the distant evolutionary past.

Indeed, the possibility always remains that these orthogenetic sequences could have automatically dissipated themselves immediately after they were used to generate a new species. This would have had the additional benefit of gradually "streamlining" the orthogenetic code through a reduction in the amount of encoded information contained within it, which in turn would have substantially reduced the likelihood for a subsequent mistake in the production of new species. Unfortunately, though, it would have also made these orthogenetic sequences impossible to detect in the present; that is, unless the evolution of life on earth isn't finished yet.

Nobel laureate Walter Gilbert[29] has attempted to explain the origin of "junk" DNA in terms of traditional evolutionary theory. According to Gilbert, since the first living cell is thought to have arisen in a type of primeval soup, through a series of random arrangements and rearrangements of spontaneously occurring organic molecules, Gilbert believes that the first self-replicating molecules *themselves* had to have been stretches of nonsense as well. On this view, the "junk" DNA of today would simply be a remnant of those nonsense sequences that originally gave rise to the first living cell.

Although Gilbert's theory is superficially quite appealing, a deeper examination reveals a number of important weaknesses that render it highly implausible. For one thing, Gilbert simply assumes far too much, without any attempt to justify his assumptions. He assumes: 1) the prior existence of a coherent biocentric universe, 2) the prior existence of a life-supporting world, 3) the prior existence of stable atoms and molecules that can spontaneously combine to form a living cell, and 4) the prior capacity of chance to haphazardly form a living cell solely out of random shufflings of atoms and molecules. But it is precisely these prior assumptions that the Deistic Evolutionist believes were made possible by the deliberate activity of an Intelligent Designer. Thus, *given* all of these pre-existing conditions, life obviously could have developed "on its own" into the plethora of living creatures we have today. The whole point, however, is to give a plausible explanation for these pre-existing conditions, because they are what has made the evolution of life possible.

The non-theistic evolutionist, of course, *cannot* provide a plausible explanation for these pre-existing conditions (apart from attributing them to blind chance), so he is forced to accept them as mere givens. In the act of doing so, however, he not only avoids the entire point made by the Deistic Evolutionist, he also takes maximal advantage of the Deistic Evolutionist's explanations without giving an Intelligent Designer any of the credit for them. *It is for this reason, then, that the theistic hypothesis must be regarded as being more plausible overall.*

Gilbert's position is also strongly disconfirmed by two additional considerations: 1) the outrageous unlikelihood that life could have ever arisen by chance alone, even given the prior existence of coherent atoms and molecules, and 2) the high-level functionality that seems to have been served by these "junk" sequences, not only in the evolution of life, but also in present-day gene regulation as well.

Orgel and Crick have proposed yet another possible reason for the existence of "junk" DNA sequences that we have already briefly alluded to. Since the name of evolutionary game, at least for the neo-Darwinian, is to produce as many copies of oneself as possible, the "natural" inclination of these "junk" DNA segments, according to this view, must also be to reproduce themselves as much as possible (hence the name "selfish DNA"). However, since natural selection operating at the macro level is unable to exert its pruning effects directly within the genome, there is potentially nothing but the size of the chromosomes to stop the relentless duplication of these "selfish" DNA segments.

The problem with this conceptualization is that there is little or no concrete evidence that genes naturally "want" to reproduce themselves as much as possible. While animals in the macro world may want to reproduce at a maximal rate, this is only because of a well-understood hormonal drive. The DNA segments themselves do not possess this hormonal drive for self-duplication; they merely seek to reproduce themselves in order to carry out the normal activities of cellular life. But this is a far cry from the relentless reproduction imagined by Crick and Orgel. Moreover, such a mindless duplication of structure seems to be inconsistent with the near perfect efficiency of space, structure, and function that has been discovered to exist at all levels within the cell.

Another intriguing possibility concerning the functionality of "junk" DNA is that these repeating sequences might actually be serving as a type of on-board "nucleotide reserve," whose function would be to provide the raw genetic material for later programming changes that would in turn result in the spontaneous production of new characters and new species.

> The silent segment [of DNA] consists of a high degree of repetition of certain sequences with a scattered distribution throughout the genome. This may be crucial in mutations since it may allow sudden genetic varia-tion through a translocation of elements in the nucleotide sequence and through quantitative changes by means of an increase or decrease of nucle-otides. The genome, it appears, mutates through sudden phase changes induced by changes in the silent DNA.[30]

Although these programming changes could conceivably originate in a formative type of energy field surrounding the earth, it seems more likely that they would originate from within the genome itself, in response to external environmental cues for change.

> Some scientists envisage shocks faced by the genome to which it responds in a programmed manner. Sensing mechanisms, it is believed, alert the genome of immanent threat, and the genome responds by restructuring itself, assuring its own survival, as well as that of the cell. Such restructur-ings produce mutant individuals which in turn can lead to speciation when populations of mutants enter into competition with other species within a clade.[31]

The internal mechanism for this type of spontaneous nucleotide change could conceivably be mediated by a delicate interplay between quantum effects at the sub-molecular level and external cues at the gross environmen-tal level. Indeed, it could very well be the case that the postmodern move-ment towards organismic holoscience could be the missing informational link between "junk" DNA, on the one hand, and the spontaneous rise of new species, on the other. As physicist David Bohm and others have pointed out,[32] there seems to be a deep connection between all parts of the universe, to the point that the cumulative informational content of the entire universe seems to be imprinted on the smallest types of atomic particles. If this type of holographic perspective turns out to be correct, then one could postulate that the informational content for the appropriate evolutionary transforma-tion of all species on earth might somehow be contained in all matter every-where. According to this way of thinking, the matter contained within the genome itself would somehow direct the reprogramming of these "junk" DNA segments so as to produce new life forms whenever the historical time was right. On this holographic view, the actual nucleotide arrangement in "junk" DNA remains unordered until some type of larger cue for order arises.

However, it may simply be that the repetitive segments of "junk" DNA allow for a type of evolutionary experimentation by the cell via new gene arrangements, without causing any significant interruption in present-day functioning. Susumu Ohno first advanced this notion in his landmark book *Evolution by Gene Duplication.*[33] He argued that if only one copy of each gene existed within the genome, the genome would not be free to experiment with it in another functional capacity. But if *two* copies of the gene existed, one could go on serving its useful role in protein synthesis, while the other could be used to initiate bold new evolutionary changes.[34]

In *Hen's Teeth and Horse's Toes*, Gould affirms Ohno's original idea concerning the possible role played by introns in the evolutionary process:

> Suppose all working genes could only exist in one copy that coded for an essential protein. How then could substantial evolutionary change ever occur? What will supply the essential protein while evolution monkeys about with the only coding sequence that produces it? But if a gene can repeat itself, then one copy might continue to code for the essential protein, leaving the other free to change. Thus, potential flexibility for evolutionary change has often been cited as the primary significance of repetitive DNA.[35]

However, immediately after Gould affirms the possible functionality of repetitive DNA within the larger evolutionary process, he rejects the notion that this functionality might explain *why* these repetitive sequences exist in the first place within the genome, not because such a possibility is judged to be incoherent, but because it implies the dreaded existence of Aristotelian Final Causation:

> The argument [that gene duplication played an important role in evolution] is sound and may represent, in fact, the major *effect* of gene duplication for evolution. Yet unless our usual ideas about causality are running in the wrong direction, this flexibility simply cannot be the adaptive explanation for why repetitive DNA exists. Selection works for the moment. It cannot sense what may be of use ten million years hence in a distant descendant. The duplicated gene may make future evolutionary change possible, but selection cannot preserve it unless it confers an "immediate significance." Future utility is an important consideration in evolution, but it cannot be the explanation for current preservation. Future utilities can only be the *fortuitous effects* of other direct reasons for immediate favor.[36]

If, on the other hand, we postulate the existence of a Grand Designer who has deliberately chosen to create the living realm through natural evolutionary pathways, then He may very well have ordained at least some of these repetitive sequences to be the raw material upon which evolution could subsequently act to produce new species. This being the case, it seems a bit premature for a scientist to reject an otherwise tempting theory simply because it is at odds with his standing world view.

On the very next page, Gould proposes yet another possible function for these repetitive sequences: that of genetic regulators that act to control the expression of those genetic sequences that do in fact code for proteins.[37] This is precisely what the Deistic Evolutionist also believes to be the case, though his view requires a much broader source of controlling information, which would indeed go so far as to include the genetic information for the evolution of all species on this planet. In this scheme, the various introns of the genome could conceivably provide the impetus for the evolution of the entire biosphere by preferentially rearranging themselves between protein-encoding exons, thereby changing the types of creatures that are produced by changing the types of proteins that are coded for. Just as the preferential rearrangement of the various spaces and punctuation marks in a paragraph of text can radically alter its meaning, so too can the preferential rearrangement of introns within the genome radically alter the type of creature that is coded for.

Working with collagen IV genes in the mouse, Buttice, Kaytes, D'Armiento, Vogeli, and Kurkinen have obtained evidence that introns have indeed played a substantial role in gene evolution.[38] These researchers have analyzed the various amino acid sequences in collagen IV mouse genes and have concluded that they probably evolved in response to a number of intron-mediated interruptions in those exons that code for proteins.[39]

Other important physiological substances, such as the various immunoglobulins, have also been shown to have evolved in response to a similar process of intron-mediated "exon shuffling."[40] There are three possible ways that this exon shuffling could have come about in these molecules: either 1) many existing introns have changed position, 2) many ancestral introns have been removed, or 3) many new introns have been added.[41] There also could have been some combination of these three factors.

Interestingly enough, these intron movements appear to have taken place with such a remarkable degree of precision and specificity that some researchers are having a difficult time believing they could have been due to chance alone. Rogers, for instance, notes that:

> Intron movement cannot be a general explanation for [these] distributions, as many of the discordant introns would have to have moved across conserved coding sequences or across a non-integral number of codons. While

schemes for achieving this can be devised, and there even appears to be one example in a carbonic anhydrase gene, the calculated probability of the required double frameshift events (or of the genes surviving a transitional state) seems much too low to invoke such events as a general phenomenon.[42]

This conclusion clearly assumes that any realistic explanation of these intron movements must be random in nature. But is this conclusion justified? For our purposes the answer must clearly be no, because the possibility of random intron movement is one of the central questions that is at issue here. The majority of genetic researchers, however, don't even admit the possibility of intelligent direction in the evolutionary process, so they refuse to recognize that there is any larger philosophical question that needs to be answered in this area. They simply assume that deliberate intron movement *cannot* be a general explanation for the various intron patterns found in genes, because the notion of any intelligent direction to these movements is unthinkable, and this is in spite of the fact that intelligent control is evident throughout the genome.

Rogers goes on to point out that "many authors have tried to interpret intron distributions in terms of a mixture of removal and movement of introns, but the difficulty of phase-shifting movement must cast serious doubt on these interpretations. In contrast, some gene families for which phylogenies can be traced show patterns that clearly indicate intron insertions."[43]

The possibility of phase-shifting movement is, of course, only a problem if one rejects any possibility of intelligent control behind intron movement. As soon as one admits the possibility of intelligent control, however the possibility of phase-shifting movement becomes much easier to bear. Moreover, since many clear patterns of intron insertion are known to exist, the experimental evidence appears to be firmly on the side of intelligent control.

After examining the most recent molecular evidence surrounding intron patterns in genes, Rogers notes that there are only two possible explanations for them:

If most introns have been inserted, an explanation is needed for the apparent semi-regularities in their distribution: the fairly uniform size of exons and the tendency in some genes to map near protein structural divisions. These patterns could be caused by sequence specificity in the insertion process, or by selection for efficiency of splicing after insertion, which might depend on local exon sequences, on the proximity of other splice sites, or on the maintenance of secondary structure in the pre-mRNA.[44]

The evidence clearly seems to be in favor of sequence specificity in the original insertion process. There are simply too many elaborate intron patterns throughout the living world to have been due to selection for efficiency after insertion. It is also hard to see why there would have been so many support structures and processes within the genome favoring the intelligent manipulation of introns if intron movement were merely the exclusive result of chance processes. The existence of these support structures and processes is clearly much more consistent with the hypothesis of intelligent genomic control than it is with pure randomness.

However, as soon as we affirm that there was sequence specificity in the original insertion process, we are then led to the deeper question of how these introns could have been so preferentially located. Since the very notion of sequence specificity precludes a time-consuming process of natural selection acting upon random movements, the only other conclusion we are left with is that this original specificity was caused by an intelligent program orchestrating the entire process of intron movement. The Deistic Evolutionist clearly favors this latter explanation.

This type of intelligently-directed exon shuffling seems to be entirely capable of generating the biosphere out of a primordial group of all-purpose base sequences. Just as a group of tinker toys can be sequentially rearranged to look like any number of different structures, so too can the various introns and exons in the genome be sequentially rearranged to represent the many different members of the living world. This is the beauty of intelligent contrivance.

Of course, there is always the possibility (greatly preferred by non-theistic evolutionists for obvious reasons) that there was a genuinely random distribution of introns throughout evolutionary history. In this case, natural selection would have preserved only those rearrangements that turned out to have significant survival value.

This possibility is hard to believe for several reasons. For one thing, it is hard to believe that a purely random distribution of introns within the genome could have produced even one coherent organism that could have survived the rigors of natural selection. There are simply too many biological structures that must be precisely coded for, and randomness alone simply does not seem to be capable of producing this result, even with the help of cumulative selection. There simply hasn't been enough time in the history of life for chance intron rearrangements to have produced the millions of different species we have on this planet. For not only did life arise on the earth just as soon as it possibly could, it is also a well-known fact that most species arose *suddenly* in the distant past. This directly counters the possibility that a gradual series of selection-mediated changes could have been responsible for creating the biosphere.

Indeed, the very idea that chance-mediated processes could have generated the entire biosphere seems to be incoherent on a purely intuitive level as well, as it is tantamount to saying that a random rearrangement of spaces and punctuation marks in the Bible could have accidentally produced the

Bhagavad Gita. Most people would find this possibility too incredulous to deserve serious consideration, especially given the sudden appearance of most species throughout the historical record. But if we deny any significant creative role to these chance rearrangements, then we are left with only one other possibility: namely, that some form of intelligent agency has been responsible for effecting these preferential rearrangements.

9.3 The Orthogenetic Content of the Genome

We have seen how the repetitive segments within the genome seem to contain a great deal of information regarding the nature of the evolutionary process. There are five possibilities regarding this presumed orthogenetic content:

1. All the genetic sequences that might have originally led to the production of new species have physically dissipated; hence, they will not be discernible in any form today. In this case, the "junk" DNA we can presently observe would have some other non-orthogenetically-related status (such as present-day gene regulation).

2. These evolutionary genetic sequences have been dissipated on an informational level only (meaning that they are no longer able to transmit useful information); hence, some physical remnant could remain. This physical remnant could well turn out to be the seemingly meaningless nucleotide repetitions observed in "junk" DNA. If so, this would still allow for the possibility that these repetitions could serve other present-day needs as well.

3. These orthogenetic sequences have not been fully dissipated in either a physical or an informational sense with the passage of time; they are simply being masked now through the work of nuclear regulatory enzymes. Hence, they can still be studied today for evidence of orthogenetic informational content.

4. The repeating sequences found in "junk" DNA constitute an on-board "nucleotide reserve" within the genome itself, whose function is to provide the raw genetic material for the later reprogramming of the genome by some as yet unknown type of internal or external force, which may or may not be located somewhere within the genome.

5. There never were any orthogenetic evolutionary sequences in DNA to begin with. Thus, no remnants of these non-existent sequences will ever be found. This would mean that the repetitive sequences found in the genome today never had anything to do with any type of orthogenetic programming. In this case, they would either be relegated to some sort of present-day regulatory function, or else they would be genuinely useless.

The existence of nuclear editing enzymes would seem to make either (2), (3), or (4) above the most likely, since the activity of these enzymes seems to imply that the repetitive segments themselves serve (or served) an important enough purpose to justify their continued existence and subsequent removal during the the present-day process of protein synthesis. While the possibility remains that these repetitive sequences could have always been meaning-less, such a possibility seems inconsistent with both known evolutionary history, on the one hand, and the incredible functional efficiency of the cell itself, on the other.

When we say that the genome of the first living cell might have contained the genetic instructions for the evolution of all subsequent species, it is important to understand that this does not necessarily mean that *all* the information for these transformations had to have been simultaneously pres-ent in the first living organism. It is also possible that the very first creature could have contained only the genetic information that was needed for the very *next* evolutionary transformation in line. In this case, with each subse-quent change in species, the orthogenetic sequence would correspondingly be altered to the point that the next species in line would automatically be coded for. This particular coding process would have had the advantage of conserving the precious informational space within the DNA molecule, but it would have also required a fantastically complicated instructional system in order to function properly, one that would have had each change in spe-cies dictate a corresponding change in the orthogenetic nucleotide sequence, which in turn would have dictated the evolution of the next species "in line," and so forth. Such a system, though incredibly complicated, is not inconceivable, nor is it beyond the creative ability of an Intelligent Designer.

If we assume that the evolutionary production of new species is more or less finished at the present time, such a "domino-type" view of these orthogenetic sequences would explain the apparent informational disorder contained in "junk" DNA: no informational fidelity would remain because there would be no more animal types to actualize. Accordingly, the repeating nucleotide sequences of "junk" DNA might only represent the spent genetic remnants of nucleotide sequences that were once meaningful.

Another tantalizing possibility, which is consistent with some of the most recent experimental[45] findings in this area, is that the original genome was only programmed with the *capacity* for altering itself in response to environ-mental input, *not* with the actual information for any given evolutionary change beforehand. This Lamarckian capacity for self-programming would have greatly simplified the subsequent evolutionary process by allowing these programming changes to occur a step at a time, in response to external environmental cues for change.

On this view, the repetitive DNA sequences in the genome would serve two possible functions: 1) to provide the informational capacity required for self-programming, and/or 2) to provide a standing nucleotide reserve to be used whenever it would be time for actual programming changes to take place.

Nevertheless, the possibility always remains that "junk" DNA could in fact be worthless, and that there could be no orthogenesis at all in evolution. But even if this possibility turns out to be true, we still need to constantly be on guard to protect the openness of our world views from the extremely limiting effects of scientific arrogance. We must be careful to refrain from making any absolute statements about the nature of reality that are based solely on our present-day ignorance, for it could very well be the case that new discoveries in the future could end up radically transforming our overall world view. The important "take home" point here is that until a given hypothesis can repeatedly be confirmed in a scientific fashion, we must remain open to other possibilities, and not limit those possibilities in accordance with our own present degree of ignorance.

9.4 A Possible Relationship Between Introns and Homeotic Genes

With the previous discussion as a backdrop, we are now in a position to ask ourselves about a possible relationship between introns and the homeobox as far as evolution is concerned. There seems little question that these two parts of the genome have worked together during the evolutionary process, as the previously cited work of Schugart, Kappen, and Ruddle shows. Several duplications of large genomic regions—mediated through the extensive use and rearrangement of introns—are known to have occurred in the evolution of the homeobox, and further evidence of this type of intragenomic cooperation seems to be forthcoming.

It may be that the homeobox, working either alone or in concert with another part of the genome, somehow contains the "master plan" that enables the evolving host species to respond to the environment in a constructive manner. Introns may or may not be a part of this master plan, but even if they aren't, they nevertheless appear to have played a major role in supplying the raw materials for its execution. One thing, however, seems obvious: there is far more intelligence in the genome than was ever previously expected, and there seems little doubt that it will end up having played an important role in the overall evolutionary process.

9.5 Polyploidy

The phenomenon of *polyploidy* in the botanic world provides striking confirmation of the fact that a single massive macromutation *can* produce a new species in a single generation. It has been known for some time now that polyploid plants, which are hermaphroditic and therefore capable of self-fertilization, can actually produce a new species in a single generation through a doubling of their chromosomes during cell division.

A related phenomenon known as *allopolyploidy* can also produce a new plant species in a single generation, through the creating of a hybrid between two similar plant species containing different numbers of chromosomes. While such hybrids are usually sterile, due to the lack of viable pairing partners for the chromosomes, it sometimes happens that all of a parent cell's chromosomes during meiosis (sexual cell division) will enter the sperm or egg cells, when normally only half do so. The subsequent diploid gamete (which is a germ cell containing the full number of adult chromosomes) can then fuse with another diploid gamete to produce a *tetraploid* offspring. Since the newly-formed individual has twice the normal number of chromosomes, it is a new species.

Polyploidy is acknowledged to have been of great evolutionary importance in the plant kingdom. Indeed, 33 percent of flowering plants (angiosperms) and 70 percent of grasses are thought to have been of polyploid origin.[46]

Significantly, polyploid plant species have been shown to be hardier and better adapted to certain niches than their immediate diploid ancestors. This is important, because it shows that new species that have been created in a single generation can instantly be well-adapted to their environment, without having to go through multiple generations of refinement via natural selection. This is good news for domesticated plant breeders, because both agricultural plants like wheat and ornamental plants like tulips can repeatedly be improved in this manner.

Up until recently, polyploidy was thought to have been of minor evolutionary importance in the animal kingdom, because it was assumed that gene dilution, sexual imbalance, and a lack of genetic diversity in polyploids would promote sterility and therefore bring them to an evolutionary dead end. Today, however, it is becoming increasingly evident that polyploidy has played a major role in the evolution of fishes, amphibians, and reptiles. Indeed, natural populations of polyploid amphibians and reptiles can currently be found throughout North and South America, Africa, Europe, and Asia.[47]

According to University of Connecticut biologist R. Jack Schultz, the evolutionary transition from fish to amphibian was one of the most important and complex transitions in the entire animal kingdom, because a large number of structural and functional changes had to have been incorporated into the amphibian genome. This theoretical expectation has been confirmed by the marked increase in amphibian DNA levels relative to those found in fish.[48] Polyploidy is thought to have been originally responsible for providing this increase.[49]

The evolution of amphibians from fishes involved a substantial number of new adaptations of all which had to be genetically coded for. Assuming that many of the loci in fish are already committed, mutations of new functions would be deleterious. The suggestion of Ohno and his colleagues, that numerous uncommitted loci made available by polyploidy can be redirected to code for new adapations, provides a reasonable solution to the problem.[50]

Polyploidy also seems to have played a role in the evolutionary history of insects as well. While there are no polyploid insects above the species level, the polyploid insects that do exist are better adapted to their environment than their bisexual diploid ancestors.[51] This further suggests that the phenomenon of polyploidy may have been responsible for a signficant number of the beneficial adaptations regularly seen in nature.

Other polyploid animal species are also known to be particularly well-adapted to their environment. This high adaptability has been attributed to an increase in the overall number of genes, an increase in heterozygosity, and to the process of gene recombination in general.[52]

We can infer from this increased adaptability that very rapid speciation can indeed occur in the wild without the help of natural selection. From this inference it is but a step to conclude that the entire animal kingdom could have sequentially arisen in response to self-contained genetic factors.

Polyploidy thus provides us with an empirically verifiable method of major saltational change that can take place in a single generation. Consequently, it can no longer be argued that the production of a new species in a single generation is inconceivable or impossible. To the contrary, it is very much a real world possibility, and in fact regularly takes place throughout the world.

We mustn't, however, assume that polyploidy is the *only* mechanism by which nature can rapidly produce new species. In all likelihood it is only one mechanism among many for rapid saltational change. As such, it can be viewed as a kind of evolutionary precedent, insofar as it tells us that: 1) nature does in fact have at least one mechanism to rapidly generate new species, and that 2) if it can do it in one way, it is more likely to be able to do it in other ways as well.

9.6   RNA Recoding and Rapid Evolution

Earlier we saw how ribosomes are capable of directly affecting the course of protein synthesis by reinterpreting the genetic message contained in the mRNA molecule. This is called "RNA recoding," and it provides us with yet another possible mechanism for extremely rapid speciation during the evolutionary process. RNA recoding works through the process of frame-shifting: the ribosome simply skips over one or more bases in the mRNA molecule until it finds the one it wants.

Frame-shifting is important because it is capable of completely altering the genetic information contained in the mRNA molecule. Since each amino acid is specified in the genetic code by a three-base sequence called a codon, a frame-shift of even a single nitrogenous base can completely transform the information contained in the code itself. For instance, consider the following base sequence: TTG CCT TAT GTA. If we frame-shift to the right by a single base, a completely different sequence is produced: TGC CTT ATG TA. These altered codons correspond to a totally different sequence of amino acids, so they would end up specifying a very different protein. Hence, even a modest frame-shift can completely change the identity of the protein that is synthesized on the ribosome. And since proteins are the structural and metabolic agents that comprise all living organisms, it follows that a sufficiently elaborate series of frame-shifting events could conceivably produce two or more different species out of the same sequence of codons. In fact, if the genetic code in the DNA molecule has been pre-programmed with a sufficient level of information, it is conceivable that an entire kingdom of different species could be produced from a single DNA molecule by a strategic series of frame-shifting events.

This isn't as outrageous as it may initially seem, because we already know that the frame-shifting mechanism itself is entirely capable of operating in this manner. However, in order for the above scenario to be possible, two additional factors need to be present: 1) a pre-programmed genetic code, and 2) a pre-programmed set of ribosomes that are capable of coordinating their frame-shifting events to produce a coherent series of species.

To the non-theistic evolutionist, of course, these possibilities are absurd to the highest degree, because he explicitly denies any form of Intelligent Design in the world; he therefore doesn't believe that the genome could possibly be programmed with such a sophisticated level of evolutionary information. But what if God *does* actually exist, and what if He *has* in fact decided to utilize an inwardly-directed evolutionary process to do His creating? In this case, it is no longer so outrageous to believe that the genetic code could have been pre-programmed with all the structural information for the entire living world, or that the ribosomes could have been programmed to coordinate their frame-shifting events with certain environmental cues.

9.7 Holism, Reductionism, and the Origin of Orthogenetic Information

If the existence of some form of evolutionary program could in fact be substantiated one day, the big question we would then need to ask ourselves is this: Where did the information in the program *itself* ultimately come from? It would of course be unthinkable to assume that it had all come together purely by accident in the genome of the first life form, because chance processes are intrinsically incapable of producing such a monumental feat. Indeed, evolutionists currently believe that nucleic acids were able to evolve the way they did only because of a unique combination of organic molecules and environmental pressures acting over huge stretches of time, because this is the only conceivable way that it could have occurred by chance alone. In this orthodox conceptualization, the existence of an evolutionary program in the genome of the first living cell would be tantamount to a miracle.

Thus, if it could somehow be shown that the genetic instructions for the evolution of all life on earth were in fact contained in the very first primordial cell, the debate between theistic and non-theistic evolutionists would be closed forever, for the following reason: the *a priori* existence of a complex set of genetic instructions specifying the future development of all life on earth would *itself* demand the existence of some type of genetic programmer, which, in all probability, would turn out to be the Creator Himself.[53]

The existence of some form of orthogenetic evolutionary program within the genome would have the effect of satisfying the persistent demands of the vitalists, who have argued that the force responsible for differentiating life from non-life must reside *outside* the explanatory realm of purely physical laws. A complex genetic program would satisfy this vitalistic requirement, because information *per se* is not subject to physical and chemical laws; it is only the physical *vehicle* which carries this information (the DNA molecule) that is subject to them. Thus, the existence of a genetic evolutionary program would satisfy both the vitalists *and* the reductionists: the vitalists would have their vital force that exists outside the domain of purely physical laws (transcendent genetic information), while the reductionists would be assured that once this information is contained within a physical vehicle (the DNA molecule), the vehicle *itself* would obey all known physical and chemical laws.

The upshot of this discussion is that the phenomenon of life isn't a manifestation of a miraculous "elan vital" at all; it is simply the result of the miraculous imposition of a tremendous amount of order onto inanimate atoms and molecules by means of the information contained in the genetic code. That is to say, inanimate matter becomes living when it becomes part of a larger system that has itself been meticulously organized by the genetic machinery. Thus, the molecules *themselves* are not living; it is, rather, the larger *gestalt* of order that they are a part of that is "alive." Mayr agrees with this conclusion, insofar as he points out that "the differences that do exist between inanimate matter and living organisms are due [only] to the organization of matter in living organisms."[54]

This of course is a holistic way of looking at biology, and it stands in direct opposition to the more typical reductionistic approach that has dominated the scientific realm for the greater part of this century. One simply cannot uncover the miracle of life by continuously dissecting the cell *ad infinitum*, just as one cannot detect a symphony in action by analyzing the various musical notes themselves. One can only discover the miracle of life by looking at the larger organizational picture of the cell, just as one can only be fully aware of a symphony by listening to all the notes being played *simultaneously*. Reductionism may be able to provide us with the genetic reasons for the larger cellular order, but in order to find the elusive miracle of life itself we must revert back up to the level where the genetic instructions are translated into macromolecular order.

Put another way, biology cannot be reduced to physical science alone, only to information. However, the very nature of information is that it always points to something else besides itself. As far as the genetic information in the genome is concerned, this "something else" appears to be none other than the great Designer behind the entire universe itself.[55]

Even if our proposed evolutionary programming of the genome turns out to be the result of a Lamarckian sort of self-programming in response to external environmental cues for change, a Larger Intelligence nevertheless seems to be necessary to make this original capacity for self-programming possible. After all, where else could this original self-programming capacity *itself* have come from? It would appear to be far too sophisticated to be attributed to blind chance alone. It is one thing to say that blind mutations happen only according to the laws of chance, but it is quite another to say that the genome has learned to program itself because of a similar series of chance-mediated accidents. Remarkably enough, recent experimental evidence is increasingly suggesting that some form of Lamarckian self-programming has in fact occurred in the evolution of new proteins and enzymes.[56] If this turns out to be true, the religious implications associated with such a finding would appear to be almost beyond question.

9.8   The Great Explanatory Power of Masking Theory

According to the orthogenetic scenario we have been discussing in this chapter, there is no *a priori* reason why the very first life form couldn't have contained all the genetic information for the evolutionary development of the entire biosphere. Or alternatively, there is no *a priori* reason why some external source couldn't have infused the proper genetic instructions into the genome at the appropriate time in evolutionary history.

However, as Taylor has pointed out, if these genetic instructions were actually present in the first living cell, it would have been necessary for them to remain masked until the appropriate time would come for them to be released. Although it seems as though some sort of environmental feedback would have been necessary to initiate this unmasking process, the possibility also remains that God could have directly programmed each unmasking into the genome in advance. It seems more likely, though, that some sort of critical balance was probably struck between the genome and the environment, in which the unmasking process itself would have been regulated by some form of environmental feedback. Or, in the case of Lamarckian self-programming, the environment would have probably played a major role in directing the self-programming of the genome.

In any event, the cumulative effect of this unmasking or self-programming would have been a "saltation," or sudden evolutionary leap, to another species. This would fit in well with the known paleontological evidence of "punctuated equilibria": vast periods of species stability punctuated by relatively brief periods of rapid change. We know, for instance, that the DNA molecule can code for the immediate transformation of one type of animal into another, since the frog begins its life as a gill-bearing, fish-like creature, only to become transformed in the fullness of time into a lung-bearing, land-walking amphibian. To be sure, if such a dramatic single-generational change can be programmed into frog genes, there would seem to be no *a priori* reason why the evolution of all life forms on earth couldn't have also been programmed into the genome as well.

This type of genetic unmasking or patterned self-programming would account for one of the most remarkable facts in all of evolutionary history: the independent invention of the eye in at least forty separate evolutionary lineages. It is *very* difficult to believe that such a profoundly complex organ could have randomly formed so many separate times. Who could possibly believe, for instance, that the profound molecular complexity displayed by the cornea, retina, and optic nerve could have *ever* been duplicated by chance in so many phylogenetically distinct creatures? The very complexity of the organ, along with the incredible amount of structural coordination that is routinely seen in all types of eyes, demands that we acknowledge the existence of some sort of common genetic blueprint for the eye's origin.

The rise of human intelligence, which seems to have evolved against tremendous odds, also supports this fundamental orthogenetic concept. Given the apparent importance and "rightfulness" of human consciousness, along with the incalcuable odds against the development of *any* type of intelligence (in fact, the odds are so great that even the non-theistic evolutionists themselves believe that no other forms of intelligent life will probably ever be found anywhere else in the galaxy), it suddenly becomes reasonable to suspect that the potential for human intelligence was somehow programmed into the first living cell.

Certainly it cannot be denied that the *potential* for intelligence was present in the world from the very beginning, whether it was actually intended by a Higher Power or not. The very fact that the first living cell *did* eventually evolve into human beings proves that the potential for intelligence did actually exist in the first living creature. The only remaining issue is whether or not this potentiality was deliberately *intended* by a Higher Power or not. Given the reality of this primordial potential, along with the stupendous, unsearchable complexity of even the simplest life form (not to mention human consciousness and intelligence), it would seem overwhelmingly likely that this potentiality *was* in fact intended by some sort of Higher Power all along.

This concept of weak orthogenesis isn't as inimical to modern evolutionary thought as many would like to believe. One of the most common concepts taught to modern biology students is the so-called "biogenetic law," which asserts that "ontogeny recapitulates phylogeny," or that the development of the embryo of any given species recapitulates or repeats the key points in that species' evolutionary descent. Although this biogenetic law has largely been refuted by careful research,[57] it is still taught as fact in many classes of evolutionary biology. However, the critical point that most proponents of the biogenetic law don't seem to realize is that if ontogeny (embryogenesis) recapitulates phylogeny (past evolutionary development), then this past development must in some sense have been as purposive as embryonic development is; that is, it must have been orthogenetic.[58]

Interestingly enough, there is an orthogenetic assumption in the very origin of the word "evolution," which, in the original Latin (*evolutio*) means "to unroll" or "to unravel." Thus as far as the original meaning of the word "evolution" is concerned, the historical rise of species is attributable to the unraveling of a set of self-organizing instructions that were contained in the very first life form.

Of course, one way to prove the existence of a set of orthogenetic instructions in the genomes of living cells is to engage molecular geneticists in the empirical search for it. But even if it were found one day, the interpretation of the molecular code within it would undoubtedly prove to be much more difficult. Even so, recent advances in molecular genetics, information science, and cryptographics have been so dramatic that the future elucidation of this type of evolutionary program will always remain a possibility. If and when this ever occurs, the ongoing debate between theistic and non-theistic evolutionists will clearly be resolved once and for all.

9.9 Speciation Problems in Light of Masking Theory

A recurrent problem regarding the origin of species concerns Mayr's insistence that there be some type of geographic separation before true speciation can occur. The trouble with this sort of reasoning is that there are obviously habitats such as lakes where speciation has freely occurred despite the clear lack of geographic separation.[59]

In Africa's Lake Tanganyika, for example, there are well over a hundred species of cichlid, even though no absolute geographical boundaries between incipient species could have ever occurred there. This type of phenomenon is very difficult to explain in the absence of some sort of orthogenetic unraveling. Taylor's masking theory, on the other hand, accounts for this phenomenon very well, as it claims that speciation can occur with or without geographical separation, whenever the environmental cues for change become appropriate. The Lamarckian concept of genetic self-programming also fits in well with this hypothesis, since living creatures can easily speciate without being geographically separated if they are simply responding to predetermined environmental cues for change.

The great geneticist Richard Goldschmidt also noticed that "there is no reason, at least as far as the factual material goes, to suppose that isolation makes subspecies develop into species. . . . Isolation or no isolation, the subspecies are diversifications within the species, but there is no reason to regard them as incipient species."[60] Again we see that there seems to be some other factor at work in the speciation process besides mere isolation and other sorts of random factors.

9.10 Parallel Evolution and Other Adaptational Mysteries

Our weak orthogenetic hypothesis also provides a tantalizing explanation for the mystery of parallel evolution. As long as the genes specifying the development of parallel structures already exist in the genome, it suddenly becomes easy to understand how these similar structures could have simultaneously evolved in separate lineages. The appropriate genes would merely have become unmasked whenever the time became appropriate.

The mysterious return of certain mammals (such as whales and dolphins) to the sea is also duly accounted for by both masking theory and the Lamarckian theory of genetic self-programming. Indeed, it is immensely difficult to see how this return to the sea could have ever taken place *without* some form of inner directedness. It is clear that no type of mammal could possibly survive in the sea for more than a few minutes without the simultaneous existence of a number of fully formed, life-facilitating adaptations. But these adaptations could never have been formed piecemeal by natural selection, because the incipient creatures would have quickly been eliminated by natural selection. It is this realization that led Ernst Mayr to remark that these evolutionary events seem "as decisively directed towards perfect adaptation in the new medium . . . as if someone had directed the course of evolution."[61]

We have already mentioned the remarkable transformation that routinely takes place between fish-like tadpoles and frogs, which are amphibians. It is apparent that the genes which specify this transformation already exist within the tadpole, but if this is true, then why couldn't it also be true that the first transformation from fish to amphibian was *also* mediated by a similar unmasking of pre-existing genes?

> Is it possible that the fish carries or carried a battery of genes specifying 'amphibian' in a suppressed state and that these were suddenly activated? And similarly for other major evolutionary advances. If so, a great many puzzling facts suddenly fall into place.

> It becomes easy to understand why twelve mammal lines began to exhibit similar characteristics. All were carrying the same, or similar, sets of masked genes which began to be activated about the same time, perhaps because they were triggered by the same environmental circumstances. All instances of parallel evolution become understandable.

> We have seen that molelike creatures, almost indistinguishable anatomically, developed independently in Asia and in South America. Is it not easier to believe that they did so by the unmasking, in similar situations, of similar genes than to suppose that the same group of mutations occurred twice, in different places, by pure chance? And when we are asked to believe that it occurred four times, as with the anteaters, credulity fails.[62]

Taylor's masking theory can also be used to explain why a certain species of frog in New Guinea bears its young alive, in the same way that mammals do, instead of laying eggs like all other frogs. There is certainly no way for natural selection to explain such a strange occurrence, but masking theory accounts for it quite nicely: the genes for bearing live offspring exist in all frogs, but for some reason, they have only become unmasked in the New Guinea specimen. The same thing can be said about the only species of shark from the genus *Mustelus* that has a placenta, even though all sharks more or less live in the same habitat.

And then there is the baffling case of "evolution turned backwards"— when certain creatures are born in a certain relatively advanced state, and then "devolve" back into a more primitive way of life. Taylor cites the case of the Cnidarians—which include jellyfish, sea anemones, and coral—all of which secrete a tiny larval form that is actually more advanced in an evolutionary sense than its adult counterpart, since it is a free-swimming creature with a rudimentary backbone. Strangely, though, it soon settles down on a rock and becomes transformed into a much less mobile creature, such as an anemone or a coral.

While it could be argued that such instances of "evolution in reverse" actually help to *increase* a species' capacity for survival in one way or another, one can't help but wonder why more species haven't reverted back to a safer, more primitive way of life.[63] Indeed, humans were able to evolve intelligence *in spite* of the fact that it originally constituted a strong reproductive *liability* in our most distant ancestors, both prenatally and postnatally.[64] As we have seen, the evolution of intelligence was a reproductive liability in the prenatal sphere because highly evolved nervous systems require an unusually long gestation period, and the longer the gestation period, the more danger that is naturally incurred by both the mother and fetus alike. In the postnatal sphere, the evolution of intelligence was also a reproductive liability because it directly entails a longer period of time to raise and educate the young, and the longer it takes to produce viable adults, the more susceptible a population is to harmful influences, both from within the population and without.

In spite of these negative selective influences, the evolution of intelligence happened anyway. The best way to account for this intriguing fact clearly isn't in terms of some sort of accidental interplay between random mutations and natural selection. It is, to the contrary, to be found in a purposeful unraveling of the inner genetic potential for intelligence that took place in the ancestral line of creatures that eventually led to humanity.

Taylor's masking theory fits in quite nicely with our basic contention that, in one way or another, God was responsible for creating the entire animal kingdom. It is certainly plausible that God could have programmed the entire evolutionary history of life on earth into the very first living cell, in which case the proper genes would have tended to become unmasked in response to certain environmental influences. Indeed, this idea of a Divinely-programmed genome slowly unraveling itself over time in response to the various forces of natural selection, solves virtually every problem in traditional evolutionary thought. It accounts for the spontaneous origin of life, as well as for the relatively sudden appearance of all subsequent life forms.

The Lamarckian self-programming theory is similarly useful; it simply delays most of the specific genetic programming to the actual evolutionary process itself, during which time it delegates the programming responsibility onto the self-programming capacity of the genome, working in concert with specific environmental stimuli. In this case, God would have programmed the genome to *program itself* in response to external environmental cues for change.

9.11   God and the Existence of a Master Evolutionary Program

The fact that many introns are capable of self-splicing, protein synthesis, and self-propagation as autonomous elements within the genome, is clear evidence that they are part of a vast organizational network that has been fine-tuned to extraordinary accuracy. Without this extreme functional fidelity, the random actions of introns would destroy the functional cohesion of the cell in short order. But this clearly has not happened. Therefore, some sort of larger master plan must exist, either within introns or in connection with them. The function of this master plan would be to orchestrate the many different elements within the cell into a coherent pattern.

The very existence of a master evolutionary program would directly imply the existence of a larger Creator, Who would have been responsible for originally creating it, either through direct intervention or through the actions of intermediary physical forces. Once created, though, this evolutionary program would have been capable of directing itself into increasingly greater levels of species diversity and complexity, by working in concert with the ever-changing nature of the physical environment.

Interestingly enough, this is directly analogous to the way we humans were presumably made, since it is clear that we were not created in our final form. Rather, we were given the inner potential to grow in response to our own free-willed choices, in the same way that life seems to have been given the ability to grow autonomously in response to local environmental pressures. This Divine delegation of the developmental process onto the creatures preserves their freedom over against their Creator, and gives the resultant biosphere greater significance and meaning than it ever would have possessed otherwise in a strictly deterministic, robot-like world.

9.12 The Return of Goldschmidt's "Hopeful Monster"

The belief that evolution occurs by sudden leaps (saltations) is not a new one. The famous geneticist Hugo De Vries, working at the turn of the century, often spoke about the sudden production of new species. Many other seminal thinkers have agreed with him. O.H. Schindewolf, for instance, one of Europe's top paleontologists in the 1930's, even went so far as to explain the reptile-to-bird gap by saying that a reptile laid an egg and out hatched the first fully-developed bird![65]

It remained for world-renowned Berkeley geneticist Richard Goldschmidt to make this idea of "quantum evolution" famous with his "hopeful monster" theory, set forth in his controversial book *The Material Basis for Evolution*. Upon noting that scientists had been searching in vain for transitional fossils for over a hundred years, Goldschmidt came to the momentous conclusion that *no* such fossils were probably *ever* going to be found. As a consequence, he suggested that a new theory was needed to help account for the obvious saltationism that has repeatedly been observed throughout the fossil record.

Goldschmidt found the basis for his new theory in the fact that every once in a while, a two-legged sheep or two-headed turtle was born. He reasoned that if such a thing could happen naturally from time to time, then it might also be possible for a completely new species—a "hopeful monster"—to be born in a single generation. For Goldschmidt, then, each occurrence of a gap in the fossil record was actually caused by the birth of a new "monster."

Although Goldschmidt's theory was initially met with all manner of ridicule and criticism (due to the evolutionary establishment's strong commitment to gradualism), he is now well on his way to being vindicated after all, thanks in large part to recent revelations in molecular genetics and to the rise of punctuationalism in modern evolutionary thought. While it is possible to conceive of this punctuationalism in terms of traditional gradualist scenarios, Goldschmidt's "hopeful monster" theory provides a much more direct explanation for it.

In order for any type of "hopeful monster," though, to be born in a single generation from a completely different species, it is clear that the genome of the parent species must first be able to radically alter itself in a very precise and coordinated fashion, so that it can produce coherent and viable offspring immediately. But before this can even remotely be possible, the basic genetic machinery for enabling it to happen must first be in place.

Goldschmidt found much evidence for this macromutational machinery in the genomes of ordinary creatures. He observed that species are separated by "bridgeless gaps," which are themselves generated by "systemic mutations" that are distinct in kind from the micromutations that merely produce varieties within a species. In order to bring about these systemic mutations, Goldschmidt invoked the activity of rate genes and other genetic factors in the inherited developmental program, which purportedly enabled relatively small changes in genotype to be amplified into huge changes in phenotype, even to the point of producing new species in a single generation.

> For a long time I have been convinced that macroevolution must proceed by a different genetic method. . . . A pattern change in the chromosomes, completely independent of gene mutations, nay, even of the concept of the gene, will furnish this new method of macroevolution. . . . So-called gene mutation and recombination within an interbreeding population may lead to a kaleidoscopic diversification within the species, which may find expression in the production of subspecific categories. . . . But all this happens within an identical general genetical pattern which may also be called a single reaction system. The change from species to species is not a change involving more and more additional atomistic changes, but a complete change of the primary pattern or reaction system into a new one, which afterwards may again produce intraspecific variation by micromutation. One might call this different type of genetic change a *systemic mutation*, though this does not have to occur in one step. . . . Whatever genes or gene mutations might be, they do not enter this picture at all. Only the arrangement of the serial chemical constituents of the chromosome into a new, spatially different order; i.e., a new chromosomal pattern, is involved.[66]

Of course, this type of global chromosomal reorganization intrinsically requires a larger developmental program to guide it in the proper direction;

and indeed, there is mention of just such a developmental program in Goldschmidt's text.[67] However, no effort is made to describe the nature or origin of this developmental program; it is merely assumed to exist in a superintendent role over the saltational production of new species.

At other points Goldschmidt seems to hint that random genetic processes alone could have accidentally generated new species from time to time. However, it is very hard to see how hopeful monsters could ever be produced in appreciable numbers in the absence of some sort of larger evolutionary program, and without the benefit of multi-generational fine-tuning via natural selection. Although it is conceivable that an across-the-board series of random mutations could spontaneously produce a viable new species in a single generation, it certainly isn't likely. In fact, the odds for this kind of fluke occurrence are so infinitesimal that they can be considered to be essentially zero.[68]

The truth of the matter is that these relatively rapid bursts of speciation have occurred millions of times in the distant evolutionary past. This fact in and of itself would seem to completely invalidate any possibility of a chance-mediated speciation process.

More evidence against a chance-mediated process of speciation can be found in the surprising *regularity* that seems to have characterized the introduction of new species in the distant past.[69] By comparing the number of amino acid differences in pairs of species in the fossil record with a known period of divergence from a common ancestor, molecular biologists have allegedly been able to construct a "molecular clock" that is said to roughly approximate the pace of speciation throughout the evolutionary process.[70] What they found was a surprising amount of regularity in the actual pace of speciation, which directly contradicts the notion of speciation by natural selection. Although neo-Darwinian theorists have attempted to by-pass this powerful piece of evidence by arguing that irregularities in the pace of speciation have tended to even out over long periods of time, they have "also been forced to face the possibility that regularity of the molecular clock reflects an evolutionary process not mediated by natural selection."[71]

But if the process of rapid speciation in the evolutionary past was not mediated by natural selection, what else could possibly have mediated it? What other factor could have possibly produced new, viable species so rapidly and regularly that few, if any, transitional forms were ever needed to bridge the gap? Given the evidence at hand, it would seem that the only plausible explanation for these "anomalies" is to be found in the existence of some sort of evolutionary program in the genomes of all species, which would have enabled the regular and rapid production of new, viable species whenever the time was right.[72]

Surprisingly, Gould defends Goldschmidt's "hopeful monster" theory, but he refuses to admit that the sudden appearance of such a viable monster would instantly invalidate the neo-Darwinian paradigm. Instead, he maintains the the sudden production of new species can be perfectly consistent with the traditional evolutionary picture, since relatively small changes in embryology are known to produce radical changes amongst adults.

The fallacy in this line of argument is that we're not talking solely about embryological changes as far as the sudden production of new species is concerned. We're talking about profoundly complex *genetic* changes within the genome itself, and not even the most radical evolutionary theorist is prepared to say that small genetic changes can suddenly yield a new species entirely by accident. Because of pleiotropic considerations, a single genetic change can have devastating consequences for the viability of an organism, since it will inevitably exert a number of powerful effects throughout the body. Hence, a single genetic change *must* be accompanied by corresponding changes in *all* the other genetic systems as well, otherwise the organism will be horribly malformed and subsequently destroyed by natural selection. This idea harks back to Cuvier's holistic contention that "every organized being forms a whole, unique, and perfect system, the parts of which mutually correspond and concur in the same definitive action by a reciprocal reaction. None of these parts can change without the whole changing.[73]

Cuvier, of course, had no knowledge of modern genetics, so he based his conclusions solely on functional considerations. Cuvier intuitively saw that the body's many parts are all profoundly interdependent upon one another, so it was a relatively simple step for him to conclude that one bodily system could never change without throwing the entire system out of kilter. The same thing, of course, is true for *all* complex mechanical systems.

In addition to these functional considerations, though, we now know that the genome is a fantastically complicated structure whose systematic intricacy we are only beginning to understand. Chief among these complexities is the phenomenon of *pleiotropy*, in which a single gene cooperates with a variety of other genes to produce a series of different phenotypic effects. This being the case, a single genetic mutation will in all likelihood damage a number of different systems in the body, which would seem to explain why the vast majority of random mutations are deleterious.

Thus, in order for a brand new species to suddenly be produced in a single generation, a tremendous number of genes must simultaneously mutate in toto before a viable organism can be produced. With this in mind, it is virtually inconceivable that all of these genetic changes could simultaneously take place purely by accident. This is why Ernst Mayr could say that the sudden production of a new species in a single generation would be indistinguishable from a miracle.[74]

It is true, as Gould says, that relatively small embryological changes can result in extreme changes in adulthood. Indeed, the human embryo at certain stages of its development is virtually indistinguishable from that of a cat or mouse. However, it is the genetic program in the DNA molecule itself that is of paramount importance here as far as adult species are concerned, and not embryological factors *per se*. But as we have seen, small, uncoordinated genetic changes are simply incapable of creating a new species in a single generation. Hence, any sort of belief in Goldschmidt's "hopeful monster" theory *necessitates* a belief in a controlled and directed series of genetic alterations, which are themselves consistent *only* with some sort of inner evolutionary program. While such an orthogenetic force may be "weak" (meaning that the directed variations may not all be optimal), it is still an orthogenetic force just the same.

The providential evolutionists of the previous century, such as Richard Owen and St. George Jackson Mivart, would have wholeheartedly embraced this radical idea of speciation in a single generation. They too believed that the various species were initially formed by "preordained" monstrous births, in response to some sort of inner trigger for change. Owen, for instance, argued for an "innate tendency to deviate from parental type, operating through periods of adequate duration . . . [as the] most probable nature, or way of operation, of the secondary law, whereby species have been derived from one another."[75]

Surprisingly, an increasing number of modern biologists are returning to this explicitly saltational view of the speciation process. This new field of research is called *epigenetic evolution*, and it seeks to show how inner genetic and ontological restraints could have been responsible for directing the evolutionary process.

For those biologists who take it seriously, epigenetics has made the idea of genetically sudden changes plausible once again. The creation of a viable new pattern of development may result from a small mutation affecting the very early stages of growth, thereby switching the process into a new direction. A few now believe that such changes represent the only source of new characters, and they explicitly identify themselves with the long-neglected views of Goldschmidt and Schindewolf. The "hopeful monster" has now returned to evolution theory. Even if these sudden changes are not the basis of all speciation events, they may be the source of those major new initiatives in the direction of evolution that lead to the formation of new types or classes. In this case, the Darwinian emphasis on adaptation may be misguided, since the character of a viable developmental path may be determined by purely internal factors. Once a fundamentally new structure has appeared, it will be exploited by adaptive evolution, but the basic pattern of the structure may be determined by deeper forces that do not depend upon selection. Here again we see elements of an older anti-Darwinian tradition resurfacing in modern biology.[76]

It is clear from this quotation that the underlying assumptions of the modern epigenetic evolutionists are fully compatible with those of the Deistic Evolutionist, insofar as both postulate an inner epigenetic source of control over the speciation process. The Deistic Evolutionist simply goes one step further and asserts that this entire system of epigenetic control was itself designed and instituted by an Intelligent Creator.

Notes

1. Letter from Ernst Mayr to FJT dated December 23, 1982.
2. Ernst Mayr, "How Biology Differs from the Physical Sciences," *Evolution at a Crossroads*, (Cambridge: The MIT Press, 1985), p. 46.
3. Ibid., p. 59.
4. Rupert Sheldrake has postulated the existence of another source of morphological order besides DNA: morphogenetic fields. These would purportedly supplement the tremendous ordering capacity of the gemome.
5. Rutherford Platt, "DNA the Mysterious Basis for Life," *The Reader's Digest* (October, 1962), p. 148.
6. David Bohm, "Postmodern Science and a Postmodern World," *The Reenchantment of Science*, David Ray Griffin, ed. (Albany: SUNY Press, 1988).
7. While the orthogenetic tendencies we have been discussing may be mediated through the DNA itself, they don't have to be directly programmed into the genome from the very beginning. Rather, some sort of external formative field or even a Divine "lure" could have caused the DNA of each major species to "mutate" in whatever way was most appropriate. In this case the source of the genetic programming would be external to the genome, and would only get "piped into" it whenever the time was right.
8. Mark Caldwell, "How Does a Single Cell Become a Whole Body?" in *Discover*, Vol. 13, No. 11, Nov., 1992, pp. 88–93.
9. Ibid., p. 88.
10. Ibid.
11. Ibid.
12. The homeobox is able to function in this capacity because it is part of an extremely elaborate gene switching mechanism, which controls the differentiation of each of the embryo's different tissues. Thus, depending on which part of the homeobox is turned on at any one time, a brain or a foot might end up getting formed.
13. I don't mean to imply that the exact same homeotic base-pair sequences can be found in all species that contain the homeobox. A certain small percentage of base-pair differences is known to exist between species. I simply mean to say that the same overall *group* of homeotic genes can be found throughout those species that contain the homeobox, and that these genes function in a similar manner.
14. Ibid.
15. Michael T. Murtha, James F. Leckman, and Frank H. Ruddle, "Detection of Homeobox Genes in Development and Evolution," *Proceedings of the National Academy of Science*, Vol. 88, December, 1991, p. 10713.
16. Ibid., p. 89.
17. Claudia Kappen, Klaus Schughart, and Frank H. Ruddle, "Two Steps in the Evolution of Antennapedia-Class Vertebrate Homeobox Genes," *Proceedings of the National Academy of Science*, Vol. 86, July, 1989, pp. 5462–5463.

18. Klaus Schughart, Claudia Kappen, and Frank H. Ruddle, "Duplication of Large Genomic Regions During the Evolution of Vertebrate Homeobox Genes," *Proceedings of the National Academy of Science*, Vol. 86, September, 1989, pp. 7067–7070.
19. Ibid., p. 7070.
20. John H. Rogers, "The Role of Introns in Evolution," *Febs Letters* Vol. 268, No. 2, August, 1990 p. 339.
21. Ibid., pp. 339–340.
22. Loomis and Gilpin, of the University of California at San Diego, have conducted important research in this area. Their results were reported in John L. Casti's *Paradox Lost* (New York: William Morrow and Company, 1989).
23. Stephen Jay Gould, *Hen's Teeth and Horse's Toes* (New York: W.W. Norton and Company, 1983), pp. 175–176.
24. Ibid., p. 176.
25. Ibid.
26. See John Gribbin, *In Search of the Double Helix* (New York: Bantam, 1985), pp. 318–320.
27. An "exon" is the part of a gene that actually codes for protein synthesis.
28. Please refer to Roger Lewin's report in *Science*, Vol. 213, 1981, p. 634, for more information on this fascinating subject.
29. See John Gribbin's *In Search of the Double Helix*, pp. 314–317.
30. Ervin Laszlo, *Evolution: The Grand Synthesis* (Boston: Shambhala, 1987), p. 80.
31. Ibid., p. 81.
32. David Bohm, "Postmodern Science and a Postmodern World," *The Reenchantment of Science*, David Ray Griffin ed., (Albany: State University of New York Press, 1988), pp. 57–68.
33. Susumu Ohno, *Evolution by Gene Duplication* (New York: Springer, 1970).
34. The previously cited work of Schugart, Kappen, and Ruddle (1989) supports Ohno's hypothesis, as it too suggests that duplication of large genomic regions occurred during the evolution of vertebrate homeobox genes. It also provides a major conceptual bridge between the respective roles of introns and homeotic genes in the evolution of new species.
35. Stephen Jay Gould, *Hen's Teeth and Horse's Toes*, pp. 169–170.
36. Ibid., p. 170.
37. Ibid., p. 171.
38. Giovanna Buttice, Paul Kaytes, Jeanine D'Armiento, Gabriel Vogeli, and Markku Kurkinen, "Evolution of Collagen IV Genes from a 54-Base Pair Exon: A Role for Introns in Gene Evolution," *Journal of Molecular Evolution* (1990) 30, pp. 479–487.
39. Ibid., pp. 483–487.
40. Rogers, "The Role of Introns in Evolution," p. 340.
41. Ibid., p. 341.
42. Ibid.
43. Ibid.
44. Ibid., pp. 341–342.
45. See G.Z. Opadia-Kadima's article "How the Slot Machine Led Biologists Astray," in the *Journal of Theoretical Biology* (1987) *124*, 127–135.
46. William D. Stansfield, *The Science of Evolution* (New York: Macmillan Publishing Co., 1977), p. 241.
47. James P. Bogart, "Evolutionary Implications of Polyploidy in Amphibians and

Reptiles," *Polyploidy*, Walter H. Lewis, ed. (New York: Plenum Press, 1980), p. 341.

48. R. Jack Schultz, "Role of Polyploidy in the Evolution of Fishes," *Polyploidy*, Walter H. Lewis, ed. (New York: Plenum Press, 1980), pp. 313–314.

49. S. Ohno, *Evolution by Gene Duplication* (New York: Springer-Verlag, 1970).

50. R. Jack Schultz, "Role of Polyploidy in the Evolution of Fishes," p. 333.

51. Juhani Lokki and Anssi Sauri, "Polyploidy in Insect Evolution," *Polyploidy*, Walter H. Lewis, ed. (New York: Plenum Press, 1980), p. 277.

52. Ibid., p. 329.

53. Environmental influences could also be instrumental in the programming of the genome, but only as an adjunct to, and not a substitute for, a certain minimum degree of orthogenetic programming within it.

54. Ernst Mayr, "How Biology Differs from the Physical Sciences," *Evolution at a Crossroads*, p. 53.

55. Although there are those who believe that some advanced form of extraterrestrial intelligence could have originally programmed this life-giving information into the genome, it seems much too remote a possibility to be taken seriously, especially given Brandon Carter's powerful use of the Weak Anthropic Principle to argue *against* the existence of ETIs. Specifically, Carter has argued that since ours is the smallest and youngest universe that is capable of producing life through natural evolutionary pathways, we may very well be the only form of intelligent life in the entire universe, especially given the fact that ETIs have yet to make an unmistakable appearance in our world.

56. See G.Z. Opadia-Kadima's article "How the Slot Machine Led Biologists Astray," in the *Journal of Theoretical Biology* (1987) *124*, 127–135.

57. Luther D. Sutherland, *Darwin's Enigma* (Santee: Master Book Publishers, 1988), pp. 118–120.

58. Although most modern evolutionary researchers are spared the responsibility for dealing with this problem, due to their complete rejection of the biogenetic "law," its persistence in the schools nevertheless reveals how firmly entrenched teleology has become in careful observations of ongoing biological processes. Both cells and complex organisms are inescapably teleological in nature, since their very development and continued survival proves that their biochemical functioning must be goal-oriented. In order to avoid the obvious religious implications of this type of biological teleology, though, non-theistic evolutionists have devised a new term, *teleonomy*, to imply goal-directedness that is not intended by a Higher Power.

59. Taylor, *The Great Evolution Mystery*, pp. 149–154.

60. Richard Goldschmidt, *The Material Basis of Evolution* (New Haven: Yale University Press, 1940), p. 136.

61. Quoted in Taylor's *The Great Evolution Mystery*, p. 160.

62. Taylor, p. 180.

63. Taylor's masking theory can easily explain why creatures such as jellyfish, sea anemones, and coral are born in a more advanced state than their adult counterparts: the genes for being fishlike are contained in all Cnidarians, but they are only unmasked for a brief period of time, during each creature's larval stage. The reversion to a more primitive way of life is concurrent with a masking of these fish-like genes.

64. C.O. Lovejoy, *Life in the Universe*, J. Billingham, ed. (Cambridge: MIT Press, 1981), p. 326.

65. Although George Gaylord Simpson has publicly disavowed Schindewolf's unor-

thodox idea, he has nevertheless admitted that it was based on a literal reading of the fossil evidence.

66. Ibid., pp. 205–206.

67. Ibid., p. xxix.

68. Statistical non-possibility is considered by mathematicians to be a mere 1 in 10^{40}, while the probability for a single successful saltation has been calculated to be *thousands* of orders of magnitude less than this. For all practical purposes, then, the probability for the random occurrence of a single massive saltation is essentially 0.

69. Stephen Jay Gould, *The Panda's Thumb*, pp. 129–130.

70. As Michael Denton and others have pointed out, the only way to avoid an indictment of traditional evolutionary theory based on the relatively constant differences of amino acid content in homologous proteins is to assume that all such families have undergone a constant rate of change per unit of absolute time. It is this constant rate of change that has been termed the "molecular clock." Although this position is weakened by a number of severe problems, my point here is that even if we accept it as true, it undermines standard evolutionary theory on other grounds.

71. Ibid.

72. On this view, the opportunism that appears to have been operative throughout the rise of species would be explained by the supposition that each species, having *already* been produced by the operation of an orthogenetic program, would *then* be subject to the local selective demands of the environment.

73. Georges Cuvier, *Revolutions of the Surface of the Globe* (London: Whittaker, Treacher and Arnot, 1829), p. 60.

74. Ernst Mayr, *Populations, Species, and Evolution* (Cambridge, MA: Harvard University Press, 1970), p. 253.

75. Taken from Neil Gillespie's *Charles Darwin and the Problem of Creation*, p, 92.

76. Peter J. Bowler, *The Eclipse of Darwinism* (Baltimore: The John Hopkins University Press, 1983), p. 223.

CHAPTER 10

Self-Organization and the Prospect
of Directed Evolution

To my mind it accords better with what we know of the laws impressed
on matter by the Creator, that the production and extinction of the past
and present inhabitants of the world should have been due to secondary
causes.

CHARLES DARWIN

10.1 The Role of Evolutionary Genes in the Origin of Species

In "An Organizational Interpretation of Evolution," UCLA molecular
geneticist John Campbell[1] explores the fascinating hypothesis that evolutionary genes exist and are therefore the chief guiding force behind evolutionary change.

Campbell begins by noting how evolutionists in the past have deliberately
denied the many evolutionary roles played by genes in order to avoid the
accusation of vitalism. Instead:

... evolutionists reverted to the mechanical paradigm of physics, in
which inert objects move only in passive response to exogenous forces
pushing upon them from outside. Evolution became change that the external environment forces upon the hapless species instead of a function
that organisms are structured to carry out. In this Darwinian perspective,
species do not evolve in an active sense; they only get evolved by an
external natural selector. They do not have causal roles in their evolution.[2]

Today, however, with the advent of modern molecular genetics, this anti-
quated paradigm is being replaced by a far more dynamic and progressive
view that is finding extensive support in the laboratory. Much to their surprise, molecular geneticists have discovered the genome to be an enormously complicated structure that is able to produce a wide variety of useful
functions in the maintenance of life.

For instance, the genome has recently been found to be comprised of a
series of related gene copies that are organized as multigene families,
wherein a given protein may be coded for by a number of related coding
sequences.[3] As Campbell points out, this "enormously increases the capac-

ity of DNA to catalog, process, and express genetic information. It also allows—and demands—evolution to proceed quite differently than for simple, single-gene copies. For example, when two or ten or a thousand similar gene copies are tightly linked together, selection becomes unable to operate on mutations in a single copy. The individual gene is lost in the crowd, and natural selection is able to survey only the adequacy of the family as a whole."[4]

Campbell further notes that genes are not static purveyors of information that are faithfully handed down from generation to generation. They are, rather, what he calls "profane molecules," in the sense that they are the "chemical substrates upon which enzymes operate."[5] Accordingly, Campbell claims that the structure of the genome can be—and is—deliberately altered by the organism in a variety of different ways.[6] He even lists 20 different genomic enzymes whose sole function is to process the structure of the various genes themselves.

The activity of these enzymes within the genome is controlled by an elaborate system of genetic "governors" whose larger role is to regulate how the structure of the DNA molecule is to be altered in relation to the specific needs of the organism. These gene-processing enzymes render the genome:

> . . . far more fluid and dynamic than had been imagined earlier. . . . *They probably are the source of most of the genetic variability important for evolution. This is significant because enzymes are notable for the specificity of the chemical transformations that they catalyze, while the hallmark of classical mutation is its presumed randomness. Profane molecules thus offer patterned variation for natural selection.* Even those mutational changes not actually catalyzed by enzymes are picked over and winnowed by multiple systems of sophisticated error-correcting enzyme pathways to leave a small pool of highly edited mutant alleles for selection (emphasis mine).[7]

In other words, Campbell is saying that the genome is fully equipped to alter its own restructuring in response to a wide range of external stimuli. He even claims that the particular algorithms that are carried out by the genetic governers are able to produce "patterned variation" for natural selection to act upon. This is certainly a far cry from the chance variations spoken of by the neo-Darwinians, and is thus much more consistent with the Deistic Evolutionist's perspective, which affirms the existence of some sort of inner directionality to the variations themselves. Whether these patterned variations are the result of an internal genetic program, or an external field that is capable of influencing the genome, is thus largely beside the point. What is important is that the variations themselves seem to possess some degree of directionality to them.

Campbell goes on to describe yet another recent finding that provides further support for the Deistic Evolutionist's position: the discovery of elaborate sensing devices in the cell whose sole function is to bring relevant information from the environment to the DNA molecule.[8] As it turns out, certain genes can only be "turned on" to produce their corresponding enzymes when an externally-derived substrate is present. This "inducibility" confers a large degree of fitness upon the organism that possesses it, since it prevents a cell from having to produce large quantities of an enzyme if the enzyme isn't actually needed.

Campbell even goes so far as to assert the existence of genes whose chief purpose is to "promote and direct the process of evolution."[9] As an example of this type of "evolutionary gene," Campbell cites the *transposon*, which functions in bacteria to allow genetic information to "hitchhike" from cell to cell, and even from species to species, on larger structures called *transmissible plasmids*.[10] Transposons can also be found in eukaryotes as well, where they are deemed to be related to genomic rearrangements and to larger speciation processes.[11]

Margaret Kidwell, of the University of Arizona, and Marilyn Houck, of Texas Tech University, have recently found direct experimental evidence of this type of "horizontal" transfer of genetic material from species to species.[12] They have identified a jumping gene called the "P element" that moved from one species of fruit fly, *Drosophila willistoni*, to another, *Drosophila melanogaster*, through the surprising agency of a mite, *Proctolaelaps regalis*.

This sort of horizontal genetic transfer has profound implications for our understanding of evolution, since it can initiate speciation events virtually overnight. In support of this position, University of Georgia molecular geneticist John McDonald has pointed out that transposable elements can function as genetic regulators, producing sudden macromutations through the initiation of new regulatory networks that express themselves phenotypically in new patterns of development.[13] These new developmental patterns could very well turn out to be the agency through which new species are introduced into the biosphere.

Indeed, Jeffrey Pollard, a developmental biologist at the Albert Einstein College of Medicine, believes that transposons may at least partly be responsible for producing the punctuated pattern of evolution that is evident throughout the fossil record.[14] Pollard believes that environmental stressors may increase the rate of gene jumping, which would have the effect of making species evolve faster by substantially increasing their mutability.

Campbell uses the term *evolutionary driver* to designate biological structures whose primary function is to further evolutionary development. One category of evolutionary driver, which functions to enable an organism to adapt to its present-day surroundings, is termed *sensory evolution*. While such a capacity seems too Larmarckian to possibly be true, Campbell cites two different instances that prove it: the repressor transposon Tn917 for *Streptococci* and a broad-based informational system in *E. coli*, which is able to evaluate the status of the entire organism and transmit the information to the genome for processing.[15] He notes how similar mechanisms abound in higher organisms as well, such that it is even possible that "the entire morphology of an animal can serve as a sensory device for detecting developmental stress during embryogenesis and regulating the exposure of developmental genes to selection accordingly."[16]

With this experimental data in mind, Campbell concludes that the crucial question for evolutionists isn't *whether* this type of sensory evolution occurs, but *how extensively* it has occurred throughout evolutionary history.[17]

The peak of Campbell's article concerns his postulation of *projective evolution* in the wild. Projective evolution refers to the capacity of organisms to evolve "according to what will occur in the future instead of what the environment is like at the present."[18] Although this is clearly a teleological view of the evolutionary process, Campbell is nevertheless convinced that it has occurred many times throughout evolutionary history. He even believes that "it has become possible to identify specific genetic and physiological structures that could allow a species to evolve projectively, and to look for evolution that such structures might have directed. In particular, we now know that higher organisms have several adaptations that reasonably could be recruited to serve projective evolutionary functions."[19]

Campbell cites the following five criteria that an evolutionary driver must possess if it is to be considered truly projective in nature:

1. Access to a variety of information sources concerning itself and the environment.
2. The ability to analyze this information in such a way as to determine which physiological responses will be adaptive.
3. Direct access to the genes.
4. Access to the reproductive system.
5. The ability to induce anticipatory changes in the organism's various physiological adaptations.[20]

In spite of the direct religious implications that projective evolutionary drivers undoubtedly possess, Campbell believes that "the most advanced animals have realized mechanisms for evolving projectively, and that their most significant achievements have been directed by identifiable projective evolutionary drivers."[21]

To further his case, Campbell cites several instances of domestication as direct examples of projective evolution in action. The domestication of dwarf strains of rice and wheat through artificial selection is cited as a particularly good example of projective evolution, since these dwarf strains were bred to grow optimally in an environment of fertilized tropical soil that had not yet come into being.[22] Although he admits that this is necessarily a special case, he argues (correctly, I think) that its specialness should not detract from its importance.[23] Indeed, Campbell notes how one of the central themes of Darwin's *Origin of Species* is that changes in domesticated species are ultimately evolutionary in nature.[24]

Campbell's most radical assertion is that the end-directedness exhibited by living organisms is evidence of a type of reverse causality in nature, wherein matter that is sufficiently organized "becomes sensitive to causes arising from the future instead of just the past."[25] He even goes so far as to claim that such an openly teleological view of nature need not be inconsistent with an objective scientific interpretation.[26]

In order to bridge the gap between objective science and a teleological view of reality, Campbell invokes the notion of *future self-reference*, which refers to information about the future status of the system that will eventually contain it. Future self-reference is deemed to be revolutionary because it enables effects to precede their causes in the real world.

Campbell concludes his remarkable article with a scathing reference to the orthodox evolutionary establishment's extreme prejudice against a scientific teleology:

> . . . nearly every scientist who has written on the general nature of evolution has felt compelled to show how deftly he can skate toward the abyss of teleology without falling in (Davies, 1961). Anyone who recognizes that scientific paradigms are postulates instead of absolute truths must be surprised that evolutionists feel so strongly compelled to rationalize away evolutionary teleology as a mirage, instead of searching for the meaning or significance of its end-directedness. Evolutionists seem more dedicated to defending current philosophical viewpoints that to extending their understanding. The abuse and philosophical intractability of teleology in evolution theory during the past century is no reason to dismiss the issues behind it today. To understand its end-directed properties is the most important reason for studying the uniquely complex natural process of evolution. I do not hold that we should accept nebulous teleology as an explanation. But we should investigate the mechanisms that allow finalistic behavioral characteristics where they emerge. Involvement of future organization in the dynamics of the present, if it occurs, would be a most important discovery to make. *The poorest possible reason for rejecting projective evolution is that it may imply a substantial alteration of our conception of reality* (emphasis mine).[27]

Campbell's many courageous points are well taken. Nature does indeed seem to exhibit many goal-directed qualities that are hard to understand in the absence of some degree of projective evolution. The ultimate question, as Campbell has pointed out, thus isn't *whether* projective evolution actually occurs, but *how* and *why* it occurs. It would seem that the only reasonable way to make sense of this type of projective evolution is in terms of a Grand Designer, Who can accurately anticipate the future and influence the present accordingly.[28]

10.2   Self-Organization and the Rise of Species

In the orthodox neo-Darwinian scenario, organisms are largely considered to be "accidental accumlations of successful characters, grafted onto one another piecemeal, and once grafted, hard to change."[29] Those adaptations that did in fact arise in the wild are thus considered to be mere historical contingencies, which could just as easily have turned out to be otherwise.[30]

In order to evaluate the cogency behind these assumptions, Stuart A. Kauffman has posed an interesting question: if we imagine the evolutionary process from the Precambrian to the present to have recurred a number of times, what sorts of organisms could we expect to find?[31] The orthodox, neo-Darwinian perspective rests on the assumption that other types of creatures, with other types of adaptations, could very well result. This assumption follows inevitably from the larger assumption that there is absolutely no directionality to the evolutionary process whatever, besides the ever-present struggle for survival. Since there is no directionality, there is no intrinsic necessity for the same structures and forms to be repeated.

Such a view, according to Kauffman, is unrealistic, because it fails to consider those self-organizing properties that seem to be inherent in all life-forms.[32] If these self-organizing properties do in fact exist, they would constitute ahistorical biological universals that largely act independently of natural selection. These biological universals would thus produce their own adaptive forms independently of natural selection, which, on this view, would be relegated to the more conservative role of choosing the most well-adapted forms for continued survival.

Kauffman argues that it is precisely these self-organizing properties that seem to be responsible for the fact that virtually all metazoan and metaphyton phyla follow the same branching developmental pathways, in spite of the fact that other modes of ontological development do occasionally occur.[33] Although it is possible that this similarity in the developmental process throughout the various phyla could simply be the result of recurrent selection for a common property that confers great adaptive advantage, Kauffman argues that the competing explanation is far more realistic: namely, that organisms possess a built-in set of self-organizing properties that render the final forms they assume largely inevitable.[34]

The Deistic Evolutionist's perspective on the evolutionary process is based precisely upon this affirmation of the self-organizing power of living organisms. On this view, organisms possess the intrinsic capacity to organize themselves along developmental lines that have largely been pre-determined by information that is either contained within, or is accessed by, the genome. It is these pre-determined forms that provide the raw material for natural selection to act upon.

As Kauffman points out, evolutionary theory "has grown almost without insight into the powerful self-organizing properties of complex systems, whose features are just beginning to be understood."[35] Given the congruence of this point of view with the known facts, one wonders how traditional evolutionary dogma could have ever ignored these vital self-organizing properties to begin with.

It would seem that the reason for this neglect has far more to do with the non-theisic assumptions of the modern scientific community than it does with any actual data conveyed by living beings themselves. For as soon as one affirms the existence of a larger set of self-organizing principles in the biosphere, one is automatically led to question *where* these ingenious principles themselves could have come from. Since it is hard to see how these self-organizing principles (which, by the way, openly speak of Aristotelian final causation in nature) could have ever originated by blind chance, the only other reasonable explanation credits them to the purposeful activity of a Grand Designer. By hypothesis, then, it is the fear of affirming an openly teleological, theistic-type world view that has led several generations of evolutionists to ignore the powerful self-organizing properties that are now known to be endemic to the entire living world.

10.3   Orthogenesis and Autoevolutionism

A. Lima-de-Faria has coined the term "autoevolutionism" to explain the self-organizing power of the evolutionary process throughout history. Specifically, he defines autoevolutionism as "the transformation phenomenon which is inherent to the construction of matter and energy."[36]

This is an important definition, insofar as it seems to trace the self-organizing power of the evolutionary process back to the inherent structure of the atoms and molecules themselves. This was Darwin's original deistic view of biological evolution, and it is one that is finding increasing support in the empirical sciences.

Lima-de-Faria uses his idea of autoevolutionism to account for the obvious degree of orthogenesis found in the evolutionary process itself:

> In the framework of autoevolutionism, orthogenesis appears as the direct result of the canalization inherent to the evolutions that preceded biologi-

cal evolution, and as a result of the autonomous evolutions that occur within the cell and the organism.[37]

For Lima-de-Faria, then, the mere existence of coherent atoms and molecules in a suitable environment is sufficient to get the evolutionary process moving in a certain direction. The Deistic Evolutionist would largely agree with this point of view, insofar as he believes that the Creator is more than creative and ingenious enough to have been able to infuse the potential for the entire biosphere into the first subatomic particles at the Big Bang.

10.4 Molecular Drive and the Process of Concerted Evolution

Molecular geneticist G.A. Dover of Oxford University has coined the term "molecular drive" to explain how an *internally* driven process of genomic change can introduce new traits into a population. Because it is internally driven, the phenomenon of molecular drive is operationally distinct[38] from natural selection and random genetic drift, and this constitutes its primary point of interest for us.

Traditionally, geneticists were of the opinion that genes were passively carried about on chromosomes, which in turn led to the belief that genes and chromosomes follow the same sorts of shuffling patterns. Today, however, it is a well-known fact that "the behaviour and segregation of genes is out of phase with that of chromosomes," and because of this, the long-term dynamics of chromosomes are decoupled from that of the genes themselves."[39] Because of this freeing up of the genes from the behavioral patterns of the cell's individual chromosomes, "it is possible to envisage a long-term change in the genetic composition of a population as a consequence of internal mechanisms inducing a non-Mendelian segregation of genes, in addition to that brought about by differential or accidental survival of individual phenotypes."[40]

Dover defines the process of molecular drive in terms of this kind of non-reciprocal DNA transfer within the cell:

> Molecular drive is the process by which mutations are able to spread through a family (homogenization) *and* through a population (fixation) as a consequence of a variety of mechanisms of non-reciprocal DNA transfer within and between chromosomes, such as gene conversion, unequal crossing-over, transposition, slippage-replication and RNA-mediated exchanges. These mechanisms, in their different ways, can induce a gain or loss of a variant gene in an individual's lifetime, leading to non-Mendelian segregation ratios.[41]

This distinction between genic and chromosomal segregation patterns is at the heart of Dover's molecular drive hypothesis. It is significant for the

Deistic Evolutionist because it provides a tantalizing mechanism for the *internal* generation of biological novelty, quite apart from the external effects of natural selection. This is highly significant, because it means that there are genetic mechanisms for the *internal, self-driven* production of phenotypic novelty within the cell. This being the case, it is no longer ludicrous to believe that the genome is capable of producing coherent adaptations on its own, without the shaping influence of natural selection.

Of course, Dover still hasn't provided the internal genetic algorithms which determine the precise behavior of the various genes themselves; he has only provided the internal genetic mechanisms through which this self-driven change can take place. This is enough, though, because it means that there is indeed a molecular pathway by which the genome can evolve itself in response to its own internally generated mechanisms for change.

Part and parcel with the concept of molecular drive is Dover's idea of *concerted evolution*, which refers to the coherent and concerted pattern of genetic variation within a species which makes it viable. Without this phenomenon of concerted evolution, genes would never be able to change in tandem with one another towards a multiplicity of unified functional ends. Molecular drive, then, is the process which is invoked to account for the observed pattern of concerted evolution in nature.[42]

Once a new genetic pattern has been initiated within the genome, Dover believes that other genes will fine-tune themselves to its presence, not through an externally-mediated process of natural selection, but through an internally-mediated, molecularly driven process of genetic reorganization.[43] Because of this, "we can no longer assume that organisms have evolved necessarily as a consequence of a tight adaptive relationship with the biotic and physical environment."[44]

In other words, Dover sees the genome itself, and *not* the external agency of natural selection, as being primarily responsible for the generation of biological novelty within a population. In view of this radical change in perspective, Dover coins yet another term, *adoptation*, to refer to internally-generated types of adaptations. This is in contrast to the traditional, neo-Darwinian concept of externally-mediated adaptations, which are formed in direct response to the external agency of natural selection.

In the neo-Darwinian format, then, it is the environment itself that can be understood as providing the central "problem" for living organisms, which is then "solved" by a subsequent selection from a randomly-occurring subset of individual variants. In Dover's molecular drive format, on the other hand, the "problem" is presented by the internally-mediated changes that are taking place within the genome itself, while the "solution" is seen as emanating from within the selective constraints of the environment.[45]

The significance of these observations cannot be overestimated, because they are finally providing the long-sought-after empirical evidence for self-driven genomic change that the Deistic Evolutionist has been postulating all along.

Notes

1. John H. Campbell, "An Organizational Interpretation of Evolution," *Evolution at a Crossroads*, David J. Depew and Bruce H. Weber, eds. (Cambridge: The MIT Press, 1985).
2. Ibid., p. 133.
3. Ibid., p. 134.
4. Ibid.
5. Ibid.
6. Ibid., p. 135.
7. Ibid., pp. 135–136.
8. Ibid., p. 136.
9. Ibid., p. 137.
10. Ibid., p. 138.
11. Ibid.
12. John Rennie, "DNA's New Twists," pp. 123–126.
13. Ibid., p. 126.
14. Ibid.
15. John Campbell, "An Organizational Interpretation of Evolution," p. 147.
16. Ibid., p. 148.
17. Ibid.
18. Ibid.
19. Ibid.
20. Ibid., p. 149.
21. Ibid.
22. Ibid.
23. Ibid., p. 150.
24. Ibid.
25. Ibid., p. 154.
26. Ibid.
27. Ibid., pp. 163–164.
28. Even if we hold that, due to a voluntary self-limitation, God does not directly influence the present, He still could have designed the original molecular structures of living creatures in such a way that *they* could anticipate the future with their present behavior.
29. Stuart A. Kauffman, "Self-Organization, Selective Adaptation, and Its Limits," *Evolution at a Crossroads*, David J. Depew and Bruce H. Weber, eds. (Cambridge: The MIT Press, 1985), p. 170.
30. Ibid.
31. Ibid.
32. Ibid., p. 171.
33. Ibid., p. 172.
34. Ibid.
35. Ibid., p. 202.
36. A. Lima-de-Faria, *Evolution Without Selection* (Amsterdam: Elsevier, 1988), p. 271.
37. Ibid.

38. G.A. Dover, "Molecular Drive in Multigene Families: How Biological Novelties Arise, Spread and are Assimilated," *Trends in Genetics*, 2, (6), 1986, pp. 159–165.
39. Ibid., p. 159.
40. Ibid, p. 160.
41. Ibid.
42. Ibid., p. 161.
43. Ibid., p. 164.
44. Ibid.
45. Ibid.

CHAPTER 11

On the Role of Natural Processes in the Creation

God never wrought miracle to convince atheism, because his ordinary works convince it.

FRANCIS BACON

11.1 God is Natural

Much of the reason for the scientific community's rejection of a Divine Creator centers around the persistent belief that a supernatural Being would only create using miraculous Fiat, instead of gradual natural processes. Since the world has obviously evolved over billions of years of gradual change, it follows from this assumption that a supernatural God probably does not exist.

The problem with this type of two-dimensional reasoning is that it is based more on a childish, colloquial view of the Divine Being than it is on any rigorous theological understanding of God's most probable nature. As the ancient Stoic philosophers were well aware, if God exists at all, then He is at once the most natural entity in the entire universe. They even had a name for this naturalistic side of God: the *Logos*, which is Greek for "logic." For the Stoics, then, if God existed at all, He *had* to be the Logos, or Logical Power, behind the operation of the natural world. Not surprisingly, the Apostle John also referred to God as the Logos, or Logical Word:

> In the beginning was the Word [Logos], and the Word [Logos] was with God, and the Word [Logos] was God (John 1:1).

These ancient thinkers had the presence of mind to realize that it was this aspect of God as Logos that generated the logical principle of cause-and-effect that is found throughout the natural world. We can substantiate this conclusion by noting that the formal definition of the word "natural" is usually taken to mean "that which naturally exists in the universe apart from the works of man." By this definition, God is clearly the most natural thing we know of, since He has existed apart from the works of man for eternity. In fact, He is so natural that He is actually *supernatural*, not in the sense of negating the natural, but rather in the sense of *transcending* it, by acting as the Creative Source from which all that is natural flows. To the extent that this view of God is valid, it follows that everything is probably "natural" on God's higher plane of reality, at least insofar as these events flow naturally from God's innermost Being, entirely apart from the works of man. However, if we could compare these events with events in our own realm of causation, they would in all likelihood seem *beyond* the natural, not because they aren't natural themselves, but because they are part of a much higher level of emergent causation, whose effects are not immediately comprehensible in the human sphere of events. Higher levels of emergent causation thus may *seem* supernatural when compared with lower levels, but that isn't because they occupy a different ontological reality than the natural; it is simply because these higher levels are inherently more advanced. To a caveman, for instance, a helicopter would seem positively miraculous, not because it is truly supernatural, but rather because it utilizes a level of natural causation that is far beyond his realm of comprehension. To us, on the other hand, a helicopter isn't anything special at all, because we are intimately familiar with this level of natural causation.[1]

Now, if we extrapolate this principle of emergent causation all the way out to the Divine Realm, we find that it is distinctly possible for it to be just as "natural" as our own world is, in the sense that the same cause-and-effect principles that apply here in our world may in fact apply there as well. However, since these higher levels of causation are presumably so much more advanced than the levels we are familiar with, they would rightfully be expected to seem supernatural to us, when in reality they could merely represent higher, emergent levels of the same natural reality. It is in this fashion that we can conceive of the supernatural realm in an entirely "natural" fashion, while simultaneously retaining all of its alleged supernatural properties.

In other words, the natural and the supernatural may not constitute two mutually exclusive realms at all. Rather, they may constitute two different aspects of the *same* realm, i.e., they may simply refer in a relativistic fashion to the various emergent levels of causation that occur in an entirely natural universe. On this view, that which is above one's own level of causation appears to be supernatural, not because it is wholly other than the natural, but because higher levels of emergent causation are by definition "super" to all lower levels. We can thus define the natural and the supernatural, not in terms of any distinct absolutes *per se*, but rather in terms of where a given event occurs relative to one's own vantage point. To a mouse, then, the everyday world of human events would clearly seem to be supernatural, not because it routinely violates the natural law of cause-and-effect, but simply because it exists on a much higher level of emergent causation, where the very complexity of its organization naturally produces effects that seem to be supernatural.

Another way to define that which is natural in the universe is in terms of whatever flows naturally out of the will and power of God," because these are events that would take place entirely apart from the works of man. According to this definition, the natural processes that are involved in universal and biological evolution can be seen as being natural results of God's Creative Activity. On this view, God's supernatural nature doesn't preclude Him from acting in a wholly natural manner; it rather *enables* Him to act naturally, since it functions as the larger cosmic force that *allows* the natural cause-and-effect processes that are at work in the universe to operate and have their being. This means that natural cause-and-effect processes can regularly be utilized by a supernatural God as His natural mode of creative action. This in turn means that the natural "evolutionary" patterns that are regularly observed in the universe can represent the natural manner in which God has chosen to act in the cosmos.

The upshot of this discussion is that any rejection of a supernatural Creator that is based on the existence of natural evolutionary processes is a serious mistake that can only be attributed to a profound naïvité regarding the essential nature of God's Inner Being. A supernatural Creator is, by virtue of His very supernaturalness, also the quintessential *natural* Being as well.

We see, then, that the popular distinction between the natural and supernatural realms is terribly confused. For as long as we define the natural as everything that exists apart from the works of man, it follows that there can't be two distinct realms of causation in existence; only one (since the human race clearly originated apart from the works of man). This unified realm of causation is both supernatural, because it emanates out of the direct or indirect activity of God, *and* natural, because it exists apart from the works of man, and because it presumably operates according to the law of cause-and-effect. Within this unified realm of causation, events can appear to be either "natural" or "supernatural," depending on where they occur relative to one's own vantage point.

The upshot of the foregoing discussion is that our traditional notion of God as Creator needn't be entirely supernatural in nature. God can and does act to control the universe by means of the physical laws He has created; in this sense He acts naturally, not supernaturally. At the same time, though, the very operation of those laws, and indeed, the very existence of the physical universe itself, requires an endless stream of supernatural "miracles" (defined here as events that would otherwise not take place in the absence of the Divine Will), so in this sense reality is also supernatural.[2] Paradoxically, then, God seems to use a supernatural means to support an exclusively natural cause-and-effect universe.

11.2 Can God Act Acausally?

It is difficult to determine precisely what we mean when we refer to the "law of cause-and-effect." Most scientists and philosophers simply take it to mean that any given effect can occur only when its corresponding cause is first engaged in. (There may, of course, be more than one possible cause for any given effect.)

However, if by this causal law we simply mean that everything that occurs must have a sufficient reason for its occurrence, the law cause-and-effect seems to reduce to a virtual tautology, which says that there must be a sufficient reason for everything that there is a sufficent reason for. To the extent that this is true, the law of cause-and-effect may be a metaphysical principle that applies in *all possible* worlds, and not just in this one, since it is hard to conceive of anything that could ever occur that did not have a sufficient reason for its occurrence.[3]

This view of the causal law accords well with the traditional doctrine of omnipotence, as it seems perfectly reasonable to assert that everything an omnipotent God does must have a sufficient reason for its occurrence (namely, that God has performed it). On the other hand, some have taken the law of cause-and-effect to represent a fundamental *limitation* of the Divine power, insofar as it seems to restrict God's capacity to elicit certain effects to a prior production of the appropriate causes. However, if we simply recast this causal law in terms of the Principle of Sufficient Reason, there no longer seems to be anything to detract from God's omnipotent power, i.e., the notion that there must be a sufficient reason for everything that occurs seems to be entirely consistent with the doctrine of omnipotence as it has been traditionally conceived.

Indeed, it is hard to see how the hypothetical Divine capacity to produce certain effects in the *absence* of a sufficient reason for their occurrence could be construed as enhancing the Divine power in any meaningful way. It may even be logically contradictory. For to the extent that the Divine election to produce a certain effect is *itself* a sufficient reason for the effect's occurrence (mediated, of course, through the natural realm of cause-and-effect), it follows that it is logically impossible for God to produce an effect acausally, i.e., without deliberately electing to produce it.

This argument reduces to the following:

1. The law of cause-and-effect can be reduced to the Principle of Sufficient Reason, which says that all effects must have a sufficient reason for their occurrence.
2. The Divine election to produce a certain effect is *itself* a sufficient reason for the effect's occurrence (mediated, of course, through the appropriate physical or spiritual processes).

3. To produce an effect acausally according to this definition, God would have to choose to produce a certain effect without choosing to do so, which is blatantly contradictory.

4. It is therefore logically impossible for God to choose to produce any given effect acausally, i.e., without choosing to do so.

5. Logically impossible states of affairs cannot be said to limit the Divine power.

6. Therefore, God's "inability" to act acausally according to this definition cannot be said to limit the Divine power in any significant way.

11.3   The Process View

For the process theologian, the terms natural and supernatural, when applied to God, refer to God's relative degree of power vis-à-vis His creation. Thus, on the process view, a natural God is one who does not possess all the power in the universe and never did, since He necessarily shares it with an eternally existing world of partially self-determining finite actualities. A supernatural God, on the other hand, is one who originally possessed *all* the power in the universe, and who thereafter voluntarily created the universe *ex nihilo*. According to this definition, the process God is a wholly natural Being who creates using natural processes because He has no other choice. In stark contrast to this type of process deity is the Deistic Evolutionist's supernatural God, who *voluntarily* creates a universe in which natural processes are His only mode of action. Both views thus affirm God's exclusive use of natural processes; they only differ on the amount of power God originally possessed, vis-à-vis the rest of the universe, and how He went about using that power.

We can therefore use a new term, *Supernatural Naturalism*, to describe the Deistic Evolutionist's conceptualization of God's creative power in the world. On this view, the Divine power is supernatural, insofar as it emanates from an utterly transcendent Being who originally had all the power in the universe (before He chose to enact a voluntary self-limitation by creating human freedom). At the same time, though, the Divine power is also natural, insofar as it exists naturally apart from the works of man, and operates solely according to natural cause-and-effect processes.

Accordingly, the issue of the "naturalness" of the world, and even of all possible worlds, is not a major point of disagreement between the process and Deistic Evolutionist's positions, at least as long as we define the natural in the above-stated manner. The main point of disagreement revolves instead around how the Divine power is conceptualized. The process thinker, as we have seen, assumes that God must be a wholly "natural" being, insofar as he believes that there was never a time when God possessed all the power in the universe. The Deistic Evolutionist, on the other hand, assumes that

God is ultimately a "supernatural" Being, insofar as he believes that there *was* indeed a time when God possessed all the power in existence; namely, before He created the world *ex nihilo.*

11.4 God Isn't Limited by Time

It is commonly believed that if an omnipotent God did indeed create the world, He would have done so "instantly." It is thus inconceivable to many that such a Creator would have voluntarily taken billions of years to accomplish His creative goals, when He presumably could have done otherwise. As a consequence, when these individuals see that modern science has documented a long and slow process of evolutionary ascent leading up to our present state of global development, they automatically conclude that God *couldn't* have been involved with it.

This type of reasoning is faulty because it assumes that a supernatural God must be limited by time. As Augustine, Aquinas, and many other theologians have pointed out, however, this temporal limitation is by no means obvious. Even if we assume that God is temporally, rather than timelessly, eternal (i.e., that some form of time does apply to God), God's unique position in the cosmos would *still* enable Him to transcend the normal limitations of time, presumably through some sort of relativistic effect.

The Bible assures us that God is beyond the normal confines of time, as St. Peter tells us that "with the Lord one day is as a thousand years, and a thousand years as one day" (2 Peter 3:8). Indeed, many orthodox theologians have maintained that God actually *created* time in the beginning,[4] along with the rest of the universe. The science of modern cosmology agrees with this assertion, insofar as it too holds that time itself was created at the Big Bang.[5] But even if the reality of time is a metaphysical "given," and therefore must apply in all possible worlds, it would seem that God's unique vantage point as transcendent universal Creator must nevertheless grant Him a large degree of immunity from the ordinary confines of time.

One of the most pervasive reasons for believing that God is actually limited by time has been the reality of evolution. Indeed, it is very hard to see why God would have resorted to the long and drawn-out evolutionary process to do His creating unless He *were* in fact limited by temporal matters. Historically speaking, since no good reason for God's voluntary use of the evolutionary process was ever found, it was assumed that either evolution itself was a farce, or else that God was in fact temporally limited, and so had no choice but to utilize the evolutionary process in His creation. In contradistinction to this historical dichotomy, the Deistic Evolutionist postulates a third alternative, which states that God freely chose to create the universe in a gradual evolutionary manner, not because He had to, but because He voluntarily *chose* to do so, in order to be consistent with the necessary nature of the Human Definition.

It is important to understand, though, that God's voluntary decision to create the universe in this gradual manner is only a problem as far as the *human* perspective on creation is concerned. For God—who is presumably beyond the normal confines of time altogether—this "long" stretch of time is immaterial (both literally and figuratively). That is to say, since both types of creation—instantaneous and gradual—presumably take approximately the same amount of "time" for God, it makes sense to suppose that He would have chosen the mode of creation that was most consistent with His desired end product (which for the Deistic Evolutionist is humanity).

Indeed, the necessity for time *itself* seems to be derived from the intrinsic time-based nature of the human developmental process. The very notion of an "evolutionary" sequence of personal development from conception to completion directly *implies* a need for time, since it takes time to grow from one stage of character assembly to another. Time thus appears to be a metaphysical prerequisite for the existence of the developmental process itself, which, in turn, would seem to justify the deliberate creation of time *ex nihilo*, as a necessary universal property for the instantiation of the Human Essence.[6]

11.5 Divine Delegation

As we have seen, there are two ways in which we can view God's role in natural cause-and-effect processes. On the one hand, we can view Him as the Stoics did, as the Logos, or Logical Mediator, between cause and effect. This would give Him an indirect Hand in everything that ever occurs, not through the production of natural efficient causes *per se*, but rather through the metaphysical linking between cause and effect. On the other hand, we can restrict our analysis to the realm of efficient causation only; that is, to the direct and immediate causes of the events themselves. This limitation would effectively remove a naturalistic God from direct participation in world-based affairs.

Of course, the discipline of modern science *presupposes* the prior existence and validity of this causal law. At this level of analysis, the role of God as Logos is *not* duly considered, since science concerns itself only with the immediate (i.e., efficient) causes of events, and not with the indirect, underlying *cause* of these causes.

Now, as long as we restrict ourselves to this superficial level of analysis, we find that the events of the natural world occur, not in direct response to God's creative hand, but as a consequence of the Divine delegation of efficient causes to the natural realm. Indeed, everywhere we look, we find evidence of this Divine delegation—virtually everything that we can observe seems to occur in response to world-based efficient causes.

This notion of a complete Divine delegation whenever and wherever possible is consistent with the postulate that God does nothing for man or the universe that they can do for themselves. Since they *can* produce all (or virtually all) of their efficient causes on their own, God is apparently content to let them do so in order to be consistent with this particular postulate, which seems to be derived from the necessary nature of the human character structure (see chapter 12). At the same time, though, since neither man nor the universe is capable of providing a metaphysical foundation for this causal law, God Himself can be expected to provide it.

This doctrine of Divine delegation explains the many self-organizing principles that are increasingly being discovered in the natural world. It also explains why God is not directly intervening in the world on man's behalf every time something goes wrong: since man *can* clearly do a vast number of things for himself, God is opting not to do these things for him, not because He doesn't care about humanity, but rather so He can remain consistent with the necessary nature of the Human Definition, which seems to require that God do nothing for man that man can do for himself.

We can even go so far as to assert that these self-organizing natural processes are the creative "tools" that God has used to implement His creative behavior in the universe, in much the same way that a paintbrush is the physical tool that an artist uses to implement his own creative behavior. However, just because an artist uses a paintbrush instead of his fingers in the creative process, doesn't mean that his final product belongs to him any less. Similarly, just because God uses natural processes as His creative tools, instead of directly creating things by miraculous Fiat, doesn't mean that His final product belongs to Him any less, either.

Notes

1. Indeed, the Deistic Evolutionist believes that there are levels of natural causation that are *infinitely* "super" to our own. This postulation enables him to affirm the existence of bona fide miracles without forcing him to abandon the necessary naturalness of the whole of reality. On this view, God *could* presumably have created the present universe more or less instantaneously (with respect to itself), not by violating the Principle of Sufficient Reason, but by utilizing radically higher instances of it.
2. We could even go so far as to say that anything God does is supernatural *by definition*, since nothing at all would presumably exist apart from the Divine Will.
3. The events of the quantum world are often cited as being "acausal," but this assertion is far from being proved. Indeed, how could we ever know this to actually be the case unless we were to somehow gain infinite knowledge about the individual events of the quantum world? For all we know, genuine quantum causes may actually exist, but due to our own scientific ignorance, we can't yet detect them.

4. The primary question at issue here isn't solar time *per se* (since there was obviously a time before the sun and earth were created), but rather the metaphysical distinction between "before" and "after."

5. Paul Davies, *The Mind of God* (New York: Simon & Schuster, 1992), pp. 49–50.

6. The law of cause-and-effect also seems to be a metaphysical prerequisite for the existence of the human developmental process. The reason for this can be traced to the behavioral component of this growth paradigm: If humans are to be capable of gaining their own knowledge and development for themselves (so they can forge their own independent identities in the process), they must be capable of eliciting certain effects by engaging in certain causative behaviors. Implicit in this requirement is the deeper need for a cause-and-effect world in which this self-directed process of growth can take place.

PART III

A Theological Justification for the Evolutionary Process

CHAPTER 12

The Reality and Necessity of Evolution as a Cosmic Process

> The issue of the compatibility of God and evolution is second to none in importance today.
>
> DAVID RAY GRIFFIN

12.1 The Validity of the Evolutionary Paradigm

In order to be successful, any proposed synthesis between evolution and creation utilizing the traditional doctrine of omnipotence[1] must first account for two things: 1) the reality of the evolutionary process in nature, and 2) the issue of why an all-powerful Creator would choose to create the world gradually through a long and drawn-out evolutionary process, instead of instantaneously by Divine Fiat.

To begin with, the word "evolution" itself simply means "change with respect to time." In this general sense the truth of evolution is self-evident, because everything in our experience changes over time.

Literally speaking, the word "evolution" also means a process of gradual unfolding, as we have seen. The reality of this more specific form of evolution is also plainly evident to anyone who carefully examines the nature of the physical world. Seen in this context, evolution is ultimately a historical[2] *process*, and it is this process-oriented character that in turn strongly suggests the existence of some form of cosmic evolution, for all of the visible universe is in process. Indeed, according to the most recent physical evidence, the "concrete" world we take for granted may not have any ultimate static reality at all. Rather, sub-atomic particles such as electrons, protons, and neutrons seem to derive their being from the existence of an evolutionary-type process of "becoming," which produces certain "static" qualities merely as a side effect. As Holmes Rolston III has pointed out:

> Perhaps the most fundamental notion of all is not matter or motion, space or time, but energetic and evolutionary process, not being but becoming. There are, absolutely, no things, no substances, but only events in a space-time something, not bodies that move in empty space over time, but a series of moving changes with continuity, forming all the "identity" there

is, a relative rather than an absolute identity in an incurably successive world.[3]

When viewed over time, this universal process of becoming is evolution in action. The reality of evolution is thus proven in the life cycles of stars, galaxies, and indeed, in the very equivalence of matter and energy, where it is the physical "process" represented by Einstein's famous equation $E = MC^2$ (in which energy equals matter times the speed of light squared), that governs the interconversion of matter and energy.

The phenomenon of evolution, however, is not limited to inanimate matter. Living creatures also experience a very real type of evolution in their own development from microscopic beginnings to full adulthood. We humans experience the ultimate form of this type of evolution: self-conscious development towards full psychospiritual maturity over a span of several decades.

Indeed, everywhere we look in the visible universe, we invariably find this same gradual process of evolutionary development, be it in the life cycles of plants, animals, stars, galaxies, or even the entire universe itself. This raises an intriguing metaphysical question: why is it that human beings share an important quality—namely, the reality of their own developmental process—with the remainder of the entire known universe? There are two possible ways to explain this phenomenon. First, it is possible that the developmental process itself is a totally natural (and perhaps necessary) property of everything that exists. If so, we would then expect everything that exists, including both humans and non-humans, to inevitably possess this fundamental developmental nature. A second way to view this ubiquity of the developmental process in nature is to regard it as a *non-essential* quality that was deliberately imposed upon the cosmos by an External Being for a particular reason.

In trying to decide between these two possibilities, the one thing we can say with a fair degree of certainty is that it *is* possible to conceive of a non-evolving, static cosmos of utterly concrete objects that would remain the same over vast eons of time. On the basis of this *a priori* observation, the developmental process itself doesn't appear to be a metaphysically necessary characteristic of universal existence *per se*. It is thus *possible* that the developmental process in all its many forms was deliberately chosen and subsequently imposed upon physical reality by God for a Higher Reason. And indeed, judging from the profound importance of the developmental process in nature, it stands to reason that such a Higher Purpose, if it exists at all, would in all likelihood be closely tied to the overall Purpose God had in creating the universe.

An important clue can be found here in the central importance of the developmental process in comprising the human identity structure. *It ap-*

pears as though it is logically impossible[4] *for man to be fully human in a deep psychospiritual sense in the absence of this all-important developmental process.*[5] This is an extremely important point, for if it can be shown that the Human Definition necessarily requires the developmental process as one of its essential defining properties, we will then have attained a possible reason for the *ex nihilo* creation of the developmental process, not just in humans, but also in the rest of nature as well (through a series of critical corollary assumptions). Our first task towards this end will thus be to demonstrate the necessity of the developmental process in the underlying Human Definition. From there, we will attempt to ascertain humanity's relative degree of importance in the larger scheme of things, and once this is accomplished, we will then try to see if there is any possible connection between the developmental process in humans and the biological process of evolution itself.

12.2   A Word of Caution

Before moving on, the reader is forewarned that the anthropocentric material in this section will seem implausible and even far-fetched if it is viewed from the atheistic and positivistic perspective of modern science. Everything changes, however, if the same material is viewed from a theistic perspective, because God could easily have designed the entire universe with human beings in mind.

Remarkably, this sort of theistic world view is becoming more and more scientifically respectable with each passing day, due to a wealth of recent findings in cosmology and particle physics which seem to indicate the presence of Intelligent Design throughout the universe. Indeed, this evidence for contrivance is so compelling that physicist Paul Davies has even gone so far as to admit that, given what we know about the history of life, "the impression of design [in the universe] is overwhelming." On this score, modern science seems to be returning full circle to its theistic roots.

This being the case, it behooves us to give the notion of Intelligent Design a fair philosophical hearing. We can do this by first *assuming* the prior existence of a Designer for the sake of argument and then extrapolating out from this assumption the various ramifications that would be entailed by such a possibility. The purpose of this type of theoretical maneuver is to see what would actually be entailed in a God-centered universe, so we can then compare our hypothetical findings to the known characteristics of our own universe. If the fit turns out to be too good to be attributed to chance alone, we will then have attained further evidence for the validity of our theistic world view.

12.3 The Role of the Developmental Process in the Human Definition

We humans tend to take the ubiquitous process of psychobiological development for granted, and for good reason: it is such an integral part of our own experience that it's hard to notice in and of itself. Yet without it—and this is the important point—we would cease to be human. Our humanity is inextricably tied to the reality of this developmental process, whether we are aware of it or not.

When we see a newborn baby, for instance, we automatically *assume* the prior existence and validity of the developmental process in humans, so we unconsciously tend to acknowledge the infant as a person who is existing at more or less the beginning of its developmental rise to maturity. Although such a developmental affirmation displays an important faith in the way things are, we must dig deeper in order to understand *why* things are this way. Indeed, as we are about to see, true insight into the structure of the universe and the nature of the human condition only *begins* when we start to question the origin and function of this developmental process in man.

Although one may or may not agree with the existence of transcendent Platonic forms or essences, it cannot be denied that certain requirements must be fulfilled if a given being is to be described as "human." Among these essential attributes are self-consciousness, the dual capacities for rational thought and emotional feeling, and a potential freedom[6] of choice. Although these various capacities must be possessed[7] to one extent or another by any being purported to be human, they are not directly related to the process of development *per se*, i.e., it is possible to conceive of their existence in the absence of such a developmental process.

However, there are two additional aspects to the Human Definition that *are* intimately related to this developmental process. They are: 1) a fully unique and independent psychospiritual identity, and 2) a full possession of one's own personality, with its inner database of self-acquired knowledge.

At first it may seem as though these additional qualities are too nebulous and abstract to be rationally tangible, but a deeper examination reveals that this is not so. After all, as personal beings we are largely *comprised* of a unique and independent psychospiritual identity that is to varying degrees self-possessed.

It is a well-known fact that each of us is fundamentally different from everyone else who has ever existed on this planet. Moreover, each of our personalities is distinct (i.e., independent) in the sense that our identities are not directly connected to, or derived from, any other type of being at the present time. While we may have ultimately originated from the procreative activity of our parents, the process of being born physically separated us from a complete co-identification with Mother forevermore. And while many of us continue to psychologically identify with either or both of our parents long after we are born, we are still physically and psychologically separate individuals, and it is this existential separation that confers upon us the distinct potential for a truly independent psychospiritual identity. While we may be internally related to one another in such a way that our identities are partially being self-created *out of* our relationships, we are still ontologically separate individuals with firm boundaries between our personalities.

There are thus two distinct aspects to a person's overall independence of identity: a physical aspect and a psychospiritual aspect. The process of birth confers upon us a physical independence of identity, in the sense that it physically separates us from Mother. This physical separation sets the stage for a subsequent psychospiritual separation, which proceeds to one extent or another throughout life. Indeed, the overall goal or *telos* of life can be thought of as the perpetual struggle to forge an independent psychospiritual identity for oneself to coincide with one's physical independence of identity, which one has possessed from birth onwards. Thus, each of us is now a self-contained personality structure, with a psychospiritual identity that is progressively becoming more and more unique over time.

While it may be difficult to conceptualize what is meant by the term "independent identity," we all know how to recognize one because each human personality in existence is a concrete example of one. The challenge is to figure out which qualities actually comprise this independence of identity, so that we can in turn posit the possible routes by which such an identity can be attained.

One of the most important aspects of a person's independence of identity is undoubtedly the knowledge database that all humans must have in order to be able to live with equanimity in the world. It turns out that this knowledge database cannot be externally conferred upon man by God without the former automatically being transformed into a preprogrammed robot. The reason for this is not far to seek: As soon as God instills any type of knowledge or experience into man that man could have acquired for himself, He will have automatically preprogrammed man's inner database *by definition*, and this in turn would automatically transform him into a preprogrammed automaton.[8] Needless to say, such a robot-like quality is totally at odds with the presumed requirement that man be a self-motivated "independent self." How can such a robot-like creature be an independent, self-contained entity as long as its internal database, and hence its overall behavior, is being determined by an External Power?

In short, the very idea of preprogramming a being in order to control its behavior is intrinsically incompatible with the traditional notion of freedom as it has normally been ascribed to human beings. Robots, of course, respond to environmental stimuli by calling upon their own inner database of knowledge that they were initially programmed with. Their responses therefore tend to be predictable, two-dimensional, and, as a consequence, not very noteworthy. Humans, in contrast, respond to environmental stimuli by calling upon their own *self-programmed* database of knowledge and experience, and this ends up making all the difference in the world to them, because it confers an authenticity and creativity to their lives that could never be duplicated in an externally programmed automaton. For instance, humans are capable of responding to a given environmental stimulus in any number of creative ways, not only because they are behaviorally free to do as they please, but also because their internal database of knowledge has *itself* been obtained in a self-directed, creative manner. The end result of this behavioral creativity is a being with a completely independent locus of self-consciousness, whose actions truly matter in the overall scheme of things.

Going one step further, it is evident that if man is to be an independent moral agent, capable of freely doing either good or ill with his behavior, he *must* possess a certain amount of knowledge and experience in his life, in order to be able to direct his behavior in whatever direction he finds most appropriate. The prevention of behavioral evil is also intimately related to the specific content of this knowledge database, because it takes a certain amount of practical real-world knowledge to be able to act in such a way as to avoid producing any destructive consequences with one's behavior. A certain level of moral awareness is also required if these destructive consequences are to avoided, since it is the extent of this moral awareness that compels the individual to use his self-attained knowledge in either a constructive or destructive fashion.

The need for real-world knowledge and moral awareness in a free-willed agent is thus beyond question. It is, rather, the task of getting this knowledge and moral awareness *into* such an agent that turns out to be the real problem, because due to the intrinsic definition of any robot-like mechanism, it is logically impossible for God to miraculously infuse this knowledge and moral awareness into any type of being's mind without automatically transforming it into a pre-programmed robot.

It now becomes instructive to note the traditional definition of the word "robot." A robot is generally defined as a mechanism that acts in accordance with a certain body of data that has been preprogrammed into it.[9] A human, in contrast, can be defined as a being that acts in accordance with data that has been *self-acquired.* According to these definitions, it was logically impossible for God to infuse any practical, real-world data into the human mind, because in the very act of doing so He would have programmed man's behavior *by definition*, and so would have automatically transformed him into a preprogrammed robot.

But it isn't as if the only thing that man would have lost is his autonomous nature if he were to have been externally preprogrammed by God. He also would have lost the most precious aspect of his humanity as well: his spontaneous and uniquely human personality characteristics. So, instead of behaving like a bona fide, self-determining human being, our preprogrammed "person" would have been condemned to behave like a mindless automaton. Nowhere has this fundamental truth been better portrayed than in the old "Star Trek" episode entitled "Return of the Archons." In this science fiction drama, a human-like being by the name of Landru gains a type of immortality by copying the contents of his entire mind into an advanced supercomputer. Upon doing this, the part human, part computer then attempts to eliminate all the humanly-derived evil on its planet by controlling (or reprogramming) the minds and personalities of all the people that live there, so as to force them to behave in a non-destructive manner. Landru "succeeds," and all humanly-derived evil on the planet is effectively abolished. This elimination of evil, however, comes at an extremely high price: the citizens themselves are automatically transformed into mindless sheep, who are clearly more robot-like than they are human.

The crew of the Enterprise soon come to realize the tremendous injustice that is taking place on Landru's planet. For while there is no longer any behavioral evil to speak of in the alien society, this "goodness" has only come about through the inadvertent creation of the greatest of all evils: the absolute destruction of each person's independent character structure. As a consequence, Kirk implores the computer to give up its possession of the planet's citizenry. At first Landru resists him, arguing that it had been programmed to produce only good for the people. Kirk then correctly retorts that in the computer's sincere attempt to produce only good on the planet, it had inadvertently produced the *greatest* of all evils: the complete destruction of each person's inner creativity and power for self-determination. This fundamental contradiction causes the computer to self-destruct, at which point the people immediately return to normal again.

This normality is soon evidenced by the occurrence of several domestic squabbles and barroom brawls, which the crew of the Enterprise are greatly pleased to see happening, since they indicate a return to a healthy state of affairs on the planet. This type of preference for self-motivated behavioral evil, instead of mindless bliss, reveals what is perhaps the most fundamental of all human truths: namely, that the higher goal of independent identity formation in man not only necessitates the temporary existence of a certain amount of behavioral evil in the world (which results from the temporary lack of full character development in man), it also *justifies* it as well, since there is by hypothesis no other logically possible way to create beings who are genuinely free and self-determining.

On this view, God was intrinsically incapable of preprograming humanity in order to prevent behavioral evil because of the destruction of character that would have inevitably resulted. But if God was unable to preprogram man because of the intrinsic requirements of the Human Definition, there is only one other way in which man could possibly have attained his essential knowledge database: *by starting out at the very beginning of the developmental process and getting it for himself. It is precisely here that the developmental process in humans has its ultimate origin and value.*

It is also here that the problem of moral evil has its ultimate origin as well: since humans must undergo a gradual process of self-attained character development in order to be fully human, it follows that they must begin their lives in a relatively undeveloped, and therefore immature, state of being if they are to be able to qualify as being genuinely human. This lack of full character development is itself manifested as a lack of knowledge, a lack of psychospiritual maturity, and a lack of moral awareness in people. But these are precisely the qualities that are needed if moral evil is to be prevented in human society, because people need to know *what* to do, *how* to do it, and *whether* to do it if they are going to be able to avoid producing behavioral (i.e., moral) evil in their lives. Therefore, any free-willed being who is deprived of a certain critical amount of knowledge, maturity, and moral awareness will inevitably be susceptible to the production of behavioral evil. This is why the problem of evil appears to be implicit in the very details of the Human Definition: because man must gradually develop in order to be fully human, and this means that he must also suffer the consequences of being *undeveloped* at the present time. Unfortunately, this directly entails a huge susceptibility to moral evil. On the other hand, this propensity steadily decreases as one grows more mature, until it is finally banished altogether when one reaches one's own state of full character development.[10]

It would seem, then, that many of the specific qualities of human life can be traced back to the metaphysical limitations surrounding the necessary nature of human knowledge. These limitations can be summarized in the following conditional statement: *If* we are to be genuinely human, then we *must* acquire our own knowledge for ourselves; it *cannot* be given to us from without.

Indeed, this process of acquiring one's knowledge and development for oneself turns out to be so fundamental to the uniquely human experience that it is apparently involved in the forging of each person's most intimate inner qualities. These are the idiosyncratic characteristics that we naturally associate with being human, which have the effect of making each person absolutely unique in the end.

A good portion of this psychological uniqueness appears to be derived from how the individual happens to view the *undeveloped* aspects of his or her inner mind. That is to say, a significant chunk of each individual's psychological uniqueness seems to come, not just from what he or she happens to know, but also from how he or she chooses to view and respond to that which *isn't* yet known. Each individual has his or her own unique way of responding to this great unknown, and it is this unique response that determines many of the more subjective aspects of an individual's inner character structure. However, it is important to realize that this aspect of human personality is impossible to attain *by definition* in the absence of a gradual process of psychospiritual development. How can there be a cognitive and developmental unknown to respond to if a person is *already* fully developed and totally preprogrammed from the start?

Of course, one could argue that God could have miraculously duplicated this unique individualistic response *instantaneously*, but even if this were possible (and it doesn't seem to be), He still couldn't have infused these unique personality characteristics into a live individual without simultaneously converting it into a preprogrammed automaton.

It is often suggested that God could have created beings who *thought* they were free and unique, but who really weren't deep inside. It is argued that God, acting as a Master Hypnotist, could have given us the post-hypnotic *impression* that we were free and unique, while in actuality we would be so rigidly programmed that we would be incapable of ever engaging in moral evil.[11]. The problem with this possibility, of course, is that while *we* wouldn't know about this grand act of deception, God *would* know, and it is precisely this Divine Awareness that makes such a deceived being not worth creating in the first place. Certainly if we had the choice to either be our present selves or to be thoroughly deceived in the above manner, most of us would choose to be the way we are now, even though it necessarily entails a certain amount of behavioral evil.

Another important part of a person's inner identity structure is determined by *how* he actually comes to fill in his own internal database of knowledge. That is to say, it isn't just what one knows in life that determines one's inner sense of uniqueness, it is what one learns and becomes while attaining this fundamental knowledge that makes each person truly unique. There are, of course, as many different ways to obtain a given body of knowledge as there are moments in history, since the various circumstances surrounding each person are utterly unique; therefore, the contribution of each individual learning experience to the overall personality structure is equally unique. The end result of this global emphasis on uniqueness is the automatic production of a series of totally unique human personalities.

A third aspect of man's intrinsic definition that is made possible by this gradual process of development is his existential "ownership" over his own personality. This is a complex subject with many far-reaching implications, but it boils down to a single assertion: *the more effort one employs in obtaining a given item, the more one will end up "owning" that item in a deep, existential sense.* Put another way, we need to expend a significant amount of effort in trying to obtain a given item before it can truly be said to "belong" to us.[12] Such an assertion makes immediate intuitive sense to us: a car that we pay for with our own hard-earned money is more "ours" than one that is purchased with someone else's money. We can even go so far as to say that a car that is built with our own hands "belongs" to us more intimately still than one that is built by someone else, even if it is purchased with our own money.

The implications of these principles of ownership for human identity formation are both clear and straightforward: in order for man to claim—in the deepest and most inexorable sense possible—true ownership over his own thoughts and feelings (and indeed over his entire personality), he must do everything he possibly can to attain his own knowledge and personality development by his own individual effort. Accordingly, a personality that is externally bequeathed upon man by God would not only rob man of his own unique and fully independent identity, it would also rob him of full existential ownership over his own personality and knowledge database as well.

Indeed, what good is even an *infinite* knowledge database and a *perfect* personality if these qualities don't fully belong to one in the deepest possible manner? It is for this reason that we can point to the property of full ownership over one's own thoughts and personality as being yet another essential feature of the Human Definition. But if it is impossible to be fully human in the absence of a fully-owned personality, then we are again forced to conclude that a gradual process of development is an absolutely essential ingredient in the process of human identity formation, since it is only through a self-attained developmental process that humans can come to fully possess the contents of their own personalities.

A good way to visualize the contribution of the self-driven developmental process to the formation of the human identity structure is in terms of a primary process (that of development) automatically producing a secondary byproduct (an independent human identity). According to this conceptualization, as one struggles to overcome one's lack of knowledge and development in the world by living and learning as decisively as possible, one *automatically* forges an independent and self-possessed identity for oneself as an inevitable side effect of the process of development. On this view, the uniqueness and independence of the human identity structure is simply an epiphenomenon of the developmental process itself. *The critical insight to be gained here is that there is no other logically possible way for an independent human identity to be obtained apart from this evolutionary-type developmental process.* This is why we (and, as we are about to see, the larger universe itself) are gradually evolving towards greater and greater levels of becoming: because there doesn't appear to be any other logically possible way for the human identity structure to be formed.

12.4   Why "Data Disks" Cannot Be Used in the Programming of Human Beings

As we have seen, the achilles heel of the human race is epistemological in nature: it revolves around the problem of how knowledge can be infused into people's minds without violating their basic humanity and transforming them into robots.

It has been suggested that one way to resolve this problem (contingent upon the existence of the appropriate technology, of course) would be to add practical knowledge and "experience" into people's brains via miniature "floppy disks." This, it has been asserted, would significantly add to our knowledge database and would thereby make us less prone to moral evil, without making us any less human.

This is surely the crux of the matter when it comes to the question of whether or not mature humans could have been created ready-made. For if knowledge and experience can be externally derived and then inserted into the human mind with no further expenditure of effort, and with no underlying violation of the Human Definition, it follows that the particular route of knowledge acquisition that is used for the assembly of intelligent beings is not really an essential factor in determining their intrinsic degree of "humanness."

The Deistic Evolutionist, of course, is convinced that the external inputting of knowledge into the mind in this manner *would* automatically violate the Human Definition. Besides the intuitive feeling that something sacred would be violated by such a process, four additional arguments can be raised in support of the Deistic Evolutionist's position.

The first argument is of the "slippery slope" variety. It has to do with the observation that an agent's method of knowledge acquisition seems to naturally follow an all-or-none format in its basic character: either an agent must gain all of its knowledge on its own through its own hard effort in the world, or else it will quickly gravitate over to the *opposite* extreme, where all, or virtually all, of its knowledge will be externally administered, with no further effort being expended on the agent's part.

The reason for this is tied to the pain and suffering that is typically associated with self-acquired knowledge. Knowledge that one gains for oneself generally causes one a tremendous amount of hardship, *and it is precisely this hardship that would motivate any sentient being to exclusively utilize an easier method of knowledge acquisition if one actually existed.* Based solely on this almost universal preference of pleasure over pain, any sentient being would naturally prefer to have all, or virtually all, of its knowledge externally copied into its brain, instead of having to invest so much personal time and effort trying to reach the same end product.

It would seem, however, that if this type of self-programming were actually possible, the situation at both the individual and societal level would quickly deteriorate into sheer, non-productive anarchy. Few people would be driven to do anything at all besides acquiring additional data disks to load into their brains, and one could even imagine entire world wars being fought to gain access to these "priceless" disks.

But even if the distribution of these data disks in society were totally peaceful, something much more qualitatively ominous would nevertheless result from their continued use. Whereas the mind's data bank would quickly become well-stocked by the persistent use of these disks, the individual's innermost essence of personality—the "I" who is the ultimate arbiter over *how* this knowledge is to be utilized—would undoubtedly suffer severe consequences from the use of this type of artificial knowledge, because the maturation of the ego seems to be inextricably tied into *how* knowledge and experience are actually acquired for the self. What's more, there doesn't seem to be any type of "data disk" that could externally provide this fundamental psychospiritual maturity, because the maturation of the personality appears to be qualitatively different than the mere possession of knowledge *per se*. It rather seems to be related to the nebulousness of the personality's own psychospiritual substance; to its state of development vis-à-vis its own process of self-assembly. In this developmental paradigm, knowledge and experience constitute a valid *means* for effecting this personality development; they are *not* identical or cosubstantial with it.

In other words, it is the process of acquiring knowledge through hard work that develops the personality. Thus, to simply add knowledge into the brain with data disks would bypass the personality altogether, leaving it just as immature as before. This is one of the chief reasons why the use of external data disks would end up violating the Human Personality Definition: because neither knowledge nor experience are cosubstantial with the "I" that constitutes who we really are in our innermost being.

If this is true, and if it is also true that the goal of life is for humans to acquire their own knowledge and development for themselves, it follows that humans would need to begin the developmental process at the earliest possible starting point, so they can gain as much knowledge and development on their own as possible. On this view, both the personality and the mind's inner database would need to begin the developmental process in as immature a state as possible, so that a coordinated state of mutual development could subsequently take place.[13]

Of course, this entire discussion begs the question of why a completely different type of disk could not be created that would contain the entire psychospiritual personality *itself* in a fully assembled state of being. There are two ways to answer this question. First, even if it were actually possible to artificially create a "naked" psychospiritual self in a fully mature ontological state, it would still require the external inputting of knowledge and experience in order to be functional, and the very act of inputting them into the mind would irrevocably violate the being's potential humanness in all the ways previously discussed.

The second reason why a fully-assembled psychospiritual self cannot be externally administered by disk is that the self appears to be irreducible by its very nature, i.e., it does not appear to be possible to reduce the self to the static form of a disk that can arbitrarily be copied onto a vacuous recipient. Rather, the self appears to be an ontologically fundamental unit that by its very nature must stand on its own. Intuitively speaking, one can see how ridiculous it would be to have one's innermost sense of self or "I-ness" reduced to mere numbers, or to some type of static magnetic pattern. In this sense the self appears to be an intrinsically irreducible, and therefore non-transferable, ontological unit.

One of the new "Twilight Zone" TV episodes deals with this very issue. In this intriguing story, which takes place sometime in the future, human technology has advanced to the point that human memories can be added and removed from the mind at will. They can also be stored in a computer for future use.

Because of their priceless value, these memories command a very high price tag. In order to capitalize on this burgeoning new industry, one individual who happens to be down on his luck chooses to sell the memory of his high school graduation to a professional "memory broker" in order to earn some much-needed cash. At first, he doesn't seem to be any worse for the transaction; he just can't seem to remember when, or even if, he ever graduated from high school. Predictably, the same man ends up coming back several times in the future to sell more memories, until eventually, he becomes a fragmented and incoherent individual who can't even pass a basic interview to get a job. Understandably distraught at what has become of him, he returns to his memory-broker and forces him, at gunpoint, to give him his precious memories back. Tragically, he finds that his memories have already been sold to other people. Consequently, the best his memory-broker can do is to give him *other* people's memories for free. The poor man has little choice but to accept the offer, even though he has no idea how these other memories will ultimately affect him.

Predictably, the instantaneous infusion of other people's memories into the vacuum of his innermost soul causes him to become even *more* fragmented and incoherent than before, because his mind now contains the conflicting memories of a large number of different people. At the episode's conclusion, we find our miserable protagonist making a fool out of himself in yet another interview, because the details of his life have now become too confusing and contradictory to make any kind of sense at all. It thus becomes evident that both his life and mind have been ruined forever.

Upon seeing this highly suggestive "Twilight Zone" episode, one can't help but feel that something sacred has been violated in this man's life. Evidently, one cannot manipulate memories in this manner (or the knowledge and experience that go into them), without toppling the entire edifice of one's deepest personality. This is because one's own innermost sense of self is not only *based* on the specific content of these memories; its fundamental structure is also directly determined by *how* these memories are actually acquired. Since each bit of knowledge and experience that the individual attains for himself results in a corresponding alteration in his innermost state of development, it follows that these memories (along with their attendant knowledge and experience) cannot retroactively be removed from the mind without the entire personality structure, which has used these memories all along as a structural foundation, being obliterated as well. It would be like attempting to remove all of the bricks on the first floor of the World Trade Center; the entire building would immediately come tumbling down.

Moving in the opposite direction, we find that we cannot just arbitrarily insert memories (or data disks) into a fledgling personality either, because the innermost self would still suffer equally severe consequences. If the self is only able to grow in response to knowledge that is self-acquired through a hard-won deposit of time and effort, it follows that the input of externally-derived knowledge and experience into the mind would completely *bypass* the developmental structure of the self altogether, thereby leaving it just as immature as it always was.

We can perform a "thought experiment" in order to verify this claim. If we were to take a computer disk containing, say, the ability to read French fluently, and then we were to somehow input it into our minds, the most that could conceivably result from such a procedure is that we would suddenly be fluent in French. It is hard to see how this input of knowledge would have any effect at all on how mature we would be deep inside, or how we would feel about our innermost selves. We would simply remain the same sort of people we always were, only we would be able to add the ability to speak a foreign language to our list of intellectual capacities.

If we would attempt to do the same sort of thing with a young child, two things would probably result. First, the child's innermost personality structure would probably not be altered in the least bit by the external input of knowledge. Indeed, even if all the knowledge in the universe were to be copied into his mind, it is hard to see how this would have any significant effect on who he really was deep inside. This leads to the second problem that such a procedure would entail: the child's psychological maturity level would clearly be insufficient to handle such a massive input of knowledge in this manner.

The same sort of situation would probably exist in *any* sort of individual that was being programmed from without. Not only would his innermost state of psychospiritual development probably remain unaffected by this rapid input of knowledge, his relatively immature state of being would also turn out to be grossly ineffective at handling this degree of force-fed information.

This constitutes yet another reason for tying a being's state of psychospiritual development to the overall process of knowledge acquisition: not only does the act of acquiring knowledge serve to increase the developmental state of an individual's innermost personality, it also makes it much more likely that he or she will be able to *handle* this self-acquired knowledge in an appropriate manner.

What it all boils down to is this: even if it *is* actually possible in principle to input externally-derived knowledge into human-like beings, such a procedure can still never be performed on genuinely *human* beings, as long as we count among their essential defining characteristics the property of freedom. For as long as we define "humanhood" as the capacity to act freely in response to freely-attained knowledge, and as long as we define "robothood" as the compulsion to act in response to externally-administered knowledge that has *not* been freely-attained, we find that it is logically impossible to have a bona fide human being who has been externally programmed with knowledge that it could have acquired for itself.

The one thing that seems almost beyond question is that the very existence of an externally-derived database makes it much more likely that the agent in question will behave in direct accordance with the specific content of its programming. Since such an agent could not engage in any type of action whatsoever without calling upon the specific content of its inner database, it follows that *all* its behaviors will be determined in one way or another by the specific content of this database. It simply would not know how to do anything at all in the absence of this internal source of knowledge. It would seem to follow, then, that an agent's behavior *is* necessarily tied to the specific content of its inner database, either directly, through the unmitigated *determining* of its actions, or indirectly, through the determining of its *underlying basis* for action.

To the extent that this is true, however, the agent in question cannot be said to be acting freely in relation to its programming. For as long as we define freedom as the lack of *any* external compulsion on an agent's behavior, then a database that has its origin outside the agent would *necessarily* limit that agent's freedom. It follows, then, that in order to be *truly* free, an agent must acquire its own database for itself, along with the capacity for manipulating it in whatever way it sees fit. This in turn requires a developmental process that is entirely self-directed.[14]

While it is possible that God could have created preprogrammed (i.e., unfree) beings who were programmed to *think* they were free, it is logically impossible for God to have created preprogammed beings that were *in fact* free. And since a good God would clearly not want to create self-deceived beings, it follows that God could not have created preprogrammed beings that were both undeceived and free at the same time, even if He were genuinely omnipotent (since omnipotence does not include the power to do the logically impossible). This is probably why God did not originally avail Himself of the presumed "possibility" of creating ready-made beings that always acted rightly: because no such possibility actually exists, even though we often like to think that it does.

12.5   Are Humans Worth Creating?

The entire foregoing discussion begs the question of whether or not humans themselves are *worth* producing in the first place, especially since they seem to have entailed so many existential difficulties in their creation, not the least of which is the behavioral malfunctioning (i.e., moral evil) that is a natural consequence of their partial character development. Judging from the fact that we currently exist in spite of these difficulties, it is evident that our existence has been judged worthwhile in spite of its tremendous metaphysical "price," and the reason for this is not far to seek: as the alleged children of the Great Creator Himself, we by hypothesis have an ultimate destiny that is so great that we can hardly conceive of it at the present time. Before we can "inherit" it, however, we must first become "worthy" by completing our own development. Hence, the true issue here is whether the eventual good of a fully formed human character structure is worth the necessary metaphysical "cost" of its production (in terms of physical and moral evil). I can think of no better way to answer this question that by quoting St. Paul himself:

> For I consider that the sufferings of this present time are not worthy to be compared with the glory which shall be revealed in us (Romans 8:18).

In fact, we can go so far as to say that human existence is worth *infinitely* more than its temporary metaphysical cost, because the future good of human existence, which is infinite by definition in this traditional eschatology, *infinitely* outweighs its finite metaphysical cost in terms of the temporary production of evil.

Based solely on this observation, we must reject Ivan Karamazov's protestation in Dostoyevsky's *The Brothers Karamazov* that the supposed goodness of humanity can never be worth such a tremendous metaphysical cost. For as long as we assume that the future good of humanity will be infinite in both duration and extent, and that our present suffering is a necessary ingredient in the production of this infinite good, then this good must *infinitely* outweigh any finite cost *by definition*. Even if the foundation of such an infinite good must of necessity be built on the horrible tears of billions of tortured young children, we must nevertheless affirm the ultimate value of this Lofty Goal.

Going one step further, if we assume the process of human identity formation to be logically impossible in the absence of a gradual process of self-attained development, we find that this developmental process has suddenly taken on a huge importance in the overall scheme of things, at least insofar as man himself is concerned. *It is so important, in fact, that it appears to be the central paradigm upon which most of physical reality itself is based.*

In order for this to be true, we must posit human development as one of the most important goals in the entire universe; otherwise, why would the rest of physical reality be based upon it? We seem to be supported in this conclusion by man's unprecedented degree of inner complexity, along with the inherent miraculousness of human consciousness itself. Indeed, it is because human consciousness is *so* unsearchably miraculous and complex that it suddenly becomes rational to look elsewhere for a sufficient explanation for it. This is precisely what Nobel laureate Sir John Eccles has done in his book *The Wonder of Being Human* (Boston: Shambhala, 1985). In this outstanding work, Eccles comes to the radical conclusion that the only way to account for the miraculous nature of human consciousness is by appealing to a Higher Spiritual Power.

Interestingly enough, this is exactly what the Bible has been telling us for thousands of years. According to the Bible, God is actually reproducing Himself in a finite capacity on this planet in the form of human "children," who are allegedly being created in God's own psychospiritual "image." Indeed, to the extent that God possesses a free-willed, self-consiousness personality (albeit in Infinite Form), the superficially grandiose assertion that humans are being created in the image of God has a certain ring of truth to it, since these human qualities are in point of fact the most advanced forms of complexity in the entire known universe, and therefore appear to be inexplicable in the absence of a Divine Origin.

This realization immediately presents us with a strange paradox: we know that we are exceedingly imperfect beings, yet we also know that we are the most complicated things that have ever been discovered. These two assertions appear to be vaguely incompatible with one another. After all, how could we possibly be the most complex things in existence, in spite of our many gross imperfections? Intuition, reason, and common sense all tell us that this is probably not the case; *surely* such an imperfect being as man, by virtue of his very imperfection, could never be the most complex thing in existence. Yet, at the same time, nothing in the entire known universe even *approaches* the organized complexity of the human brain.

Of course, one could attempt to adopt the Weak Anthropic Principle, in conjunction with the creative power of blind chance, to explain this apparent anomaly. One could simply say that out of all the finite actualities in existence, human beings just happened to become the most complicated. On this view, it is necessarily the case that we humans are one of the most complex things in existence, because we couldn't possibly be aware of this status if we weren't.

According to the Weak Anthropic Principle, then, an extreme amount of biological complexity is a necessary precondition for conscious awareness *per se*; therefore, we couldn't possibly have observed the universe to have been otherwise. Accordingly, it is our own state of self-awareness, which is made possible by our extreme amount of inner complexity, that acts as a fundamental selective mechanism. It is this form of retroactive selection that makes it "necessary" that we be one of the most complicated things in existence.

We mustn't, however, be fooled by this type of necessity. For although it is necessarily the case that intelligent observers must possess a great deal of inner complexity in order to be self-conscious, it does *not* follow that this ontological relationship makes it necessary that such a profound state of complexity should exist in the first place.

That is to say, the metaphysical necessity that exists between complexity and self-consciousness may be a necessary *precondition* for the existence of intelligent observers, but it is not a *sufficient* condition. Something else needs to be added to make this possible; namely, the addition of a sufficient *causal* explanation for this complexity. It is for this reason that the Weak Anthropic Principle can never be used to account for the ultimate origin of intelligent life.

But even though this necessary relationship between complexity and self-consciousness is not a sufficient condition for the existence of intelligent observers, it is still possible that human beings in all their complexity could have come into existence by chance alone. If this were indeed the case, then it would have been just a fluke (facilitated by the Weak Anthropic Principle, of course) that we humans turned out to be one of the most complicated things in existence.

Fortunately, there is a much better explanation for why we humans are such profoundly complex beings, in spite of our many imperfections. According to the ancient Church fathers, we are as complicated as we are because we are merely crude copies of a much more perfect Original. On this view, a much more perfect spiritual Being *does* in fact exist in the heavens, and we are directly patterned after Him; this explains why we are the most complicated things we know of. On the other hand, our tremendous imperfection is alleged to result from the fact that we have yet to approximate this Perfection in our own lives, since we are still growing towards our own full development.

This latter view—which corresponds to the Biblical assertion that humans were created in the image of God—has the great advantage of appealing to our intuition and common sense. It would be an odd universe indeed if the most complicated things in it—namely ourselves—turned out to be, in spite of our many imperfections, the most complex things in existence. It is far easier to believe that we humans are patterned after a much more perfect Original.

At any rate, as long as we assume that man is being created in the image of God, and that God possesses a supremely personal character structure (both statements of which have been affirmed by traditional theologians for centuries), then we have an additional reason for positing a fixed content to the Human Definition: Since man's character structure is presumably patterned after the nature of God Himself, the Human Definition is what it is because God's definition is what *it* is. Consequently, since God is a completely unique Independent Self who owns His own Personality in the deepest and most inexorable sense possible,[15] it stands to reason that man, who is being created in the image of God, must also possess similar qualities (albeit in finite form).

Interestingly enough, man does indeed seem to be in the process of obtaining these important psychospiritual qualities for himself through the gradual process of self-attained development. Unfortunately, due to the intrinsic nature of these qualities, they can only be had at a very high "price": that of the many metaphysical necessities that are inevitably imposed on the world by the developmental process itself.[16] But even though this process of development invariably brings with it a whole host of problems, it cannot in any case be avoided without the simultaneous forfeiture of the underlying humanity of man.

Now we are in a position to understand how man could possibly be the "center" of the universe in terms of his overall importance and meaning. The very notion of the human character structure being patterned after the Divine Spiritual Image *automatically* carries with it a tremendous degree of importance (assuming, of course, that we believe it to be true in the first place). Indeed, to the extent that this assumption turns out to be valid, it is hard to see how any finite being could be *more* important than a literal "child" of the awesome Creator Himself.

12.6 *De Re* Necessity and the Deistic Evolutionist's Position

To sum up what we have covered thus far, the Deistic Evolutionist believes that there is indeed such a thing as a Human Essence within the Mind of God. He further believes that this Human Essence corresponds to a finite replica of the Divine Spiritual Image, set in the form of an independent psychospiritual agent, i.e., he believes that the Human Essence is comprised of those characteristics that would enable a being who possessed them to be a genuine "child of God." It is for this reason that the Deistic Evolutionist believes that God chose to instantiate this particular essence from among an unlimited number of other possible essences: because it is the only one that corresponds to a finite representation of the Divine Psychospiritual Image.

Moreover, the Deistic Evolutionist believes that the Human Essence necessarily entails a certain constellation of essential properties, which define it and therefore make it what it is. Just as the creation of a triangle necessarily entails a geometrical shape with three sides, so too does the creation of a genuine human being necessarily entail the simultaneous instantiation of certain essential properties. These essential properties[17] presumably include free will, the capacity for rational thought, and the need for a self-guided developmental process, beginning at the simplest possible starting point and progressing in a stepwise fashion toward a relative state of full character growth. Going one step further, the Deistic Evolutionist also believes that virtually all of the structural details of our world can be derived in one way or another from the necessary properties that are entailed by the Human Essence.

In short, the Deistic Evolutionist believes that the notion of *de re* necessity—in which each possible object or essence necessarily requires a particular constellation of essential properties in order to obtain self-identity—is very real, and can be used to explain virtually all of the basic features of human existence, including the reality of universal and biological evolution.[18]

12.7   The Primacy of the Developmental Process in the Grand Universal Scheme

We went through the entire foregoing discussion to show two things: 1) the importance of the developmental process to the overall Human Definition, and 2) the importance of man to the cosmos itself. The first assertion above appears to be true enough, as it appears to be logically impossible for man to be human in the above-stated sense in the absence of this self-guided developmental process. The second assertion is open to doubt, however, especially to those who are unconvinced of the existence of God.

It is, however, possible to indirectly demonstrate the importance of man to the universe by showing two things: 1) that man is far and away the most complicated and advanced entity in the entire known universe, and 2) that the entire universe, to the farthest reaches of the most distant galaxy, has been "fine-tuned" in such a way as to make human life possible on this planet.[19] The first proposal, as we have seen, is already accomplished, insofar it is a widely-acknowledged fact that, apart from the creative power of the entire universe itself, human beings are, for better or for worse, the most complicated and advanced things that are currently known to exist.

Remarkably, an impressive amount of empirical data can be marshalled in support of the second proposal as well. Using the Anthropic Principle as a basic theoretical guide, a number of physicists and cosmologists have been able to show that life is only possible on this planet because of a striking number of cosmic "coincidences" involving the fundamental constants of nature, which have all mysteriously worked together against tremendous odds to make a universe fit for biological habitation. Because these fundamental constants pervade the entire physical realm, there is a very real sense in which the whole universe is centered around the stipulation that life should be able to exist. On this view, we are indeed the "center" of the universe after all.[20]

The reason I am going to such lengths to demonstrate the overall importance of man in the cosmos is that it may not be a mere coincidence that the very same developmental (i.e., evolutionary) process that is exhibited by the universe at large also may be one of the essential properties of its most complex inhabitant—man. Indeed, if man is so important that: 1) he occupies the privileged position of being the most advanced entity in the entire known universe, and 2) the entire physical universe is centered around his own existence and survival, then perhaps it is not too unreasonable to postulate an *extreme* level of cosmic importance for man. In this particular anthropocentric conceptualization, we can postulate that one of the most important ingredients in the Human Definition—namely, the developmental process itself—has been deliberately infused into the overall character of the universe from the very beginning, so as to make it a suitable home for developing human beings.

Such an explicitly anthropocentric position isn't as outrageous as it may initially seem. For as long as we assume that the developmental process itself is a necessary aspect of the Human Definition, and that humans, as alleged children of God, are among the most important entities in the entire universe (and are therefore worth creating in and of themselves), then in the interests of cosmic unity and environmental appropriateness, God may indeed have found it necessary to infuse the entire physical universe with the same developmental quality that appears to have been so essential to the Human Definition. The interwoven structure of the universe itself seems to corroborate this view of universal self-consistency, since many of the same basic evolutionary principles can be observed to exist at several different levels of physical reality.

However, there may be an even deeper function to this universal principle of self-consistency than mere aesthetics: human development as we now understand it appears to be impossible in a static, non-evolving world and universe. Indeed, if the goal of human life is for man to attain his own full development through his own free-willed behavior in the world, then it is reasonable to expect that God would have created a world that would have facilitated man's growth to maturity in as many different ways as possible.

Assuming this to be true, one of the most effective ways for God to have achieved this end would have been to immerse man in a world that shared his own basic "evolutionary" nature. For in this way, developing humans could seamlessly "fit into" their developing world, with the result that the various interaction dynamics that would constantly go on between them would end up facilitating human development in the end. On this view, had the world been created in a static, non-evolving fashion, developing humans would have been totally out of place.

One of the chief reasons why they would have been out of place in such a world is that there would have been no natural way for their developmental progress to be manipulated "from within," so to speak, so that it could be optimally facilitated without requiring constant input from God Himself. In a developing (i.e., evolving) world, on the other hand, many natural opportunities for facilitating human development would automatically present themselves. These growth-facilitating opportunities would largely operate via the process of *generalization*, in which man would unconsciously come to internalize a set of growth-facilitating principles that had been deliberately infused into the physical world for this explicit purpose.[21] By becoming intimately familiar with these principles on a deep unconscious level, he would then be more likely to behave in ways that are consistent with them. This in turn would help him to deal in an optimal manner with the many problems and pitfalls that are inevitably associated with the developmental process, so that his chances for achieving his developmental goal would be maximized in every possible way. *This alone provides sufficient reason for God to have infused the physical world with the same evolutionary processes of development that are a necessary part of the Human Definition.*

Now we are in a position to understand why God would have opted to create the universe "gradually" over billions of years instead of instantaneously, which He presumably *could* have done if the traditional doctrine of omnipotence[22] is adhered to: because for the sake of structural consistency and the overall facilitation of human development, He was compelled to implement the same evolutionary processes in the larger universe that are an essential part of the Human Definition.[23]

On this view, although God could conceivably have created the physical universe without a succession of evolutionary events, He could *not* have created man as we have defined him without an unfolding succession of developmental events, for, as we have seen, to do so would have constituted an intrinsic violation of the Human Definition. It is important to realize, however, that such a "limitation" of God's creative power does *not* limit His omnipotence, because the task being proposed is alleged to be a logical contradiction in terms. Since there is presumably no such thing as a "human being" in the absence of this type of self-driven developmental process (owing to the intrinsic demands of the Human Definition), it does *not* limit God's power to say that He cannot create a human being instantaneously. For as Aquinas has pointed out, logically impossible propositions cannot be said to limit God's power because they amount to ontological zeroes, and omnipotence minus zero still equals omnipotence. For some strange reason, though, we humans have the curious capacity to dream up logically impossible states of affairs, but such a capacity doesn't mean that these states of affairs could ever actually exist in reality. It also doesn't mean that we have succeeded in dreaming up a task that an omnipotent God could not perform, for as C.S. Lewis has assured us, "meaningless combinations of words do not suddenly acquire meaning simply because we prefix to them the two other words 'God can.' It remains true that all *things* are possible with God: the intrinsic impossibilities are not things but nonentities. It is no more possible for God than for the weakest of His creatures to carry out both of two mutually exclusive alternatives; not because His power meets an obstacle, but because nonsense remains nonsense, even when we talk it about God."[24]

12.8 The Developmental Parallelism Between Cosmic and Human Evolution

In summary, four critical points have been made concerning the nature of the evolutionary process:

1. When defined as an incremental process of gradual development, the process of evolution as a universal phenomenon is very real. The affirmation of this fundamental point puts us in agreement with the vast majority of scientific observations on this subject, as well as with the overall character of process thought.
2. The same type of evolutionary process also characterizes human psychospiritual development as well.
3. The reason why humans develop in an evolutionary manner is that man as he has been traditionally defined would cease to be human in its absence. (This of course is assuming the existence of an omnipotent God.)
4. God has therefore chosen to pattern the nature of the entire physical universe after this general evolutionary paradigm, for the sake of structural consistency and human growth facilitation, in order to make the world an appropriate home for human character development.

In order to further clarify these vital points, more needs to be said regarding the various similarities between human development and the process of cosmic evolution.

The first point of similarity is that the human developmental process is characterized by growth from the most fundamental starting point possible: the fertilized egg. Thereafter, growth only takes place in a gradual, self-driven fashion (at first biologically, then volitionally), in such a way that out of a plethora of conceptual and experiential possibilities, only those most fit to survive actually get incorporated into the individual's overall personality. Again, the purported reason for this self-motivated growth from humble beginnings is so that man can gain as much of his own knowledge and development—and therefore as much of his own identity—as he possibly can through his own hard effort, because this is by hypothesis the only way that a genuinely independent and self-possessed human identity can be formed.

A corollary to this basic developmental principle states that *God cannot do anything for man that man can do for himself.* This corollary follows from that part of the Human Definition that requires man to gain as much of his own development as he possibly can through his own free-willed behavior in the world. Since man *can* act to acquire his own knowledge and development throughout most of his life (because of the inherent capacity for self-directed growth that he has been given), he is subsequently obliged to do so in order to remain consistent with his own definition.

The physical component of the human developmental process supports us in this conclusion. As Stephen Jay Gould[25] has pointed out, when compared to other primates, humans are born essentially as "embryos." That is to say, they are born completely helpless and defenseless, whereas other primates are born in a far more advanced state of development.

The traditional neo-Darwinian explanation for this phenomenon is that due to their anomalously large brain size, humans *must* be born long before they "should" be, so they can fit through the human birth canal.[26] Thus, natural selection is said to have favored a relatively short gestation period for humans (short in comparison to man's own internal developmental rate, not in comparison to the gestation times of other primates, which are still shorter than man's), in spite of the fact that it makes it necessary for the human to be born in a completely helpless and defenseless state of being.

Although this may be true on a purely physical level, one wonders why larger pelvises in humans weren't *also* selected for, so that human infants could spend more time developing in the womb. This undoubtedly would have had tremendous survival value for the human race, since it would have enabled humans to be born in a much more advanced state of development. On the other hand, it could also be the case that human pelvises are about as large as they're intrinsically capable of getting; if so, then the survival of the human species would depend on infants getting born when they're still small enough to fit through the birth canal.

While it is possible that this physical explanation is all the reason there is for this curious phenomenon, other, more spiritual explanations also fit the facts. Adolf Portmann, a Swiss zoologist, believes that humans must leave the womb so early in order to fulfill mental requirements.[27] Since humans are learning creatures, Portmann argues that they must leave the confining and unchallenging womb in order to enter the fascinating and stimulating world of the extrauterine environment.[28]

Although Portmann seems to be on the right track, the Deistic Evolutionist would go one step further and argue that humans must be born as "embryos" because of the intrinsic demands of the Human Definition, which necessitate the self-development of the personality from the earliest possible starting point. Since it is possible for humans to be born at such a relatively early stage of development, and since the experience of being a post-natal infant seems to make a significant contribution to the individual's emerging personality structure,[29] the Human Definition would seem to require an "early" birth in humans, since one of its implicit demands is that incipient human beings begin their post-uterine development from the earliest possible starting point. On this view, the size of the infant's brain relative to the size of the birth canal is only of secondary importance, since God could presumably have made the female pelvis larger from the very beginning if He really wanted to.

Primates, on the other hand, have no need for these early post-natal experiences, because they are not destined to individuate nearly as extensively as human beings. Therefore, they have no need to be born at such an early stage of development, especially given the fact that it would constitute a major survival liability for them. As a consequence, they are born in a much more advanced state of development than humans are, with the result that they are much more capable of surviving in the wild.

Another interesting facet of human development that is supportive of the Deistic Evolutionist's basic case concerns the unusually long time it takes for humans to grow up. As W.M. Krogman has pointed out, "Man has absolutely the most protracted period of infancy, childhood and juvenility of all forms of life, i.e., he is a neotenous or long-growing animal. Nearly thirty percent of his entire life-span is devoted to growing."[30]

Gould believes that the adaptive significance of this phenomenon can be found in the unique capacity of the human brain to learn by experience:

> To enhance our learning, we have lengthened our childhood by delaying sexual maturation with its adolescent yearning for independence. Our children are tied for longer periods to their parents, thus increasing their own time of learning, and strengthening family ties as well.[31]

The Deistic Evolutionist would again go one step further and say that it isn't just human learning that is enhanced by such a protracted childhood; it is the development of the human psychospiritual identity *itself* that is optimally enhanced. For insofar as our identity is comprised of all the free-willed learning experiences we undergo in our lives, it follows that the *more* developmental territory we experience, the richer and deeper our identities will become as a consequence. On this view, the human developmental process is as protracted as it is because of the intrinsic demands of the Human Definition.

It is thus the process of self-attained development from the smallest possible beginnings that seems to be the overall paradigm upon which the Human Definition is necessarily based. Interestingly enough, the universe itself also seems to be based on this very same paradigm, insofar as it too began from the smallest possible starting point (an infinitely dense "singularity"), only to subsequently "grow" through successive evolutionary stages to the present state of universal complexity.[32]

The details of this cosmic process of self-organization are nothing short of remarkable. Cosmologists tell us that the entire universe suddenly exploded into being approximately 15 billion years ago, in an unprecedented cataclysm of heat and light called the "Big Bang." In the massive state of cosmic expansion that followed, subatomic particles gradually came to be formed entirely through natural processes. Some time thereafter, these particles spontaneously began to organize themselves into increasingly complex aggregations of matter, again due entirely to natural forces such as gravitation and electromagnetism. Stars eventually resulted from some of these aggregations, the larger varieties of which came to manufacture heavy elements like carbon deep in their interiors. These heavy elements, which are essential for life, were then spewed into space several billion years later in huge supernova explosions. This initiated the final stage of the life-making process, which saw these freed up particles spontaneously organizing themselves into solar systems, planets, and eventually, people.

Throughout this entire cosmic drama, we find the same two principles at work that also characterize the human developmental process: 1) the most fundamental starting point possible, and 2) an incremental, self-guided process of growth that takes place entirely in accordance with the law of cause-and-effect. The chief difference between these two developmental systems is that the process of human growth is driven primarily by the conscious and unconscious strivings of the inner self, whereas subatomic particles simply behave in a manner that is consistent with their own inner nature.[33] In both cases, the emphasis is on self-actualization, or the full realization of each system's inner potential for growth. Moreover, because both processes are self-driven, both are able to retain a critical sense of freedom and independence for themselves.

It is thus the phenomenon of self-directed growth from humble beginnings that functions as the common denominator that links both man and the universe together in a basic evolutionary partnership. From these humble beginnings, both have followed a gradual, self-driven evolutionary process, and both have "snowballed" their way into producing truly impressive levels of order and complexity.

The phenomenon of biological evolution also seems to have followed this same basic principle of self-development from the smallest possible beginnings. Life apparently began in the primordial seas nearly four billion years ago as a single cell, and it has grown enormously in both complexity and diversity since then, through a continual struggle against the "pruning" effects of natural selection.

12.9 Discussion

It is nothing short of remarkable to realize that the same basic evolutionary processes can be found in such widely varying areas of the cosmos as biological evolution, human psychospiritual development, and the ongoing expansion of the universe itself. It is a large thought indeed to realize that the Big Bang[34] singularity, the first primordial cell, and the human fertilized egg, are all different representations of the same basic developmental process, yet the parallels are unmistakable.

Professor Holmes Rolston of Colorado State University has noticed this fundamental similarity between biological evolution and the process of human psychospiritual development:

> The notion of a Newtonian Architect who from the outside designs his machines, borrowed from Paley for his Watchmaker God, has to be replaced (at least in biology, if not in physics) by a continuous creation, a developmental struggle in self-education, where the creatures through "experience" become increasingly "expert" at life. This increased autonomy, though it might first be thought uncaring, is not wholly unlike that self-finding that parents allow their children. It is a richer organic model of creation just because it is not architectural-mechanical. It accounts for the "hit and miss" aspects of evolution. Like a psychotherapist, God sets the context for self-actualizing. God allows persons to be imperfect in their struggle for fuller lives . . . *and there seems to be a biological analogue of this.* It is part of, not a flaw in, the creative process (emphasis mine).[35]

The Deistic Evolutionist builds on Rolston's observations in two fundamental ways, by asserting that: 1) man cannot be fully human in the absence of a self-driven developmental process, and 2) for the sake of structural consistency and the overall appropriateness of man's developmental environment, God has deliberately designed the entire universe to grow in accordance with this same basic developmental paradigm.

An additional comment needs to be made here on the self-driven nature of the evolutionary process. As we have seen, the developmental unfolding that has given rise to everything in our universe is characterized by an incremental process of growth that naturally builds on everything that has come before. This is important because it ensures two things: 1) that each intervening step in the overall developmental distance will be covered, and 2) that each developmental stage that is acquired will take place entirely under the organism's own direction and self-driven capacity. As we have seen, these characteristics are important for the human developmental process precisely because they ensure that each aspect of the personality—and therefore the entire personality itself—will be self-acquired in an entirely autonomous fashion (apart, of course, from the original capacity of the self to grow and develop, which clearly could not have been self-acquired), and this, in turn, ensures that man will eventually be able to attain a genuinely independent and self-possessed identity for himself.

Now, if we attempt to extrapolate out to the universe itself this principle of self-attained growth through all relevant stages of development, we find that the universe too must grow through all the relevant stages of its own development (cosmic egg, Big Bang, galaxy formation, supernova explosions, etc.) before humanity can evolve. On a biological level, this principle translates into the need for all the relevant evolutionary stages between the first proto-cell and the first humans to have been traversed as well. Significantly, this appears to have been precisely what happened.

Indeed, this basic similarity between biological evolution and the human developmental process goes deeper still. As we have seen, it is necessarily the case that man must gain his own knowledge and development for himself if he is to remain consistent with the Human Definition. While he may have been given the initial *capacity* to program himself from the very beginning, it is important to understand that this capacity is only fulfilled when man actually interacts with his environment on a daily basis.

Interestingly enough, recent findings indicate that the biosphere itself may have evolved through a similar process of cellular self-programming.[36] As we have seen, the genome of each species seems to be equipped with the capacity to program itself in response to external input from the environment. This of course is directly analogous to man's capacity to program his own mind with the knowledge he acquires from his own day-to-day interaction with the world.

A final point of similarity between biological evolution and the process of human development concerns the notion of contingency. Non-theistic evolutionists commonly point out that the historical course of evolution appears to have been utterly contingent, insofar as the details of our past history could conceivably have been otherwise. On this view, if evolution were to happen again, not only would other types of creatures probably evolve, there is no guarantee that humans would even appear at all. This profound degree of contingency is taken to be strong evidence *against* the existence of an Intelligent Designer, since it is assumed that such a Being would have been much more deterministic in His chosen method of creation.

There are two ways to deal with this potentially serious criticism. First of all, it is far from obvious that any *absolute* form of contingency has ever actually existed in the material realm. Although limited forms of contingency do seem to appear throughout the evolutionary record, these only occur within an overall backdrop that itself does *not* appear to be contingent. That is to say, neither the entire ecological order, nor the evolutionary rise of species, appear to have been a fluke occurrence of nature. Rather, both seem to exhibit some form of overall direction, in which contingent forces can and do act in limited ways to help produce the final product.[37]

Thus, while the biosphere may have evolved in response to forces that *appear* to have been absolutely contingent, the possibility remains that they were either *relatively* contingent (occurring within the overall backdrop of some degree of determinism), or not contingent at all. On these two latter views, the appearance of absolute contingency would simply reflect our own inability to precisely determine the subtle causative forces that have been employed by the natural realm.

However, to the extent that the forces of evolution have in fact possessed some degree of contingency, it is always possible that that this would have been the Deity's preferred method of creation. This hypothesis is supported by the observation that the human developmental process displays a similar form of contingency to that which is seen in evolution. One way to explain this type of similarity, as we have seen, is in terms of a deliberate patterning of the physical world after the necessary nature of the human developmental process. The alternative explanation, however (and one that is much more appealing to the non-theistic evolutionist), is that human development is contingent simply because the evolutionary process that gave rise to it is also contingent.

There is little doubt that much of human development is contingent in nature. Humans clearly mold their personalities in response to decisions they choose to make in their daily lives. From this observation it follows that, to the extent that these decisions are themselves contingent (i.e., could have been otherwise), the human developmental process *itself* must be contingent as well, insofar as the final product that obtains (a concrete, self-made personality) could conceivably have been otherwise. The point is simply that if the Divine Intention was to pattern the evolutionary process after the various dynamics of human character development, then we would expect evolution itself to have also displayed a similar type of contingency in its own formation.

A further role for contingency in the evolutionary process centers on the conditions necessary to facilitate human freedom. As many authors have noted through the years, it is difficult to see how freedom could possibly exist in a strictly deterministic universe. French philosopher Henri Bergson shared this basic sentiment, and even thought that this fundamental incompatibility between freedom and determinism should be extended to the progressive nature of the universe as a whole. For Bergson, an inevitably progressive universe was itself deterministic, so some form of genuine contingency was needed in order to make room for human freedom and creativity. Bergson found the contingency he was looking for in Charles Darwin's opportunistic view of the evolutionary process.

Many other thinkers, including John Dewey, Charles Peirce, and William James, also saw the chief value of Darwinism in terms of its destruction of determinism. They saw evolution as "the growth of 'cosmic reasonableness,' through which a rational order emerged from a primitive, unpersonalized chaos. Here the idea of progress was reintroduced, but in a subtler form that did not impose a preordained structure on the final goal. Progress is possible, but it need not proceed inevitably in a single direction, because life has the freedom to create its own future."[38]

We see, then, that an omnipotent Creator did indeed have sufficient reason for designing contingency into the evolutionary process, because some form of contingency appears to be a necessary prerequisite for the existence of human freedom. This is a momentous realization indeed, because it means that the apparent contingency of evolution can no longer be counted as *ipso facto* evidence against the existence of an Intelligent Designer.

12.10 Human Rationality and Natural Selection

The intrinsic nature of human rationality also bears a striking resemblance to one of the most prominent aspects of the evolutionary process: natural selection. As Rolston has pointed out, human rationality has a kind of "groping" quality to it.[39] In the struggle to attain a rational view of the world, humans spontaneously produce a wide range of possible thoughts, only a few of which are selected by the rational center of the mind for permanent inclusion into the individual's overall world view. Thus, the very basis of human rationality seems to depend on a significant overproduction of possible thoughts, so that the best can be chosen to remain.

Each individual life also tends to "grope" towards an ultimate (self-determined) destiny as well. A multitude of existential possibilities present themselves to us on a daily basis, yet it is our own free choices that select which possibilities will ultimately be realized.

Interestingly enough, the evolution of the biosphere also seems to have had a similar groping quality to it. Although the overall scope of the evolutionary process has been towards progressively greater levels of complexity, a great deal of groping has also taken place in the gradual ascent of life up the phylogenetic ladder; dozens of unsuccessful plant and animal varieties have apparently been produced for every successful one that has been able to escape nature's selective hand.

At first this process of groping would seem to be inconsistent with the existence of a Perfect Designer, for one would superficially think that He wouldn't have had to try so many times to get things right with His creatures, especially when the creatures themselves seem to have experienced so much pain and suffering throughout the evolutionary process. But what if the ultimate criterion for determining the "rightness" of the creation isn't the successful production of different biological forms *per se*, but rather the capacity of the various species to grope towards progressively higher levels of being? This is an altogether different type of question that changes the entire focus of the problem concerning God and evolution, but it is nevertheless precisely what we would expect if: a) groping is an intrinsic property of the Human Definition, and b) God has deliberately chosen to pattern the entire physical world after the necessary nature of human development.

On this view, nature gropes because man gropes. While man has the inner *capacity* for rationality, he is evidently unable to actualize it until he first emits a wide range of possible thoughts, only a few of which will later be chosen for inclusion into his growing base of rationality. Man also possesses the capacity for attaining certain goals in his life, but he must first be exposed to a wide range of existential possibilities before he can actualize any one of them. In the same way, nature also clearly has the capacity for "upward" evolution, in the sense that it is capable of producing a wide range of possible forms for natural selection to act upon. But before it can actualize this potentiality, it must first produce all or nearly all of these possible forms and then allow the selective power of the local environment to choose the most appropriate ones for continued survival.[40]

Given these intriguing possibilities, the question we must now ask ourselves is this: if humans must continually grope towards their own full development in order to obtain a fully individuated and self-possessed character structure, might it not also be possible that nature is doing the same thing for the same reason? That is to say, might not the physical universe itself also be struggling to attain *its own* self-possessed identity during the process of cosmic evolution?

12.11 Extinction and Human Development

The history of life on earth has been fraught with five major extinctions on the way to *Homo sapiens*. Although each of these great dyings have led to a temporary setback in the gradual ascent of life up the phylogenetic scale, each setback has been duly followed by substantial increases in complexity. The general pattern in the evolutionary process, then, has been several steps forward, a step or two backward, followed by several steps forward again, and so on.

This jagged ascent upward is curiously analogous to the well-known process of human psychospiritual development. People also gradually grow more mature through a painstaking process of repeated fits and starts, in which a number of severe setbacks are experienced on the way to eventual psychospiritual maturity. This remarkable degree of similarity in the respective trajectories of evolution and human development provides further evidence that the process of evolution may have been directly patterned after the human growth paradigm.

While we're on the subject of extinction, it might be useful to address a major problem that some thinkers have had with the idea of providential evolution. It is widely believed that several historical extinctions were actually caused by random astronomical phenomena, such as comets impacting on the earth, which would have presumably had no direct causal connection with the evolutionary trajectory of life on earth. Indeed, without at least one of these great dyings (the one that doomed the dinosaurs), humans arguably would have never evolved. This apparent contingency has led many to believe that there is probably no such thing as providential evolution, since the cosmic and terrestrial events that have led to human beings seem to have been mediated by chance alone. Such a strong degree of cosmic contingency is deemed to be inconsistent with the workings of an Intelligent Designer.

The trouble with this short-sighted view is that it fails to consider the wider web of causation that seems to be operative throughout the universe. As David Bohm and others have pointed out, the entire universe seems to be connected through some sort of larger implicate order, through which causally disconnected phenomena can nevertheless work together towards the realization of certain constructive ends. Indeed, we already know that, despite overwhelming odds to the contrary, the universe itself has evolved in such a way as to make life possible. This cosmic "fine-tuning" is all the more remarkable because it has involved a large number of apparent coincidences in distant branches of physics, which themselves appear to be unrelated in the absence of a larger coordinating force.

Now, if the universe as a whole could have accomplished such a tremendous feat from the Big Bang onward, why couldn't it have also arranged for a few strategic comets to hit the earth at the proper time, so as to facilitate the eventual evolution of human beings? Or, as Thomas Burnet would have argued, why couldn't God have originally set the universe in motion in such as way as to cause these well-timed celestial impacts several billion years later?

Best of all, this deistic explanation doesn't bring us back to the much maligned God-of-the-gaps, because it doesn't try to place God in a causative role within the universe *in place of* natural processes. To the contrary, it merely asserts that God is the One who orchestrated these natural processes in the first place, and this sort of indirect explanation is entirely consistent with the naturalistic findings of modern science.

12.12 The Importance of Man's Environmental Mileu

Getting back to the nature of human development, it would be a mistake to disregard the vast importance of man's environmental mileu in determining his routine thoughts and behaviors. As B.F. Skinner[41] and other behavioral psychologists have repeatedly shown, the specific features of any given environmental mileu make a tremendous difference in how organisms behave within it, and this is true whether the organism in question is a guinea pig or a human being. While humans may possess a greater degree of freedom and self-determination than guinea pigs, their specific behaviors are nevertheless greatly influenced by the way in which their environment is set up. Free acts, after all, can only take place within a concrete environment. And since it is the specific nature of any given environment that determines the types of free behaviors that can take place within it, it follows that the free acts of humans can be greatly influenced by the way in which their overall environment is constructed.

As Skinner has repeatedly demonstrated in the laboratory, behavioral environments can be designed in such a way as to make almost any conceivable type of behavior more likely to occur. Although Skinner performed the majority of his experiments with rats, we have good reason to believe that the same basic behavioral principles can also be applied to human beings as well. Assuming this to be the case, it makes sense to suppose that God would have wanted to design man's earthly mileu in such a way as to make certain growth-facilitating decisions and behaviors more likely. He would have wanted to do so because of the tremendous potential for anarchy that is inherent in *any* self-conscious being that is only partially developed. Partially developed beings *need* to be guided in the proper direction, because their intrinsic naïvité and irresponsibility make it exceedingly unlikely that they would ever be able to grow in the proper direction without external assistance.

This Divine manipulation of the environment becomes all the more understandable when we consider the types of limitations that God freely chose to place on Himself when He originally elected to instantiate the Human Essence. Since the property of free will intrinsically prevents God from coercing an individual to perform any given behavior, the only remaining way for God to channel free-willed humans in the proper direction is through the indirect behavioral method of strategic environmental manipulation.

This gives God the ability to make certain growth-facilitating human behaviors more likely without any violation of their essential freedom.

Humans need to be familiar with two things in order to be able to grow properly: 1) the nature of their own inner reality, and 2) the nature of those behaviors that will help them facilitate their own development. However, due to their profound naïveté and lack of self-awareness (which are the inevitable consequence of their partial character development), humans are typically ignorant of these two very relevant factors. It follows, then, that the best way to facilitate human development is for these growth-facilitating factors to somehow be *infused* into the physical environment, so that humans can be conditioned into becoming intimately familiar with them, thereby increasing the likelihood that they will behave in a growth-facilitating fashion.

The Deistic Evolutionist believes that God achieved this effect by patterning the structure of the physical world after the fundamental features of the human psychospiritual world. For in so doing, God was able to indirectly condition a certain amount of growth-facilitating knowledge into man without any subsequent violation of man's free will. The advantage of this symbolic arrangement, as we have seen, is that it provides humans with an important physical referent for dealing with those intangible aspects of the developmental process that would otherwise remain unknown.

12.13   A Universe of Unbroken Wholeness

We will now further examine the Deistic Evolutionist's assertion that, for the sake of self-consistency and human growth facilitation, God has deliberately chosen to pattern the structure of the physical universe after the necessary nature of human development. The Deistic Evolutionist believes that it was necessary for the physical universe to be patterned after the human character structure, and not the other way around, because he is convinced that the underlying definition of man is *not* free to vary, whereas he believes that the overall character of the physical universe *is* much more flexible, especially in the hands of an omnipotent God who creates *ex nihilo*. For the Deistic Evolutionist, then, man must necessarily represent the starting point for any cosmic building program, because his intrinsic definition purportedly could not have been otherwise (though his actual instantiation in reality *could* obviously have been otherwise).

If we assume this to be the case, it follows that everything revolved around God's decision to instantiate the Human Essence in reality. For once this decision was made, the character of the rest of the universe had to be extrapolated out from the necessary properties and requirements of the Human Definition. Although it is conceivable that God could have designed the universe in a completely different manner, wholly unrelated to the intrinsic demands of the Human Definition, this would have had two very undesirable effects: 1) it would have made the universe a discontinuous, non-unified place, and 2) it would have created an inappropriate developmental environment for human beings. Since both of these consequences would have been inconsistent with God's developmental plan for mankind, He instead chose to create a universe of unbroken wholeness, centered around the intrinsic requirements of the Human Definition.

The chief advantage of a unified creation, as we have seen, is that it has the capacity of facilitating man's growth to maturity in a number of important ways. Such a capacity follows from the fact that a physical world patterned after the human character structure offers an "inside route," as it were, to the influencing of man's overall developmental progress. In a unified creation, man's physical world can deliberately be manipulated to make certain behavioral skills more likely to develop. Then, through the process of generalization, these skills can unconsciously be generalized over to the psycho-spiritual realm, where they can subsequently act to facilitate human development in a variety of different ways.

Interestingly enough, modern physics has largely verified the existence of a unified, holistic universe. Both Einstein's theory of relativity and modern quantum mechanics lend support to this notion of an unbroken wholeness in nature (although they do so in different ways). Physicist David Bohm has taken this idea one step further by proposing an underlying *implicate order* to the universe, in which the entire cosmos—including human consciousness—is actively enfolded in each of its constituent parts.[42] To the extent that Bohm's vision is true, it means that we are truly one with the universe after all, and that everything in existence is working together for a common goal, which for the Deistic Evolutionist is nothing less than the full development and eventual deification of man.[43]

12.14   The Biblical View

The Deistic Evolutionist's belief in a fundamental patterning of the physical world after the human psychospiritual world is not new. It was proposed nearly 2000 years ago by no less an authority than St. Paul himself:

> For the creation was subjected to futility, not of its own will, but because of Him who subjected it, in hope that the creation itself also will be set free from its slavery to corruption into the freedom of the glory of the children of God. For we know that the whole creation groans and suffers the pains of childbirth together until now. And not only this, but also we ourselves, having the first fruits of the Spirit, even we ourselves groan within ourselves, waiting eagerly for our adoption as sons, the redemption of our body (Rom. 8:19–23, NAS).

In the above passage, St. Paul is asserting the unfinished nature of the entire cosmos. This is why he says that it has been laboring with "birth pangs" until the present time: because it is still in the process of getting "born." More importantly, he indicates that the reason why the universe was originally subjected to this "futility" of partial assembly has to do with the "revealing" (i.e., the development) of the "sons of God," who are none other than earthbound human beings.

In other words, St. Paul is telling us that the creation was deliberately subjected to the "futility" of being corruptible (less than perfectly developed), not for its own sake, but for the sake of the facilitation of human development. This statement directly implies that the physical world has been deliberately patterned after the necessary nature of the human developmental process, so that it can facilitate human growth in every possible way.

Once humans attain to the glory of being children of God (i.e., once they become "liberated" into their own full character development), we are told that the creation itself will also be set free from its "slavery to corruption," since it will then have already served its purpose in facilitating the overall developmental process. This is why we are told that the creation "groans" and "suffers the pains of childbirth" until now: because we humans are the ones who are gradually getting formed as future "children of God." We groan and suffer because the process of character development is intrinsically painful. Likewise, the entire creation also "groans" as well, because it too must suffer the bondage of being less than fully developed, since its underlying structure has presumably been designed to parallel the presently incomplete nature of the human character structure.

The purpose of all this cosmic striving, of course, is the eventual revealing of the fully-assembled "sons of God," which will presumably take place when our inner process of character development is more or less completed. At this point, we will finally be considered "worthy" enough, by virtue of our own completed development, to be "adopted" into God's own Spiritual Family. St. Paul himself would have thus agreed with the Deistic Evolutionist's assertion that the entire physical universe has been patterned after the necessary nature of the human developmental process.[44]

Another important Biblical figure who would have also agreed with this limited anthropocentric perspective is Jesus Christ. Jesus also believed that the physical world had been deliberately contrived by God in such a way as to facilitate human development. Indeed, His famous New Testament parables *assume* a direct functional relationship between the workings of the physical world, on the one hand, and the essential features of the human developmental process, on the other. This analogical relationship, of course, would have only been valid in a physical world whose underlying structure had been directly patterned after the most fundamental aspects of human development.

Notes

1. I understand the traditional doctrine of Divine omnipotence to mean that God originally created the universe *ex nihilo* (out of nothing), and that He is by definition capable of performing any act that is not logically impossible.
2. See Brian Swimme's article "The Cosmic Creation Story," David Ray Griffin, ed., *The Reenchantment of Science*, (Albany: SUNY Press, 1988), pp. 47–56.
3. Holmes Rolston, *Science and Religion* (Philadelphia: Temple University Press, 1987), p. 60.
4. I understand logical impossibility in this sense to refer to the intrinsic impossibility of a given object or definition to remain identical with itself once one or more of its essential properties have been removed.
5. It is only the human personality, and not the human body, which I am arguing could not have been formed instantaneously by supernatural Fiat. By hypothesis, then, if human beings (in this psychospiritual sense) weren't to be included in the creation, the world and the entire animal kingdom could have conceivably been formed instantaneously by miraculous Fiat. As we are about to see, though, the inclusion of humanity into the Divine Creative Scheme seems to have changed everything, in the sense that the logically necessitated developmental process for man simultaneously may have put a strong limitation on the way the rest of the world and universe could have subsequently been created.
6. I use the term "potential" here to denote the idea that, while humans may possess free will in an ideal sense, their freedom is greatly limited in the real world by all sorts of internal and external limitations.
7. It is possible to argue that a being could in fact be human and still lack some of these so-called essential properties, such as self-consciousness or the capacity for rational thought. A good example of this would be a person in a coma. It is important to understand, though, that it isn't the mere possession of these properties in the exclusively here-and-now that qualifies a being as human; it is, rather, the *potential* for these properties in a relatively normal state of affairs that makes this essential qualification. Thus, a person who isn't in a coma *would* ordinarily possess these properties, and so *would* in fact qualify as being human, even while unconscious in a coma. A cow, on the other hand, could never satisfy these essential criteria for humanhood under any possible set of circumstances, so it could never be considered as human.
8. While it may be true that our knowledge isn't *totally* responsible for determining our affections and motivations, it nevertheless influences them to such a profound extent that we would still be transformed into robots if we were given external knowledge by God.
9. I am assuming that this preprogrammed database contains within it the sufficient conditions for determining how the entity will behave in a variety of situations.
10. In saying that we are all striving towards the goal of full character development, I don't mean to imply that there is a final *static* state that we are all aiming for. To the contrary, it would seem as though there is no true end to the human developmental process at all, either in this world or in any other. Nevertheless, there would still seem to be a state of *relative* character completion for the personality, in which it will have attained enough knowledge and development to enable it to avoid producing any more moral evil with its behavior.
11. Actually, we cannot use the term "moral" to describe the behavior of a being that is programmed to produce only good. Morality presupposes the existence of a real *choice* between good and bad, as Ninian Smart has deftly pointed out in "Omnipotence, Evil, and Supermen" *Philosophy*, Vol. XXXVI, No. 137 (1961).

12. Of course, this isn't to say that some things can't belong to us instantly with little or no effort of our own being expended to obtain them. Even so, we still don't feel like we own these items to the same extent that we do those things we work hard for. The very process of struggling to obtain something seems to create a "bond of ownership" that deeply connects us to the item in question.

13. Implicit in this conceptualization is the assumption that the initial structure of the human personality has been deliberately reduced to the minimum possible state of development that would still qualify as "human." Again, this temporary privation of the infantile self's fundamental structure appears to be simultaneous with its almost complete lack of knowledge and experience, because it is only in this parallel state of developmental privation that the self-driven process of knowledge acquisition can be used to "pull" the psychospiritual self's inner state of assembly towards increasingly greater levels of maturity.

14. The only aspect of the human developmental process that is not self-directed is the inner *capacity* for growth, which clearly must be supplied by God from without.

15. Just as God's intrinsic quality of Self-Existence obviates any need to find a creative cause to His Own Being, so His intrinsic quality of Self-Possession obviates any need for Him to have worked to attain it.

16. The use of the word "price" in this context brings to mind the Biblical assertion that we are "bought for a price" (Col. 3:4). In this passage St. Paul seems to be referring to a similar type of metaphysical necessity to the one we have been describing; one that is associated with the loftiness of our eventual destiny as fully developed "children of God."

17. While the actual identity of these essential human properties is subject to debate, there is little question that the larger Human Essence itself is in fact comprised of a certain defining set of essential properties. We should never make the mistake of rejecting this essentialist view of human nature outright, just because we cannot identify humanity's essential properties with certainty.

18. *De re* necessity is to be distinguished from *de dicto* necessity, which is the necessity associated with propositions. Thus, the *de dicto* mode of necessity refers to what we say about the real world, while the *de re* mode refers to the intrinsic necessities that surround the things themselves. For a thorough description of these two modes of necessity, please refer to Alvin Plantinga's classic work *The Nature of Necessity* (Oxford: Oxford University Press, 1974).

19. Saying that the entire universe has been fine-tuned in such a way as to make human life possible does not preclude the existence of other life forms in the cosmos. The same "tweaking" of initial conditions that has made earthly life possible could very well have made other forms of life elsewhere in the cosmos possible as well.

20. M.A. Corey, *God and the New Cosmology*, pp. 230–231.

21. I am not referring here to the knowledge of specific scientific facts about the developmental process *per se*, since they would largely have been inaccessable to the majority of pre-scientific humans down through history. I am simply referring to a general process of unconscious conditioning, which would be mediated through the specific features of the world-based developmental process, and which as a consequence would instill in people a broad unconscious awareness of the relevant developmental principles.

22. Process thinkers, such as David Ray Griffin and John Cobb, would reject this notion of omnipotence, as they would assert that God could not have created the world instantaneously, even if He wanted to, because of the metaphysical

limitations that are alleged to be an inherent part of universal reality. The Deistic Evolutionist, on the other hand, believes that while God *could* have conceivably created the world instantaneously, had He had sufficient reason to do so, He simply chose not to, in order to remain consistent with the developmental requirements of the Human Definition. Deistic Evolution thus differs from process thought in that the former places the metaphysical limitations that affect God on the logical necessities that surround human character formation, whereas the latter places these metaphysical limitations on the inherent nature of the "finite actualities" themselves.

23. Paradoxically, a 15 billion year creation takes about as long in God's own frame of reference as an "instantaneous" creation does, since He is presumably beyond the ordinary confines of time altogether. The primary issue here, though, is the utilization of a vast succession of evolutionary events in the creation, and not the Divine perception of a certain amount of "time" *per se.*

24. C.S. Lewis, *The Problem of Pain* (New York: Macmillan Publishing Company, 1962), p. 28.

25. Stephen Jay Gould, *Ever Since Darwin*, pp. 70–75.

26. Given the fact that the human brain is only 23% of its final size at birth, compared to 40.5% for the chimpanzee and 65% for the rhesus monkey, it is hard to see how brain size alone could be the primary factor in determining how long human fetuses spend in the womb.

27. Adolf Portmann, "Die Ontogenese des Menschen als Problem der Evolutionsforschung." *Verhandlungen der Schweizerischen Naturforschenden Gesellschaft* (1945), pp. 44–53.

28. Ibid.

29. Modern depth psychology also believes in the importance of infantile experiences in determining the later course of psychological development. (See Arthur Janov's *The Primal Scream*, (New York: G.P. Putnam's Sons, 1970).

30. Taken from Gould's *Ever Since Darwin*, p. 68.

31. Gould, *Ever Since Darwin*, p. 68.

32. Although most physicists still continue to posit the existence of a Big Bang singularity, Stephen Hawking has recently suggested that due to quantum gravitational effects, a singularity may not have been necessary after all. For our purposes, though, the findings of modern cosmology continue to show that the universe began from the smallest possible starting point.

33. In process thought, even the subatomic particles themselves are able to perceive or "prehend" the environment. Significantly, this capacity for prehension is thought to differ only in degree from human consciousness, not in kind.

34. Even if there was no Big Bang singularity at the beginning of the Hubble expansion, there nevertheless had to have been some sort of "primordial egg" which the universe began expanding from. It is this cosmic egg that the Deistic Evolutionist is primarily interested in here.

35. Holmes Rolston III, *Science and Religion* (Philadelphia: Temple University Press, 1987), p. 131.

36. G.Z. Opadia-Kadima "How the Slot Machine Led Biologists Astray," *Journal of Theoretical Biology* (1987), *124*, 127–135.

37. If the natural order has been precisely determined to produce free (i.e., contingent) acts, it is difficult to say whether or not these acts are truly contingent. On the one hand, one would think that since they are part of a larger predetermined system, they cannot be absolutely contingent. On the other hand, *any* type of free act would seem to require some form of concrete base from which

to proceed. On this view, absolutely contingent acts are intrinsically impossible, because some type of foundation for action needs to be predetermined. It would seem, then, that the only forms of contingency that can occur in our universe are relative forms, which occur within an overall backdrop of a natural realm that has been predetermined to produce free acts. This is the view held by the Deistic Evolutionist.

38. Peter J. Bowler, *Evolution: The History of an Idea*, p. 241.
39. Rolston, *Science and Religion*, pp. 128–129.
40. Genetic change thus doesn't have to be entirely preplanned (strongly orthogenetic) *or* completely directionless (not tending to benefit the creature in any way). Rather, *both* features can simultaneously exist in the phenotypic expression of the genome. There can thus be a kind of diffuse directionality to the evolutionary process, but only at the expense of the production of a wide range of possible characteristics.
41. B.F. Skinner, *Beyond Freedom and Dignity* (New York: Knopf, 1971).
42. David Bohm, *Wholeness and the Implicate Order* (London: Routledge & Kegan Paul, 1980).
43. The Eastern Orthodox Church shares this basic view of man's overall importance in the grand universal scheme.
44. The reason for this conclusion, once again, isn't far to seek: the only appropriate place where evolving, partially-developed human beings can be "at home" is in an equally evolving, partially-developed cosmos.

CHAPTER 13

The Legitimacy of Moderate Anthropocentrism

What is Man, that Thou art mindful of him?

PSALM 8:4

The credo of the Deistic Evolutionist is based on a limited (i.e., moderate) anthropocentric view of cosmic reality. On this view, humans are *one* source of importance in the universe, though not necessarily the *only* source of importance. The stronger anthropocentric view, in contrast, claims that humans are the *only* source of importance in the universe. This latter position is rejected by the Deistic Evolutionist out of hand because of its unreasonable, counterintuitive nature.

Although moderate anthropocentrism is a good deal less offensive to the modern mind than its stronger counterpart, it is still viewed with suspicion by many modern thinkers. Yet, as astrophysicist Brandon Carter has pointed out, just because we aren't special in *every* way doesn't necessarily mean that we aren't special in *any* way.[1] Indeed, it is *necessarily* the case that our location in the universe be privileged to the extent of being compatible with our own existence as observers.[2] This doctrine is known as the Anthropic[3] Principle, and it is revolutionary because it seeks to re-establish the importance of humanity in the overall cosmic scheme.

As Barrow and Tipler[4] have shown, the unique type of postdictive reasoning employed by the Anthropic Principle has led to one inescapable fact: against all the odds, the entire universe has mysteriously assumed just the right underlying configuration to enable life to evolve on this planet. This biocentric quality extends down to the smallest subatomic particles, and dates all the way back to the Big Bang itself, because the fundamental constants of nature have apparently occupied their present life-facilitating values from the very beginning, some 15 billion years ago. (This is an astonishing realization in and of itself, because it means that nature's constants have not gone through a trial-and-error process of natural selection[5] since the Big Bang. Rather, they have occupied their present life-supporting values from the very beginning, and this constitutes perhaps the most compelling evidence of all for Intelligent Design.)

What this means, of course, is that the *entire* universe, and not just our small localized region, is permeated with the *same* biocentric qualities that have enabled life to evolve on this planet. It follows from this observation that, at least in terms of the constants themselves, we and all the other forms of life on this planet are *in point of fact* the structural "center" of the universe, insofar as the entire universe possesses the same underlying structural values that have enabled life to evolve on this planet (and perhaps elsewhere). A strong interpretation of this phenomenon claims that these values have actually been *determined* by the stipulation that some form of life should be able to exist in the universe.[6]

At least on an underlying structural level, then, we are perfectly justified in proclaiming the phenomenon of life to be the foundational "center" of the universe.[7] After all, if life is so important to the universe that the physical requirements for its existence have somehow influenced both: a) the initial conditions displayed by the Big Bang, and b) the specific values of the fundamental constants themselves, then these earth-based life forms (of which we are presumably chief) must be important indeed in the overall scheme of things; perhaps not *all* important, but important just the same.

The Anthropic Principle in its various manifestations, then, is basically an attempt by some members of the scientific community to account for the fact that many different aspects of the physical universe, down to the actual values of the physical constants themselves, seem to have been deliberately predesigned for supporting biological (and especially human) life. As a consequence, instead of the universe being indifferent to the needs of humankind (and to all the other forms of earthly life), as we have repeatedly been told in the past, we are now learning that the universe has actually *catered* to the specific physiological needs of earth-based life forms *from the very beginning*, which explains why we were able to evolve in the first place. As it turns out, every one of nature's fundamental constants—which conspire together to determine the overall character of the macro universe—has been exceedingly fine-tuned to a *single* precise value *out of a virtual infinity of possible choices*. For some mysterious reason, it just so happens that *each* of these seemingly "arbitrary" choices is an essential prerequisite for the development of carbon-based life forms, including humans.

This fundamental connection between biological life on earth and the underlying structure of the universe is so intriguing that many scientific theoreticians are beginning to sit up and take notice. John Wheeler, for instance, one of the modern pioneers of quantum mechanics, has questioned whether the actual subatomic particles *themselves* are somehow tied into making life possible, since "the physical world is in some deep sense tied to the human being . . . We are beginning to suspect that man is not a tiny cog that doesn't make much difference to the running of the huge machine but rather that there is a much more intimate tie between man and the universe than we heretofore suspected."[8]

An even more surprising testimony of the centrality of human life to the universe has been proposed by modern quantum physicists. In place of the completely objective universe that we were raised to believe would exist even in the absence of man, we are now being told that there may be no objective reality at all apart from the observership of some sort of living consciousness.[9] The strong form of this statement, dubbed "The Participatory Anthropic Principle" by John[10] Wheeler, asserts that intelligent observership is somehow necessary to give the universe its very *existence*! This is certainly a far cry from the utterly pessimistic notion that we are unimportant in the overall scheme of things.

Given this strong scientific support[11] for a moderate anthropocentric view of reality, one wonders how the opposing assertion, known in cosmological circles as the Principle of Mediocrity, was able to draw such a huge following in the first place. In fact, moderate anthropocentrism in and of itself has no *a priori* implausability at all, in spite of its widespread unpopularity in modern intellectual circles. On the contrary, it possesses a tremendous degree of *a posteriori* truth and validity, as we will be arguing throughout the remainder of this book. Humility as a personal ideal is fine, but when it comes to the underlying features of the universe in the large, most of the relevant evidence seems to be pointing towards a moderate anthropocentric view of reality.

Indeed, what kind of "evidence" was ever used to discredit anthropocentrism to begin with? Historically speaking, the original criterion that was used for rejecting anthropocentrism was "geographical" in nature: Copernicus' discovery that the earth revolves around the sun, and not vice versa, signaled the end of anthropocentrism in the modern age.

In a limited sense, of course, Copernicus was absolutely correct; the earth is not the literal center of the universe, but who says that it has to be in order for us to be important in the overall scheme of things? It is a childish notion indeed to assume that we need to literally be at the physical center of the cosmos in order to be important to it. In the final analysis, our astronomical location in the universe is totally unrelated to the possibility that we might be important to it. Indeed, Copernicus, who was ironically a thoroughgoing anthropocentrist himself, was well aware of this fact, as he believed that, in comparison to the vast size of the universe, the displacement of the earth from this cosmic center is actually very slight.[12]

The criterion of physical size has also been used to count against the spectre of anthropocentrism in the modern world. Carl Sagan, for instance, has repeatedly reminded us about how small and insignificant we are in the face of the vast sizes and distances found in the heavens.[13] But since when did physical size ever equal overall significance in any larger metaphysical sense? Is a giraffe more significant than a man simply by virtue of its size alone? Obviously not, since there is no direct correlation between physical size and the ability to produce things of higher intrinsic value, like sonnets or symphonies. While we may be infinitesimally small in terms of physical size, we're the biggest things we know of in terms of structural complexity, creative capacity, and reflective self-consciousness.

Interestingly enough, there *is* a sense in which man (and the rest of the biosphere) does indeed exist at the "center" of the universe. When the various observable objects in the universe are plotted on a size-mass diagram, we find that the human body is poised midway between the size and mass of the universe, on the one hand, and the size and mass of subatomic particles, on the other. Although there is no proof that this curiosity bears any direct relationship to the true place of humankind in the cosmos, it nevertheless remains as an intriguing testimony to the profound mystery that surrounds the meaning of our existence.

In actuality, there are several other criteria besides size and astronomical location that are far more relevant in determining humanity's relative degree of importance to the cosmos. These criteria include an object's internal degree of complexity and its capacity for reflective self-consciousness. When these more relevant criteria are taken into consideration, man suddenly occupies a far more central position in the cosmos, since his body is easily the most complicated mechanism in the entire known universe, and his mind is uniquely capable of the miracle of self-consciousness.[14]

In recent years, however, a much more important argument has gradually surfaced against this anthropocentric world view. It is concerned with the tremendous amount of time it took after the Big Bang for humans to appear and to rise to any degree of significance on this planet. In the words of Bertrand Russell, "If the purpose of the Cosmos is to evolve mind, we must regard it as rather incompetent in having produced so little in such a long time."[15]

However, with the tremendous increase in our cosmological understanding in recent years, a devastating anthropocentric rebuttal to this objection has suddenly made itself known: carbon-based life forms intrinsically *require* a universe as big and as old as our own in order to exist, because they are physiologically dependent on an adequate supply of carbon and other heavy elements, which weren't in existence in any appreciable quantities immediately following the Big Bang. Instead, they had to be "cooked" for billions of years in the interiors of dying red giant stars, and then subsequently released into the cosmos via colossal supernova explosions.

When this striking fact is taken into consideration (along with the other temporal stipulations on planetary and organic evolution), it turns out that ours is the *youngest* possible universe that could have evolved carbon-based life forms through natural evolutionary pathways.[16] Furthermore, given the fact that the universe is expanding, ours is also the *smallest* possible universe that could have evolved life through these same natural pathways.[17] Thus, it would take a universe as big and as old as the present one just to evolve a *single* race of intelligent beings. Accordingly, as long as we accept the stipulation that life must evolve through natural evolutionary pathways, the vast size and age of our universe is perfectly compatible with an anthropocentric world view.

Indeed, given the intrinsic power of an omnipotent Creator, it is no longer outrageous to presume that such a Being might have created our overwhelmingly large universe just for the sake of human-like beings. To be sure, if He were anything other than the infinite Creator of the universe, this possibility would be totally unacceptable. But since He *is* presumably all-powerful (at least on the Deistic Evolutionist's view), the present size of our universe is no more daunting than if it were one-tenth this size. It follows from this observation that an omnipotent God could indeed have created the entire cosmos primarily for the sake of mankind.[18]

While many of the original opponents of anthropocentrism did not have access to our modern scientific understanding regarding cosmic evolution, there are still a great many scientifically-trained professionals today who continue to believe that we are unimportant in the larger scheme of things, just because of our small size and lack of geographical centrality in the universe. It would seem that these individuals are responding more to an *existential* intuition regarding man's place in the universe than to any type of raw physical data *per se*.

Indeed, it is our seemingly bleak existential plight in the cosmos that constitutes by far the most serious argument against an anthropocentric world view. For in a very real sense we seem to be alone in the universe. If God is actually in control of the whole affair, He obviously isn't directly communicating with us, at least not in a way that is immediately obvious. Even when horrific evils, such as those seen during the Holocaust, have threatened entire population centers with utter doom, the Powers that be, if they exist at all, have remained curiously silent. As a consequence, sensitive thinkers on the subject have concluded that we must *not* be very important in the overall scheme of things, for if we were, we wouldn't be forced to suffer so intensely, or to feel so alone in the universe.

There is a problem, however, with this sort of existential reasoning. For while it may be more compelling than the ridiculous criteria of physical size and astronomical location, it totally neglects another plausible explanation for our apparent aloneness in the universe: namely, that a Supreme Being might in fact exist, but for reasons having to do with the ultimate welfare of man, He may be choosing to remain silent for the present time. John Hick makes this very point in *Evil and the God of Love*, arguing that a certain amount of "epistemic distance" between God and man is a logically necessary precondition for the existence of genuine human freedom. The basic idea here is that if God were to immediately make Himself known to us in all His incomprehensible Glory, we would quickly become so overwhelmed that we would lose all our freedom to do as we pleased. But God doesn't want to force us to come to Him against our will; He wants us to *freely* come to Him whenever we are ready to do so, because this is the only type of love that is intrinsically worth having. It is significant to note, however, that the only logically possible way God can achieve this goal is by temporarily making Himself unavailable to the human race in any direct fashion.

Once again we see that the apparent evidence against anthropocentrism turns out to actually support it when all the relevant options are duly considered. God only "neglects" man so that his freedom—and hence his basic humanity—can be maximized to the greatest possible extent.

What this means, of course, is that God's apparent absence from the world cannot be used as unequivocal evidence against a limited degree of anthropocentrism in the cosmos. For if God's purpose for mankind can be conceived in such a way as to render inevitable His temporary absence from the world, then this absence can be properly accounted for from within the confines of the theist's anthropocentric view of reality.

Notes

1. Brandon Carter, *Confrontation of Cosmological Theories With Observation*, M.S. Longair, ed. (Dordrecht: Reidel, 1974), p. 291.
2. Ibid.
3. As I pointed out in *God and the New Cosmology*, the Anthropic Principle should actually be called the "Humanoid Principle," because other human-like beings could contribute an equal amount to its overall validity. In order to avoid any unnecessary confusion, though, I have elected to bow to convention by retaining the conventional "anthropic" nomenclature.
4. Barrow and Tipler, *The Anthropic Cosmological Principle*, pp. 288–289.
5. Ibid., p. 288.
6. From here on out I will be assuming the centrality of humanity in the overall world scheme, not because all the other creatures on this planet are unimportant, or because no other forms of intelligent life may exist in the universe, but because humans appear to be the most highly evolved creatures in our own biosphere.
7. If it turns out that life as we know it only exists on our own planet, then in this sense the earth alone will be the center of biological value in the universe. If other life forms exist elsewhere, then the phenomenon of life in general will constitute a more dispersed "center" to the universe.
8. John A. Wheeler, interviewed in Florence Helitzer's "The Princeton Galaxy," *Intellectual Digest*, No. 10 (June 1973), p. 32.
9. Barrow and Tipler, *The Anthropic Cosmological Principle*, pp. 468–471.
10. Ibid., p. 22.
11. As we have seen, the scientific data in no way suggests that we are the *most* important beings in the entire universe. For all we know, thousands of other intelligent civilizations could very well exist which could be every bit as important as we are, if not more so. As a consequence, the discovery that we are important to the cosmos should cause us to be *more* humble, and not less, vis-à-vis our relationship to the rest of creation.

12. Nicholas Copernicus, *On the Revolution of the Heavenly Spheres*, transl. C.G. Wallis, ed. R.M. Hutchins (Encyclopedia Britannica, London, 1952), Book 1, Ch. 6.
13. Carl Sagan, *Discovery*, Vol. 4, No. 3, March, 1983.
14. Although it could be argued that I am arbitrarily taking our own features to be important criteria in the overall scheme of things, I would counter that these criteria are not arbitrary at all. To the contrary, intelligence and the ability to act decisively in the world are obviously important in an objective sense, since they alone are capable of producing the awesome levels of creativity that humans routinely enjoy. They are also important insofar as they allow the making of deliberate large-scale changes to the overall structure of the cosmos. For instance, humans can, by virtue of these objectively important criteria, act to deliberately destroy their own planet, whereas no other entities in the entire known universe are capable of doing so. On a more positive side, this same capacity can also be used for equally *good* ends if it is properly used.
15. Bertrand Russell, *Religion and Science* (New York: Oxford University Press, 1968), p. 216.
16. Barrow and Tipler, *The Anthropic Cosmological Principle*, p. 385.
17. Ibid.
18. It must be continually borne in mind, though, that human beings don't have to be the *only* intelligent life forms in the universe in order for them to be important in the overall scheme of things. The cosmos could in fact be *teeming* with intelligent life, without the overall importance of man being diminished one iota.

CHAPTER 14

The Morality of Evolution

The Lord God may be subtle, but He isn't mean.

ALBERT EINSTEIN

Not one sparrow falls to the ground without your heavenly father knowing.

JESUS CHRIST

As we saw in Chapter 1, the biggest problem Charles Darwin had with the idea of a Divinely-directed evolutionary process had nothing to do with the physical evidence itself; it was centered instead on the problem of the morality of evolution. Darwin was well aware of the many horrors that go hand-in-hand with organic evolution, and he understandably had a hard time believing that a good and loving God could have been responsible for creating such a pain-filled natural process.

In this chapter we will explore the prospect of animal suffering in more detail, in order to see if it is possible to reconcile the pain of evolution with the existence of a good Creator.

14.1 Do Animals Really Suffer?

Implicit in the assertion that a good God has deliberately chosen to create the world through normal evolutionary pathways is the assumption that He has found the sacrifice of millions of animals throughout evolutionary history to be morally defensible. One of the primary criticisms of this assumption has to do with the tremendous amount of pain and suffering that was supposedly experienced by millions of innocent creatures throughout evolutionary history.

David Ray Griffin, for instance, has raised the question of whether or not the alleged suffering of millions of other species throughout evolution just for the sake of one species (humanity) can be considered to be morally justifiable.[1] Such an objection, of course, is based on the assumption that animals are indeed capable of suffering in a self-conscious, aversive manner, much as humans are.

There is, however, no good evidence indicating this to be the case. Although the lower animals clearly experience physical pain, this is a long way from saying that they actually *suffer* the way humans do. For one thing, the lower animals don't seem to be capable of conceptualizing pain the way humans can; thus, while they may feel pain as an aversive physical sensation, it seems very unlikely indeed that they actually suffer the way humans do. The immediate prospect of death, for instance, isn't nearly as aversive to the lower animals as it is to human beings, since humans are able to conceptualize their own doom, whereas the animals apparently cannot. Moreover, physiologically-based protective mechanisms such as the the endorphin system[2] are operative throughout much of the animal kingdom. These protective mechanisms act to dull the sensation of pain whenever an animal's body is significantly damaged. While humans also possess this endorphin system, it is evidently most efficacious in instances of pure physical pain. The psychospiritual conceptualization of suffering, which seems to be unique to humans, is apparently not affected to any significant degree by the endorphin system, except insofar as the endorphins themselves are capable of reducing the intensity of pains that are purely physical in origin. Animals, on the other hand, only seem to experience the physical sensation of pain; therefore, the endorphin system can presumably act to greatly reduce or even eliminate the amount of pain they feel.

Strong anecdotal support for this position has been provided by David Livingstone, who became famous as the man Henry Stanley combed the continent of Africa in search of. As Livingstone describes in his book *Livingstone's Africa*, he was on a low grassy hill when he was attacked by a large lion:

> I heard a shout. Staring and looking half round, I saw the lion just in the act of springing upon me. I was on a little height; he caught my shoulder as he sprang and we both came to the ground below together. Growling horribly close to my ear, he shook me as a terrier does a rat. The shock produced a stupor similar to that which seems to be felt by a mouse after the first shake of a cat. It caused a sort of dreaminess in which there was no sense of pain nor feeling of terror, though (I was) quite conscious of all that was happening. It was like what patients partially under the influence of chloroform describe, who see all the operation but feel not the knife. This singular condition was not the result of any mental process. The shake annihilated fear, and allowed no sense of horror in looking round at the beast. This peculiar state is probably produced in all animals killed by carnivora; and if so, is a merciful provision by our benevolent Creator for lessening the pain of death.

Given our present understanding of endogenous pain-killing systems, Livingstone's conclusion is particularly convincing. And when we add to this the animal kingdom's apparent lack of self-consciousness and their resultant inability to conceptualize pain and suffering, we find that the animals are well-insulated from the many pains that are inevitably associated with the evolutionary process.[3] This would seem to protect the moral integrity of a Creator who chose to use billions of years of evolution to produce the human race.

But even if we assume that animals do in fact suffer to a morally significant extent, we would only be justified in criticizing God for creating them in this manner if they existed totally on their own, since a suffering animal world in and of itself would appear to be a terrible thing for a good and loving God to create. However, it is abundantly clear that the animals do *not* exist in isolation from the rest of the world. They are, to the contrary, intimately intertwined with virtually all aspects of the natural order, including the existence of human beings.

It is thus possible that the animal world could serve its highest purpose, not in terms of its own independent existence, but in terms of its larger role within the overall global economy, which would include its role in the process of human development. Indeed, to the extent that animals are necessary ingredients in the human developmental process, it would seem to follow that any pain they would experience would at least partly be justified by the larger Goal that is supposedly intended for humanity. For just as the present reality of human suffering can be justified by a future Good that it has helped to bring about, so too can the present existence of animal pain be similarly justified, especially insofar as it is necessarily entailed in the realization of this Goal. The Bible supports this overall view with its contention that a human being is worth many sparrows (Luke 12:7). This is an intuitive assertion that most everyone would agree with, yet implicit within it is the possibility that the animals could, in addition to possessing their own intrinsic value, have a higher instrumental value that is directed towards facilitating human development.

Indeed, part of the reason why animals seem to suffer as much as they do may be to stimulate *human* compassion and responsibility. In this sense, their suffering *is* morally significant, but only insofar as it is incumbent upon humans to do everything in their power to reduce it.[4]

14.2   Those Infamous Ichneumons

In addition to the pain and waste engendered by the evolutionary process, there is yet another moral objection to the idea that a good and loving God is ultimately responsible for creating life on this planet. It has to do with the "vicious" predator-prey nature of the biosphere. A good and loving God, it is said, would almost certainly have created a more harmonious natural order than the "dog eat dog" one we presently have.

Many specific examples of cruelty in the wild have been cited over the years as being inconsistent with the idea of a good and loving Creator. The infamous "ichneumon fly"—which really isn't a fly at all, but a wasp—is probably the most frequently cited objection of this kind.

The ichneumon fly has evolved a "horrible" mechanism for nourishing its newly-hatched larvae within the body of a suitable host, usually a hapless caterpillar. Upon finding such a rich food source, the female ichneumon uses her ovipositor tube to inject her eggs directly into the caterpillar's body.

Once the eggs hatch, they begin feeding on the still-pulsating tissue of the caterpillar's body. Since a dead caterpillar isn't nearly as nutritious as a living one, the larvae have the good sense to eat only the inessential parts of the caterpillar first, leaving the crucial organs for last. This preserves the life—and hence the nutritiousness—of the caterpillar until the last possible moment.

It is easy to see how the ichneumons could have been perceived as constituting a severe threat to the possible existence of a benevolent Creator, particularly in the realm of natural theology. After all, these "wicked" organisms subject the poor caterpillar to the worst possible means of torture: a gradual ingestion of its internal organs piece by piece, while it is still alive and sentient, and yet unable to do anything about it. Why, it is asked, would a good God ever create such a grisly means of torture in the first place, when there are undoubtedly less terrible ways of providing nutrition to newly hatched larvae?

There are two notable problems with this type of criticism. To begin with, it severely anthropomorphizes the lower forms of God's creation. Caterpillars, on this view, are thought to have a capacity for feeling and conceptualizing pain that is remotely comparable to humans; therefore, the torture they feel at having their insides slowly eaten away must be real.

There is no doubt that many of us feel a strong temptation to anthropomorphize the various members of the animal kingdom. There is also no doubt that such a view is almost certainly mistaken. It is a virtual certainty that the lower forms of life, such as ants and caterpillars, are unable to feel and conceptualize pain the way humans can. Thus, the "suffering" of a caterpillar that has been victimized by a procreating ichneumon isn't even *remotely* comparable to the suffering that would be experienced by a human in a similar circumstance. But if this is actually the case, then we can't properly fault God for creating such a "horrible" natural process.

Indeed, faulting God in this manner is itself based on a value judgment that views the world in terms of a potential hedonistic paradise. Thus, to the extent that our world falls short of this ideal, it is deemed to be evidence that the world could not have been the product of a good God.

However, the function of our world in the Divine Economy is presumably not to be a hedonistic paradise *per se*, but rather to be a "vale of soul-making," as John Hick has pointed out.[5] On this view, human development, and not mindless pleasure, is the chief aim of the creation. Accordingly, anything that can play a substantial role in facilitating this development is deemed to be important and desirable, *even if it happens to appear undesirable when viewed in terms of itself.*

According to the Deistic Evolutionist, one of the most important sources for this type of growth facilitation is a physical world that has been patterned after the necessary nature of the human developmental process. To the extent that this assumption turns out to be true, we immediately have in our possession a potential justification for *any* type of natural "evil" or physical symbol that can be shown to play an important role in the facilitation of human development.

The ichneumons, by hypothesis, constitute precisely this sort of physical symbol. They seem to represent those "predatory" aspects of the human psychospiritual world that constantly seek to "feed" on our innermost souls whenever they are allowed to do so. Certainly it cannot be denied that there are inner evils that act for all the world like "spiritual ichneumons," insofar as they perpetually seek to lodge themselves inside our innermost souls, where they try to "eat away" at us until we are killed. Drug addiction and certain forms of mental illness provide excellent cases in point: they possess approximately the same relationship to their human host (in the psychospiritual plane) that the ichneumon fly possesses with its caterpillar host (in the physical plane).[6]

This utilitarian explanation has been criticized on the basis of the overly concealed nature of the ichneumon's life, which renders it largely inaccessible to human view. According to this objection, the ichneumons are unable to facilitate human growth in the proposed manner because they have been invisible to the vast majority of humans who have ever lived. Since they can't be seen, they can't function to facilitate human growth even indirectly.

The Deistic Evolutionist responds to this objection by pointing out that his world view assumes that the *entire* physical world has been patterned after the necessary nature of the human developmental process. Therefore, to the extent that this assumption is true, we would expect *all* levels of physical reality to reflect this basic patterning, and not just those that are visible to the human eye. It is thus the entire symbolic result of this essential patterning that acts to *cumulatively* facilitate the human growth process, and not any one specific example *per se.*

What this means is that while most people down through history have not been directly aware of the ichneumon's existence, they *have* been aware of other equally important physical symbols in the natural world that serve the same sort of symbolic function that the ichneumons do: that of providing a symbolic physical referent for those psychospiritual evils that can parasitize our innermost souls if they are allowed to do so. The Deistic Evolutionist believes that it is the unconscious perception of these symbols that conditions us to think and act in certain defensive ways in response to them, and that these conditioned responses can then help us to develop sufficient cognitive and behavioral skills for battling the many evils within us.[7] The point is simply that if we choose to evaluate our world in terms of its overall soul-making capacity, we must deem the ichneumons to be an important part of physical reality, since they are part of a larger environmental mileu that, as a whole, serves to symbolically represent a significant source of evil in our lives.[8]

14.3 Evolutionary Waste and the Prospect of Intelligent Design

Many have attacked the process of evolution by natural selection as being too wasteful a means to be used by a benevolent Creator. The Deistic Evolutionist responds to this attack by pointing out that such assertions are all a matter of priority and perspective. For if the psychospiritual development of human beings is as important as it seems to be, then anything that is essential to this process will automatically be considered worthwhile in the end, even if happens to temporarily involve a certain amount of suffering and "waste." We need to keep in mind Jesus' assertion that human beings are worth more than many sparrows (Luke 12:7). Judging solely from this presumed value differential between man and other species, we must conclude that any natural process that is necessary for the unfolding of mature human beings will turn out to be justifiable in the end, because this goal will presumably be so glorious that it will end up justifying all the necessary sacrifices that led up to it.

This leads us to the critical notion of perspective that applies to any type of metaphysical interpretation of the natural realm. From our limited viewpoint, it seems cruel and wasteful for a good God to sacrifice so much "innocent" animal blood in His creation of the human race. However, from the perspective of the Deity, who is presumably outside the ordinary confines of space-time, He is able to see *right now* the glorious goal that we are all still striving for on this planet. Next to this immaculate goal, the sacrifice of a certain number of animals can only be seen as being worthwhile in the end, especially if there is some degree of necessity associated with this particular method of creation.[9]

We mustn't forget that this is how nature works on the large scale as well. Huge amounts of entropy (disorder) are regularly sacrificed to produce small conglomerations of order in the universe. Huge supernovae are utilized to synthesize a relatively small quantity of those heavier elements that make up the majority of our world and bodies. A tremendous amount of heat is generated by our sun, just to warm the tiny fraction of its radiant area in which we live. Huge numbers of eggs are fertilized by fish and amphibians, only a few of which actually live on to adulthood. Even Jesus warns us that "many are called, but few are chosen" (Matt. 22:14). Apparently, the metaphysical "cost" of order in the universe inevitably entails the production of large amounts of disorder. Perhaps this is what St. Paul had in mind when he wrote that we were "bought for a price" (Col. 3:4).

We can see this same basic principle at work in the realm of human creativity, where huge quantities of disorder and perspiration are typically required to generate a comparatively small amount of creative inspiration. (Accordingly to Edison, the actual ratio is 99% perspiration and 1% inspiration.) When we apply this principle to the realm of biological evolution, we find that many evolving animals must be sacrificed to produce the amount of evolutionary order we currently have in the world. In view of these thermodynamic considerations, we see that God was only being consistent with the Law[10] of Entropy (which He presumably created) when He instituted such a "cruel" and "wasteful" evolutionary process.[11]

Of course, this raises the question of why an omnipotent God couldn't have created a fully-ordered, non-entropic universe to begin with. Presumably He could have, but it is possible to show that such a universe would not have been an appropriate home for developing human beings.

There are two very important reasons for this. For one thing, the Entropy Law is an essential prerequisite for the existence of predictability in the world. If the Entropy Law were not in effect, the normal course of causation in the world would be severely disrupted, with the tragic effect that we would be unable to predict the consequences of our actions, even in relatively simple interactions with the environment.[12] Friction, for instance, could not be counted upon in a non-entropic world to slow things down or to produce heat, because these effects are based on the prior validity of the Entropy Law. Even worse, it would be impossible to predict the consequences of *any* state of affairs in a non-entropic world, because order could then spontaneously increase or decrease entirely of its own accord, and there would be no way to predict ahead of time what would actually happen.

As it stands now, the Entropy Law enables us to predict with certainty that things will gradually get more disordered with the passage of time, and it is this basic predictive ability that gives us a stable environmental foundation to act upon. A non-entropic world, by contrast, would be a madhouse of arbitrary causes and effects in which no reliable form of prediction would be possible, and this in turn would destroy any chance for coherent human action. Indeed, because this unpredictability would necessarily extend to all aspects of our interaction with the environment, it would destroy our freedom of choice as well, since it would reduce the internal coherence of the choices themselves. Free beings, however, clearly need a coherent set of behavioral alternatives to choose from. Therefore, it follows that we must live in an entropic world if we are to be truly free.

The Entropy Law also turns out to be a metaphysically necessary precondition for the existence of time, because it helps to define the direction in which time inexorably flows (from order to disorder). But time itself is an indispensible part of the human growth process, because the very idea of a gradual developmental process implicitly *assumes* the existence of time. We can see this most clearly in the need to distinguish between early, middle, and late stages of development. Without a uni-directional flow of time, these distinctions would be impossible. The question thus isn't *whether* time is needed for humans to develop in, but rather *what kind* of time is needed for this grand ontological task.

As Stephen Hawking[13] and others have pointed out, it is vitally important that the psychological arrow of time, or the direction in which we perceive time to flow, be in the same direction as the thermodynamic arrow of time, which is the direction of steadily increasing disorder in the universe. This means that we *must* live in an entropic universe if we are to be capable of perceiving the flow of time properly.

We see, then, that God could *not* have created a non-entropic world without simultaneously destroying the possibility for human growth and freedom. Indeed, to the extent that: a) these two qualities are essential parts of the Human Definition, and b) that God's overall goal was to create human beings, it follows that God *had* to have created an entropic world. This would explain why an omnipotent God, who presumably could have created a non-entropic world, nevertheless chose to create an entropic one: because only the latter type of world is compossible with the human character structure as it has been empirically observed to be.

This would appear to be the reason why there is no "free lunch" to be had anywhere in the cosmos: because it is in the very nature of entropic systems for order to be "paid for" by the production of comparatively large amounts of disorder. It follows from this thermodynamic relation that the most highly evolved forms of order in the entire known universe—namely ourselves—could only have come about through the production of tremendous quantities of disorder.

The "waste" that is generated by the process of evolution by natural selection is perhaps the premier example of this type of entropic process. However, since this "waste" is, by hypothesis, an essential part of the human developmental process (which itself appears to be the only logically possible way for humans to come into existence), it is no longer "waste" at all when it is viewed from a larger, holistic perspective: it is, rather, an *essential ingredient* in the overall cosmic economy.

Those who routinely criticize God for creating this type of world are thus guilty of two important oversights: 1) not realizing the metaphysical need for an entropic world in a universe populated by free-willed, developing human beings, and 2) not realizing the tremendous thermodynamic "cost" of order in an entropic universe. Order isn't a "free" everyday phenomenon in the cosmos; it is, rather, the result of a complex and highly articulated reversal of the natural physical tendency towards increased entropy or disorder. Consequently, any significant production of order in the universe (such as that found in the evolution of life) is bound to entail some degree of thermodynamic "cost."

This observation, in turn, raises an even *deeper* objection by the atheologian. It centers around the presumed omnipotence of the Divine Power, and it is usually stated in the following manner: If God is truly omnipotent, then surely He could have produced the desired end product (fully actualized humans) without going through all the trouble and waste of the last four billion years of evolutionary development. The advantage of this alleged possibility is that it would have enabled us to bypass all the evil and suffering that have occurred on this planet throughout the millennia.

This is the infamous "problem of evil," and it is undoubtedly the number one problem facing traditional theology. It is a problem because the existence of evil seems to constitute evidence against a good and all-powerful Creator. At the very least, it seems to indicate that God's creative efforts were probably limited by some type of constraining factor.[14]

This latter assertion isn't as heretical as it may initially seem, because even the most traditional theologians readily admit that God is limited or constrained by His own nature. Thus, the true issue here isn't *whether* God's creative behavior has been constrained, but *where* this constraining factor is to be located. There are only two possibilities: it can either be located within the Divine Substance or outside of it. Process theologians take the latter course, insofar as they believe that God is necessarily limited by: 1) a pre-existing world of self-determining actualities, and 2) by several constraining metaphysical principles that are believed to apply in all possible worlds. This is a dualist scenario that is unacceptable to the orthodox theologian, because it necessitates that we do away with the traditional doctrine of omnipotence.

Fortunately, there is another way to conceptualize this apparent limitation that does not entail any significant compromise of the Divine Power. All we have to do is place this Divine locus of limitation within God's own Being, because it doesn't count against God's omnipotence to say that He is "limited" by some necessary aspect of His own nature. For instance, God's intrinsic goodness clearly limits His freedom to be evil, but this isn't normally taken to count against His possible omnipotence. The same thing can be said for God's other intrinsic qualities as well.

In other words, since these "limitations" are understood to always result in a maximal production of goodness, they cannot in the end be considered to be true *limitations* at all. For while God may be free to do whatever He wants, this is only within the realm of the Divine Power. The Divine Goodness, on the other hand, necessarily constrains the Divine Power to do only that which leads to a maximal production of good. Therefore, God's capacity to produce good is unlimited. Similarly, His capacity to bring about pure evil is essentially nil, not because He doesn't have the power to create it, but because the Divine Goodness always acts to constrain the Divine Power, so as to bring about exclusively good results.

What this means is that God always acts as an integrated unit, with all of His intrinsic qualities cooperating with one another to bring about the best possible result. Hence, the Divine Will never acts in isolation from the Divine Goodness, or from the Divine Rationality. All three work together to bring about the desired product. Hence, the Divine Power is always tempered by the Divine Goodness and by the Divine Rationality. This is the Thomist concept of the Divine Simplicity, and it explains why God never chooses to bring about genuine evil in the world. In a good universe, however, this "inability" cannot be considered to be a genuine limitation of the Divine Power. It is, rather, a perfect *enhancement* of the Divine Freedom to produce maximal goodness.

It follows from this concept of the Divine Simplicity that in God's perpetual quest to produce maximal goodness, He cannot resort to the logically impossible[15] in order to prevent certain evil events from occurring. The reason for this is that there isn't any coherent course of action for Him to pursue in such instances. Logically impossible states of affairs are ontological zeroes, so they cannot properly be called "things" at all. They are, rather, "no-things" in the deepest sense of the word, so they could never be said to comprise a task that is beyond God's ability to perform. For some strange reason, though, we humans have been given the capacity to imagine logically impossible states of affairs as though they were truly attainable. But just because we can imagine these absurdities doesn't mean that they could ever really exist in reality, or that God's "inability" to bring them about puts a limit on His omnipotence. As C.S. Lewis has so aptly put it, "nonsense remains nonsense, even when we talk it about God."[16]

It is at this point that the Deistic Evolutionist makes two critical assumptions: 1) that the Human Essence necessarily entails the temporary existence of evil, and 2) that this was the only essence that was "good enough" for God to create. Needless to say, there is no way we can objectively confirm these assumptions. The most we can do is to hypothetically assume their validity, so we can extrapolate out from them in order to see where they might lead. When we do this (i.e., when we assume the truth of the two above assumptions), a startling conclusion quickly presents itself: God could not have brought about an instantiation of the Human Essence without simultaneously bringing about the temporary existence of evil, and this would have been the case no matter how much power He had at His disposal, because not even an infinite amount of power can bring about two logically contradictory states of affairs simultaneously. It is in this fashion that the

Deistic Evolutionist seeks to preserve the traditional concept of omnipotence in the face of all the evil in the world.

The validity of this train of argument, however, relies on a further assumption; namely, that it was logically impossible for God to have created man instantaneously by Divine Fiat. This appears to be a highly defensible proposition, for as we have seen, the Human Essence seems to necessarily entail a gradual process of self-attained knowledge and character development for man. To the extent that this is indeed the case, we find that the instantaneous creation of mature human beings ready-made is a logical contradiction in terms, which means that it doesn't even have a *potential* reality in the cosmos.

Going one step further, if it was logically impossible for God to have created mature humans ready-made, it may have also been logically impossible for Him to have created man's physical world instantaneously as well. This would especially be true if some aspect of the Human Essence required the physical world to be patterned after the necessary nature of human development. If this were actually the case, it would explain why God chose to create the world through natural evolutionary pathways, instead of instantaneously by miraculous Fiat.[17]

This essentialist viewpoint offers a bold answer to Einstein's famous question concerning the amount of choice God had in creating our world. For as long as we take the Human Definition to be our theoretical starting point, so we can extrapolate from it the various universal qualities that must exist if this essence is to be instantiated, we find that God had *no choice at all* in how the basic features of the world were to be created, since the Human Definition *itself* has apparently specified all the important details.

Thus, insofar as the problem of evil is a necessary byproduct of the Human Definition, its present existence *cannot* count against God's omnipotence or benevolence. The most it can do is count against His overall wisdom in desiring to instantiate the Human Essence in the first place. On the other hand, since God can purportedly see the ultimate glory that we are all presently striving for on this planet, He is the only entity who is in a position to decide whether or not all the evil in our world will ultimately turn out to be justifiable, all things considered. The very fact that we do presently exist, in spite of evil, would seem to indicate that this evil will indeed turn out to be justifiable in the end. But this will only be the case if some larger degree of necessity is associated with this mode of creation, since there would appear to be no reason why a good God would pursue such a pain-filled creative process if a less agonizing alternative were immediately available to Him.

Notes

1. David Griffin, *God, Power, and Evil* (Philadelphia: The Westminster Press, 1976), pp. 191–192.

2. Endorphins are endogenously-occurring morphine-like substances that are automatically released when the sensation of pain in an organism becomes sufficiently intense. The analgesia that is subsequently produced is similar in efficacy to morphine and its analogues.
3. This, however, should not be taken to mean that it is OK to deliberately subject an animal to painful stimuli. To the contrary, *our* moral integrity appears to be dependent on precisely the opposite course of action. We should do everything we possibly can to prevent animals from experiencing pain, because they undoubtedly feel it, and because deliberate cruelty is never justified.
4. Again, such a statement should not be taken to mean that animals are incapable of feeling a significant amount of pain, or that humans can ever be justified in their wanton abuse of animals. To the contrary, animals are *obviously* capable of experiencing a profound degree of physical pain (at least from our own point of view). And since we are the ones who are are largely in control of these painful stimuli, it is our moral duty to eliminate them whenever possible.
5. John Hick, *Evil and the God of Love*, pp. 302–309.
6. There even appears to be a physiological component to this developmentally-derived symbol: cancer. Just as a malignant tumor tends to "eat away" at us until it is either surgically removed or until it actually kills us, the "terrible" ichneumon fly also tends to parasitize its host to the very end if it is allowed to do so.
7. Of course, this begs the question of why God had to build humans in such an evil-prone way to begin with. The reason for this, according to the Deistic Evolutionist, is that the temporary propensity for evil is an essential property of the Human Definition, which itself is presumably the only end product that God found worthy enough to create.
8. The ichneumons also undoubtedly serve a valuable function in the larger ecological order as well, by keeping down the population of crop-destroying caterpillars.
9. This is a version of the "aesthetic argument" for the justification of evil on this planet. Just as the existence of dark splotches on a painting can be justified by virtue of their essential contribution to the meaningfulness of the larger whole, the "dark splotches" of physical and moral evil in the world can also be justified, not in terms of their own intrinsic value, but in terms of their essential contribution to the meaningfulness of the larger whole.
10. The Law of Entropy states that the total amount of disorder in the universe is perpetually on the increase. It is also known as the Second Law of Thermodynamics.
11. Although God may have created the Law of Entropy, it seems likely that there are certain intrinsic features of this law that were necessary to the overall creative process, at least with respect to the creation of human beings. So while God may have created the law itself, He presumably did *not* create the metaphysical need for this type of law vis-à-vis His overall creative intention—that of creating humanity.
12. Barrow and Tipler, *The Anthropic Cosmological Principle*, p. 176.
13. Stephen Hawking, *A Brief History of Time* (New York: Bantam, 1988).
14. Some even go so far as to assert that the reality of evil shows that God cannot possibly exist.
15. This statement is based on the presumption that it is logically impossible for a particular essence to be instantiated, and yet for it *not* to exude those essential properties that necessarily comprise it.
16. C.S. Lewis, *The Problem of Pain*, (New York: Macmillan Publishing Company, 1962), p. 31.

17. Process theologians have proposed an alternative explanation for why God utilized the process of evolution to do His creating. They believe that it is metaphysically impossible for God to create *any* complex entity instantaneously, not just in this world, but in all possible worlds. They thus want to move the locus of metaphysical necessity from the necessary nature of the Human Essence to generic reality itself.

PART IV

The Implications of Deistic Evolutionism for Theology

CHAPTER 15

Deistic Evolution and Modern Philosophical Theology

To someone who could grasp the universe from a unified standpoint the entire creation would appear as a unique truth and necessity.

J. D'ALEMBERT

15.1 Creation *Ex Nihilo*

One of the chief theoretical presuppositions of Deistic Evolutionism is that God did indeed create the world *ex nihilo*. This means that, prior to the creation, God was the only entity in existence, and that He freely used His power to create the entire physical universe "out of nothing." This renders God a supernatural Being by definition, insofar as He originally possessed all the power that could possibly be had in the cosmos.

Human beings are the beneficiaries of this primordial power, since their existence is presumably due to the free exercise of God's creative will. However, due to the structural limitations that are an intrinsic part of the Human Definition (and which appear to be ultimately derived from God's own rational nature), the Deistic Evolutionist believes that there was only one logically possible way for humans to be brought into existence: through the gradual process of psychospiritual development, beginning at the smallest possible starting point and moving on to progressively greater levels of self-attained maturity. It is this intrinsically necessary developmental process that presumably constitutes the ultimate constraint on the type of universe God was able to create.

On this view, God began His creative venture with a "blank slate," so to speak, insofar as there were no pre-existing metaphysical limitations on the type of world that God could have created. He merely had to choose the identity of His creative goal and then faithfully bring every aspect of it into being. The Deistic Evolutionist is thus committed to a moderate voluntaristic position, insofar as he believes that God originally had the power to freely choose the types of limitations that would subsequently apply to His creation.

It is important to note, however, that these limitations do not reflect back to any inherent deficiency or weakness in God's Power; they merely represent the necessary "limitations" that are an inherent part of all finite objects. On this essentialist view, every coherent object has its own necessary nature; therefore, any attempt to instantiate a particular essence necessarily limits the types of properties that can subsequently be brought into being. In this respect God is no different from man, insofar as He is necessarily "limited" by the intrinsic nature of whatever it is that He freely chooses to create. Thus, if God originally chose to create a universe of triangles only, He would subsequently be "limited" to creating three-sided objects whose internal angles add up to 180 degrees.[1] This conceptualization of the Divine Power is fully consistent with the traditional doctrine of omnipotence, insofar as these creative "limitations" have nothing to do with God's inherent degree of power. They are an intrinsic part of the creative process, because they merely require that God be "limited" to creating the type of world that He freely chooses to create. Power is clearly not an issue here, because no conceivable amount of power could enable God to do otherwise.

This moderate degree of voluntarism stands in stark contrast to the types of divine limitations envisioned by process philosophers, which are thought to apply to *all* possible worlds. The Deistic Evolutionist only acknowledges one such metaphysical limitation, as we have seen, and that is the one that necessarily limits God to instantiating those essences (and their attendant properties) that He freely chooses to create. This view, however, falls short of a stronger voluntarism, because it does not assert that God has the power to determine the types of properties that are exhibited by the objective essences themselves. The Deistic Evolutionist believes this to be a fundamentally incoherent position, insofar as he believes that essences and their properties are inextricably tied to one another *by definition*. The moderate voluntaristic view, by contrast, states that God only has the power to choose the identity of those essences that He wants to instantiate in the first place; He does *not* have the power to determine the types of properties that are exhibited by these essences.

It is for this reason that the Deistic Evolutionist believes that God was "limited" to creating an evolutionary-type world where humans must gradually grow to their own full maturity: because self-attained growth is presumed to be an essential defining property of the Human Definition. So is free will; therefore, God had no choice but to relinquish some of His own power when He decided to create substantially free human beings.

The important thing to realize here, though, is that this Divine Self-Limitation was entirely free, insofar as God freely chose to relinquish some of His power to His creatures, in order to be consistent with the necessary nature of the Human Definition. Furthermore, since God's instantiation of the Human Essence is presumed to have been totally free (and therefore uncompelled), His subsequent "limitation" by its intrinsic properties is entirely consistent with His sovereignty and all-power.

In other words, due to the "eternal verities" that necessarily surround the Human Definition, God's election to instantiate the Human Essence in reality intrinsically required Him to give up some of His power to His creatures.[2] On this view, even though God has freely brought the world into existence *ex nihilo*, and even though He has voluntarily chosen *what* to bring into existence, the inherent nature of these voluntarily chosen items are nevertheless themselves pre-determined, in the sense that their basic definitions are eternal necessities, and so are therefore beyond Divine Decision.

These "eternal verities," however, should not be thought of in a dualistic fashion, because they are *not* an external force limiting God's Power. Rather, they are an *internal*, self-limiting feature of the Divine Mind, in which they seem to be roughly analogous to God's own thoughts or ideas. This interpretation of essences as being internal to the Mind of God has the great advantage of preserving the traditional monotheistic conception of the Godhead; it also protects God's presumed omnipotence from the power-limiting effects of an external metaphysical principle.

15.2   Deistic Evolution and Process Thought

Interestingly enough, most of the attributes of the physical realm postulated by process theologians fit in well with the underlying dictates of the Human Definition. For instance, process thinkers posit the existence of a somewhat animated physical realm, in which the freedom of self-determination exists all the way down to the most fundamental building blocks of nature. It thereby acknowledges only a difference in degree, and not one in kind, between human freedom and the freedom exhibited by the physical particles themselves. In the same way, it acknowledges only a difference in degree, and not one in kind, between human consciousness and the "prehensive" consciousness of the smallest physical particles.

The Deistic Evolutionist sees this fundamental similarity between the physical world and the psychospiritual nature of human life as the ultimate example of the way in which the physical world has been patterned after the necessary dictates of the Human Definition. Since the properties of freedom and self-consciousness are presumably indigenous to the Human Essence, and since the nature of the physical realm must by hypothesis be patterned after this Essence, it follows that the physical particles themselves must also possess these fundamental characteristics as well. This is an alternative explanation for the apparent animation and prehensive consciousness of the physical world.

Process thinkers also consider creativity to be the most fundamental aspect of universal reality. In its spontaneous prehension of all past events, each act of becoming in the universe is said to exhibit a certain amount of creativity, insofar as even the smallest events themselves are thought to intrinsically possess a certain amount of creative freedom for self-determination. This universal creativity is directly analogous to human creativity, for as we have seen, the larger goal of human development is intrinsically creative by its very nature. For the Deistic Evolutionist, it is this developmental creativity, which is presumed to be an essential property of the Human Definition, that has rendered it necessary for the physical world to exhibit a similar degree of creativity.

Process thinkers also view time in terms of this universal process of becoming. As David Ray Griffin has pointed out in a recent essay, "time is real only if the present moment creates something that was not already there in the past; only if this is a real addition, adding something to the sum total of reality, is time irreversible in principle."[3]

The underlying assumption of this process view is that time is a necessary feature of the creative process itself, insofar as creativity requires the temporal succession of events in order to allow the emergence of new levels of form. It is precisely here that the Deistic Evolutionist also sees time as ultimately originating, since he recognizes that the developmental process itself intrinsically requires "time" to take place in. On this view, the temporal nature of the world *itself* has been deliberately patterned after this metaphysical requirement of the Human Definition.

Overall, then, the Deistic Evolutionist agrees with the process theist in terms of the way in which the underlying nature of the physical world is perceived. It is only on the fundamental issue of *why* the world is this way that the two positions radically differ from one another. For the process thinker, the inherent creativity of matter is the eternal "given," so the Creator had no choice but to evolve man out of these fundamentally creative particles. On this view, man is a free being, not because he has externally been given this capacity by an omnipotent Being, but because freedom and creativity necessarily exist in *all possible* worlds.

For the Deistic Evolutionist, on the other hand, the only "given" is the necessary nature of the Human Essence, which God has, by hypothesis, freely chosen to instantiate in reality. On this moderate voluntaristic view, it is only because the Human Essence necessarily entails a temporal, creative, and developmental format that the otherwise contingent physical realm possesses these characteristics, not because all possible worlds must possess them.

The process theologian further believes that God's power is necessarily limited by the inherent metaphysical limitations that are thought to surround a pre-existing society of "finite actualities." In this dualistic mode of thinking, God took some 15 to 20 billion years to do His creating because He was inherently unable to do otherwise, due to the intrinsic power possessed by these pre-existing actualities. The process theologian thus believes that

God would have created the universe instantaneously had He had the power to do so, because this would have done away with the tremendous amount of pain and suffering associated with the evolutionary process. From the process point of view, then, the phenomenon of universal evolution is a lasting testimony to the many metaphysical limitations that are thought to surround God's creative power.[4]

As we have seen, the Deistic Evolutionist agrees that there are certain limiting factors that necessarily act to constrain God's creative power, but he chooses to locate these limitations elsewere, in the necessary natures of the created objects themselves, rather than in any metaphysical limitation of God's power that would apply in all possible worlds.

This is a critical point, because the entire character of God revolves around this important distinction. For instance, the process deity, by virtue of the many metaphysical limitations that necessarily act upon him in all possible worlds, is an entirely naturalistic God of limited power, who has no choice but to enter into a dualistic battle with a pre-existing world of self-determining actualities whenever He chooses to create something. The Deistic Evolutionist's God, on the other hand, is a supernatural and fully omnipotent Being who is only limited by the logical constraints that are an inherent part of His own Faculty of Reason. Originally the only Being in existence, this self-limited Deity voluntarily chose to create the universe *ex nihilo* at some point in the past, not arbitrarily, but in total harmony with the logical constraints that naturally surround the Human Definition.

For the process thinker, then, those metaphysical factors that supposedly acted to constrain God's creative power are necessarily eternal in nature, so they would have existed in any possible world that God would have created. As a consequence, they were *not* chosen by Him, either directly or indirectly, when He decided to create the world. For the Deistic Evolutionist, on the other hand, these limiting factors are logical and not metaphysical, so they are more directly related to *what* God has chosen to create, rather than to any pre-existing world of metaphysical necessities *per se*. On this view, God freely chose the logical limitations that would subsequently apply to Him, *via* His voluntary election to create humanity. The Deistic Evolutionist thus believes that once God has freely opted to pursue a particular creative goal (in this case humanity), the structural content of what He will subsequently create is *not* free to vary; it is only the *possible existence* of these invariant necessities that is free to vary. In other words, God is free to choose whether or not to create man, but having made the decision to create him, God is *not* free to alter *what* He creates or *how* He creates it, since these creative decisions are intrinsically predetermined by the logical necessities that necessarily surround the Human Character Definition.

The chief difference between Deistic Evolutionism and the process position thus boils down to a distinction between the moderate voluntarism of the Deistic Evolutionist and the absolute naturalism of the process theist. The process theist believes that the various internal qualities of the universe (apart from its degree of organization) were all beyond Divine decision, insofar as they are presumed to have been metaphysically necessary features of a pre-existing material realm. The Deistic Evolutionist, on the other hand, believes that God *deliberately imposed* these qualities on the material realm for a Higher Purpose: that of facilitating the growth of human beings.

This latter view is characteristic of a moderate voluntaristic approach, because it asserts that God is only able to determine the particular qualities that will be exhibited by the universe by choosing the specific nature of what He wants to create ahead of time.. A strong voluntarist approach would say that God could have determined the specific qualities possessed by the universe *regardless* of the end product He was trying to create.[5]

15.3 Discussion

Apart from rendering certain theological problems, such as the fact of evil and the process of evolution, easier to understand, there seems to be no good *internal* reason why the metaphysical limitations spoken of in process thought must extend to *all* possible worlds. Surely their apparent existence in this world cannot be used in and of itself to justify their extension to all possible worlds.

Much of the reason for this type of generalization in the process literature seems to be that no other good reason can be found to explain why God would have utilized the evolutionary process to do His creating, or indeed, why He would have tolerated the problem of evil at all. It is simply assumed that if God *could* have avoided these problems in the creation, He *would* have. Therefore, since He hasn't avoided them, it is automatically concluded that He must not have originally had the power to do so.

This conclusion wouldn't be so problematic if the process thinker were to stop here, because it is possible, as we have seen, to identify the locus of metaphysical necessity in the universe in the essential nature of *what* God has freely chosen to create, instead of in the metaphysical structure of reality *per se*. Significantly, though, the process theist does *not* stop here; he goes one step further and extends the locus of metaphysical necessity from our own world to *all possible* worlds. Since no good reason for the realities of evil and evolution can be found, none is deemed to exist, so the metaphysical limitations that are thought to have produced these problems are assumed to exist in all possible worlds. The rationale here seems to be that if these limitations exist in all possible worlds, then God couldn't help but be limited by them in this actual world.

But what if the process of development turns out to be one of the essential properties of the Human Definition? More importantly, what if the Human

Essence turns out to be the only one that was "good enough" to fulfill the lofty demands of the Creator? If so, then a larger justification for the evolutionary process (and for the reality of evil) will have been in existence all along. Best of all, this justification turns out to be perfectly consistent with the traditional doctrine of omnipotence, so we don't have to sacrifice our concept of the Divine Power in order to believe in the reality of evolution.

Indeed, with this justifiable reason in hand, it no longer becomes necessary to postulate a series of metaphysical limitations in all possible worlds, as the process theists have done. It is only necessary to postulate a limitation in this particular world *only*, since the Human Essence does indeed seem to entail a discrete set of creative boundaries that would not be necessary in other possible worlds where humans do not exist. To the extent that this hypothesis is correct, we can say that the process theist has confused an essential property of the Human Definition for an essential metaphysical limitation of generic reality itself.

Notes

1. While this self-evident assertion may sound trivial, it becomes important if one believes that God freely chose to instantiate the Human Essence in reality. For if this were indeed the case, then God was automatically "limited" to instantiating only those types of properties that are consistent with the Human Essence. But what if certain weaknesses or evil propensities are also part of the Human Definition? In this case, God would have no choice but to bring them into being, provided of course that He found the Human Essence desirable enough to instantiate to begin with.

2. For more on the intrinsic nature of the eternal verities, please refer to G.W. Leibniz's seminal work on the problem of evil, entitled *Theodicy* (La Salle, IL: Open Court Publishing Company, 1985).

3. David Ray Griffin, in an as yet unpublished manuscript, "Time, Creativity, and the Origin of the universe: A Response to Stephen Hawking," p. 68.

4. David Ray Griffin, *God & Religion in the Postmodern World* (Albany: SUNY Press, 1989), pp. 69–82.

5. A deeper inspection of the strong voluntaristic approach, as we have seen, reveals it to be unintelligible for the following reason: the creation of any concrete end product *by definition* requires that its internal properties be consistent with its intrinsic identity. Thus, not even an omnipotent God could create a triangle with four sides, since the very designation of the identity of the end product simultaneously determines the particular properties it must possess in order to be itself. Since the strong voluntaristic approach claims that God could have created just any universe He pleased, regardless of what it was that He was trying to create, it turns out to be incoherent after all. The moderate voluntaristic approach thus turns out to be a far more intelligible alternative, insofar as it does *not* posit a God who determines the specific properties that each possible thing will possess if it is to be self-identical; it simply posits a God who determines what will and will not exist, and so *indirectly* determines the character of the universe by determining what it is that He wants to create.

CHAPTER 16

Supernatural Naturalism

I want to know how God created this world. I am not interested in this or
that phenomenon. I want to know His thoughts, the rest are details.

ALBERT EINSTEIN

The type of providential evolution we have been discussing in this book
is not new. It falls under the rubric of a larger philosophical position, known
as theistic evolutionism, which has existed in one form or another since the
days of ancient Greece. In this broad conceptual framework, God is seen
as utilizing the natural cause-and-effect processes inherent in the world to
accomplish His creative ends.

Theistic evolution has been attractive to many because it seems to possess far greater explanatory power than either non-theistic evolutionism or
non-evolutionary creationism. For by employing the scientist's natural
cause-and-effect processes within a larger theistic framework, the theistic
evolutionist is able to provide a satisfactory account of both the directedness
and the miraculousness of evolution, while still remaining within the naturalistic realm of the physical scientist. Theistic evolution thus offers the best
of both theoretical worlds.

Indeed, at the turn of the century, theistic evolution was actually a dominant force in both the scientific and religious communities. It gradually lost
influence, however, not because its major presuppositions were found to be
at odds with the findings of modern science, but rather because its underlying belief system was directly contradicted by the philosophical credo of
the modern worldview.[1]

That is to say, given the development of the modern scientific worldview,
which includes an affirmation of the philosophical ideals of predictive determinism, reductionism, and scientism, the notion of theistic evolution came
to be understood as a contradiction in terms, largely because these conceptual ideals were seen as being incompatible with any type of Divine influence
in the evolutionary process.[2]

For instance, the modern scientist likes to believe in a physical reality
that is, at least in principle, entirely predictable, and hence deterministic.
In order for this scientific ideal to be realized, though, a completely passive
material realm must be posited in which no "caprice" or spontaneity can be
allowed. A Divine Creator cannot be allowed for the same reason: because

it would introduce an element of unpredictability into the entire realm of nature, and this would seem to take away from the very foundation of science itself.[3]

The modern scientist also likes to believe in the ideal of complete reductionism, in which all things in principle can be explained in terms of their component parts alone. Such a view necessarily espouses only "upward causation," from the parts to the whole. The "downward causation" found in holistic and organismic philosophies, in which the causal influence runs from the whole to the component parts, is thus largely denied, because its affirmation would seem to imply the existence of a larger Intelligence that is itself perceived as being antithetical to the entire scientific pursuit.[4]

Finally, the modern scientist's affirmation of scientism—which is the belief that there are no genuine explanations apart from objective scientific ones—also works to oppose the acknowledgment of a Divine Creator, even if He is understood to work exclusively through the naturalistic process of cosmic evolution. It is in this fashion that the underlying suppositions of the modern world view virtually guarantee a state of animosity between theism and modern science.

However, it isn't logically necessary for the relationship between God and evolution to be mutually contradictory. To the contrary, it is possible to conceive of the Divine Creative Influence as acting in a purely naturalistic, cause-and-effect manner.[5] Such a naturalistic God is not disconfirmed by the existence of a temporally-based evolutionary process; He is supported by it. It is this type of naturalistic Creator that makes theistic evolution a viable theoretical alternative in the scientific attempt to account for the evolution of life.

16.1 Theistic Naturalism vs. Supernatural Naturalism

Within the broad category of theistic evolutionism, there are two theoretical subdivisions that correspond to a fundamental distinction between two radically different conceptualizations of the Divine Power. In the first conceptualization, known simply as *theistic* or *process naturalism*, God does not have supernatural power over the evolutionary process. He doesn't even have ultimate control over what does and does not exist, because He didn't create the world *ex nihilo* to begin with. He simply orchestrated the design of the present universe out of a pre-existing realm of finite actualities, which in and of themselves are thought to necessarily possess a certain amount of creative self-determination. On this view, God created the world using a temporal process of evolution because He couldn't possibly have done otherwise. This is the controversial position held by the process-oriented followers of Alfred North Whitehead and Charles Hartshorne. It is also the position espoused by David Ray Griffin in his series of books on Constructive Postmodern Thought.[6]

The second conceptualization of the Divine Power, known as *Supernatural Naturalism*, stands in stark contrast to the theistic naturalism of the process philosopher. On this view, God created the world using a temporal process of evolution, not because He had to, but because He voluntarily *chose* to do so, in order to be consistent with the Higher Purpose He originally set for Himself when He freely elected to create the world. This is the position held by the Deistic Evolutionist, who believes that it is the necessary nature of humanity, and not a pre-existing set of metaphysical limitations *per se*, which determined the type of universe that God created.

This is an eminently reasonable way to look at the phenomenon of creation, for it is a commonly observed fact that the end product of any creative endeavor necessarily determines *what* is actually created and *how* it is produced. In the assembly of an automobile, for instance, it is necessarily the case that the end product will possess several wheels, at least two doors, and an engine. It is also the case that a predictable sequence of engineering steps will be utilized to produce the end product, including the production of blueprints, the assembly of the engine, the molding of the body, and so forth. In the same way, the Deistic Evolutionist holds that God's primordial decision to create human beings inevitably established a firmly demarcated upper and lower bound on both *what* was to be created in the universe and *how* it would be produced.

It is precisely here at God's voluntary decision to create a certain type of world in a particular way that a major point of disagreement exists between the process position and the Supernatural Naturalism of the Deistic Evolutionist. The process thinker believes that a supernatural God, who unilaterally chooses to create a certain type of world, inherently retains the power at all times to retract or violate that which He has voluntarily created. The process theist wants to argue this position because he believes that any type of freedom that is arbitrarily (or voluntarily) given to the creatures by an omnipotent Being can be arbitrarily removed at any subsequent point. To the extent that this assertion is correct, it would seem to compel a good God to temporarily retract free will from His creatures from time to time in order to prevent certain evil events from occurring. Since these strategic retractions do not seem to have taken place (as the horrific evils of Hiroshima, Auschwitz, and Bosnia well illustrate), the process thinker concludes that God must not be a supernatural and omnipotent Being after all.

The Deistic Evolutionist believes this to be a faulty conclusion because he believes that its underlying premise is equally mistaken. It does *not* necessarily follow that whatever is arbitrarily given by an omnipotent Being can be arbitrarily removed at any subsequent point. To illustrate, let us suppose that an omnipotent God has voluntarily chosen to instantiate a series of essences with certain essential properties in the world. It is clear that once He has acted upon this desire, He is no longer free at any subsequent point to retract any of these essential properties from His creation; that is, unless He also desires to retract those essences that are partially comprised by them. Essences cannot be separated from their implicit properties by their very nature, because the lack of even a single essential property would destroy the integrity, and hence the identity, of any given essence *by definition.* This is why a supernatural God cannot arbitrarily remove the property of free will from His creatures from time to time in order to prevent certain evil events from occurring: because free will appears to be one of the essential defining properties of the Human Essence; hence, it cannot be temporarily removed without causing irreparable harm to the instantiated Form.[7]

Now, if it is true that a supernatural God can indeed be restricted by that which He has voluntarily chosen to create, one of the process philosopher's chief arguments against Supernatural Naturalism is automatically invalidated. The process thinker, as we have seen, believes that if the Deity were truly omnipotent, He would strategically use this power to prevent the occurrence of certain evil events in the world, by temporarily suspending the freedom that He has voluntarily given to His creatures. But if the intrinsic definition of these creatures explicitly *forbids* this type of suspension, or if the greatest possible good for the greatest number of people necessarily excludes it, then it follows that God's failure to intervene in the world in order to prevent certain evil events from occurring does *not* necessarily count against His goodness or all-power.

A similar argument can be used to reject the process thinker's use of evil as evidence against a supernatural God. For as long as the unique combination of properties comprising the Human Essence necessarily entails a certain amount of evil in the world, it follows that humans cannot exist *by definition* without a certain amount of evil also existing, even if a supernatural God is responsible creating it all. On this essentialist view, God's possible supernaturalness turns out to be superfluous to the present existence of evil in the world.

16.2 The More Plausible View

To the extent that the Divine Choice to create a particular object necessarily entails the choice of a certain constellation of metaphysical properties that are implicit in the definition of the object itself, the position held by the Deistic Evolutionist would seem to be more plausible overall than that held by the process theist. For not only does Deistic Evolutionism preserve the traditional view of God held by the majority of theologians throughout recent history, it does so by showing how the specific properties of the natural world spoken of by the process theist are *necessarily entailed* by God's election to instantiate the Human Essence.

For the Deistic Evolutionist, then, God could not have created a world of bona fide human beings without also giving the world the same types of properties that are described in process circles. And since there is no empirical way to tell the difference between an eternally existing material realm that necessarily possesses these properties, and a fully contingent world created *ex nihilo* by God to possess these same properties for a Higher Purpose, we must in the end rely on the view that seems more plausible overall, given the current evidence at hand. Since all of the properties displayed by our world can be shown to be necessarily entailed by God's free election to create human souls, and since it is vitally important to protect the Divine Freedom and Power from any theoretical diminution if at all possible (because this is the view of the Godhead that has traditionally been understood as being most consistent with the underlying definition of the word "God"), the Deistic Evolutionist believes his own moderate voluntaristic approach to be the more plausible view overall.

16.3 William Paley and the Deistic Evolutionist's Position

Although the Deistic Evolutionist's position has much in common with the arguments for Design contained in William Paley's *Natural Theology*, one sharp distinction should be noted. Whereas Paley saw the existence of naturally-occurring complexity as being evidence for Divine Intervention into an otherwise mundane realm of natural processes, the Deistic Evolutionist doesn't necessarily see this intervention as occurring at any specific point in time since the original creation. Rather, he sees it as occurring primarily at the very *beginning* of the creation. In support of this notion, he points out that God could very well have programmed the entire history of cosmic evolution, including the rise of earthly life, into the very first sparks of the Big Bang, so that once the initial conflagration occurred, the subsequent process of cosmic development could have taken place entirely on its own, utilizing only the intrinsic self-organizing properties of atoms and molecules, which would have been specifically designed for this purpose.[8] As far as the Deistic Evolutionist is concerned, then, God need not have interjected a single efficient cause into the universe at any point in time since the Big Bang, since He *could* have set up the entire cosmos in such a way that all the desired end products could have arisen naturally within it.

Thus, the existence of a self-driven, self-contained cosmos doesn't necessarily preclude the possibility that God could nevertheless be causing certain events within the physical system itself by purely natural means. Given God's presumed omniscience and omnipotence, it is possible to imagine a deliberate manipulation of the various forces that went into the Big Bang, so that any number of specific events in the distant future, including earthquakes, hurricanes, and famines, could have been deliberately caused by God through an entirely "natural" cause-and-effect means.[9]

This possibility is particularly attractive, because it allows us to reconcile the obvious cause-and-effect character of the universe with God's presumed freedom to cause certain events within it. The point is that we don't have to give up our scientific belief in a naturalistic, self-driven universe in order to believe that God can cause certain specific events within it.

It is important to note at this point that the Deistic Evolutionist's emphasis on natural causation within the larger universal order doesn't necessarily conflict with the traditional Christian belief of *Divine Intervention* as the ultimate cause of all that exists. The Deistic Evolutionist simply believes that most of this intervention occurred at the *very beginning* of the present cosmic expansion, whereas the traditional theist believes that the history of life has been replete with a large number of different interventions.

There are thus two general areas where the bulk of specific interventions could have occurred. The first is at the very beginning of the present cosmic epoch, while the second spreads out these interventions throughout the entire history of the universe. In the first possibility, God would have acted to bring about a physical universe that was so self-sufficient (in terms of the efficient causes within it) that it would have been able to evolve intelligent life entirely "on its own." Indeed, it would seem that this deistic view is actually more worthy of the Supreme Being than the standard theistic view, since a creation that is so advanced that it can build itself is intrinsically more impressive than a creation that must be assembled piecemeal at various steps along the way.

The choice thus isn't between the use or non-use of natural processes *per se* to bring about physical complexity in the universe, but rather between a realm of *Divinely-contrived* natural processes, on the one hand, and a realm of natural processes that could supposedly exist in the absence of God, on the other. It is precisely here that the standard Design Argument for the existence of God leads directly into the Cosmological Argument, because there is no good reason for supposing that we would even *have* a realm of natural processes in the absence of a Supreme Being.

This is where the marvelous complexity of the natural realm begins to figure prominently in the Deistic Evolutionist's overall argument. For by telling us in no uncertain terms how efficient and impressive the natural processes of the universe are in creating things like the human brain and the DNA molecule, this complexity tells us (albeit indirectly) that in all likelihood, a Divine Intelligence probably *was* responsible for contriving the whole affair.

Before we move on, it should be pointed out that the particular brand of deism espoused by the Deistic Evolutionist is not absolute, because it does not strictly forbid Divine Intervention within the present universal scheme. It merely requires that this intervention be absolutely necessary for effecting the greatest possible good for the greatest number of people (which leaves open the possibility for a specific Divine Incarnation). Furthermore, even the most heroic forms of deism nevertheless require a deeper metaphysical *foundation* for the day-to-day functioning of the universe, and this is where the continuous creative activity of God comes into play. For it would appear as though specific Divine Input is required *at each moment* of cosmic history in order to keep the entire universe in proper working order. This is a radical conclusion that is based, not just on the presuppositions of traditional theology, but also on the most recent findings of modern quantum physics.

We are distinguishing here between two different types of Divine Activity in the world: direct *intervention* in the form of Divinely-generated efficient causes, and indirect causal *support* for the entire physical realm, through the providing of an appropriate metaphysical foundation for its continued existence (perhaps via the continuous creation of an all-encompassing quantum field).

This being the case, it would seem to be a mistake to simply assume that the "scientific" realm of efficient causation could ever exist solely on its own, with no underlying metaphysical foundation, since the causal chain of naturalistic events *itself* requires sufficient metaphysical support in order to be functional. This is where the Deistic Evolutionist invokes the need for God as the metaphysical "ground" of all being. On this view, God supports the existence and functionality of the entire natural realm, even though He may or may not have interjected any specific efficient causes into it after the Big Bang.

Support for this fundamental position can be found with the ancient Stoics, who believed that if God existed at all, He *had* to the Logos, or Logical Mediator, between cause and effect, who tied all efficient causes to their corresponding natural effects. This is directly analogous to the Deistic Evolutionist's view of God as the metaphysical ground of all being. Since no form of natural causation can apparently exist in the universe without an adequate metaphysical foundation for its existence, it follows that the Supreme Being may in fact be functioning in this capacity. The recent quantum idea of God as the "Ultimate Observer," who observes the entire universe into being, is strongly supportive of this conclusion. To the extent that this is true, the ancient Stoic philosophers would seem to have anticipated one of the most profound discoveries of modern quantum physics.[10]

Notes

1. David Ray Griffin, *God and Religion in the Postmodern World* (Albany: SUNY Press, 1989), p. 74–78.

2. Ibid., p. 74.

3. Ibid.

4. Ibid.

5. Ibid., pp. 80–81.

6. See David Griffin's *The Reenchantment of Science* (Albany: SUNY Press, 1988), and *God and Religion in the Postmodern World* (Albany: SUNY Press, 1989).

7. This would appear to be why we are able to limit the freedom of our fellow citizens without making them any less human, and yet why God may not be able to do the same: because we act in an outer way only, while God's actions extend to the innermost definitions of things. For instance, if you lock me up in a closet for an hour, you have effectively limited my outer freedom without rendering me any less human. While God could conceivably do the same, His actions would seem to penetrate much deeper, since He is the One who has initially given us our defining freedom in the first place. We, on the other hand, cannot by any stretch of the imagination take away another person's freedom at its innermost root. The most we can do is to externally limit its expression. This is why we can't destroy the humanity of others by outwardly limiting their freedom. God, by contrast, does indeed have the power to destroy our humanity by taking away our freedom, because He is capable of acting on the inner definitions of things. While it isn't necessary that He always act on this innermost level, God's very identity as Creator could conceivably blur the distinction between these two levels, so that any action on one level could end up having an effect on the other. This would make it difficult for God to outwardly limit our freedom without simultaneously compromising our inner defining property of free will. The one thing we can say for sure is that God cannot arbitrarily remove our inner property of free will without simultaneously destroying our humanity (that is, to the extent that free will is an essential property of the Human Definition). On the other hand, it may be possible for God to externally limit the expression of our freedom without taking away our inner defining property of free will.

8. God would still be needed in this deistic scheme to provide the universe with a metaphysical foundation for its moment-to-moment existence.

9. Of course, this isn't to say that God ever directly caused any specific natural disaster in this manner. It is merely to say that God is theoretically *capable* of causing specific natural events in the universe without directly violating the law of cause and effect.

10. See Barrow and Tipler's *Anthropic Cosmological Principle*, pp. 440–444.

CHAPTER 17

Conclusion

Science and religion are very much alike. Both are imaginative and creative aspects of the human mind. The appearance of conflict is a result of ignorance. We come to exist through a divine act. That divine guidance is a theme throughout our life; at our death the brain goes, but that divine guidance and love continues. Each of us is a unique, conscious being, a divine creation. It is the religious view. *It is the only view consistent with all the evidence* (italics mine).[1]

SIR JOHN ECCLES
NOBEL LAUREATE

17.1 The Downfall of Darwinism

Throughout this book we have seen how the various tenets of non-theistic evolutionism are directly contradicted by a large body of scientific evidence. This evidence is so convincing that "it is astonishing to realize that the theory is still faithfully adhered to and vigorously defended within many sectors of the scientific establishment."[2]

In response to this vast body of conflicting evidence, many within the traditional evolutionary community are gradually coming to their senses. World-renowned paleoicthyologist Colin Patterson, for example, author of the book *Evolution* and senior paleontologist of the British Natural History Museum, has recently gone through a complete change of heart concerning the validity of non-theistic evolutionism. In 1981 he explained his heroic change of position to his colleagues at the American Museum of Natural History:

Last year I had a sudden realization. For over twenty years I had thought I was working on evolution in some way. One morning I woke up and something had happened in the night; and it struck me that I had been working on this stuff for twenty years and there was not one thing I knew about it. That's quite a shock, to learn that one can be so misled so long . . . So for the last few weeks I've tried putting a simple question to various people . . . Can you tell me anything you know about evolution, any one thing, any one thing that is true? . . . All I got was silence.

The absence of answers seems to suggest that . . . evolution does not convey any knowledge, or, if so, I haven't yet heard it. . . . I think many people in this room would acknowledge that during the last few years, if you had thought about it at all, you have experienced a shift from evolution as knowledge to evolution as faith. I know that it's true of me and I think it is true of a good many of you here. . . . Evolution not only conveys no knowledge but seems somehow to convey antiknowledge.[3]

The above quote is all the more remarkable because it is coming from one of the pillars of modern evolutionary thought. One can scarcely imagine the impact he must have had on his unsuspecting colleagues as he tried to get them to realize how wrong they've actually been over the years.

17.2 The Role of Bias in Modern Evolutionary Interpretations

It is no accident that the majority of evolutionists working today seem to be either atheistic or agnostic in their fundamental orientation towards a possible Creator. The very nature of science itself seems to exert a strong selective effect on the type of people who ultimately decide to become scientists. While it may be true that the modern scientific movement was originally founded upon a strong theistic foundation, many modern-day scientists have nevertheless lost touch with the religious roots of their profession, and a significant proportion of these individuals can even be described as being openly anti-theistic.

Indeed, many atheists seem to be drawn to scientific careers precisely *because* of the non-theistic nature of the hard sciences. There is currently the widespread perception amongst many learned individuals that our modern scientific understanding has somehow done away with the need for an Intelligent Designer. Much of the reason for this belief can be traced to a fundamental inability to see how God could have used natural cause-and-effect processes to create and maintain the present universal order. The popular consensus seems to be that if God exists at all, He must be a "miraculous" type of Deity who does everything by supernatural Fiat, because this is the primary way God has been portrayed in the popular culture. So, when people learn that the world works exclusively by natural cause-and-effect processes, they conclude that a supernatural Creator must not exist. Training in the hard sciences only helps to buttress this overall perception, because our modern scientific texts completely ignore the possibility of Intelligent Design; instead, they choose to focus exclusively on the enormous complexities that are inherent in the scientific realm, and this only deepens the perception that there can be no such thing as a supernatural Creator.

The general feeling behind this train of thought seems to be that if one can understand how the world works in the apparent absence of God, then one has somehow dispensed with the need for a Creator altogether. Many non-theistic scientists subscribe to this way of thinking because it supports their overall world view. They want to believe that if they can figure out how nature works in strict mechanistic detail, then they will also be rewarded with information about why it exists, where it came from, and what its overall purpose happens to be. Furthermore, if a Divine Influence isn't found to be directly needed in order to explain the workings of the natural world, then it is typically concluded that such an Influence probably never existed to begin with.

The Principle of Objectivity is often correctly cited as a further justification for God's exclusion from "hard-core" experimental science. Since God obviously cannot play a direct role in any type of experimental procedure, the Principle of Objectivity requires that God be totally left out of this particular mode of scientific inquiry. It is important to understand, however, that this type of exclusion is only appropriate within the immediate confines of the laboratory. Once the scientist steps out of this self-imposed boundary and begins speculating on the origin and meaning of life, it is clear that the Principle of Objectivity no longer applies. This is why it cannot be used as a legitimate scientific justification for atheism: because the very process of posing this type of assertion automatically takes one outside of the epistemological boundary in which the Principle of Objectivity applies.

The preponderance of atheism within the scientific community can thus be traced to two important contributing factors: the inherently non-theistic nature of the scientific process itself (which is largely derived from the Principle of Objectivity), and the high proportion of atheists that seem to be naturally drawn to the scientific profession. As it turns out, it is precisely this atheistic majority that seems to have played a significant role in the development of non-theistic evolutionary theory over the years. Being atheistically-inclinded from the start, many of these evolutionary scientists have brought a strong anti-theistic bias to the study of evolution, and it is precisely this anti-theistic bias that seems to have led to a fundamental misinterpretation of the existing scientific evidence.

It is a well-known fact that accuracy in any form of interpretation is much more difficult for a strongly biased observer than for an unbiased one. The reason for this, of course, is that people who are biased have a tendency to misinterpret the known facts in favor of their bias. Indeed, insofar as the notion of Intelligent Design is in fact correct, this would appear to be precisely what has happened in the orthodox evolutionary community: atheistic scientists, who clearly have a tendency to be biased against the notion of a Divine Creator, have inadvertently allowed their anti-theistic feelings to skew their interpretation of the existing scientific evidence in favor of a non-theistic world view. To the extent that this assertion is true, it would explain why so many of their conclusions have not held up under objective scrutiny: because they are trying to explain theistically-oriented evidence in a non-theistic manner.

Many scientists use the Principle of Objectivity to openly support the validity of their anti-theistic bias. They correctly point out that God *must* be left out of physical science if their pursuit of objective knowledge is to remain scientific. A problem arises, though, when this deliberate exclusion of theistic ideas is carried over into the realm of scientific theorizing, because the Principle of Objectivity only applies to hard-core experimental science, and *not* to scientific conjecture *per se*.

There are thus two general areas of thought in the field of evolutionary biology: a strictly experimental area, which studies objectively measurably quantities in the laboratory, and a metaphysical area of fact interpretation, which seeks to provide a reasonable understanding of the known facts. The Principle of Objectivity clearly applies to the first area *only*, and not to the second. But even though this may be true, religious and philosophical matters pertaining to the evolutionary process can nevertheless be discussed in a logical and sensible fashion as a philosophical extension of the scientific method.

In other words, the quest for objectivity in the field of evolutionary biology necessitates that the issue of God be treated in two distinct ways: on the one hand, it dictates that religious matters should be totally excluded from the laboratory, while on the other hand, it requires that they nevertheless be *included* in the area of metaphysical fact interpretation.

With this in mind, it is easy to see how evolutionary scientists could have become confused over this issue. In their continual effort to be objective,[4] they have erred by leaving God out of *both* investigative arenas, when in fact they were justified in excluding Him from the experimental arena *only*. In order to be truly objective, then, evolutionary biologists need to do two things: 1) they need to distinguish between the experimental and metaphysical areas of their research, and 2) they need to exclude religious matters from the experimental area *only*. To the extent that they fail to do this, they run the risk of being severely mistaken in their overall metaphysical conclusions.

This leads us to consider what is perhaps the most serious problem of all that is associated with the use of an atheistic bias in evolutionary theorizing: it causes the theorist to literally wager *everything* on the non-existence of God. For by leading him to stubbornly avoid all common-sense interpretations of the known facts whenever they happen to point in a theistic direction, this bias drives the theorist to inadvertently set himself up for an across-the-board failure if God turns out to actually exist in the end.

It is clear that the existence of such an institutional bias in the name of science deeply jeopardizes the evolutionary establishment's ability to perform balanced appraisals of the known facts. As a result, there is a potential for serious error in the field of evolutionary biology that is unrivaled anywhere else in the entire range of scientific analysis.

Much of the reason for this interpretive vulnerability can be traced to the fact that, as Karl Popper and others have pointed out, the very field of evolutionary biology is *itself* unscientific, since its assertions are largely untestable and therefore unfalsifiable. It follows, then, that when this type of "pseudoscience" is coupled with a strong atheistic institutional bias, a significant chance for serious interpretive error is bound to result.

It is ironic, but in the very act of attempting to be objective via the Principle of Objectivity, non-theistic evolutionists have inadvertently become non-objective, due to the serious anti-theistic bias that is invariably produced. One simply cannot be objective if one is heavily committed to avoiding certain types of conclusions.[5]

Nevertheless, a significant proportion of modern-day evolutionists have resolutely committed themselves to a non-theistic way of looking at the world. As a direct consequence of this theoretical self-limitation, they aren't free to draw any type of conclusion they want from the existing evidence; they are instead confined primarily to conclusions that end up supporting the traditional evolutionary picture in one way or another.

This is a very difficult limitation to be repeatedly subjected to, because as we have seen, orthodox evolutionary theory is frequently contradicted by the objective scientific data. Indeed, this divergence between theory and observed fact in modern evolutionary biology can be so pronounced that traditional theorists are often forced to adopt severe contortionist measures in order to render their theories compatible with the evidence. But no matter how many theoretical heroics are utilized to sanitize the objective data, the theistic alternative almost always turns out to be simpler and more reasonable in the end.

In saying this, however, I am not suggesting that we return to an outdated "God-of-the-gaps" explanation to account for the many marvels of the evolutionary process, because there is little doubt that a "natural" explanation will be found for all of them. I am therefore not disputing the truth or validity of any of the major facts of evolution. I am merely arguing that the process of evolution *itself* is unintelligible in the absence of a larger Creator.

17.3   The Anti-Empirical Effect of Neo-Darwinian Dogma

As we have seen, evolutionary scientists are so confident about the validity of their theory that they have elevated it to the level of self-evident fact, the so-called "fact of evolution." Such a presumption, however, clearly mitigates against any sort of objectivity in the nature of their reasoning, for as long as one accepts something as a fact, it no longer becomes necessary to demonstrate its overall validity. Indeed, this recognition of the "fact of evolution" in the scientific community is so intense that objections to it are routinely met with outright hostility. This hostility, as Michael Denton points out:

> . . . is readily understandable in terms of the sociology of knowledge because, as the biological community considers Darwinian theory to be established beyond doubt "like the earth goes round the sun," then dissent becomes by definition irrational and hence especially irritating if the dissenters claim to be presenting a rational critique. It is ironic to reflect that while Darwin once considered it heretical to question the immutability of species, nowadays it is heretical to question the idea of evolution.[6]

This confidence in the truth of the neo-Darwinian paradigm extends to the very core of its theoretical formulation, since the principles that comprise it are usually stated in a self-evident, tautological manner, as we have previously seen. In other words, evolutionary theorists are guilty of the fallacy of circular reasoning, since they have unknowingly posited the truth of their conclusions in their theoretical premises. This explains why they can be so confident about their theory's validity, as philosopher of science Paul Feyerabend has so aptly pointed out:

> [This] . . . semblance of absolute truth is nothing but the result of absolute conformism. For how can we possibly test, or improve upon, the truth of a theory if it is built in such a manner that any conceivable event can be described, and explained, in terms of its principles? The only way of investigating such all-embracing principles is to compare them with a different set of equally all-embracing principles—but this way has been excluded from the very beginning. The myth is therefore of no objective relevance, it continues to exist solely as the result of the effort of the community of believers and of their leaders, be these now priests or Nobel prize winners. Its "success" is entirely man made.[7]

Even the word "evolution" itself is fraught with all manner of confusion, because of the extreme lack of precision in its general usage.[8] As Philip Johnson has pointed out:

> Much confusion results from the fact that a single term—"evolution"—is used to designate processes that may have little or nothing in common. A shift in the relative numbers of dark and light moths in a population is called evolution, and so is the creative process that produced the cell, the multicellular organism, the eye, and the human mind. The semantic implication is that evolution is fundamentally a single process, and Darwinists enthusiastically exploit that implication as a substitute for scientific evidence. Even the separation of evolution into its "micro" and "macro" varieties—which Darwinists generally resist—implies that all the creative processes involved in life comprise a single, two-part phenomenon that

will be adequately understood when we discover a process that makes new species from existing ones. Possibly this is the case, but more probably it is not. The vocabulary of Darwinism inherently limits our comprehension of the difficulties by misleadingly covering them with the blanket term "evolution."[9]

The solution to this linguistic problem is twofold. First, we need to distinguish between the different possible meanings of the word "evolution" whenever we use it. We can't expect to think accurately about this immensely complicated subject if the terms we use are imprecise and muddled. Second, we need to refrain from using the term "evolution" (especially in its non-theistic, accidental sense) in a completely factual manner, because once again, it is the factual nature of non-theistic evolutionism that we are trying to prove in the first place. The coherence and accuracy of our conclusions regarding the history of life depend on how well we can live up to these twin linguistic goals.

Unfortunately, orthodox neo-Darwinian theorists have failed to do this. In the words of Philip Johnson, they have "taken Darwinian descent as a deductive certainty and [have] . . . sought to flesh it out in detail rather than to test it."[10] In so doing, they have taken present-day phylogentic relationships and have prematurely concluded that they *must* indicate an accidental process of ancestral descent, because their theory told them that these ancestors *had* to be there.[11]

To help remedy this persistent problem, Johnson has delivered a potent challenge to the orthodox evolutionary establishment. He has simply requested that they evaluate the existing scientific evidence "independently of any assumptions about the truth of the theory being tested."[12] Johnson concludes that such a request is bound to make evolutionists uncomfortable, because they have been trained, not to empirically demonstrate the validity of their theory, but to take its truth for granted.

17.4 Projection

When the nature of modern scientific reasoning is closely examined, a subtle philosophical bias can be observed to underly virtually all scientific explanations. This bias has to do with the belief that naturalistic explanations alone are capable of accounting for all known physical phenomena, since supernatural explanations (albeit through indirect, secondary means) simply aren't possible. Since supernatural explanations aren't possible, the non-theistic scientist can only conclude that naturalistic forces alone were responsible for "creating" the miracle we call life.

It is this hidden assumption that leads to the arrogant confidence of the non-theistic evolutionist when it comes to the "fact" of evolution. Since human beings and other forms of life obviously exist, the non-theistic evolutionist automatically concludes that a sufficient explanation for their existence must itself exist. However, since the entire field of scientific inquiry is based on an implicit rejection of *all* forms of supernaturalism (including those that operate via secondary causes), it seems to follow that some form of Darwinian naturalism *must* have been responsible for generating the biosphere.

This sort of non-theistic reasoning is based on an extremely subtle substitution into the Principle of Sufficient Reason, which itself states that everything that exists must have a sufficient reason for its existence. However, because the philosophical basis of modern science precludes the existence of all forms of supernatural explanation, the non-theistic scientist finds it necessary to add a naturalistic proviso to the Principle of Sufficient Reason, so that its updated form states that everything that exists must have a sufficient *naturalistic* reason for its existence. The net result of this philosophical sleight of hand is that all scientific explanations are limited to the naturalistic realm only.[13] Indeed, this limitation is so absolute that it even excludes the indirect action of a supernatural Creator, who would have employed secondary naturalistic means in His creation of the world. Ironically, this was the sort of deistic Creator envisioned by Darwin, but Darwin's modern-day followers have almost completely ignored this fact. Instead, they have opted to convert their deceased leader into an unabashed atheist, so that they can justify their institutional atheism.

It doesn't seem to matter to these individuals that the vast majority of naturalistic explanations are at odds with the existing scientific evidence, because extreme subservience to empiricism is *not* what science is all about. If it were, as Philip Johnson has pointed out, neo-Darwinism would have long ago been confined to microevolution, where its scientific, philosophical, and religious implications would have been unremarkable. To the contrary, the most important scientific priority is:

> . . . to maintain the naturalistic worldview and with it the prestige of "science" as the source of all important knowledge. Without Darwinism, scientific naturalism would have no creation story. A retreat on a matter of this importance would be catastrophic for the Darwinist establishment, and it would open the door to all sorts of false prophets and mountebanks (at least as naturalists see them) who would try to fill the gap.

> To prevent such a catastrophe, defenders of naturalism must enforce rules of procedure for science that preclude opposing points of view. With that accomplished, the next critical step is to treat "science" as equivalent to truth and non-science as equivalent to fantasy. The conclusions of science can then be misleadingly portrayed as refuting arguments that were in fact disqualified from consideration at the outset. As long as scientific natural-

ists make the rules, critics who demand positive evidence for Darwinism need not be taken seriously. They do not understand "how science works."[14]

The upshot of the foregoing discussion is that what often passes for "scientific truth" in evolutionary circles actually amounts to little more than an automatic projection of the scientific community's cumulative atheism onto the existing scientific evidence. It is for this reason that we can say that the atheistic ideas concerning life's origins that are being brandied about by evolutionary scientists tend to say more about the nature of the atheistic scientists *themselves* than it does about the true nature of life's origins *per se.* Even Gould has conceded the fact that scientific "truth" often turns out to be nothing more than "prejudice inspired by prevailing social and political beliefs."[15] In this case, the prevailing social belief is a profound scientific prejudice against the notion of Intelligent Design. According to the Deistic Evolutionist, it is precisely this atheistic prejudice that has caused evolutionary biologists to misinterpret the existing scientific evidence in such a way as to validate their *own* non-theistic beliefs.

We mustn't forget that the human mind is an incredibly powerful shaper of reality that tends to see only what it wants to see in the larger world of reality.[16] In order to make this sort of reality-twisting possible, the mind tends to *predetermine* what it wants to believe, so that it can then spontaneously pick and choose from among the existing facts *only* those qualities that are in support of the desired conclusion. This reality-twisting mentality is actually a familiar holdover from childhood, as young children characteristically tend to twist their perception of the existing facts so that they can see only what they want to see in their day-to-day lives. In this sense we can say that their understanding of the real world tends to be more fantasy-based than reality-based.

In contrast, true adulthood is based more on reality than fantasy. It is characterized by a ruthless commitment to reality regardless of cost, which is made possible by the routine subordination of one's own inner biases to the information that is supplied by the larger world. The truly mature individual thus doesn't see only what he wants to see in his day-to-day life; he sees what objective reality shows him, whether it conforms to his own inner biases or not.

This psychological principle is valid for all people, including evolutionary scientists. Indeed, insofar as the non-theistic evolutionist twists his interpretation of the existing facts in order to have them conform to his predetermined world view, he is guilty of a severe failure of adequate reality-testing.[17]

A similar problem with reality-testing exists in the paranoid schizophrenic, who sees a certain constellation of real-world facts and then misinterprets their overall meaning by misinterpreting their actual connection to one another. The purpose of this fundamental act of misinterpretation is to have the "truth" of reality fit the particular version of it he wants to believe. The non-theistic evolutionist does the same sort of thing, insofar as he projects his inner prejudices onto the data that is before him, so that the final end product can be manipulated in the "proper" direction.[18]

It is easy to see that the paranoid schizophrenic has engaged in self-serving act of reality-twisting, because it is next to impossible to argue him out of his irrational beliefs. The reason for this, of course, is that his beliefs are intimately tied into his own inner needs and prejudices, so they are actually functioning to keep his entire state of mind intact. But the same thing can be said for the reality-twisting evolutionist, insofar as he too cannot easily be argued out of his beliefs, due to their extreme personal significance for him.

In extreme cases, both the paranoid schizophrenic and the reality-twisting evolutionist totally close their minds off to the possibility that they may be wrong.[19] With the paranoid, this profound cognitive rigidity is to be expected, since he clearly has a mental problem. With the reality-twisting evolutionist, on the other hand, it is inexcusable.

Indeed, many learned individuals have come to the conclusion that the non-theistic evolutionist's world view is quite literally crazy. Consider, for instance, the words of Montreal psychiatrist Karl Stern, who believes that the modern evolutionary view of cosmogenesis "is crazy. And I do not at all mean crazy in the sense of a slangy invective but rather in the technical meaning of psychotic. Indeed such a view has much in common with certain aspects of schizophrenic thinking."[20] Stern's point is that when one separates one's self from the scientific dogma that is perpetrated in non-theistic evolutionary circles, the notion that our glorious world could have been formed by chance alone, in response to a blind and meaningless cosmic billiard game, is preposterous enough to be classified as a frank delusion.

In defense of the traditional evolutionary perspective, however, it should be pointed out that much of the reason for its presumed lack of interpretive accuracy can be traced to the intrinsic ambiguity that is associated with the scientific attempt to connect concrete effects in the natural world with their corresponding historical causes. Unfortunately, the dynamics of biological causation aren't so easy to pin down. The fact is, there is often no direct one-to-one correspondance at all between causes and effects in the natural realm. The same effect can often be produced by a number of different causes, so identifying the correct cause of any given effect typically requires a careful and unbiased perusal of *all* possibilities, and not just the ones that happen to fit into one's pre-established world view.

What is thus required in both the paranoid schizophrenic and the reality-twisting evolutionist alike is a deliberate abandonment of all preconceived notions and inner prejudices, so that a fresh and objective view of the available evidence can be obtained. Unfortunately, this is much easier said than done, since both the paranoid and the reality-twisting evolutionist's inner prejudices are deeply rooted in the subconscious part of their respective psyches. Thus, both typically have an unconscious ax to grind, whether they are aware of it or not.

In the paranoid, this unconscious agenda is usually tied to his own childhood, where a certain degree of pain and fear is typically found to have surrounded his relationship to one or both parents. These negative emotions are retained throughout adulthood as an unconscious series of repressions which, in the right circumstances, can subsequently be projected onto the real world in the form of profoundly irrational beliefs. When this unfortunate circumstance occurs, the feeling usually turns out be correct, but the thought isn't. The feeling is correct in these instances because it has been derived from an unconscious reservoir of pain that is actually felt by the individual. The thought, on the other hand, is not correct, because it is the result of an old feeling that is being projected onto present-day circumstances. It thus has absolutely no causal connection associated with it in the present.

To illustrate, consider the example of a young child whose mother is often tormented by a wild and unpredictable father. To a young and defenseless child, this type of insane behavior is both inexplicable and overwhelming in its emotional scope. Indeed, it is typically experienced as being *so* exquisitely painful that the resulting feelings are automatically pushed back into the unconscious mind, where they remain for a lifetime.

In fact, we can go so far as to say that, because of the intrinsic power of these repressions, they will inevitably have the effect of slanting her adult mind in their direction, insofar as they will end up coloring her day-to-day perceptions and feelings in some manner, usually mediated by some sort of vague emotional discomfort. However, since she won't be able to realize that her discomfort is originating in the past instead of the present, she will feel compelled to look for a sufficient reason in her present-day life for why she is feeling so bad. Curiously, the actual reason she chooses will typically have some sort of continuity with the past origin of her pain. For instance, if the primary source of her childhood suffering was her father, she might identify another significant male in her current life, such as her husband, as the central cause of her suffering.[21] However, it is also possible that she could choose a larger organization, such as the Republican or Communist Party, as the primary cause of her discomfort.

Once she chooses an appropriate present-day cause for her suffering, she will unconsciously proceed to project her unconscious emotional pain onto it. This in turn will cause her perception of reality to be skewed in the conceptual direction of her projection. What this means is that she will tend to interpret the meaning of her present-day life *in terms of* her past pain.

This is why she will end up being so convinced that her paranoid suspicions are true: because the underlying feelings that are fueling them *are* real; it is only her present-day *suspicions* that are grossly in error, since they are rooted in the present instead of the past, where they belong.

Interestingly enough, some strongly committed evolutionists appear to suffer from a similar type of projective problem, only in this case the repressed feeling seems to involve some form of aversive religious experience from childhood. To the extent that this is true, the emotional content of this repression would unconsciously be projected onto the evolutionist's present-day understanding of the scientific world, where it would subsequently cause him or her to misinterpret much of the "empirical" evidence in favor of an atheistic view of reality.

However, religiously-oriented repressions emanating from childhood aren't the only cause of present-day intellectual projection in the scientific realm. One need only have a strong non-theistic bias for *any* reason to be able to project in this manner.[22] For instance, many evolutionists sincerely believe that they cannot be "good" scientists if they allow themselves to believe in God. Therefore, in the interests of being scientific, they unconsciously proceed to interpret *everything* in their day-to-day lives from a non-theistic point of view.

We mustn't forget that we in the West have been weaned on the various doctrines of non-theistic evolutionism (including the related doctrines of humanism and materialism) for most of our lives. Not only have we been bombarded with these ideas by the mass media since we were young children, we have also been taught to accept them *as fact* in our school systems from the first grade onward. As a result, since we couldn't help but internalize many of these humanistic ideas while we growing up, and since one of the unspoken credos of our modern society is that science is gospel, it was a virtual certainty that we would grow up believing in the various tenets of non-theistic evolutionism. This in itself appears to be the largest source of bias in the non-theistic evolutionary community.

This educationally-instilled bias has further been exacerbated by the historical opposition between science and the Church. It is only natural to oppose religion when one learns that the Church once tortured and executed scientists out of its fear of scientific truth. Indeed, this historical fact tends to give one the irresistable impression that religious people are the bad guys, and that scientists are the good guys. This impression, in turn, is buttressed by the realization that it was the scientists who turned out to be right in the end, at least when it came to such strict scientific issues as the nature of gravity and the earth's physical location in the universe.

Given this historical and educational backdrop, it was inevitable that many of us would grow up being firm believers in the non-theistic theory of evolution. However, it is equally clear that this culturally-sanctioned process of indoctrination does not in itself constitute a justifiable reason for holding a given theory to be true. There is only one such justifiable reason in the realm of scientific discourse: the intrinsic persuasiveness of the physical evidence itself.

No one formulates a conceptual conclusion in an ideational vacuum. The very process of drawing conclusions is based upon a core conceptual foundation that one subsequently builds upon in sequential fashion. That is to say, the process of conclusion-making is based upon a progressive series of extrapolations from a core set of foundational assumptions. It is for this reason that one's conclusions can only be as accurate as the foundational assumptions upon which they are based. Thus, if one's foundational assumptions turn out to be mistaken, it is inevitable that the conclusions that are based on them will be mistaken as well. As a consequence, the accuracy of one's overall world view is almost entirely dependent upon the accuracy of one's foundational assumptions about life.

These foundational assumptions can themselves be grouped into three distinct philosophical categories: the atheistic orientation, the agnostic orientation, and the theistic orientation. Due to the all-inclusive nature of one's basic religious orientation, it follows that one's actual choice in this sphere will have a profound influence on virtually every aspect of one's world view, including the nature of the conceptual conclusions that one draws about life. This is why so much revolves around whether or not we believe in the existence of a Supreme Being: because it is *how* we choose to answer this question that determines the direction in which we will subsequently build our conceptual edifices. This being the case, one thing seems certain: if God actually exists, then the only orientation towards life that will turn out to be accurate in the end is the theistic one. On the other hand, if God doesn't exist, the converse will be true.

It follows, then, that if we want to be as accurate as possible in our intellectual conclusions about life, we first need to determine which religious orientation we want to assume. It is this initial choice that needs to be as objective and unbiased as possible, because it determines the direction in which virtually all our later conclusions will go. Hence, once we make this initial decision, it is inevitable that we will be subsequently "biased" or slanted in most of our conceptual formulations. However, as long as we choose the "right" religious orientation, being biased in this manner is no longer such a bad thing, since it means that we are leaning towards a fundamentally correct view of the world. On the other hand, if we choose the wrong orientation, being biased turns out to be very destructive indeed, since it means that we are leaning towards a fundamentally *incorrect* view of the world.

Of course, no one knows for *absolute* sure whether his world view is objectively correct. Therefore, the possibility always remains that any one individual could turn out to be wrong in the end. This is why we must perpetually strive to keep an open mind—so we can remain open to other possibilities in case we happen to be mistaken in our present-day beliefs.

However, even if we happen to possess a fundamentally correct view of the world, it is still possible for an unreasonable amount of bias to severely distort the accuracy of our conclusions. This is why we must always carefully weigh the evidence for any given conclusion in light of *all* the available facts, whether or not we are actually convinced of our interpretive accuracy. Since no one can be *completely* sure of his underlying position, we need to strive to be as fair and judicial as possible in *all* the conclusions we draw about life. This system of conceptual checks and balances can serve as a perpetual safeguard against the ever-present threat of ideational error in our scientific and philosophical theorizing.

Notes

1. Sir John Eccles, "Modern Biology and the Turn to Belief in God," *The Intellectuals Speak Out About God*, Roy Abraham Varghese, ed. (Chicago: Regnery Gateway, 1984), p. 50.
2. Jeremy Rifkin, *Algeny*, p. 155.
3. Ibid., p. 113.
4. Two senses of the word "objective" are being used in this discussion: a strong sense, which refers to a given object or process being physically measurable or quantifiable, and a weak sense, which refers to an idea being logically coherent and sensible.
5. While it may seem as though I am as biased *for* my position as my non-theistic counterparts are against it, I should hasten to point out that I am only very strongly *persuaded*, not biased. There is a significant difference between strong prejudicial bias, on the one hand, and reasonable enthusiastic support, on the other. In the former, one is heavily committed to a certain type of conclusion, regardless of the evidence at hand, while in the latter, one can more or less objectively evaluate the evidence and then come to an enthusiastic conclusion either for or against a given interpretation.
6. Michael Denton, *Evolution: A Theory in Crisis*, p. 76.
7. Ibid., pp. 76–77.
8. The word "creationist" is also routinely misused and misunderstood. In the popular mind, a creationist is someone who believes that God created the world in six 24-hour days and that the world is not more than 10,000 years old. While this is true in many instances, in many other instances it is not. Broadly speaking, a creationist can be defined as a person who believes that the universe was designed and built for a purpose by an Intelligent Creator. This definition clearly allows for a wide range of different creative mechanisms, ranging from an instantaneous creation by Divine Fiat to a gradual, evolutionary one. It is perfectly appropriate, then, to the use the term "creationist" to describe the Deistic Evolutionist, since he does in fact believe that the universe was designed and built for a purpose by a supernatural Being.
9. Philip Johnson, *Darwin on Trial*, pp. 69–70.
10. Ibid., pp. 73–74.

11. The true question at issue here isn't concerned with the possible existence of ancestral lines of descent *per se*; it is concerned instead with the possible accidental nature of the descent process itself. So, even if the neo-Darwinian idea of ancestral descent with modification turns out to be true, it doesn't necessarily follow that this process of descent was accidental in nature. It could just as easily have been purposeful (i.e., Divinely-intended) from the start, and indeed, the evidence seems to point decisively in this direction.

12. Ibid., p. 73.

13. Ironically, the Principle of Sufficient Reason was conceived by one of the greatest scientific theists of all time, the German philosopher and mathematician Gottfried Leibniz.

14. Philip E. Johnson, *Darwin on Trial*, p 116.

15. Stephen Jay Gould, *Ever Since Darwin*, p. 44.

16. This characteristic does not appear to be an intrinsic feature of the human mind *per se*; rather, it appears to be more a consequence of idiosyncratic emotional and psychological factors which are themselves ultimately a function of our own lack of character maturity.

17. I am not arguing that all evolutionists are chronic reality-twisters. I am only referring here to those that are.

18. I'm not saying that the non-theistic evolutionist is crazy, simply because of the content of his metaphysical beliefs. I'm only saying that there seems to be certain parallels between the dynamics of paranoid thinking, on the one hand, and the presumed tendency of some evolutionists to misinterpret the existing evidence, on the other.

19. Although I have clearly been convinced by the quality of the existing evidence that the world has been intelligently designed, I am still open to other possibilities. I have no stake in being "pig-headed" for the sake of protecting my own beliefs. I am only interested in the truth, whatever it happens to be. Thus, if my position turns out to be mistaken, I want to be the first to know it, so I can move on to a more realistic position.

20. Taken from Rifkin's *Algeny*, p. 114.

21. This is probably the greatest single reason for all the marital discord and divorce in our society. When an individual begins projecting unresolved emotional conflicts from the past onto his or her partner, it is often only a matter of time until the relationship completely dissolves.

22. For the sake of argument, I am assuming the prior validity of theism in this discussion.

Bibliography

Angrist, Stanley W., and Loren G. Hepler. *Order and Chaos* (New York: Basic Books, Inc., 1967).

Aquinas, Thomas. "The Summa Theologica," in *Great Books of the Western World*, Vol. 19, R. M. Hutchins, ed. (Chicago: Encyclopaedia Britannica, 1952).

Argyll, Duke of. *The Reign of Law* (New York: Lovell, n.d.).

Ayer, Alfred Jules. *Language Truth and Logic* (Oxford: Oxford University Press, 1936).

Barbour, Ian. *Religion in an Age of Science* (San Francisco: Harper & Row, 1990).

Barrow, John D., and Frank J. Tipler. *The Anthropic Cosmological Principle* (Oxford: Oxford University Press, 1986).

Barrow, John D. *The World Within the World* (Oxford: Oxford University Press, 1990).

————. *Theories of Everything* (Oxford: Oxford University Press, 1991).

Bogart, James P. "Evolutionary Implications of Polyploidy in Amphibians and Reptiles," *Polyploidy*, Walter H. Lewis, ed. (New York: Plenum Press, 1980).

Bohm, David. "Postmodern Science and a Postmodern World," *The Reenchantment of Science*, David Ray Griffin, ed., (Albany: State University of New York Press, 1988).

————. 'Some Remarks on the Notion of Order,' in C.H. Waddington, ed. *Towards a Theoretical Biology* (Edinburgh University Press, 1969).

————. *Wholeness and the Implicate Order* (London: Routledge & Kegan Paul, 1980).

Bondi, Herman. *Cosmology* (Cambridge: Cambridge University Press, 1960).

Boslough, John. *Stephen Hawking's Universe*, (New York: William Morrow, 1985).

Bowler, Peter J. *Evolution: The History of an Idea* (Los Angeles: The University of California Press, 1989).

————. *The Eclipse of Darwinism* (Baltimore: The John Hopkins University Press, 1983).

Brandon, Robert N. "Adaptation Explanations: Are Adaptations for the Good of Replicators or Interactors?" *Evolution at a Crossroads*, David J. Depew and Bruce H. Weber, eds. (Cambridge: The MIT Press, 1985).

Brooks, Daniel R., and E.O. Wiley. *Evolution as Entropy* (Chicago: University of Chicago Press, 1986).

Brown, Michael H. *The Search for Eve* (San Francisco: Harper & Row, 1990.

Burnet, Thomas. *Sacred Theory of the Earth* (1691), London: reprinted by Centaur Press, 1965.

Buttice G., Kaytes P., D'Armiento J., Vogeli G., and Kurkinen M. "Evolution of Collagen IV Genes from a 54-Base Pair Exon: A Role for Introns in Gene Evolution," *Journal of Molecular Evolution* (1990) 30.

Caldwell, Mark. "How Does a Single Cell Become a Whole Body?" *Discover*, Vol. 13, No. 11, November, 1992.

Campbell, John H. "An Organizational Interpretation of Evolution," *Evolution at a Crossroads*, David J. Depew and Bruce H. Weber, eds. (Cambridge: The MIT Press, 1985).

Capra, Fritjof, and David Steindl-Rast. *Belonging to the Universe* (San Francisco: HarperSanFrancisco, 1991).

Carter, Brandon. "Large Number Coincidences and the Anthropic Principle in Cosmology," *Confrontation of Cosmological Theories With Observation*, M.S. Longair, ed. (Dordrecht: Reidel, 1974).

Casti, John L. *Paradox Lost* (New York: William Morrow and Company, 1989).

Caullery, Maurice. *Genetics and Heredity* (New York: Walker and Co., 1964).

Chambers, Robert. *Vestiges of the Natural History of the Creation* (London: Churchill, 1844).

Christian, James L. *Philosophy: An Introduction to the Art of Wondering* (New York: Holt, Rineheart, and Winston, 1977).

Cicero. *The Nature of the Gods*, translated by H.C.P. McGregor (London: Penguin, 1972).

Clark, Ronald W. *The Survival of Charles Darwin: A Biography of a Man and an Idea* (New York: Random House, 1984).

Cobb, John B. *Living Options in Protestant Theology* (Philadelphia: The Westminster Press, 1962).

Coleman, William. *Georges Cuvier: Zoologist* (Cambridge: Harvard University Press, 1964)

Collins, C.B., and S.W. Hawking. *Astrophys. J.* 180, 317 (1973).

Copernicus, Nicholas. *On the Revolution of the Heavenly Spheres*, transl. C.G. Wallis, ed. R.M. Hutchins (Encyclopedia Britannica, London, 1952), Book 1, Ch. 6.

Corey, M.A. *God and the New Cosmology: The Anthropic Design Argument* (Lanham, MD: Rowman and Littlefield, 1993).

Corner, E. "Evolution," *Contemporary Biological Thought*, McLeod and Colby, eds., 1961.

Crawford, Michael, and David Marsh. *The Driving Force* (London: Heinemann, 1989).

Crick, Francis. *Life Itself: Its Origin and Nature* (New York: Simon & Schuster, 1981).

Cuvier, Georges. *Revolutions of the Surface of the Globe* (London: Whittaker, Treacher and Arnot, 1829).

Darwin, Charles. *The Origin of Species* (New York: P.F. Collier & Son Co., 1909).

Darwin, Erasmus. *Zoonomia*, 2 vol. (London, 1974).

Darwin, F. *The Life and Letters of Charles Darwin* (London: John Murray, 1888).

Davies, Paul. *God and the New Physics* (New York: Simon & Schuster, 1983).

———. *Other Worlds* (New York: Simon and Schuster, 1980).

———. *Superforce* (New York: Simon and Schuster, 1984).

———. *The Accidental Universe* (New York: Cambridge University Press, 1982).

———. *The Cosmic Blueprint* (New York: Simon & Schuster, 1989).

———. *The Mind of God* (New York: Simon & Schuster, 1992).

Dawkins, Richard. *The Blind Watchmaker* (New York: W.W. Norton, 1987).

———. *The Selfish Gene* (Oxford: Oxford University Press, 1989).

De Beer, Gavin. *Charles Darwin* (Garden City, NY: Doubleday & Company, Inc., 1909).

———. *Homology: An Unresolved Problem* (London: Oxford University Press, 1971).

DeLey, J. *Evol. Biol.* 2, 103, 1968.

Denton, Michael. *Evolution: A Theory in Crisis* (Bethesda, MD: Adler & Adler, 1986).

Depew, David J., and Bruce H. Weber, eds. *Evolution at a Crossroads* (Cambridge: The MIT Press, 1985).

Dewar, D. *More Difficulties of the Evolution Theory* (London: Thynne and Co., 1938).

Dover, G.A. "Molecular Drive in Multigene Families: How Biological Novelties Arise, Spread and Are Assimilated," *Trends in Genetics*, 2, (6), 1986.

Dyke, C. "Complexity and Closure," *Evolution at a Crossroads*, David J. Depew and Bruce H. Weber, eds. (Cambridge: The MIT Press, 1985).

du Nouy, Lecomte. *Human Destiny* (New York: Longmans, Green and Co., 1947).

Dyson, Freeman. "Honoring Dirac," *Science*, Vol. 185, September 27, 1974.

Eccles, Sir John. "Modern Biology and the Turn to Belief in God," *The Intellectuals Speak Out About God*, Roy Abraham Varghese, ed. (Chicago: Regnery Gateway, 1984).

Eccles, Sir John, and Daniel N. Robinson. *The Wonder of Being Human* (Boston: Shambhala, 1985).

Eden, Murray. "Inadequacies of Neo-Darwinian Evolution as a Scientific Theory," *Mathematical Challenges to the Neo-Darwinian Interpretation of Evolution*, P. Moorhead and M. Kaplan, eds. (Philadelphia: Wistar Institute Press, 1967).

Edey, Maitland A., and Donald C. Johanson. *Blueprints: Solving the Mystery of Evolution* (Boston: Little, Brown, and Company, 1989).

Einstein, Albert. *Essays in Science* (New York: Philosophical Library, 1934).

———. *Out of My Later Years*, rev. reprint ed. (Westport, Connecticut: Greenwood Press, 1970).

Flamsteed, Sam. "Probing the Edge of the Universe," *Discover*, Vol. 12, No. 7, July, 1991.

Flew, Antony, R.M. Hare, and Basil Mitchell, "Theology and Falsification," *New Essays in Philosophical Theology*, Antony Flew and Alasdair MacIntyre, eds. (London: SCM Press, 1955).

Freedman, Wendy L. "The Expansion Rate and Size of the Universe," *Scientific American*, Vol. 267, No. 5, Nov., 1992.

Frye, Roland Mushat, ed. *Is God a Creationist?* (New York: Charles Scribner's Sons, 1983).

Galen. *On the Usefulness of the Parts of the Body*, translated by M. T. May (New York: Cornell University Press, 1968).

Gillespie, Neal C. *Charles Darwin and the Problem of Creation* (Chicago: University of Chicago Press, 1979).

Gingerich, Owen. "Let There Be Light: Modern Cosmogony and Biblical Creation," *Is God a Creationist?* Roland Mushat Frye, ed. (New York: Charles Scribner's Sons, 1983).

Gish, Duane. *The Challenge of the Fossil Record* (San Diego: Creation-Life Publishers, 1985).

Godfrey, Laurie R, ed. *Scientists Confront Creationism* (New York: W.W. Norton & Co., 1983).

Goldschmidt, Richard. *The Material Basis of Evolution* (New Haven: Yale University Press, 1940).

Gould, Stephen Jay. *Bully for Brontosaurus* (New York: W.W. Norton & Company, 1992).

———. "Darwin's Untimely Burial—Again!" in *Scientists Confront Creationism*, Laurie R. Godfrey, ed. (New York: W.W. Norton & Co., 1983).

———. *Ever Since Darwin* (New York: W.W. Norton & Company, 1973).

———. *Hen's Teeth and Horse's Toes* (New York: W.W. Norton & Company, 1980).

———. "The Ediacaran Experiment," *Natural History*, Vol. 93, No. 2, Feb., 1984.

———. *The Flamingo's Smile* (New York: W.W. Norton & Company, 1985).

———. *The Panda's Thumb* (W.W. Norton & Company, 1980).

Grant, Peter R. "Natural Selection and Darwin's Finches," *Scientific American*, Vol. 265, No. 4, Oct. 1991.

Grasse', Pierre. *Evolution of Living Organisms: Evidence for a New Theory of Transformation* (New York: Academic Press, 1977).

Gray, Asa. *Darwiniana* (New York: Appleton, 1876).

———. "Natural Science and Religion," *Is God a Creationist?* Roland Mushat Frye, ed. (New York: Charles Scribner's Sons, 1983).

Greeley, Andrew. "Keeping the Faith: Americans Hold Fast to the Rock of Ages," in *Omni*, Vol. 13, No. 11, August, 1991.

Greene, John C. *Science, Ideology, and World View: Essays in the History of Evolutionary Ideas* (Berkeley: University of California Press, 1981).

Greenstein, George. *The Symbiotic Universe* (New York: William Morrow, 1988).

Gregory, Frederick. "The Impact of Darwinian Evolution on Protestant Theology in the Nineteenth Century," in David C. Lindberg and Ronald L. Numbers, eds., *God and Nature* (Berkeley: University of California Press, 1986).

Gribbin, John, and Martin Rees. *Cosmic Coincidences* (New York: Bantam Books, 1989).

Gribbin, John. *In Search of the Double Helix* (New York: Bantam Books, 1987).

———. *The Omega Point* (New York: Bantam Books, 1988).

Griffin, David Ray. *God, Power, and Evil* (Philadelphia: The Westminster Press, 1976).

———. *God and Religion in the Postmodern World* (Albany: SUNY Press, 1989).

———ed. *Physics and the Ultimate Significance of Time* (Albany: SUNY Press, 1986).

Griffin, David Ray, and Huston Smith. *Primordial Truth and Postmodern Theology* (Albany: SUNY PRESS, 1989).

Griffin, David Ray, ed. *The Reenchantment of Science*, (Albany: SUNY Press, 1988).

———. "Time, Creativity, and the Origin of the Universe: A Response to Stephen Hawking," in an as yet unpublished manuscript.

Hadarard, J. *Lectures on Cauchy's Problem in Linear Partial Differential Equations* (New Haven: Yale University Press, 1923).

Hadd, John R. *Evolution: Reconciling the Controversy* (New Jersey: Kronos Press, 1979), p. 31.

Hahn, Roger. "Laplace and the Mechanistic Universe," in David C. Lindberg and Ronald L. Numbers, eds., *God and Nature* (Berkeley: University of California Press, 1986).

Hall, Marshall and Sandra. *The Truth: God or Evolution?* (Grand Rapids: Baker Book House, 1973).

Hardy, Alister. *Darwin and the Spirit of Man* (London: Collins Press, 1984).

Harris, Errol E. *Cosmos and Anthropos* (Atlantic Highlands, New Jersey: Humanities Press International, Inc., 1991).

Harrison, E.R. "The Dark Night Sky Riddle: A 'Paradox' that Resisted Solution," *Science*, 226. (1984).

Hawking, S.W. *A Brief History of Time* (New York: Bantam, 1988).

Helitzer, Florence. "The Princeton Galaxy," *Intellectual Digest*, No. 10, (June 1973).

Henderson, L.J. *The Fitness of the Environment* (Glouster: Peter Smith, 1970).

———. *The Order of Nature* (Cambridge: Harvard University Press, 1917).

Henderson, Charles P. *God and Science* (Atlanta: John Knox Press, 1973).

Hick, John. *An Interpretation of Religion* (New York: Macmillan Press, 1989).

———. *Evil and the God of Love* (New York: Harper and Row, 1977).

———. "Rational Theistic Belief Without Proof," in *Arguments for the Existence of God* (New York: Macmillan, 1971).

———. *The Existence of God* (New York: The Macmillan Publishing Company, 1964).

Hickman. *Integrated Principles of Zoology* (St. Louis: The C. V. Mosby Co., 1978, Sixth Edition).

Hiebert, Erwin N. "Modern Physics and Christian Faith" in David C. Lindberg and Ronald L. Numbers, eds., *God & Nature* (Berkeley: University of California Press, 1986).

Himmelfarb, Gertrude. *Darwin and the Darwinian Revolution* (New York: W.W. Norton, 1959).

Hogben, L.T. *The Nature of Living Matter* (London: Routledge and Kegan Paul, 1931).

Hoyle, Fred, and Chandra Wickramasinghe. *Evolution from Space* (London: J.M. Dent and Co., 1981).

Hoyle, Fred. *Religion and the Scientists* (London: SCM, 1959).

———. "The Big Bang in Astronomy," *New Scientist*, V. 92, No. 1280, November 19, 1981.

———. "The Universe: Past and Present Reflections," *Engineering and Science* (November 1981).

Hume, David. *Dialogues Concerning Natural Religion* (London: Penguin, 1990).

Jaki, Stanley L. *Cosmos and Creator* (Edinburgh: Scottish Academic Press, 1980).

———. *The Paradox of Olbers' Paradox* (New York: Herder and Herder, 1969).

James, William. *The Varieties of Religious Experience* (New York: Longman, Green, & Co., 1902).

Janov, Arthur. *The Primal Scream* (New York: G.P. Putnam's Sons, 1970).

Jantsch, Erich. *The Self-Organizing Universe* (Oxford: Pergamon Press, 1980).

Jastrow, Robert. *God and the Astronomers* (New York: Warner Books, 1978).

———. *Until the Sun Dies* (New York: Warner Books, 1977).

Johanson, Donald C., and M.A. Edey. *Lucy: The Beginnings of Humankind* (New York: Simon and Schuster, 1981).

Johnson, Philip E. *Darwin on Trial* (Washington, DC: Regnery Gateway, 1991).

Jones, Philip D., and Tom M.L. Wigley. "Global Warming Trends," *Scientific American*, Vol. 263, No. 2, Aug. 1990.

Kaku, Michio, and Jennifer Trainer. *Beyond Einstein: The Cosmic Quest for the Theory of the Universe* (New York: Bantam Books, 1987).

Kappen, C., Schughart, K., and Ruddle, F.H. "Two Steps in the Evolution of Antennapedia-Class Vertebrate Homeobox Genes," *Proceedings of the National Academy of Science*, Vol. 86, July, 1989.

Kauffman, Stuart A. "Antichaos and Adaptation," *Scientific American*, Vol. 265, No. 2, Aug. 1991.

————. "Self-Organization, Selective Adaptation, and Its Limits," *Evolution at a Crossroads*, David J. Depew and Bruce H. Weber, eds. (Cambridge: The MIT Press, 1985).

Kilby, Clyde S., ed. *An Anthology of C.S. Lewis: A Mind Awake* (New York: Harvest/ HBJ Books, 1968).

Knoll, Andrew H. "End of the Proterozoic Eon," *Scientific American*, Vol. 265, No. 4, Oct., 1991.

Landman, Otto E. "Inheritance of Acquired Characteristics," *Scientific American*, Vol. 266, No. 3, Mar., 1993.

Laszlo, Ervin. *Evolution: The Grand Synthesis* (Boston: Shambhala, 1987).

Leakey, Richard, and Roger Lewin. *Origins Reconsidered* (New York: Doubleday, 1992).

Leakey, Richard. *The Making of Mankind* (New York: E.P. Dutton, 1981).

Leibniz, G.W. *Theodicy* (La Salle, IL: Open Court Publishing Company, 1985).

Lerner, Eric J. *The Big Bang Never Happened: A Startling Refutation of the Dominant Theory of Universal Origins* (New York: Random House, 1991).

Leslie, John. "Anthropic Principle, World Ensemble, Design," in *American Philosophical Quarterly* 19 (1982).

Lewin, Roger. *Complexity* (New York: Macmillan Publishing Company, 1992).

Lewis, C.S. *Christian Reflections* (Grand Rapids: William B. Eerdmans Publishing Company, 1967).

————. "Encounter With Light." Taken from *An Anthology of C.S. Lewis: A Mind Awake*, Clyde S. Kilby ed. (New York: Harvest/HBJ Books, 1968).

————. *Mere Christianity* (New York: Macmillan Publishing Co. Inc., 1952).

————. *The Problem of Pain* (New York: Macmillan Publishing Company, 1962).

Lima-de-Faria, A. *Evolution Without Selection* (Amsterdam: Elsevier, 1988).

Lindberg, David C. "Science and the Early Church," in *God & Nature*, Lindberg, David C., and Numbers, Ronald L., eds. (Berkeley: University of California Press, 1986).

Lindberg, David C., and Ronald L. Numbers, eds. *God & Nature* (Berkeley: University of California Press, 1986).

Lindsey, Hal and C.C. Carlson. *The Terminal Generation* (New York: Bantam Books, 1977).

Lokki, Juhanim, and Anssi Sauri, "Polyploidy in Insect Evolution," *Polyploidy*, Walter H. Lewis, ed. (New York: Plenum Press, 1980).

Long, A.A. *Hellenistic Philosophy* (Berkeley: University of California Press, 1974).

Lovejoy, C.O. *Life in the Universe*, J. Billingham, ed. (Cambridge: MIT Press, 1981).

Macbeth, Norman. *Darwin Retried: An Appeal to Reason* (Boston: Gambit Press, 1971).

———. "The Question: Darwinism Revisted," *Yale Review* (June 1967).

Mayr, Ernst. *Animal Species and Evolution* (Cambridge: The Belknap Press of Harvard University Press, 1963).

———. "How Biology Differs from the Physical Sciences," *Evolution at a Crossroads*, (Cambridge: The MIT Press, 1985).

———. *Populations, Species, and Evolution* (Cambridge, MA: Harvard University Press, 1970).

McDonough, Thomas R., and Brin, David. "The Bubbling Universe," *Omni*, Vol. 15, No. 1, Oct., 1992.

Mendillo, M., and R. Hart. "Resonances," *Physics Today*, 27:2 (Feb., 1974).

Midgley, Mary. *Evolution as a Religion* (New York: Methuen & Co., 1985).

Mivart, St. George Jackson. *On the Genesis of Species* (London: Macmillan, 1871).

Monod, Jacques. *Chance and Necessity* (New York: Alfred A. Knopf, 1971).

Moore, John N. *Should Evolution Be Taught?* (San Diego: Institute for Creation Research, 1971).

Moorehead, P.S., and M.M. Kaplan, eds. *Mathematical Challenges to the Neo-Darwinian Interpretation of Evolution* (Philadelphia: Wistar Institute Press, 1967).

Morgan, T.H. *The Scientific Basis of Evolution* (London: Faber and Faber, 1932).

Murchie, Guy. *The Seven Mysteries of Life* (Boston: The Houghton Mifflin Company, 1978).

Murtha, M.T., Leckman, J.F., and Ruddle, F.H. "Detection of Homeobox Genes in Development and Evolution," *Proceedings of the National Academy of Science*, Vol. 88, December, 1991.

Novikov, Igor D., and Zel'dovich, Yakob. "Physical Processes Near Cosmological Singularities," in *Annual Review of Astronomy and Astrophysics*, 11. (1973).

Ohno, Susumu. *Evolution by Gene Duplication* (New York: Springer-Verlag, 1970).

Oldroyd, D.R. *Darwinian Impacts* (Atlantic Highlands, NJ: Humanities Press, 1980).

Oliwenstein, Lori. "All the Way With RNA," *Discover*, Vol. 14, No. 1, Jan., 1993.

Opadia-Kadima, G.Z. "How the Slot Machine Led Biologists Astray," *The Journal of Theoretical Biology* (1987) *124*.

Owen, Richard. *On the Archetype and Homologies of the Vertebrate Skeleton* (London: Van Voorst, 1848).

Paley, William. *Natural Theology* (London: Baldwyn and Company, 1819).

Peat, F. David. *Superstrings and the Search for the Theory of Everything* (Chicago: Contemporary Books, 1988).

———. *The Philosopher's Stone* (New York: Bantam Books, 1991).

Peterson, Michael, William Hasker, Bruce Reichenbach, and David Basinger. *Reason & Religious Belief* (Oxford: Oxford University Press, 1991).

Plaine, Henry L., ed. *Darwin, Marx, and Wagner: A Symposium* (Columbus: Ohio State University Press, 1962).

Plantinga, Alvin. *God, Freedom, and Evil* (Grand Rapids: William B. Eerdmanns Publishing Company, 1974).

———. "Religious Belief Without Evidence," in *Rationality and Religious Belief*, C.F. Delaney, ed., (University of Notre Dame Press, 1979).

———. *The Nature of Necessity* (New York: Oxford University Press, 1974).

Platt, Rutherford. "DNA the Mysterious Basis for Life," *Reader's Digest* (October, 1962).

Polkinghorne, John. *Science and Creation* (Boston: New Science Library, 1988).

Pojman, Louis P. *Philosophy of Religion* (Belmont, CA: Wadsworth Publishing Co., 1987).

Popper, Karl. *Unended Quest* (Glasgow: Fontana Books of Collins, Sons and Co., Ltd., 1976).

Portmann, Adolf. "Die Ontogenese des Menschen als Problem der Evolutionsforschung." *Verhhandlungen der Schweizerischen Naturforschenden Gesellschaft* (1945).

Powell, Corey S. "Greenhouse Gusher," in *Scientific American*, Vol. 265, No. 4, October, 1991.

———. "The Golden Age of Cosmology," *Scientific American*, Vol. 267, No. 1, July, 1992.

Radetsky, Peter. "How Did Life Start?" *Discover*, Vol. 13, No. 11, November, 1992.

Rayl, A.J.S., and K.T. McKinney. "The Mind of God," *Omni*, Vol. 13, No. 11, August, 1991.

Raup, David M. "Conflicts Between Darwinism and Paleontology," *Field Museum of Natural History Bulletin*, Vol. 50, No. 1, January, 1979.

———. *Extinction: Bad Genes or Bad Luck?* (New York: W.W. Norton & Co., 1991).

Raymonde, *Studies in the History of Natural Theology*, (Cambridge: Cambridge University Press, 1915).

Rennie, John. "DNA's New Twists," *Scientific American*, Vol. 266, No. 3, March, 1993.

Repetski, John. "A Fish from the Upper Cambrian of North America," *Science*, Vol. 200, No. 4341, 5 May, 1978.

Rifkin, Jeremy. *Algeny* (New York: The Viking Press, 1983).

Rogers, John H. "The Role of Introns in Evolution," *Febs Letters* Vol. 268, No. 2, August, 1990.

Rolston, Holmes. *Science and Religion* (Philadelphia: Temple University Press, 1987).

Ross, Hugh. *Genesis One: A Scientific Perspective* (Sierra Madre, CA: Wisemen Productions, 1983).

———. *The Fingerprint of God* (Orange, CA: Promise Publishing, 1991).

Russell, Bertrand. *Religion and Science* (New York: Oxford University Press, 1968).

Sagan, Carl. *Cosmos* (New York: Random House, 1980).

———. *Discovery 4* (No. 3, March), 30 (1983).

Schrodinger, Erwin. *What is Life?* (Cambridge: Cambridge University Press, 1967).

Schroeder, Gerald L. *Genesis and the Big Bang* (New York: Bantam, 1990).

Schughart, K., Kappen, C., and Ruddle, F.H. "Duplication of Large Genomic Regions During the Evolution of Vertebrate Homeobox Genes," *Proceedings of the National Academy of Science*, Vol. 86, September, 1989.

Schultz, R. Jack. "Role of Polyploidy in the Evolution of Fishes," *Polyploidy*, Walter H. Lewis, ed. (New York: Plenum Press, 1980).

Scriven, Michael. "The Presumption of Atheism," in Louis P. Pojman's *Philosophy of Religion* (Belmont, CA: Wadsworth Publishing Co., 1987).

Shapiro, Robert. "Prebiotic Ribose Synthesis: A Critical Analysis," *Origin of Life and Evolution of the Biosphere*, 18, (1988).

Shea, William R. "Galileo and the Church," in David C. Lindberg and Ronald L. Numbers, eds., *God & Nature* (Berkeley: University of California Press, 1986).

Sheldrake, Rupert. *A New Science of Life* (Los Angeles: J.P. Tarcher, Inc., 1981).

———. "Modern Bio-chemistry and the Collapse of Mechanism," *The Intellectuals Speak Out About God*, Roy Abraham Varghese, ed. (Chicago: Regnery Gateway, 1984).

Simpson, George Gaylord. *The Meaning of Evolution* (New Haven: Yale University Press, 1967).

Skinner, B.F. *Beyond Freedom and Dignity* (New York: Knopf, 1971).

Smart, Ninian. "Omnipotence, Evil, and Supermen," *Philosophy*, Vol. XXXVI, No. 137 (1961).

Smith, John Maynard. *Did Darwin Get It Right?* (New York: Chapman & Hall, 1989).

Spergel, David N., and Neil G. Turok. "Textures and Cosmic Structure," *Scientific American*, Vol. 266, No. 3, March, 1992.

Stahler, Steven W. "The Early Life of Stars," *Scientific American*, Vol. 265, No. 1, July, 1991.

Stanley, S. *Macroevolution* (San Francisco: Hutchinson Publishing Co., 1979).

Stansfield, William D. *The Science of Evolution* (New York: Macmillan Publishing Co., 1977).

Stoner, Peter W, and Robert C. Newman. *Science Speaks* (Chicago: Moody Press, 1968).

Sullivan, Walter. "Evolution: A New Concept," *The New York Times* (October 25, 1964).

Sutherland, Luther D. *Darwin's Enigma* (Santee: Master Book Publishers, 1988).

Swimme, Brian. "The Cosmic Creation Story," David Ray Griffin, ed., *The Reenchantment of Science*, (Albany: SUNY Press, 1988).

Taylor, Gordon Rattray. *The Great Evolution Mystery* (New York: Harper & Row, Publishers, 1983).

Tennant, F.R. "Cosmic Teleology," *Philosophical Theology*, Vol. II, chapter IV (New York: Cambridge University Press, 1930).

Thompson, D'Arcy Wentworth. *On Growth and Form* (New York: MacMillan, 1942).

Thompson, John Arthur, and Patrick Geddes. *Life: Outlines of General Biology* (London: Williams & Norgate, 1931).

Trefil, James. *Reading the Mind of God: In Search of the Principle of Universality* (New York: Charles Scribner's Sons, 1989).

———. *The Dark Side of the Universe* (New York: Doubleday, 1988).

Trumpler, Robert J. "Absorption of Light in the Galactic System," in *Publications of the Astronomical Society of the Pacific*, 42. (1930).

Van Till, Howard J. *The Fourth Day* (Grand Rapids: Eerdmans Press, 1986).

Varghese, Roy Abraham, ed. *The Intellectuals Speak Out About God*, (Chicago: Regnery Gateway, Inc., 1984).

Voltaire. 'Atheist Atheism,' *Philosophical Dictionary* (1769), transl. and ed. P. Gay, 2 Vols (New York: Basic Books, 1955).

Waddington, C.H. *The Strategy of the Genes* (London: Allen & Unwin, 1957).

———ed. *Towards a Theoretical Biology* (Edinburgh University Press, 1969).

Wallace, Alfred Russel. *Natural Selection and Tropical Nature* (London: Macmillan, 1895).

Weinberg, Steven. *The First Three Minutes* (London: Andre' Deutsch, 1977).

Weisskopf, Victor F. "The Frontiers and Limits of Science," *American Scientist*, Vol. 65, July-August, 1977.

Westman, Robert S. "The Copernicans and the Churches," in David C. Lindberg and Ronald L. Numbers, eds., *God & Nature* (Berkeley: University of California Press, 1986).

Wheeler, John A. in Florence Helitzer's "The Princeton Galaxy," *Intellectual Digest 3*, No. 10 (June 1973).

Wiester, John. *The Genesis Connection* (Nashville: Thomas Nelson Publishers, 1983).

Wysong, R.L. *The Creation-Evolution Controversy* (Midland, Michigan: Inquiry Press, 1976).

Youngblood, Ronald. *How It All Began* (Ventura, CA: Regal Books, 1980).

Index